Marriage and the English Reformation

FAMILY, SEXUALITY AND SOCIAL RELATIONS IN PAST TIMES

GENERAL EDITORS:
Peter Laslett and Michael Anderson

Western Sexuality: Practice and Precept in Past and Present Times**
Edited by Philippe Ariès and André Béjin

The Explanation of Ideology: Family Structures and Social Systems**
Emmanuel Todd

The Causes of Progress: Culture, Authority and Change
Emmanuel Todd

An Ordered Society: Gender and Class in Early Modern England*
Susan Dwyer Amussen

Sexuality and Social Control, Scotland, 1660–1780
Rosalind Mitchison and Leah Leneman

A History of Contraception: From Antiquity to the Present**
Angus McLaren

The Children of the Poor: Representations of Childhood since the Seventeenth Century
Hugh Cunningham

A History of Youth**
Michael Mitterauer

Marriage and the English Reformation
Eric Josef Carlson

Medieval Prostitution*
Jacques Rossiaud

Wet Nursing: A History*
Valerie Fildes

Porneia: On Desire and the Body in Antiquity**
Aline Rousselle

Highley 1550–1880: The Development of a Community*
Gwyneth Nair

The English Noble Household, 1250–1600*
Kate Mertes

Country House Life: Family and Servants, 1815–1914
Jessica Gerard

FORTHCOMING

Londoners: The Family and Kinship in Early Modern London
Vivien Brodsky

The Rise and Fall of the Servant in the Twentieth Century
Kate Mertes

Women and Families: An Oral History, 1940–1970
Elizabeth Roberts

The Making of a Woman's World
Kate Mertes

*out of print
**available in paperback

Marriage and the English Reformation

Eric Josef Carlson

BLACKWELL
Oxford UK & Cambridge USA

First published 1994

Blackwell Publishers
238 Main Street
Cambridge, Massachusetts 02142
USA

108 Cowley Road
Oxford OX4 1JF
UK

Library of Congress Cataloging-in-Publication Data

Carlson, Eric Josef
Marriage and the English Reformation / by Eric Josef Carlson
p. cm. (Family, sexuality, and social relations in past times)
Includes bibliographical references and index
1. Marriage – England – History. 2. Marriage (Canon law) – History.
3. Reformation – England – History. I. Title. II. Series.
HQ615.C37 1994   93–32891
306.81'0942–dc20   CIP

ISBN 0–631–16864–8 (alk. paper)

British Library Cataloguing in Publication Data

A CIP catalogue record for this book is available from the British Library.

Typeset in 10 on 12 pt Garamond by
Puretech Corporation, Pondicherry, India

Printed in Great Britain by Robert Hartnoll Ltd, Bodmin, Cornwall
This book is printed on acid-free paper

To the memory of
Anna Bologna Mondo
and
Bridget Margaret Spufford

Those who wait for the Lord
shall renew their strength,
they shall mount up with wings
like eagles,
they shall run and not be weary,
they shall walk and not faint.
(Isaiah 40: 31)

Contents

Preface   viii

List of Abbreviations   x

Part I The European and English Context

1 The European Reformation of Marriage   3
2 Church, Crown, Lordship and Marriage in Medieval England   9

Part II Marriage and the English Reformers

3 Theology, Ritual and Clerical Marriage   37
4 Canon Law   67
5 Extraparliamentary Pressure   88

Part III Marriage and the People

6 Law and Practice in the Formation of Marriage in
   English Communities   105
7 Church Courts and Communities in Reformation England   142

Notes   181
Select Bibliography   263
Index   273

Preface

On those days when my research took me to the British Library, I would often, while returning from lunch, stop at a glass-covered case near the entrance to the manuscript room and gaze sympathetically at a famous letter from Henry VIII to Cardinal Wolsey which rested within it. In the letter, Henry declares that "wryttyng to me Is somewhat tedious and paynefull." In those postprandial visits to the display case, I discovered I had one thing in common with the monarch whose activities I spent so much time studying. This book has taken an unconscionably long time being completed, in large part because of my resistance to writing. The one part of that irksome task which I find to be a pleasure is remembering and acknowledging the many kindnesses shown to me while researching and writing this book and the dissertation on which it was based.

First, since this project began its life as a seminar paper at UCLA in 1977, I would like to thank Professor Eleanor Searle, who first interested me in the study of marriage when I was an undergraduate, and during two years of graduate study at UCLA gave unstintingly of her time and knowledge. In graduate school, Professor Steven Ozment interested me in the German Reformation and encouraged me by word and example to stake out controversial positions and defend them. I benefitted enormously from the ideal thesis advisor in Professor Wallace MacCaffrey who, in addition to wooing me away from the grip of the Middle Ages into the arms of the Tudors, was heroically patient and gave (and continues to give) me sound advice, encouragement and support.

My research was funded by the Mark DeWolfe Howe Fund of the Harvard Law School, and the Gross Fund of the Harvard History Department. I cannot imagine having been able to complete my research without my membership in Clare Hall, Cambridge, and I thank those who made and continue to make that place my second home.

Many librarians and archivists have aided and encouraged my research, particularly Dr Dorothy Owen, Mr Godfrey Waller and the staff of the Cambridge University Library Manuscript Reading Room, and the staff of the Borthwick Institute in York. I am deeply grateful to them all for their assistance with my many requests. I thank also archivists and staff at the Bodleian Library, the British Library, the Cambridgeshire County Record Office, the House of Lords Record Office, the Houghton Library (Harvard), the Huntington Library, the Institute of Historical Research, the Lambeth Palace Library, the Parker Library of Corpus Christi College, and the Public Record Office. Professor Sir Geoffrey Elton, Professor Norman L. Jones, Dr Kenneth L. Parker, Dr J.R. Ravensdale, and Dr Keith Wrightson have been generous with their time, experience and great knowledge. Dr W.J. Sheils and Dr Claire Cross tolerated many interruptions of their own work in York to help me. I thank them all.

The collection of Cambridge research students working with Margaret Spufford – "The Spuffordians" as we have come to be called – have had an exceptionally positive impact on my work, whether by challenging my arguments, providing me with additional evidence and ideas, or – most importantly – by keeping me sane with their understanding and good humor. For all of this, I would like to thank especially Amy Erickson, Judith Maltby, Chris Marsh, Derek Plumb, and Tessa Watt. Dr Spufford has herself transformed my understanding of the sixteenth century and my approach to the study of history. Her generosity with her time and her research has been beyond measure. I do not have words adequate to thank her for her support and love and the hospitality she and her husband, Dr Peter Spufford, show me.

My parents continue to be a source of extraordinary support on many levels, and in a thousand ways at least, this book could not have happened without them and their unfailing love. In the last stages of writing, I have also felt very demonstrably the support of my colleagues at Gustavus Adolphus College, especially Florence Amamoto. Finally, my thanks most of all to Doug Rorapaugh, who has patiently tolerated the intrusion of this book in his life for far too long.

Completing a project of this length in time and in words is a great relief and source of joy. That joy is diminished only by not being able to share it with the two people remembered in the dedication. I hope heaven has a library.

Eric Josef Carlson
St Peter, Minnesota

List of Abbreviations

Printed sources:

APC   *Acts of the Privy Council of England*, ed. J.R. Dasent, 32 vols (London, 1890–1907)

BNB   *Bracton's Note Book*, ed. F.W. Maitland, 3 vols (London, 1887)

CCR   *Calendar of Close Rolls*

CJ, vol. 1   *Journals of the House of Commons*, vol. 1, (London, 1803)

CPPR   *Calendar of Entries in the Papal Registers Relating to Great Britain and Ireland*

CPR   *Calendar of Patent Rolls*

CRR   *Curia Regis Rolls*

CSP, Foreign *Calendar of State Papers, Foreign Series of the Reign of Elizabeth preserved in the Public Record Office*

CSP, Span   *Calendar of Letters and State Papers relating to English Affairs preserved principally in the Archives of Simancas*

CW, More   *The Yale Edition of the Complete Works of St Thomas More*, ed. Richard Sylvester *et al.*, 16 vols to date (New Haven, 1963–)

DNB   *Dictionary of National Biography*

HMC, Bath   *Calendar of the Manuscripts of the Marquis of Bath preserved at Longleat, Wiltshire*, 5 vols to date (London, 1904–)

HMC, Salisbury *Calendar of the Manuscripts of the Most Honorable The Marquis of Salisbury, preserved at Hatfield House*, 14 vols to date (London, 1883–)

LJ, vol. 1   *Journals of the House of Lords*, vol. 1, (London, 1888)

LP   *Letters and Papers, Foreign and Domestic of the Reign of Henry VIII*, 21 vols, ed. J.S. Brewer, *et al.* (London, 1862–1920)

LW   *Luther's Works*, ed. Jaroslav Pelikan and Helmut T. Lehmann, 55 vols (Philadelphia, 1958–86)

MER   Eric Josef Carlson, "Marriage and the English Reformation," Harvard University Ph.D., 1987

RB   *The Roxburghe Ballads*, ed. W. Chappell and J.W. Ebsworth, 9 vols (London, 1871–97)

SR   *Statutes of the Realm*, 11 vols (London, 1810–28)

Strype, *Annals*   J. Strype, *Annals of the Reformation and Establishment of Religion
                    . . .* , 4 vols (London, 1709–31; repr. Oxford, 1820–40)

TRP   *Tudor Royal Proclamations*, ed. Paul L. Hughes and James F.
                    Larkin, 3 vols (New Haven, 1964–9)

VCH, Cambs.   Victoria County History of Cambridgeshire, i.e., *A History of
                    the County of Cambridge and the Isle of Ely*, ed. C.R. Elrington,
                    et al., 9 vols to date (London and Oxford, 1938–)

Research Libraries and Archive Collections:

BI   Borthwick Institute of Historical Research, York
BL   British Library
CCCC   Corpus Christi College, Cambridge
CRO   County Record Office, Shire Hall, Cambridge
EDR   Ely Diocesan Records
                    (deposited in ULC, Manuscript Room)
EPR   Ely Probate Records
                    (deposited in CRO)
HLRO   House of Lords Record Office
Ox. Bod.   Bodleian Library, Oxford University
PRO   Public Record Office, London
ULC   University Library, Cambridge

All canon law citations are according to standard form, and cited from *Corpus Iuris Canonici*, ed. Emil Friedberg, 2 vols (Leipzig, 1879–81).

Spelling and punctuation have been modernized except in the titles of pre-1700 book titles.

PART I

The European and English Context

1

The European Reformation of Marriage

In one of Sir Arthur Conan Doyle's most well-known short stories, Sherlock Holmes assisted Colonel Ross in recovering the missing racehorse Silver Blaze in time for the running of the Wessex Cup. After Holmes completed his initial investigation, Inspector Gregory asked the great detective if there was anything to which his attention should be drawn. "To the curious incident of the dog in the night-time," replied Holmes. Puzzled, Gregory responded: "The dog did nothing in the night-time." "That," said Holmes, "was the curious incident."[1] In this book, I explore a similar curious incident: the failure of the English Reformation to share in the dramatic transformation of the status of marriage, the laws which regulated it, and the courts which enforced those laws which characterized the Protestant Reformation elsewhere, most notably in what is now Germany and Switzerland.[2]

Recent scholarship on the continental Reformation suggests that many factors interacted to bring about these changes. First, reformers attacked the Roman church's teaching that marriage was one of the seven sacraments. As late as 1519, Martin Luther taught that marriage was a sacrament.[3] In 1520, however, when he fired his *Babylonian Captivity* across the bow of the church, he denounced that view unequivocally, arguing that matrimony in no way met the criteria for a sacrament: it was not instituted by Christ, but by God the Father in the Garden of Eden; it did not impart grace; and it was not necessary for salvation.[4] Luther did agree that it was of divine creation and was therefore good and proper, but he believed that the church's elaborate theological claims had grown out of the tyrannical impulses of the papacy and could not be justified from scripture. This theme was a universal one in Protestantism. No reformed church maintained that marriage was a sacrament.

Depriving marriage of sacramental status raised serious problems for the reformers since the old theology, by honoring marriage with the title of sacrament, had given the married state an important place in the economy of salvation. The reformers seemed by implication to be denying the importance of matrimony. This was precisely the opposite of what they had intended since, at the same time, they were launching their attack on what they viewed as the anti-marriage celibate ideal of the church.[5] This attack on celibacy was the second feature of the movement which affected the position of marriage in the Reformation. The leading Wittenberg figure in this cause was not Luther but Andreas Karlstadt who published the first major Protestant assault on celibacy and dramatically married in 1521, writing to the Elector that he had considered "that many poor, miserable and lost clerics who now lie in the devil's prison and dungeon might without doubt be counselled and helped by a good model and example."[6] By 1525, in Wittenberg and elsewhere, almost all of the reformers (of whom Luther was among the last) had married. Ulrich Zwingli married in 1522. He and ten other priests, with growing popular support, petitioned the bishop to allow clerical marriage, and published the petition as a pamphlet.[7] By the same year, clerical marriage was legal in Denmark, where it enjoyed wide support, and both king and magistrates resisted episcopal opposition.[8] Anton Firn became, in October 1523, the first of the Strasbourg clergy to marry. Within a year he was imitated by all of the Strasbourg reform leaders: Matthias Zell in December 1523, and Wolfgang Capito and Caspar Hedio in the summer of 1524. These married clergy enjoyed enough popular support that the Rat, fearing outbreaks of disorder in the city if they acted, resisted episcopal pressure to remove them from their pulpits.[9] By 1525, marriage had become one of the litmus tests of commitment to reform.

The reformers, unsurprisingly, found it necessary to defend their actions. In part they did this by discrediting monastic vows and requirements of celibacy as contrary both to nature and Christian freedom. More importantly, they constructed a positive justification for marriage. Preaching at Anton Firn's marriage, for example, Zell declared that in marriage alone could men achieve full perfection.[10] Praising marriage was not entirely new. Nicholas de Blony and Geiler von Kaysersberg in Strasbourg and Gabriel Biel in Tübingen, for example, had (by 1500) preached that marriage was a natural state for man, pleasing to God.[11] However, after 1521 evangelical priests made a significant advance by putting their doctrine into practice, admitting that true celibacy was such a rare gift that unmarried clergy had little hope of avoiding fornication, and that marriage was a state far more pleasing to God since through it they could satisfy their natural urges without sin as well as propagating children for the increase of the community.[12] In the process of repeatedly defending their doctrine and their actions, the reformers argued with vigor and conviction that the married state was not merely acceptable, not even merely equal to the single life, but was superior to it in every respect. Their exaltation of marriage could be applied not only to themselves but to all people.

Although these defences of clerical marriage served to a certain extent as a counterpoison to withdrawing from matrimony the honor and dignity of a sacrament, the reformers had created still another problem to resolve. The sacramentality of marriage underpinned ecclesiastical claims of legal jurisdiction over it. Once it was no longer considered a sacrament, the logic of such claims vanished. The reformers had to decide what, if any, future role the church should have in the legal regulation of marriage and, at the same time, what law should be applied.

A sustained assault on Roman canon law in general, as well as the marriage laws specifically, was the third feature of the reform movements contributing to a new treatment of marriage. Luther was the most outspoken of all in his denunciation of Roman canon law. In both his letter *To the Christian Nobility of the German Nation* and his treatise on *The Babylonian Captivity of the Church*, he denounced the arbitrary and capricious character of papal law, nurtured by the inexhaustible greed of the papacy which made laws only to peddle dispensations from them. "Let canon law perish in God's name," implored Luther, "for it arose in the devil's name."[13] In December 1520, Luther dramatized his views by staging a public bonfire, which Philip Melanchthon had encouraged his students to attend as "a pious and religious spectacle,"[14] into which he heaved books of papal law. Luther objected to the pope's creation of binding laws. Christians, he wrote, could only be required to perform what was required of them by the word of God. Strasbourg reformers also developed this theme. Matthias Zell, in his *Christeliche Verantwortung* (1523), denounced the power to make laws as the root of all evils in the church. Moreover, according to Zell, what did not rest on the word of God could not please God and was soteriologically useless, at best, and, at worst, destructive.[15]

The church's marriage laws were particularly obnoxious. Luther denounced "the shameful confusion wrought by the accursed papal law" of marriage,[16] and complained that dispensation sales had made men of God into merchants selling vulvas and genitals.[17] Both in his *Babylonian Captivity* and *Vom ehelichen Leben* (1522), he described at length the impediments to matrimony in the canons and showed that they could rarely be justified from scripture and often directly opposed it.[18] In addition to the impediments, reformers also criticized canons upholding the validity of secret marriages.[19] Criticizing marriage law attracted the support of lay elites, who were opposed to those canonical provisions which upheld marriages made without parental consent. Before the Reformation, Augsburg gave parents the legal authority to disinherit children who married against the will of their parents.[20] As long as the canon law remained in effect, however, such marriages could not actually be dissolved.

When given opportunities to change these laws, the reformers seized them, although their response and that of the laity was by no means uniform.[21] Beginning in 1553, church ordinances in Hohenlohe, and the subsequent comprehensive marriage law of 1572, required parental permission for marriage if either party was "still under the authority of his or her parents."[22] Marriages to which parents objected were voided in Augsburg. In Zurich, parental consent was required only if children were under nineteen, while in Nuremberg it was required until a boy was twenty-five and a girl twenty-two. In 1565, Strasbourg raised the minimum age for marriage without consent from twenty-four for boys and twenty for girls to twenty-five for both sexes, while Basel lowered requirements from twenty-four and twenty to twenty and eighteen between 1529 and 1533.[23] The response to the problem of secret marriages was more uniform: Basel, Nuremberg and Zurich, for example, all required the presence of witnesses for a valid marriage. Protestants also reduced the numbers of impediments, as well as the numbers of partners forbidden under consanguinity laws. In spite of variations in interpretation and practice, Protestant polities uniformly took advantage of opportunities created by the Reformation to simplify and modify the canon law, using scriptural principles as the basis for new laws.

Finally, adopting the Reformation usually created a legal vacuum which made developing a new court system a matter of some urgency. This gave reformed territories the chance to develop marriage tribunals more in harmony with the wishes both of reformers and laity. Zurich, for example, had been under the authority of the bishop of Constance. There was no tribunal within the city which had exercised matrimonial jurisdiction before the break with the bishop. However, even in cities and territories where such a vacuum did not occur, the old episcopal courts were not rebaptized and continued under the new dispensation. The hostile feelings of the laity were largely responsible for this development. Particularly in Germany, lay antipathy to the ecclesiastical courts had regularly manifested itself since at least the mid-fifteenth century.[24] Miriam Chrisman, who studied books and pamphlets written by Strasbourg laymen in the early years of the Reformation, observed that "[f]ear and mistrust of the ecclesiastical arm helped to shape the lay response to the Reform. Their eagerness to dissolve the ecclesiastical courts or to curb their jurisdiction stemmed, in part, from the fact that they saw them as arbitrary, capricious and repressive, a threat to the peace of the community."[25]

Because of this long-standing displeasure with courts run by the church, few places which took matrimonial jurisdiction away from bishops were eager to hand it over to the Protestant clergy. The reformers, for their part, did not have a uniform policy. Luther wanted nothing to do with marriage cases and believed they were entirely the business of the magistrates. In spite of this, because of his preaching and teaching about marriage, people often sought his advice in difficult cases. When a pastor from Zwickau wrote for his advice in 1532, Luther responded angrily "I'll give him something to remember me by for implicating me in such matters that belong to the government!"[26] Heinrich Bullinger, Zwingli's successor in Zurich, held a position similar to Luther's. The minister, in Bullinger's ecclesiology, was the successor of the Old Testament prophet. The pastor could thus only admonish the ruler to establish religion according to the divine word, and exhort the people to keep the covenant conditions. His function did not include discipline, even exclusion from the eucharist. The magistrate was the successor of the Old Testament kings. Like the Old Testament ruler, the magistrate alone had the power to establish religion and to discipline.[27]

Oecolampadius, however, urged the establishment of ecclesiastical morals courts, a view shared by Martin Bucer, John Calvin, and Theodore Beza.

Ultimately, whatever their position on the nature of the new courts, reformers were at the mercy of the magistrates and princes who protected them and their coreligionists. Lay leaders were understandably reluctant to create new tribunals which could tyrannize over them or which could become independent power bases undercutting their own authority and the unity of their cities or territories. In Strasbourg, for example, the political authority of the bishop had been ended in the thirteenth century. Since that time, the Senate and XXI, the two principal governing bodies, had been chipping away at ecclesiastical court jurisdiction within the city. The clergy, however, remained outside of their control because they were not required to buy Burgerrecht. In the sixteenth century, when the bishop was under severe economic pressure, his attempts to extort additional revenues from the clergy drove them to the Rat for protection. Adopting the Reformation completed the process by which the Rat ended all independent authority in Strasbourg. Bucer, therefore, argued in vain for a church polity which would create a consistory and exclude magisterial control over church matters. Instead, in 1529, the Rat established a marriage court consisting of three Senators and two Ratsherren with only an advisory role for the clergy. In Nuremberg, the council rebuffed Osiander's desire for a consistory and gave authority over marriage and morals to the city civil court. No clergymen sat on the courts which were given jurisdiction over marriage in Augsburg or in Denmark.

Courts with mixed membership were occasional solutions. Zurich adopted, in 1525, a local tribunal made up of two clergymen and four lay members (two each from the small council and great council). Appeal from this court would be to the great council. In 1539, Electoral Saxony created a consistory court of two clergymen and two lawyers. In Geneva the consistory established by Calvin was made up of pastors and elders appointed by the council. Although technically civil servants, the method and term of appointment of the pastors made them extremely independent of the magistracy. Moreover, the council was required to consult with the pastors on the choice of elders for the consistory. Thus, in spite of magisterial appointment, the Genevan consistory was the most non-lay of all of the new Protestant courts which had jurisdiction over matrimonial matters.[28] The Genevan consistory, which so many churchmen such as Bucer and Osiander would have preferred, was exceptional. As Steven Ozment notes, Protestant governments "were no keener on giving Protestant clergy jurisdiction over the moral life than they had been on letting Catholic bishops continue to exercise it."[29]

This brief survey is not comprehensive, for it is not my purpose to rehearse the German, Swiss and Scandinavian Protestant movements and their treatment of marriage law and theology. Rather, these examples have been set out to show that the "new view" of marriage emerged because of many different constituencies with different reasons for wanting to implement a change. In England, on the other hand, similar developments never occurred. Official sacramental theology was unsettled for over twenty years after the break with Rome and marriage did not finally lose its sacramental status until the Elizabethan settlement. Even then, official desacramentalization's impact was blunted by the form of the new marriage service. The celibate ideal was not attacked in England with either the vigor or immediate success that characterized such attacks elsewhere. Finally, the Roman canon law of marriage and the system of courts which applied and enforced it survived virtually unchanged until the seventeenth century. This unusual course left England more "Roman" than the Roman church, since even after the Council of Trent made significant changes in marriage law, the English church continued to use pre-Tridentine rules.

There is no simple explanation for this, and I eschew any monocausal approach to the subject in what follows. Rather, I argue that there are several factors, acting in concert, which are responsible for England's unique situation. First, I will describe the medieval canon law of marriage and its application in England, focusing on the unique *modus vivendi* which developed between the English crown and church during the middle ages. Next, I will trace debates over sacramental theology, ritual, clerical marriage, and law reform through the reigns of the Tudors, showing why those in the political nation who could have initiated some reform of marriage law and practice chose not to do so. Finally, I will argue that because the English people were largely satisfied with marriage law as it was and with the courts which enforced it, there was no grassroots lay reform movement either. No one of these parts stands alone, in my view, nor is one more important than another. For a tangled web of reasons, there was no significant constituency for marriage reform in England, and with no constituency demanding it, no reform took place.

2

Church, Crown, Lordship and Marriage in Medieval England

Medieval marriage has been the subject of much study in the past two decades. Among the most important and widely respected products of that study is *Marriage Litigation in Medieval England*, in which Professor Richard Helmholz declared that "there never was an English law of marriage apart from that administered by the Church courts."[1] This chapter argues that, in fact, there *was* an English law of marriage apart from that of the church. When the Reformation began in England, a *modus vivendi* had been in place for nearly three centuries by which ecclesiastical and secular powers *shared* jurisdiction over marriage.[2] Not only were the two authorities compatible, but their successful cooperation was essential in shaping the special character of the English reaction to the Reformation.

Until the twelfth century, the king was responsible for the administration of both secular and ecclesiastical law. Once these two became separate spheres as a result of the Investiture Controversy, the possibility of conflict between overlapping and competing jurisdictions arose. In England, after a brief crisis, the crown and the church agreed to a compromise so effective and long-lasting that it left not only the crown but the feudal nobility and the political elites of England without significant grievances against the church courts and their jurisdiction at the beginning of the Reformation.

An important component of this compromise concerned the law of marriage. Marriage was a sacrament, and thus its regulation concerned the church. However, marriage was also an act with political and economic implications and therefore of concern to feudal and manorial authorities. Reconciling these claims was a significant part of the crown's achievement in the twelfth century. To this successful synthesis belongs partial credit for English reluctance to change marriage law under the Tudors. Tracing this accommodation is the first step towards understanding marriage's fate in the English Reformation.

Long before the twelfth century, when the church began to extend and formalize its claim to legal jurisdiction over marriage, the church and the crown collaborated in efforts to reform English matrimonial practices.[3] Although the church initially faced resistance in England (as elsewhere) to its regulations against near-kin marriage, by the late tenth century royal laws reinforced papal dicta.[4] Anglo-Saxon laws also affirmed the rights of widows to be free to marry whom they wished after an appropriate mourning period, and a law of Cnut denounced forced marriage, a principle closely associated with the church, stating "no woman or maiden shall ever be forced to marry a man whom she dislike."[5]

The conquest of England (with papal support) by Duke William of Normandy and his choice of Lanfranc of Bec as archbishop of Canterbury reversed a century of decline in the English church. William summoned councils, presiding personally over many, to reform and discipline the church.[6] In his ordinance of 1072(?), William stepped towards the creation of institutionally separate ecclesiastical courts, which were not a feature of the pre-1066 ecclesiastical polity.[7] Contemporaries would have found nothing exceptional in William's intrusive practice of kingship by which, like David and Solomon, "all things spiritual and temporal alike waited upon the nod of the king."[8]

During William's reign, the Investiture Contest, initially an argument between cardinals Peter Damian and Humbert of Silva Candida on the validity of the orders of a simoniacal bishop, was becoming a quarrel about something far more fundamental: the proper relation of priestly and royal offices. From 1059, the papacy prohibited lay investiture and a conflict resulted from the refusal of the emperor to accept this decree which convulsed church-state relations on the continent until 1122.[9] William could not accept the political dimensions of the decrees against lay investiture any more than could the emperor. English bishops were feudal lords exercising secular jurisdiction, and as such were crucial to William in the process of consolidating his control. Any suggestion that he be deprived of the right to choose his barons would have been risible. For William, "[t]he management of material estates [did] not become a spiritual activity simply because bishops [were] set in charge of them".[10] But the desperate need of the pope for allies, and the genuine concern of William for the good order of the church insured that William would remain untroubled.[11] The reigns of William's heirs were marred by severe disruptions of church-state relations. At the end, however, it was the terms and not the fact of the partnership between ecclesiastical and secular government which were changed.

Until 1095 there was no trouble between the new scholarly monk-archbishop Anselm and the coarse, vulgar king William II. Then a series of conflicts began which resulted in Anselm fleeing the country and remaining exiled until William's death in 1100.[12] During his exile, Anselm drank deeply at the reformers' well. William's brother, Henry I, was compelled by his insecurity on the throne to come to terms with Anselm who made one of his conditions that the king reject lay investiture. After several years of wrangling, Henry gave up investiture and Anselm accepted the principle of doing homage for lay fees attached to church offices, and the transformation of English ecclesiastical jurisdiction was underway.[13]

Some time before 1118, a collection of the laws current and applicable during Henry's reign was compiled.[14] Virtually a textbook of contemporary theocratic government, it captures perhaps better than any other surviving document a still picture of the legal world then coming to an end. For the compiler of the *Leges Henrici Primi*, it was natural to describe county courts having jurisdiction over the due rights of the Christian faith (*debita vere christianitatis iura*),[15] and church affairs triable by the king (*placitis ecclesie pertinentibus ad regem*) including not paying Peter's Pence, refusing to render tithes, and withholding annual church dues. In adultery cases, the king had authority over the man and the bishop over the woman. Working on church festival days was subject to a heavy fine.[16] Both William and Henry I had accorded the bishop of London the right to hear cases of adultery, working on festival days, and blasphemy and perjury, and it appears likely that these rights were held and exercised by other bishops as well,[17] but these rights were not exercised in separate ecclesiastical courts, and they were exercised only by royal grant and not by virtue of episcopal authority over spiritual matters.

Ironically, this compilation was made at precisely the moment when it was ceasing to be relevant to the English legal system. Yet even as the division between lay and ecclesiastical jurisdiction hardened and found institutional reflections, and ecclesiastical causes ceased to be a form of plea pertaining to the crown and began to develop a life and procedure of their own, the cooperation which characterized the centuries when the two spheres were blurred was to continue. It was the mechanics of the partnership, and not the fact of it, which were to change as a result of the Gregorian revolution in church-state relations.

That Henry was allowed to go quietly about his old ways has led Norman Cantor to conclude that the church had failed to overthrow the church-state system of William I and Lanfranc.[18] This is misleading. First, the crisis period created for the first time the notion of the papal court as an alternative to the king's court as a source of justice. Several embassies went back and forth to Rome during the years of struggle appealing to the pope for some resolution. Those embassies brought to the pope, for his judgement, other issues of importance to the local church and brought back knowledge of new potentials and procedures. There is also evidence of matrimonial cases initiated by private parties independent of these embassies. One case petitioned for the annulment of the marriage of Matilda of Aquila with Robert de Mowbray, Earl of Northumberland and a prisoner of the king. The pope referred the case back to Archbishop Anselm, who granted the annulment.[19] The physical distance between England and Rome and the difficulties that raised in transmitting necessary information were serious barriers to the utility and popularity of litigating in Rome. Nonetheless, the trickle of litigants was to become a flood within a century. More importantly, Henry I never voiced any objections.[20] While individual cases may seem unimpressive in matter or numbers, Martin Brett notes,

> [I]n 1100 ignorance of papal practice was all but universal in England; by the end of the reign this can have been far less true . . . . If it was still true that Henry's clergy in 1135 placed more trust in a royal charter than a papal privilege, and preferred the king's court to the Pope's Curia, by then they certainly recognized the alternative, and were incomparably better informed on papal affairs than their predecessors in the days of Lanfranc.[21]

Henry's compromise conceded that there was a real difference between the spheres of the secular and the sacred. While rejecting a complete separation between clergy and laity as the Gregorians desired, it did recognize that the clergy had separate roles as subjects of the king and ministers of the church. In so doing, it admitted in principle that there were activities which were of an order over which secular authorities had no rights. It also created the potential, soon to be realized, of divided loyalties and overlapping claims of jurisdiction.

Henry had worked a small revolution in statecraft of his own. In approaching the Gregorian papacy he was always pragmatic. Henry never stood on the old theocratic principles of his father. Instead, he set the precedent for negotiating with the papacy ways in which royal dignity and English custom could appear to be protected while conceding the legitimate concerns of the church. While not an active reformer like the Conqueror, Henry supported order and discipline in the church, and approved reforming canons. Compared with the contemporaneous crippling catarrh afflicting the Empire, the dispute over Anselm's exile was only a mild cold. The willingness both sides evinced to negotiate and respect the dignity of the other cured it speedily. Henry never stood in the way of change. He simply determined to ensure that it did not race away leaving royal dignity in the dust.[22] This pattern of negotiation and compromise would be repeated over and over again in the following three hundred years. Henry's lasting contribution to church-state relations was that he recognized outdated ideology, abandoned it and, however cautiously, led England forward.

His successor, Stephen of Blois, owed his throne to the church and the efforts of his brother the bishop of Winchester.[23] Stephen's coronation was a triumph for the Cluniac belief that the most effective way to protect and reform the church was "not by fighting the secular power but by cooperating with it and converting it," and it raised the expectation of "a glorious condominium in England with two brothers, bishop and king, wielding the spiritual and secular swords in loving harmony."[24] By 1139 harmony had become dissonance. Concerns about church liberties underlay Stephen's deposition in favor of Henry I's daughter Matilda, and his restoration when Matilda proved even more antipathetic to those liberties. On three separate occasions the church determined the occupant of the throne. In addition, the pope deposed one archbishop of York and replaced him with another, with the king looking on helplessly. It was also during these years that legal appeals to the pope became commonplace, and it seems that papal judges delegate with explicit mandates to resolve legal (especially matrimonial) cases first appear at this time.[25]

The expanding legal activities of the papacy during Stephen's reign were more than a reflection of the weakness of the king and his willingness, provoked by desperation, to share power with the church. The course and solution of the struggle over lay investiture had sailed the church into uncharted waters in a ship over which no one had much control, for what began innocently enough as an attempt to reform the church in part by wresting the appointment of those responsible for directing that reform out of the unreliable hands of secular rulers quickly broadened into a more theoretical dispute upon the nature of authority itself.

Blinkered by the conventional presuppositions of his age, Gregory VII could conceive only of a unitary church-state; if the king was not in charge of it, then the pope must be. Gregory construed the superiority of the spiritual power to be not only over spiritual things, but over all things, including kings and emperors, while Henry I had taken the novel and more reasonable position that the two structures of offices were separable one from the other, that there were two swords of spiritual and temporal government, and that they could be wielded by different people.[26] However, in order for a strict division of spheres to work, the clergy would have to abandon completely both landed estates and temporal power. Since that was not about to happen, the church had to (and finally did) admit that temporal activities did not become spiritual because they were conducted by clerics, and settle for superiority over spiritual activities, conceding temporal matters to secular rulers. It was on this basis that Henry's settlement had been made, and this was the basis for resolving the larger Investiture Contest in 1122.

The compromise created an administratively united church, placing the pope in a relationship of superiority to the whole church parallel to that of a king over his kingdom, but it was an authority for which the papacy was ill-prepared. Having been admitted to jurisdiction over spiritual matters, it was soon blindingly apparent that the definition of what constituted a spiritual matter, the rules to employ when dealing with it, and the sanctions to apply against those who violated those rules remained undefined.[27]

The church was well provided with laws and rules, derived from scripture, the early councils, church fathers and the decretal letters of popes.[28] With its new role as supreme judge and legislator, the papacy found the numbers of cases initiated or appealed to Rome swelling and the clamor for legal advice becoming deafening. It became crucial to make some sense out of the inchoate mass of maxims, dicta and rescripts, "to convert the detritus of a thousand years of Church law-making into a comprehensible legacy."[29]

Around 1140, at the University of Bologna (Europe's leading law school) the Camaldolese monk Gratian compiled his *Concordia discordantium canonum* (or *Decretum*), which was speedily adopted as the definitive statement of the law up to that date, widely copied and circulated.[30] The popularity of Gratian's *Decretum* facilitated greater administrative unity in the church, and Gratian's emphasis on the pope's role as supreme judge and legislator accelerated the movement among bishops and judges to seek his opinion in legal cases.[31]

Gratian's work enjoyed great respect, but it was never an "official" code of laws and remained merely a text-book, deriving its authority from that of the authority of its components: scripture, conciliar decrees and papal decretals. The papacy's expanding role created new problems which were not addressed in the *Decretum*, and petitioners raised questions not previously asked of the popes. To deal with the deluge of requests, Alexander III (1159–81) expanded the role of papal judges delegate, having them settle locally cases which had been referred to the papacy. While issues of fact were decided locally, popes issued letters detailing the law which was to be applied by the judges.[32] As a result, there was a dramatic rise in the number of decretals after 1140. These, taken with the decrees of the councils at Tours (1169) and the Lateran (1179) meant that there was a substantial body of legal material unincorporated by Gratian which had also to be known by jurists.[33]

Between 1170 and 1210, more than fifty private collections were made to fill this need, though with no authority beyond that of the contents and subject to doubts concerning their authenticity. In 1210, Innocent III (1198–1216) commissioned Peter Collivaccinus to make an official compilation of decretals (*Compilatio Tertia*), followed in 1226 by a collection of Honorius III's (1216–27) decretals (*Compilatio Quinta*). These provided authentic texts, but did no more than supplement Gratian.[34] The 1234 publication of Raymond of Peñafort's *Decretals* was a major event. Raymond made extensive use of previous collections, shortening and modifying some passages and filling gaps with pithy decretals from Gregory IX dashed off for the occasion. In *Rex pacificus* (1234), Gregory also made the *Decretals* the first official code of law for the church; it was to be the sole basis for the resolution of future legal matters.[35]

Investigating the authority of this papal law in England has occasioned some notable scholarly blood-letting. In the *Report* of the Ecclesiastical Courts Commission in 1883, Bishop Stubbs concluded that the Roman canon law had great authority but was not binding, and the English church legislated for itself.[36] F.W. Maitland responded with crushing thoroughness in a series of essays in which he demonstrated that the church courts always considered themselves bound in principle by the authority of papal law and that English provincial and diocesan legislation simply did not provide enough material to form an adequate alternative to it.[37] More recent research has shown that the English were, in fact, the most sophisticated and well-informed adherents of the new law.[38]

Recently, some legal historians have demonstrated, without rejecting the claim that papal law was theoretically binding, that practice in the courts was not entirely consistent with the theoretical claims.[39] The most important member of this "yes, but" school of Maitland's successors is Professor Charles Donahue, whose work has suggested several modifications of the post-Stubbs-Maitland orthodoxy. First, Donahue has demonstrated that procedure in medieval English church courts occasionally deviated from what the canon law dictated, an "imperfect reception" of the law he credits to professional decision makers' resistance to constricting rules, and the need to employ procedure already more or less familiar to litigants and deponents.[40] Donahue has also argued that Maitland was incorrect in describing Roman canon law as statute law. A decretal by its nature addressed only one particular problem, and while it provided principles which could be considered binding in exactly parallel cases, it left room for interpretation and maneuver on the part of lawyers and judges that statute could not. Where gaps existed in the law, which Donahue suggests could be quite regular, the judges exercised considerable freedom in decision making.[41] He emphasizes quite correctly that legal historians have taken an anachronistic view of medieval courts. The court was a place where disputes were settled. The infrequency of sentences in ecclesiastical courts suggests that the judges rarely were pushed to the point of having to apply canon law to the issue before them. "All of this does not make the papal law any less binding," he concludes, "but it does make it considerably less important."[42] Nevertheless, it seems clear that *if* a case proceeded to judgement, it was virtually certain that an English jurist would not imagine applying any law other than the pope's if appropriate rules existed.

This leaves the problem faced by Stephen's successor Henry II of jurisdictional competition between royal and church courts, especially in the wake of the expanding claims of the pope.[43] Henry was not an enemy of ecclesiastical liberties, and his apparent interference in church matters proves upon investigation to be both justified and quite modest.[44] Nor did Henry obstruct legal appeals to Rome.[45] Henry believed that problems of unclear or ambiguous jurisdictions should be resolved by discussion on a case-by-case basis and not by stubborn appeals to ideology on either side, and Archbishop Theobald accepted this. He believed the pope might have jurisdiction in principle, but he realized the limits of papal power and that in practice it might not always be expedient.[46]

In the 1160s, as Henry struggled to improve law and order in England, one of the most frequent complaints he received concerned the inadequacy of ecclesiastical discipline in dealing with criminous clerks. Henry felt compelled to intervene, and it was over this issue that the new archbishop Thomas Becket took an unnecessarily provocative stand on the untouchability of the clergy. The pope supported Henry in the interests of harmony and Becket was forced to back away. Strengthened by this victory, Henry prepared a statement of sixteen customs of the time of Henry I, the Constitutions of Clarendon, which he demanded that all of the bishops should sign.[47] Becket's exile and eventual murder followed from their refusal. The Constitutions were hardly worth a death, as their claims were quite modest. While Pope Alexander took the tactical position that abandoning the Constitutions was essential for reestablishing good relations with Henry after Becket's murder, the Compromise of Avranches in May 1172 gave both men most of what they wanted. Henry agreed "utterly [to] abolish customs prejudicial to the church which had been introduced in his reign," a phrase sufficiently vague to leave any claims based on his grandfather's customs intact. The bishops were not required to swear to any statement of customs. The king agreed not to impede appeals to Rome, but he was allowed to take security from those he had cause to mistrust.[48] Disputes over advowsons and debts jurisdiction raised by the Constitutions were not as easily compromised. Although Alexander III had forbidden ecclesiastical courts from cooperating or collaborating with royal courts in cases of patronage, Henry resolved matters by a royal show of force: he issued a writ to the bishop prohibiting him from hearing a plea touching patronage on the grounds that such suits concerning advowsons belonged to the crown.[49] Jurisdiction over debt cases was similarly resolved by a limited writ of prohibition. Henry did not claim all debt cases, but only those of laymen, and only in suits over chattels and debts which were not "from testaments or matrimony."[50]

The writ of prohibition sounds much more aggressive than it actually was. It was rarely employed, and church courts still heard cases of debt and advowson which could easily have been prohibited.[51] As W.L. Warren notes: "This technique of haphazard veto was an ingenious piece of practical statesmanship: it asserted the authority of the crown while allowing in practice the operation of parallel jurisdictions. It left the initiative in the hands of the king without forcing the clergy to the humiliation of abandoning established claims." In other words, Henry conceded the jurisdiction of the church while retaining his own.[52] The writ of prohibition remained the basis for harmony which was not substantially disturbed during the period before the Reformation,[53] and the legal developments of the thirteenth century, which made the secular courts more effective, did not directly raise issues of jurisdiction.[54] While the abuse of prohibitions was a constant source of clerical grievance in the thirteenth century, there was a statutory form for quashing an improper prohibition and, in 1311, the king granted that judges and plaintiffs victimized by the illegal use of prohibitions would receive damages from the guilty party.

After the Compromise of Avranches, then, both courts settled down to doing their business as effectively and productively as possible. As royal courts improved procedurally and were thus more desirable to litigants, the business and profit of the ecclesiastical courts could be reduced, and there was little the latter could do about it.[55] The *modus vivendi* itself, however, was not challenged.

In only one case (bastardy) was ecclesiastical jurisdiction itself actually reduced and this has received more attention than it deserves precisely because it is so unusual. In inheritance cases which turned on an accusation of bastardy, the royal court would ask the bishop to certify whether the parents of the alleged bastard were validly married.[56] There was one wrinkle: canon law recognized as legitimate the children born before a couple married while common law did not accept retroactive legitimacy for inheritance.[57] When the exception of bastardy due to prenuptial birth was raised at common law, reference to the church courts yielded an unsatisfactory answer. The royal courts adopted the expedient of submitting to a jury the question of fact: was X born before or after the marriage of X's parents? This avoided challenging the right of the church to determine status. Pope Alexander III described Henry III as disturbed by this problem, and essentially conceded the point to the king since property inheritance was at issue.[58] Confrontation took place only because the bishop Robert Grosseteste, one of that quixotic breed of English bishops given to being more papalist than the pope, insisted not that the church should continue to hear the pleas as before but that the English law should be changed and brought into line with the canon law. At the Council of Merton in January 1236, the barons "answered with one voice that they would not change the law of the realm."[59] Grosseteste had no successors willing to tilt at that particular windmill and the matter was left to the juries in exceptions of "special bastardy."

What is so striking in this case is the reluctance of common law courts to be accused of poaching. They never asserted the right to decide status and carefully avoided the appearance of such a claim. An isolated, if influential, prelate forced the issue. In spite of the conflict which erupted, nothing shows more clearly the normal pattern of cooperation and mutual respect which existed between the two courts. The church needed the secular courts to enforce sentences of excommunication.[60] The common law courts needed the church courts to do justice in cases of debt and testament among others for which they themselves simply had no law. Even in the political crises of the thirteenth century, bishops from Grosseteste to Winchelsey who ran up the flag and cried "Church in danger" did not challenge the proper operations of the compromise which followed the death of Becket. Church and crown were partners in a cooperative venture to provide justice to the English people. Their spheres of activity had been settled in the infancy of the emerging common law under Henry II and the canon law under Alexander III. The settlement, as these things go, was remarkably durable.[61]

Henry II and his successors never attempted to circumscribe the church's matrimonial jurisdiction. Although it was at one time the appropriate object of royal legislation, at the division of spiritual and temporal matters in the twelfth century, the king conceded marriage to the church. This concession was neither automatic nor inevitable in the face of historical practice. As Georges Duby says: "In the early centuries of the Church, its leaders nearly all looked on marriage as something repugnant and did their best to keep it as far away as possible from all that was sacred." While the Carolingian church made laws regulating marriage under royal supervision, it was reluctant to become too involved. King Louis the Pious once referred a matrimonial case to the bishops who refused it as unseemly. Reliance on Roman law for ideas and language reinforced the view of marriage as a secular matter, and priests were rarely involved even in ceremonial aspects.[62]

 Several forces acted together to undo the old ways. First, people began to seek a priestly blessing over their weddings the way they did over their fields (and with much the same intention) and the church complied.[63] Second, the attack on clerical marriage resulted in the church taking upon itself to dissolve marriages as part of its disciplinary jurisdiction over the clergy.[64] Third, and perhaps most important, the concern of the church with sin and salvation led to increasing challenges to the sexual mores of the time and attempts to change behavior.[65] So complete and successful was the shift that John of Salisbury could say in 1158 in referring to the Anstey case that Henry II did right in referring to the ecclesiastical court because the question of marriage was something "which the clergy understand and of which the laity are ignorant."[66]

By the late thirteenth century there was perhaps no other field of ecclesiastical authority for which the body of law was so complete and the gaps so few.[67] Since the canon law was both effectively binding and widely available and studied in England, it is extremely important for what follows to understand in what the canon law of marriage consisted.[68]

A valid and indissoluble marriage was effected when a man and a woman who were free to do so exchanged words in the present tense indicating their consent to be husband and wife.[69] There was no necessity for any ceremony, publicity, witnesses, or consent by any other parties such as parents. The couple married themselves by their expression of consent alone.[70]

This doctrine, taken from the *Decretals*, was less ambiguous than that originally set down by Gratian. While Gratian averred that the lack of consent proved there was no marriage,[71] consent might not be all that was necessary. A letter of Pope Evaristus against clandestine marriages identified other requirements:

permission of a woman's guardian, betrothal and donation of a dowry by her parents, blessing by a priest, and so on. Without these, the union would not be lawful (*legitimum*).[72] While it was not sinful to omit requirements inadvertently, Evaristus wrote that deliberate omission made the marriage "infected."[73] Was it still valid and indissoluble? Gratian admitted it was,[74] though the exchange of consent had to be ratified by sexual intercourse. Until then, the exchange of consent had not created an indissoluble bond.[75]

Popes and canonists after Gratian supported his argument on consent. No ceremony, publicity, or parental consent were thought necessary for an indissoluble marriage. If such a marriage was alleged, the burden of proof was on the party claiming it,[76] but if both parties admitted it, the church was bound to ratify it.[77] Gratian and his colleagues were sensitive to the difficulties implicit in this formula. It would be quite easy, for example, to commit bigamy or adultery since a person already married secretly could conceal the fact of that union while taking up with another partner.[78] Conversely, it could create difficulties for a couple that married without publicity and lived together faithfully as man and wife if their failure to "go public" had kept them ignorant of a kinship bond between them.[79] If the bond was one considered incestuous by the church, their union was *ipso facto* void; by living together they were guilty of fornication. Clandestine marriages made the legitimacy of offspring uncertain, thereby clouding and confusing inheritance.

To overcome these inconveniences, teaching instruments, such as Thomas of Chobham's *Summa Confessorum* (*c*. 1210) stated that "the couple ought not to be considered married until the ceremonies were supplied."[80] Lateran Council IV (1215) decreed that those who contracted clandestine marriages be punished and a priest who had been present and blessed the union without first publicizing it according to the law was to be suspended from his office for three years.[81] The threat of punishment was not in itself successful. The English church had to respond to a crisis of undeniable magnitude: in mid-fourteenth century Rochester diocese, for example, 29 percent of all church court cases were matrimonial and 88 percent of those (46 of 52) turned on clandestine unions. In late-fourteenth century Ely diocese the figures were similar: 89 of 101 matrimonial cases concerned clandestine unions.[82]

In 1329, after more than a century fruitlessly repeating general prohibitions,[83] the church ordered priests deprived who assisted in clandestine marriages. Archbishop Stratford increased the punishment to *ipso facto* excommunication in *Humana concupiscentia* (1342), which Lyndwood held extended to all participating in the event.[84] Rochester diocesan courts even whipped those convicted of clandestine marriage.[85] Clandestine marriages were never completely eliminated, but two centuries of legislation, teaching and experience finally resulted in general compliance with church requirements.[86]

While following Gratian on the "infected" validity of clandestine marriage, later canonists rejected any requirement that consent be ratified by coitus. Twelfth century French theologians were disturbed by the implications of this for the doctrine of the virginity of Mary: if carnal knowledge was required, Mary and Joseph were not validly married. To save Mary and Joseph's marriage, they suggested that only the vows of the parties to each other were required.[87] Peter Lombard won over Pope Alexander III to this view, which was transmitted into the *Decretals* through his letters.[88]

The new law recognized two forms of betrothal (*desponsatio*), one by words in the present tense (*per verba de presenti*) and one in the future tense (*per verba de futuro*). With the first, consent alone made the bond absolutely binding. In the second case the bond held only if followed by another exchange in the present tense or if ratified by coitus.[89] Until that time, it could be dissolved by the consent of the parties or by one party marrying someone else *per verba de presenti*.[90] Contracts by future words which had not been completed could be enforced by the courts, but they were reluctant to do so since judges noted that forcing people into marriage often had unpleasant results.[91] A person who regretted a promise *per verba de futuro* could ensure against canonical compulsion by contracting *per verba de presenti* with someone else, which seems to be what usually happened.[92]

The problem which canonists and courts never resolved with any precision was that of the tense which certain words implied. As Maitland noted: "Of all people in the world, lovers are the least likely to distinguish precisely between the present and future tenses."[93] The word *volo* ("I wish," "I want") was a particular problem and arguments about its implications became one of the great judicial indoor blood sports of the thirteenth and fourteenth centuries. While, in general, it was held that contracts with the words *volo te habere* ("I wish to have you") were in the present tense, the canonists were not dogmatic, and left room for the judges to maneuver if the evidence warranted it. The great difficulty was that everyday people did not conform their everyday language to the tidy preferences of the canonists and a great many combinations of words were used in actual practice which had to be considered on a case-by-case basis, and the courts set a fairly high standard of required evidence to prove that marriage had been intended.[94]

Similar to the contract *de futuro* was the conditional contract in which the words used approximated "I take you on condition that . . ." The contract's effectiveness was suspended until the condition was fulfilled and then it was considered a contract *de presenti*. Not all conditions operated in this way. Impossible or sinful conditions were judicially ignored and the marriage declared valid as if no condition had ever been stated. If the condition was both sinful and against the substance of matrimony (for example, not to have children) the marriage was not valid. Most commonly, however, the conditions were possible and honest. The most common involved the consent of third parties: "I take you on condition that my father (mother, friends, etc.) consent." Such conditional phrases were frequently alleged in self-defense when accused of failing to fulfill contracts.[95]

The church did not hold that all people had the capacity to marry, roughly what Roman law called *conubium*.[96] In several circumstances, words *de presenti* were deemed inoperative because of impediments which fell into several categories. Preexistent contract was the most important. This is rather self-evident: Jane cannot be free to marry Geoffrey if she is married to Giles. In practice, confusion resulting from clandestine marriages, from uncertainly about the meaning of words exchanged between parties, and deliberate deceit, resulted in a consistently high number of cases in the church courts in which precontract was asserted as a bar to an alleged marriage.[97]

Neither could people marry near kin by blood or marriage. Unions made within the prohibited degrees as spelled out by the church, unless by special dispensation, were *ipso facto* null and void, and the parties were guilty of incest. One of the benefits of publicity before marriage was that it provided an opportunity for knowledge of a relationship to be made public, preventing a scandal as well as a sin.[98]

The vows of children were not binding. A marriage contracted before the age of seven was void. Between seven and puberty (legally, fourteen for boys and twelve for girls) a sort of suspended contract could be made. Upon reaching the age of puberty the children had to demonstrate consent expressly, or implicitly by peaceful cohabitation or consummation. If one or both refused to consent, the union was dissolved.[99]

Impotence was the fourth major impediment. Although coitus was not required for a valid marriage, the partners did have to be capable of it since the procreation of children and the avoidance of fornication through lawful intercourse were the two most important ends of marriage. Although there were several recognized causes of this incapacity, almost all cases alleged the natural impotence of the man. A variety of exotic methods of proof were employed. These included inspection of the virginity of the woman by other women, inspection of the man by "expert and honest men," and even delegation of a group of "honest women" to attempt to arouse the sexual desires of the man and to report the results of their endeavors to the court.[100]

Force prevented true consent, but to prevent casual use of this impediment, the church established the principle that only force which could sway a steady (*constantem*) man or woman would invalidate a contract. The court would hear testimony about events surrounding the contract and decide if the violence, or threats of violence, met that test.[101] Use of force did not render a union void automatically. If the coerced parties cohabited peacefully for a time, they could not later dissolve the marriage. At least one party had to show consistent refusal to consent or cooperate.[102]

There were, finally, a number of impediments of minor significance. If, during his spouse's lifetime, a man committed adultery with another woman, he was barred by virtue of his crime from marrying the second woman after the first wife's death if it could be shown that both parties knew he was married, and if they had compassed the wife's death or promised to marry while she was alive. In practice, this impediment was rarely raised.[103] Other impediments were error of person (marrying Alice when intending to marry Margaret), error of condition (marrying a villein when believing one was marrying a free person)[104] and disparity of cult. All of these could be overcome if, after the discovery of the problem, the marriage was ratified by consent or sexual relations. Religious vows or major holy orders nullified unions automatically.[105]

The need to learn the many impediments gave rise to the many little Latin jingles and mnemonic devices which can be found in many commonplace books, confessional manuals and court books.[106] All of these impediments could result in the dissolution of the bond of marriage: the divorce *a vinculo matrimonio*. Some of them, such as consanguinity or vows of chastity voided a marriage even if no suit was raised in the church court. These were called "diriment impediments." Others such as force and error only voided unions if the parties sought to do so. If, in spite of the impediment, they chose to live together as man and wife, the impediment was overcome.[107]

In three cases, the ecclesiastical courts would release a couple from the obligation of living together but not dissolve the bond. This form of judicial separation, called a divorce *a mensa et thoro*, was available for adultery, spiritual fornication (blasphemy, heresy or apostasy) and abuse (*saevitia*).[108] Since the bond was not dissolved, neither party was free to remarry, and the court hoped that the guilty party would mend his or her ways and a reconciliation could be effected.

To sum up. First, the exchange of words of consent in the present tense was all that was required to create a marriage bond in God's eyes. Once made, such a bond was irrefrangible. Though no ceremony, publicity or consent of other parties was necessary to make the union binding, the inconveniences that could arise from clandestine marriages – adultery, fornication, and muddled inheritances – made them desirable. Clandestine marriages were binding, but considered infected and illegitimate. Though not dissoluble, partakers would be subjected to severe punishments. Until they completed all of the desiderata of the law, they would be treated as fornicators, regardless of their status in God's eyes. Second, future tense words or words with an attached condition created imperfect unions. A later unconditional promise in the present tense, or coitus (in the first instance) or fulfillment of the condition (in the second) was necessary to make it a binding, indissoluble union. To exchange effective vows, the man and woman had to be capable, that is, there could not be supervening impediments. Some impediments made contracts null and void automatically; others made them voidable but only in the event of a judgement after trial by an ecclesiastical court at the request of at least one of the parties. A decree of nullity left the parties free to marry someone else. A decree of judicial separation did not leave either party free to remarry.

Some scholars have drawn extreme, unsustainable conclusions based on this canon law. Anthropologist Jack Goody turned from his study of African society and kinship to indict the western Christian church for making marriage too difficult in a deliberate attempt to erode the rights of kin groups and upset traditional "strategies of heirship" in order to enrich the church.[109] Georges Duby, by describing "the conflict between two radically different and antagonistic models" of marriage, argues that the ecclesiastical marriage model was fundamentally opposed to the secular lay model and its goals.[110] Legal historians such as Professors Sheehan and Donahue argue that Alexander III and his ilk undertook deliberate social engineering to undercut the authority of lords, parents and kin and "to make it easier for people to choose their marriage partners free from the control of others." For Donahue, Alexander's was "a conscious . . . attempt to use the canon law to influence the course of social development," and "represented a vision of what marriage ought to be . . . a vision far from the reality of the time in which [he] lived." For John Noonan, Gratian and his successors were responsible for creating "a giant democracy in which everyone might marry anyone."[111]

Were these scholars' views to be true, when the Reformation arrived, the English laity (especially the upper class) should have thundered for either the abolition or radical reform of marriage law. But these are distortions of reality, for in a world in which feudal and Christian society were coterminous, in which churchmen were feudal lords and shared the same interests, such an opposition would presuppose either endemic schizophrenia, or at least an ignorance of their own best interests which it stretches credibility to believe they had. Moreover, if such an opposition was taking place, it is absolutely inconceivable that medieval feudal authorities would have so casually conceded the ecclesiastical courts jurisdiction over marriage. Such claims were late developing and kings could have appealed to tradition to keep marriage in the royal purview, expanding the writ of prohibition to include matrimonial cases. That such a policy was neither adopted nor suggested argues that it is the historians and not the law-makers and law-finders of the middle ages who were blind and befuddled.

In "Power to Choose," Noonan sets out Gratian's texts against parentally compelled marriages, and then cites his dictum that there is no lawful marriage unless the girl is given by her parents, concluding that Gratian contradicted himself. According to scripture only widows had the right of free choice of spouses, yet Gratian appropriates this right for all people without scriptural warrant. According to Noonan, Gratian did this to exalt the power of the papacy at the expense of family and feudal lords. *Pace* Noonan, Gratian is completely consistent. Nowhere does he say that children should be free to choose, but only that they should be free from coercion in marriage: there is no lawful marriage unless the girl is given, not coerced, by her parents. Noonan confused choice and consent, and it is he and not the Bolognese monk who has muddled his texts.

With Professors Donahue and Sheehan the problem is rather different. The picture of conflict which they paint results from their preoccupation with the "consent only" doctrine canonized by Alexander III. While it is true that the canons do permit marriages by consent alone, it is worth asking what options the theologians had. There certainly was no scriptural warrant for a requirement of ceremony, banns, endowment or parental consent for a valid marriage.[112] Nor was the weight of tradition on the side of those who might have wanted to make such a requirement, for while Romans knew one marriage of extremely limited application, the *confarreatio*, which required a ritual for validity, the most common Roman marriages at the beginning of the Christian era were made by the couple's consent alone. Third-party consent was required only if either the man or the woman was in *patria potestas*, not *sui iuris*.[113] The German *Friedelehe* was similar. The Frankish church accepted the Roman principle, and while it might excommunicate a man for presuming to marry a girl against her parents' wishes, it does not seem to have required the permission of the bride's family to make the marriage valid.[114] Roman and Frankish society did not conceive of these marriages as indissoluble, and divorce was, for men, frequent and convenient. Thus, the church's real innovation was in the ninth century when it introduced indissoluble monogamous relationships into the law and social vocabulary of the west.[115]

It is undeniably true that clandestine marriages caused great inconveniences, and it is equally true that they were responsible for a disproportionate share of litigation. That was not the fault of canon law. Clandestine marriages had been causing inconveniences to the Romans as well and people would have continued to marry without reference to church, family or lord regardless of what Alexander III had to say. What is significant is not that they did so, but that the church punished them and made a far from toothless effort to eradicate behavior that had been part of western life for at least a millenium. Pope Alexander may have conceded validity to marriages made by consent alone, but the doctrine this represented occupied a small place in the canons described above and an even smaller place in the legal and pastoral texts. In fact, Alexander's consent theory was simply buried by and in this literature.

The canons actually protected the interests of parents and feudal lords by requiring the consent "of those in whose power [the couple] were," for a completely legal marriage.[116] More importantly, the pope explicitly allowed observing local custom to be required as well.[117] Failure to observe it could result in punishment up to and including excommunication, just as in the case of failure to secure consent, call the banns, and so on. Therein lay the potential to modify human behavior.

The canonists' overarching goal was the right ordering of Christian society, a goal shared with secular governments, and in their minds no society was orderly in which couples married willy-nilly without a care for their families' interests, their feudal responsibilities, or the health of their souls. The primary reason why English secular and church courts did not clash over matrimonial jurisdiction is because of this respect for local custom and for the rights of parents and lords. The church courts pointed the way which the secular courts followed: marriages arranged and effected without the desired consent of lords could not be dissolved because they were binding in the eyes of God, but they could be punished and they were. The laws and customs which regulated feudal marriage in this way did constitute, *pace* Helmholz, "an English law of marriage apart from that administered by the church courts."[118]

Royal and manorial courts did not attempt to dissolve marriages. They accepted absolutely the doctrine that consent alone made a marriage valid in the eyes of God, and therefore unbreakable. In fact, royal judges applied the church's definition in their own courts. For example, when Alice, the plaintiff in a suit for dower against Richard fitz Roger de Barneby, foolishly denied that she ever exchanged words of consent with Roger, she saved the court and the heir a great deal of trouble and time, for the non-existence of a valid marriage precluded the existence of a licit one, and therefore any right to dower.[119] Admitting an impediment had the same effect. Isabel, "wife" of Robert fitz Geoffrey, lost a suit for dower against her stepson, Robert's heir, when she conceded that Robert consented to marry her only after a struggle in which he lost his nose – clearly force sufficient to sway a constant man and thus prevent free consent.[120] These cases emphasize the deference to and happy acceptance of ecclesiastical jurisdiction as embodied in the definition of a sacramentally valid marriage, for the secular courts had nothing to lose in so doing.

What did concern these courts was lordship over property. It was this which gave lords a vested interest in the marriages of any of their tenants, for around the issue of marriage hung all questions of inheritance. Likewise it was this which necessitated "an English law of marriage" – a law particularly concerned with the marriages of widows, minors and wards, and with legitimacy.

Papal decretals upheld the widows' privilege of controlling their remarriage and ended the Roman requirement that they first complete the one-year mourning period called *tempus luctus*.[121] English law then followed suit. While assured their canonical rights, widows were required to make security that they would not marry without consent of their lords.[122]

Before Magna Carta and canon law combined to stop lords forcing widows to remarry, a popular arrangement was paying a fine to marry or not according to one's desires.[123] This continued after 1215 and the overlord's license to remarry was still secured by payment of a fine, although the amount of the fine seems to have decreased substantially. In 1205, Mabel Bardolf paid 3,000 marks and five palfreys to the king to control her own remarriage, and in the same year the dowager countess of Warwick offered £1,000 and ten palfreys "that she may remain a widow and not be forced to marry." After Magna Carta, the countess's successor Philippa, widow of the fifth earl, paid only 100 marks "that she not be constrained to marry as long as she prefers to live without a husband, and that she marry whom she pleases."[124] Fines continued to drop. In Edward I's reign, records show them ranging from four to 200 marks, while under Edward II the ceiling was 100 marks and fell as low as a half-mark.[125]

Even when the king granted the marriage of a widow in his gift, canonical rights were respected, and the woman's consent had to be obtained. Juliana, widow of John de Hastings, was granted to Thomas le Blont, Steward of Edward II's household, only if he could "convince . . . [her] to marry him."[126] No doubt she was under pressure to comply, but she could refuse. Refusal, or marriage without license, was not without cost: it could mean payment of a fine much higher than that which would have been paid if the widow had purchased her own marriage at the outset.[127]

Lords accepted fines after the fact, but they could hardly have done otherwise since the marriage was indissoluble. The law could only guarantee the formal seigneurial rights.[128] Glanvill stated that "the woman must marry with the consent of her warrantor or she will lose her dower."[129] This seems to have been applied both in cases of marriage without license and refusal of a marriage proffered by the king.[130] The statute *Prerogativa Regis* states: "And if they marry without licence, then the king shall take into his hands all such lands and tenements as they hold of him in dower until he is satisfied at his own will."[131] When Margery, Countess of Warwick, refused to marry a favorite of Henry III and contracted a clandestine marriage to protect herself, the king made his favorite Earl of Warwick for life anyhow. He could do nothing about the marriage itself.[132]

The marriages of villein widows presented distinct problems linked to those raised by the marriages of all villein women. Pope Hadrian IV had explicitly assured the privilege of valid marriage by consent to villeins.[133] At the same time, the control of villein marriages was becoming more important than ever to lords.[134] If a free tenant could be defined as free "because no lord controlled unsupervised his ability to make grants" and he could not be disseised for failure to obtain a lord's licence, the opposite case became essential to demonstrate unfreedom.[135] The essence of lordship over villeins lay in exercising the right to accept or reject tenants, a right no longer available to the lords of free tenants. Acceptance often took place at the time of marriage because a villein woman's husband became the tenant of her dowry or dower. A lord could not dissolve a marriage, but he could refuse to accept a tenant, or could confiscate a dower as punishment for this breach of his rights. By refusing to acknowledge the normal consequences of a licit marriage, the lord refused to acknowledge that a marriage existed.

Villein remarriage became particularly important in the land-hungry half-century before the Black Death, especially in villages such as Cottenham, on the manor of the abbot of Crowland, where custom allowed the widow to take her husband's entire holding as dower. Obtaining the marriage of a landed villein widow became the primary form of property transfer in the village, and selling marriages was a significant source of revenue for the lord, since they could fetch over £2.[136] Manorial courts could pressure a widow to take a husband, but the initiative remained hers. In November 1288, for example, Agnes Payne was distrained to provide herself with a husband by Christmas, and Sarra Byssop, specifically identified as a young widow, was ordered to marry by the next court session.[137]

Normally, a widow wishing to remarry could pay a fine to proceed. (The prospective husband could also pay it.) The fines varied with the wealth of the villein tenement; for example, they ranged between 40d and 13s 4d on the manor of Wakefield in the fourteenth century.[138] Mariotta, a villein, was the only widow to have her marriage without fine "because she is a pauper."[139] Fines could be paid retroactively, but the amount might be inflated, and forfeiture of maritagium or expulsion from dower lands were seigneurial options.[140]

When Bracton wrote "marriages ought to be free," he surely referred to consent and not cost. Royal judges soundly rejected the assertion that he meant the latter.[141] "That women could fine to determine their own marriages before or after the fact demonstrates," according to Professor Walker, "that . . . feudal overlordship, in so far as the marriage relationship was concerned, must be regarded more as a tax than an interference with freedom of choice."[142] There is something more here than that. That women *had* to fine to determine their own marriages before or after the fact was a demonstration that feudal overlordship was very much a part of the formation of marriage. While accepting the canonical rights of widows, English custom maintained its own distinct understanding of the steps which must necessarily be followed for a widow's marriage to be accepted and respected in the eyes of the law. At no point, however, did this conflict with canon law and in no way could appeal to it free one from an obligation to comply with these requirements.[143]

For unmarried women in general the situation was similar. Even before it was canonically explicit, the king recognized that a union could take place which he was powerless to dissolve, thereby forcing him (potentially) to take the homage of an enemy. Henry I tried to circumvent this by claiming the right to consent to the marriage of any daughter of a tenant-in-chief.[144] Glanvill noted that a lord must be asked to assent to the marriage of women but that he should not refuse except for "due cause"; his prohibition will not be effective otherwise. One who refused to seek her lord's consent could be disseised.[145] This sanction was employed.[146] For villein single women, as for widows, seigneurial control of their marriages was an essential part of their status. Until merchet was paid, lords refused to acknowledge the existence and consequences of their marriages, for their consent to marriages, even after the fact, which merchet represented, was at the very heart of demonstrating lordship.[147]

Marriages of wards raised an equally fundamental seigneurial right.[148] Feudal wardship created lucrative rights over both the land and the person of the heir, male or female. Magna Carta (c. 6) guaranteed that "[h]eirs shall be given in marriage without disparagement," and the Statutes of Merton (1236) and Westminster I (1275) specified permissible fines: heirs who refused honorable marriages would pay the value of the marriage to the lord before receiving seisin of their inheritances; heirs who married without permission while still in wardship were penalized twice the value of their marriage.[149] According to Bracton, if a ward married without permission, the guardian could withhold the inheritance upon the heir's coming of age "until [the guardian] has received from it up to the value of the marriage or until satisfaction has been made to him otherwise."[150]

Women passed out of their guardians' control only upon marriage, and thus required special protection. The Statute of Westminster (c. 22) forbade lords from preventing their female wards from marrying in order to keep their lands in wardship. Heiresses were to be married (subject to all of the statutory protections) by their sixteenth birthdays, or the lord forfeited his right to the marriage. Women successfully refused marriages in such cases and also sued lords who did not observe the statutory time limit set for their marriages.[151]

The canonical right of free consent was scrupulously upheld, and was probably maintained in practice as well since practically no annulment case alleges coercion by feudal lords.[152] Those cases in the rolls which read like forced, and thus invalid, marriages show that the violence was ordinarily against the guardian, while the woman was a willing accomplice of her abductor.[153] If the jury determined this to be the case, damages would be awarded to the lord.[154] Since both the canons and statutes protected the lord's right to consent, the simplest thing was to follow the widows' practice. Administrative documents and manuscript plea rolls demonstrate that heirs of both sexes did precisely that; they bought the freedom to arrange their own marriages, or married without permission and paid fines later when their guardians brought suits against them. Wards who refused suitable marriages paid the statutory penalty as well.[155]

Wards, then, like widows were guaranteed the right of indissoluble marriages made by their consent and protected by the laws and customs of England against marriages made without it. But they could be severely punished for a marriage made without their lord's agreement, however valid in the eyes of God. The full legal consequences of the union did not inhere until the consent of the lord was secured.

Secular courts had also to deal with the consequences of marriages. Could the widow claim dower? Could the widower claim tenancy by custom? Could the issue inherit? Essentially, the rule was that a marriage which had not been solemnized carried with it no rights in land. Claims for many forms of tenure were met with the counterclaim that the woman in question was not legally married in the fullest sense ("not solemnly betrothed [*desponsavit*] but privately"). If this was proved, the tenure claim was rejected.[156] For example, Robert of Norfolk claimed tenancy of the lands of Agnes, alleging that they were married secretly to circumvent the wishes of her lord and both families. The marriage was never solemnized and because she had died and was unable to show her consent, he was denied tenancy.[157]

The most common counterclaim alleged a death-bed marriage, a union *in lecto mortali*. In Del Heith's case (1306), William alleged wrongful disseisin by his uncle Peter, who responded that he held as heir of his brother John. John had married Katherine on his death bed but never married her at church door after his recovery. Because of this, Peter argued, their son William had no right as heir. The court agreed.[158] Dower also was regularly denied when it was not assigned at church door. While Maitland believed that the English law was bringing common sense and sanity to bear against the "formlessness [and] mischievous uncertainty" of the church law by requiring a public ceremony for a valid marriage, this is not the case.[159] Rather, the common law enforced the canonical requirement that "lawful endowment" take place at church door when the marriage was solemnized.[160] The rolls are packed with marriages *in lecto mortali* which, while they might be perfectly valid in the eyes of God, gave women no dower rights in the common law. While such a case could reveal a greedy stepson unwilling to yield one-third of his inheritance to his father's last wife, it could just as easily conceal a dishonest woman anxious to secure a souvenir of her paramour at the expense of his lawful heirs.[161]

Inheritance was a matter for secular courts. Pope Alexander III had conceded that without hesitation, and in any event, it was the common law courts that had the procedure to settle such cases effectively. Had the church ever claimed jurisdiction over inheritance, the litigating public would have voted with their feet and headed in droves for the royal courts. However, if the exception raised by one party for denying seisin by right of inheritance to another was one of bastardy, this raised the question of the validity of a marriage — an ecclesiastical matter. In such cases, a writ would be sent to the litigants' diocesan bishop charging him to enquire into it and report back to the king.[162]

In cases of simple bastardy, this procedure was regularly and usefully employed. In *John fitz Stephen* v. *William Shreve and Agnes his wife*, John alleged disseisin and William and Agnes excepted bastardy. After an inquiry ordered by royal writ, the bishop of Lincoln certified John's legitimacy and he recovered seisin.[163] Some cases were settled by the assize without an episcopal inquiry, but evidence suggests that this was done only when ecclesiastical evidence was available already, such as a letter from the bishop.[164]

Substantive differences did exist between canon and common law, however, which might make use of the ecclesiastical inquiry problematic. As shown above, canon law held that children born after a contract of marriage but before solemnization (called "mantle-children" because they were customarily present at the marriage covered with a cloth) were legitimate.[165] Retroactive legitimacy was not accepted by the common law courts, but the judges still wished to respect ecclesiastical jurisdiction, and fashioned a writ which, by asking a question about the dates of marriage and birth of the child in question only, dodged the question of legitimacy.[166] Some bishops recognized that this violated the spirit of church law and were reluctant to cooperate. Grosseteste ignored the writ's question by returning the delphic response *"Legitimus est,"* doing the royal courts no good at all and causing the 1236 confrontation at Merton and the subtraction of antenuptial birth cases from the church.[167]

This resolution was not as harmful to the church as it appears.[168] Alexander III merely conceded secular courts jurisdiction over seisin; nothing they did could make a child who was legitimate in God's eyes illegitimate, but the common law could refuse to permit seisin by right of inheritance. This was completely consistent: what made a prenuptial child incapable of inheriting was birth before a legitimate marriage, a marriage which had received the lord's consent.[169] In enforcing this requirement and protecting lords' rights, refusing to accept mantle-children as heirs was a logical step. The exception of special bastardy was unknown before the assizes of Henry II because it was unnecessary. After the assizes, it became a weapon in the arsenal of lords protecting their rights to accept tenants, although it could be abused by greedy family members to secure a larger slice of the patrimonial pie for themselves. Unfair it may have been to penalize children for the behavior of their parents, but it was, following the logic of lordship, a necessary evil.

Further problems were raised by children born of solemnized but later dissolved marriages. The church held that if at least one of the parents did not know of the impediment which led to the divorce and acted in good faith, the children born before the divorce were legitimate.[170] English courts took their time developing a consistent policy towards these so-called "good-faith" children.[171] Glanvill originally decided that children of parents divorced for consanguinity were capable of inheriting, but that was rejected by Bracton who accepted only those children born of parents divorced for precontract.[172]

However, that idea was ill-regarded and such children had a standing at law inferior even to mantle-children.[173] By 1400, English courts effectively held that divorce bastardized all children. Rejecting the slippery notion of "good faith," royal courts applied canon law with more relentless logic than did the church courts. Since both kinship and precontract were diriment impediments, any marriages contracted in spite of them were *ipso facto* null and void; their children were therefore the issue of no marriage and incapable of inheriting.[174] Rather than asking the church courts to rule on legitimacy, royal courts inquired about the fact of divorce, and seem not to have encountered difficulties, in spite of parallels to the problem raised by the writ of special bastardy.

Finally, another consequence of marriage with which the law had to contend was maritagium, the woman's premortem inheritance which she brought to the marriage from her family. Several sorts of suits could arise from that transfer. The first would enforce delivery of promised gifts. Glanvill said that such a plea could belong to the church courts if the petitioner so desired.[175] However, if the maritagium was in land, a writ of prohibition could be employed and, as a matter concerning lay fee, was left to king's courts. Helmholz found very few suits for delivery of maritagia of money or chattels in the church courts. Some appear in the manorial courts, which were well equipped to deal with petty debt: "It is found by inquest that John of Elm wrongfully detains from Henry Sheppard 6d of the marriage portion of his [John's] daughter."[176] It seems likely that the simplicity and availability of manorial court procedure made it the court of choice in such cases.

If the maritagium was delivered and the marriage did not take place, a related suit for recovery of goods arose. If the failure was due to ecclesiastical court action, such as blocking an incestuous union, that same court might order return of the goods.[177] If the maritagium was in land, recovery was effected in the royal courts through a writ of novel disseisin.[178] Royal courts acknowledged that recovery of moveables was not their concern.[179] They did not begin to provide a remedy in such cases until the sixteenth century when King's Bench began to take cognizance of "disappointment of expectations raised by words," or nonfeasance, as part of the evolution of *Assumpsit*.[180] In 1506, in *Lewes* v. *Style*, King's Bench heard a suit for recovery due to nonmarriage, and this jurisdiction expanded in the following years.[181]

The retardation of the royal courts was due mainly to their incapacity for providing remedies for the breach of an oral agreement, which most marriage contracts of this sort were. As the manorial courts decayed and ceased to provide petty debt remedies, Chancery stepped into the breach and early in the sixteenth century began doing a steady business in both types of suits. For example, around 1540, Thomas Dykys married Margaret Lancaster after her brother promised him 80 marks if he did. Thomas enfeoffed her in property worth 20 nobles per year as part of the agreement but her brother refused to honor his part. With no written bond, Thomas sought remedy in Chancery.[182] Recovery could also be sought there: John Downe complained in 1539 that he gave £36 13s 4d to John Bruyn in consideration of the marriage of his sister Anne with Bruyn's son, John. Bruyn died before the indentures were sealed and the marriage never took place. His executrix refused to return the money and John sought relief in Chancery.[183] If the ecclesiastical courts were responsible for preventing the marriage after a sum had been handed over, as in the case of *Prowce* v. *Hele*, suit for recovery would be made in Chancery.[184] Even the casual reader of the indices of sixteenth century Chancery cases cannot escape concluding that from its earliest days, such cases were a major component of its equity jurisdiction.

Other sorts of recovery suits seem always to have pertained to the royal courts. An heir believing himself unjustly barred from entry into his mother's maritagium would use a writ of *mort d'ancestor* for relief in the king's courts. A wife, whose husband unjustly alienated her maritagium during his lifetime, could recover after his death by a writ *cui in vita*. After the statute *De Donis* in 1285, her protection was even greater by means of the writ *formedon*. In all of these cases, although the maritagium was at issue, the source of the suit was a transfer or seisin of lay fee and belonged without question to lay courts.

Even in the cases described where lay courts absorbed roles that had once been conceded to the church, little dispute seems to have followed. Manorial courts, Chancery and King's Bench simply were better equipped to resolve suits of obligation. Except for ecclesiastical fees and tithes, debts had not traditionally been litigated in the church courts and there was no natural constituency even within the church defending the right to do so. Perhaps nowhere is the real partnership and true relationship between the two courts more obvious.

Thus, several kinds of suits could arise from marriage. Suits concerning the bond itself, either to enforce it or dissolve it, belonged without question to the church courts. Only they presumed to say what was binding in the eyes of God and what was sinful. Marriages also had certain legal consequences, most notably the lateral transfer or descent of seisin. Because of that, the common law became involved in suits which overlapped or ran parallel to the ecclesiastical jurisdiction. Generally it deferred to the church to determine the validity of a union if that was at issue. Most importantly, the secular courts applied a series of rules compatible with and complementary to those of the church to determine if the full legal rights inherent in marriage should be granted to a couple.

Academic fascination with the Alexandrine consent doctrine has obscured the "larger question" of the extent to which the church's doctrine was compatible with the social structure of England.[185] Maitland felt that a marriage was no less a marriage because a widow could not get dower or a child inherit.[186] If one asked the people so deprived, they would hardly agree. While consent alone might form a bond in the eyes of God, it must always be viewed in the context of a person's inheritance, whether of paradise or of property. Clandestine marriages were sinful and could prevent the enjoyment of the beatific vision for the perpetrators. Likewise, marriages without the consent of guardians and lords were unlawful and might bar entry into one's earthly inheritance. Both laws shared important preconceptions about the nature of a properly ordered society, and they cooperated to a remarkable extent to make that a reality through their courts and to provide resolution of problems to those who came before them.

English common law on the eve of the Reformation, then, included a law of marriage – not a competitive and contradictory system, but a compatible and complementary law rooted in the same fundamental reality which informed the canon law: that consent was only meaningful when and if people could be separated from their inheritances. This law was hammered out as part of a unique compromise between the English church and lay society. Because of it, that society moved towards the sixteenth century without serious objections either to the ecclesiastical law in general or to the marriage law of the church in particular – objections which could be the basis for some sort of efforts at reform in the years ahead.

PART II

Marriage and the English Reformers

3

Theology, Ritual and Clerical Marriage

In continental reformed polities, changes in attitudes towards marriage as well as in the laws and courts governing it, as shown above, were made possible by three developments: radical changes in sacramental theology, the legalization of clerical marriage, and wholesale attacks upon canon law. The first two themes, sacramental theology and clerical marriage, and the related theme of changes in ritual, which are explored in this chapter across the entire period during which the English Reformation took shape, were inextricably linked because of a troubling paradox in the views of reformed clergy. Their reading of scripture convinced them that marriage was not, properly speaking, a sacrament since it was neither instituted by Jesus nor essential for salvation. This, in lay eyes, seemed to devalue marriage. Yet the clergy, themselves wishing to marry and needing to justify that to their congregations, also wanted to demonstrate that marriage was of great value – superior even to celibacy – and appropriate for them. Shaping both a new theology of marriage which exalted it above celibacy and a ritual which endued marriage with dignity while stripping it of its sacramentality was a difficult task. In both cases, the English church's resolution was peculiarly its own, with significant repurcussions for this investigation.

The debate over the sacramentality of marriage began in England with the attack on Luther's works. Until 1520, Luther's works were bought and read in England, albeit by a very limited audience, without any legal restraints.[1] All of that changed after the publication of his *Babylonian Captivity* and bonfire. Pressure on King Henry and Cardinal Wolsey to denounce Luther became intense and it was met, in a bizarre mirroring of German events, by a bonfire of Luther's books on 12 May 1521, and later that year by a book: Henry VIII's *Assertio Septum Sacramentorum*.[2] Henry did not understand the serious theological issues raised by Luther and did not address them. Rather, he feared in print that Luther "robs princes and prelates of all power and authority."[3] For Henry, the principal issue was authority: the authority of tradition and of government against what he perceived as Luther's support for individualism tending toward antinomianism. Henry devoted one chapter to ridiculing Luther's views on marriage. Marriage, for Henry, was self-evidently a sacrament because the church said so. For him, that was the only proof necessary. "Has anyone, either Ancient or Modern," asked Henry, "doubted to call Marriage a sacrament without being hissed at by the church?"[4] Luther was, therefore, wrong because the church said he was wrong and there was little point in further discussion.[5] Luther framed his response in language the likes of which had rarely (if ever) been used with a monarch in Christian Europe. Accompanying the invective, he reiterated his earlier arguments, citing Erasmus's Greek New Testament against the claim that Paul called marriage a sacrament (*sacramentum*) in Ephesians 5:32. The Greek word used by Paul, following Erasmus, was simply *mysterion*. Luther denounced the church's authority, on which Henry placed so much reliance, profferring instead *sola Scriptura*: "What does your lordship defend? The seven sacraments? By whose teachings? God's or men's? Let your Thomistic lordship hear then the judgement, not of Luther, but of Him before whom the poles of the earth tremble: 'In vain do they worship me with the teachings of men.' "[6]

Thomas More responded to Luther in 1523 with a model work of vulgarity and scatology. Ignoring Erasmus, he averred: "You will find, I think, no sacrament named by the word sacrament in scripture except this one which you now stupidly attack, matrimony. Have you ever heard anyone, reader, in a matter so sacred and serious, so insolently and stupidly talking nonsense?"[7] To the claim that matrimony was never instituted as a sign of grace (necessary in a sacrament) because it was not so described in scripture, More responded:

O bold reason, and mother of many heresies. From this font Helvidius drew his venom. You admit no sacrament unless you read of its institution in a book? What book did He ever write who instituted all the sacraments? "Concerning some things," you say, "I believe Christ's evangelists." Why then do you not, concerning some things, believe Christ's church? Christ placed her over all the evangelists, who were only certain members of the church. . . . The church believes this is a sacrament; the church believes that, instituted by God, passed on by Christ, passed on by the apostles, passed on by the holy fathers, passed on thereafter from hand to hand as a sacrament, it has reached us, to be passed on by us to later generations as a sacrament, to be venerated until the end of the world as a sacrament.[8]

As for Henry, so for More. Theology, however biblical, played second chair to authority. More denied himself becoming entangled in an academic debate; he defended ecclesiastical authority and spent the rest of his energy insulting

Luther, who he called, *inter alia*, "this abuser, this cashiered friarlet, this Hussite, this Satanist from Hell, who twists the sacred scripture of Christ into a sacrilegious sense opposed to sacraments of Christ."[9] Ignoring the irony in his words, More concluded that Luther like "a blind man who is attacked and lets out a rain of blows in the direction he thinks his opponent stands and misses completely, just makes himself ridiculous." "Reverend Father Tosspot" was dismissed "to . . . preach [his] faithless faith and the religion of the Bohemian back country, where matrimony means nothing but to increase and multiply and to mate in church like a pack of dogs." Finally, More hoped that when next Luther opened his mouth "to thunder with fictitious flashes against the king" as Cacus had done against Hercules, "some Cacus should crap into it."[10]

Even when legal, Luther's teachings, in their original form, did not circulate widely in England, but Luther had unsuspecting allies in the king and More. As the passages from the *Responsio* show, both were so contemptuous of Luther, and so sure of their stand on church authority, that they believed that if people knew what Luther was arguing, they would know him for a fool. Rather than rebutting his theological arguments, both went on in this vein happily telling the whole country (albeit in Latin) that Luther did not believe marriage was a sacrament until anyone who cared to know the argument knew it.[11]

Henry certainly convinced himself that this policy was the best one. Writing to the Saxon dukes in 1524, he supposed "that there is no one with a spark either of brains or piety who has not cast out of his mind [Luther] and his madness." Henry declined further responses to Luther because there was nothing to answer, only "ravings instead of reasons."[12]

In addition to More's flailings, Luther's works were banned and burned. Bishops ordered periodic sweeps of the universities and other likely places, rounding up copies of the *Babylonian Captivity* and other works which entered England in Latin or German editions, while measures were sought against merchants and stationers to prohibit further imports.[13] At the time, many were less than sanguine about this approach than were the king and his inky attack-dog. Eustace Chapuys later reported to Charles V that book-burnings only increased the numbers of people talking about Luther and his ideas.[14] Stephen Vaughan expressed to Cromwell his concern that the government's policies only caused Lutherans to flee England, "by [which] means it is likely that new Tyndales will grow, or worse than he."[15]

By 1530, as Vaughan's animadversion suggests, William Tyndale, in exile and out of reach of English agents, had become the most irritating of many burrs under the government's saddle. His *Obedience of a Christian Man* (1527/8) was the first original English work which rejected marriage's sacramental status.[16] While noting its holy purposes and ordination by God, Tyndale denied that marriage imparted any grace. Although harassed for his New Testament translation,[17] Tyndale found that the political philosophy in the

Obedience made him popular with Henry. Any hope that his transient popularity might win some influence for his sacramental theology came to an end when Henry received a copy of his *Practice of Prelates*. At the time, Vaughan was trying to recruit Tyndale for royal service but was advised by Cromwell that Henry "nothing liked the book" for its tactless assault on the divorce, and that Henry's pleasure was that Vaughan cease trying to bring Tyndale back to England, for "he would shortly . . . infect and corrupt the whole realm . . . to the great inquietation and hurt of the commonwealth." Cromwell understated the case; Henry wanted nothing so much as to have Tyndale dead from that point on. By advising Vaughan to keep Tyndale out of England, Cromwell did more than anyone to prolong his life and activity.[18]

The ubiquitous More loosed his invective on Tyndale in a long and tedious work which touched fitfully on the marriage debate.[19] Like Luther, Tyndale was accused of denying the plain evidence of St Paul that marriage was a sacrament.[20] "If they call matrimony a sacrament," Tyndale said, "because the scripture useth the similitude of matrimony to express the marriage or wedlock between us and Christ: so will I make a sacrament of mustard seed, leaven, a net, keys, bread, water, and a thousand other things." Like Luther he denied that grace was promised in matrimony since no promise was recorded in scripture. More dismissed all of this with a reference to his denunciation of Luther.[21] Tyndale's views on the sacraments were a relatively insignificant feature of his work and probably attracted very little attention. Although More saw fit to rebut them, one has to make a serious effort to find his response, buried as it is in the hundreds of other pages of the *Confutation*.

Few works, indeed, addressed any aspect of marriage in this early period, and those largely avoided the sacramental question. Bishop Tunstall's *In Laudem Matrimonii*, written for the betrothal of Princess Mary to the Dauphin in 1518, was unoriginal. William Harrington's *Commendations of Matrimony* very briefly justified its title before tackling its real purpose: restating the canon law of marriage in a concise handbook intended for easy use by curates.[22] Juan Luis Vives's *The Instruction of a Christian Woman* (English translation, 1529), originally written for Katherine of Aragon, was so uncontroversial that it remained a popular domestic conduct book into the sixteenth-century, and had its eighth edition in 1592. Richard Whitford's *Work for Householders* (1530) produces no unorthodoxies. Whitford was a conservative Brigittine monk, who fought mightily against the dissolution of Syon, and received rough handling from agents of Cromwell in the process. Marriage is discussed briefly, with a denunciation of privy contracts and the disruptive effects of clandestine marriages.[23]

The evidence from various heresy hunts of the 1520s suggests that heretical views concerning sacraments other than the eucharist were not widespread. Sacramental theology was not a traditional Lollard concern, and most of the

government's attention was directed at Lollards of some sort.[24] Heretical views
of matrimony could predate the Reformation entirely. John Croft of Hereford
diocese was noted in 1505 for holding suspect views against the solemnization
of matrimony.[25] Richard Harman, a native of Cranbrook, the Kentish Protestant greenhouse, took a neutral position. He claimed not to know whether
marriage was a sacrament or not, holding that it was "a thing necessary and of
Christian people to be observed."[26] John Parkyn of London suggested that a
man could have two wives if a priest could have two benefices, but this was only
intended as an ironic attack on pluralism.[27] The first explicit denial of marriage's sacramental status which I have noticed dates from 1531: James Bain-
ham claimed that marriage was only "an order or law that the church of Christ
hath made and ordained by which men take to them women and not sin."[28] It
is, clearly, impossible to know what the reports omit. As Susan Brigden has
argued, individual private beliefs were frequently ignored if political circumstances did bring them to the fore, and only those beliefs which threatened
political authority tended to result in prosecution.[29]

Equally uncertain is the government's success in suppressing Protestant
books which contained heterodox views on marriage. Until 1529, responsibility for controling the distribution of heretical books belonged to ecclesiastical
authorities.[30] The most severe penalty at their command was excommunication,
which proved singularly useless. Bishop Longland suggested to Wolsey that
recognizances be employed, which he believed (probably correctly) might
induce merchants and stationers to exercise more restraint.[31] Others realized
that the supply had to be choked off at the source. John Hackett convinced the
authorities in Antwerp (identified as "the fountain of such things") to assist by
punishing the printers, but they would not act without a list of the alleged
heresies in the offending works, which Hackett failed to move Wolsey to
provide.[32]

Small print runs and a gentle intended audience meant that few books were
likely to come into the hands of people without influence, insulated from the
consequences of possessing forbidden books by social position.[33] But the small
fry who were rounded up were not without resources. Two common, successful
dodges were to claim ignorance or to claim the "know thy enemy" defense: that
the books were studied to enable the reader better to combat the heresies they
contained. This latter defense was particularly useful for clergymen and university students. Even so notorious a supplier of books as Robert Forman, the
parson of All Hallows Honey Lane (London) used this avenue of escape.[34] The
claim of ignorance is hard to evaluate given the state of Tudor communications.
Prohibitions could be effective, as in the case of a bookseller in Lynn who
refused to buy Tyndale's New Testament from a dealer because he knew it was
forbidden,[35] but the chaplain of the Staple of Calais claimed ignorance of the
same ban.[36]

Episcopal authority over books rested on the church's heresy jurisdiction. In 1530, the crown adopted the view that these books fell into the category of seditious words, over which it had authority.[37] The 1530 proclamation provided an embryonic *Index Librorum Probibitorum*, and Thomas More used Privy Council jurisdiction over "breach of proclamation" to summon offenders into Star Chamber.[38] Another proclamation followed in 1538, with the first statutory attempt at censorship of religious books in 1543 and a final proclamation in 1546.[39] This achieved little. Not until it chartered the Stationers Company in 1557 would the government have an effective means to control book printing and selling. Still, while it is easy to ridicule Tudor enforcement procedures, books were rounded up and burned (sometimes counterproductively) and people were arrested for selling and possessing them. These measures must have had some chilling effect and prevented Lutheran and other reformed sacramental teachings from enjoying the circulation or popularity that a free market might have allowed.

In spite of this history of sacramental conservatism, in July 1536, without warning or explanation, the Ten Articles, the first official doctrinal statement of the new dispensation, quietly dropped matrimony (along with confirmation, orders and extreme unction) from the list of the sacraments. This soon caused the government concern. Some people taught that marriage had been abolished, and as the king marvelled "at the malice of men that . . . would wring such seditious reports to bring his people to an evil opinion of his . . . inclination," he ordered the clergy to undertake some correction,[40] and Cromwell provided instructions for their use. They were to teach that marriage had great dignity because it was created at the beginning of time by God for mutual aid and comfort, for the preservation of mankind, for lawful succession, and (after the Fall) for generation without sin; God renewed marriage after the Flood and Christ ratified its dignity at Cana, and marriage was a channel of invisible grace.[41]

The Bishop's Book of September 1537 incorporated Cromwell's instructions in its teachings on marriage, reiterating its institution by God for several good ends, that "Christ himself did also accept, approve and allow the said institution, as well by his word, as also by his sundry works and deeds"; and that matrimony "like as the other sacraments do" consisted of both an outward sign and an inward grace. However, in concluding the section on the sacraments, it was noted that although matrimony, orders, confirmation and extreme unction had been "of long time past received and approved by the common consent of the catholic church, to have the name and dignity of sacraments, as indeed they be well worthy to have . . . yet there is a difference in dignity and necessity between them" and baptism, penance and the eucharist which were instituted by Christ personally "as certain instruments or remedies necessary for our salvation," commanded by him to be received, and had graces attached to them to forgive sins. None of these applied to the other four.[42]

In handwritten corrections, however, Henry suggested that marriage be joined to the list of major sacraments.[43] He had been encouraged by some bishops who wrote to the king after publishing the book that they regretted not having done so saying that "although it be not of so great efficacy" yet it was of great antiquity and merit. As the fourth sacrament "all men [would] have good cause to esteem it as a thing worthy of all reverence, full of cleanness, full of grace, a thing very oft and highly recommended, in both the Old and New Testament."[44] Archbishop Cranmer opposed such modifications. In his notes on *The Bishops' Book*, he observed that matrimony was not "as the others were by the manifest institution of Christ or that it is of necessity of salvation or that thereby we should have the forgiveness of sins, renovation of life and justification, etc." Richard Sampson, bishop of Chichester, noted that "though the sacrament of matrimony is a very high sacrament and instituted by God, yet it hath no convenient place with the other three sacraments of baptism, penance and the altar."[45]

Revisions were under way after 1540 which reflected the more conservative climate after diplomatic and theological attempts at an alliance with the Schmalkaldic League collapsed. On marriage, the bishops remained guardedly reformist and not conservative. While saying that they found "very much in scripture" to the effect that matrimony was holy since God had established it as a remedy for concupiscence and for the increase of the world, they found scripture unhelpful as to the number and names of the sacraments. When Cranmer finally submitted their comments to Henry for his judgement, they gave no clear answers to Henry's impatiently scribbled questions on the subject.[46] *The King's Book*, as it finally emerged in 1543, is generally regarded as conservative, but the section "Of Matrimony" is decidedly not. It repeats almost exactly the equivalent section from *The Bishops' Book*, pointedly omitting previous mention of inward grace, an essential ingredient for a traditional sacrament. Moreover, unlike the three major sacraments, none of the other four were necessary for salvation, however great their value and desirability.[47] Possibly Henry did not appreciate the significance of the changes, but even with the omission and qualifications, the prelates and the king remained torn between theological consistency and pastoral necessity. As a result, at the time of Henry's death matrimony had not reached anything near the unambiguous desacramentalization that it had in Germany.

Henry's attempts to live beyond the grave, from the unusual grant by parliament of the right to bequeath the crown by his last will, to the provisions in the will which designated the men who would become the Privy Councillors for his son Edward, could not ensure the survival of his idiosyncratic personal policies.[48] Ironically, in fact, in order to protect the royal supremacy over the church, Henry had to grant dominant roles in the government to overt Protestants itching to begin a more far-reaching reform consonant with what they knew to be occurring abroad. The first step in that direction was inadvertent when Henry entrusted the education of Prince Edward to Richard Cox and John Cheke.[49] Bishop Gardiner's eclipse and the Duke of Norfolk's imprisonment at the end of the reign removed the only effective conservative leadership.[50] Finally, in naming the executors of his will (and his son's first Privy Council) Henry turned to committed Protestants like Cranmer, his brother-in-law Edward Seymour, Lord John Russell, Sir Anthony Denny, Viscount Lisle (John Dudley), and William Herbert, brother-in-law of Queen Katherine Parr. Of the remainder, most were politiques without strong convictions in religious matters. Only Chancellor Wriothesley, Bishop Cuthbert Tunstall and Sir Anthony Browne represented any sort of religious conservatism. The statutory provision that Henry's successor be allowed to revoke any provisions made during his minority was unlikely to prove much of a hindrance to the Protestants: a prince educated by Cheke and Cox and dominated by Seymour and Cranmer would be an unlikely critic of Protestant measures taken in his name.

Restraints on further reformation would be imposed by the politics of the possible. The council, whatever its majority desired, had still to contend with parliament. If Gardiner had been extruded from the Privy Council, he was still Bishop of Winchester and the most articulate conservative in the House of Lords. While only Bishop Bonner was likely to join him in repeated attacks on council policies, the government could not rely upon such respected men as Bishops Thirlby of Norwich and Tunstall of Durham for support. These latter prelates were so indispensable to the regime, at least in the early going, that they could not be removed and the council had to tolerate a core of at least ten anti-reform votes from the episcopal ranks. An elected Commons would be no more tractable. The country was still overwhelmingly conservative, with the shortage of Protestant clergy to preach in favor of reform making immediate changes in popular opinion unlikely. The Privy Council had also to consider the impact of its religious policies on foreign affairs. War with France was a virtual certainty by 1548, and England was desperate for the support, if only by neutrality, of Charles V.[51] Thus, Somerset and his colleagues undertook a juggling act of some sophistication: their own religious convictions, the pressure of foreign affairs, and the need to maintain domestic order had somehow to be satisfied to keep the regime from crashing to the ground in a heap.

In spite of this, major and ultimately permanent changes in matrimonial doctrine were adopted when Archbishop Cranmer provided the English church with its first official and uniform marriage service. Until 1549, a variety of services had been used. The most widespread was the Sarum Use, upon which Cranmer based the new liturgy, but there were also distinct marriage services in the Hereford and York missals. The differences among them were often great; the Sequence, Gospel, and many of the central prayers were completely different.[52]

While Cranmer's communion service had been striking for its use of English, major parts of the marriage service were in "the vulgar tongue" before 1549. But several new features set his order for solemnizing matrimony apart from its predecessors.[53] First, the service now took place entirely within the church. In reality the marriage service had been an ecclesiastical matter for centuries, but the old practice of the handfasting taking place at the church door had been retained. In the old service, the couple did not enter the church until after the exchange of the ring and the prayers which followed. The Protestant service disposed of the old fiction and appropriated marriage from first to last for the church.

In the body of the church, the priest began with a new exhortation which set forth the dignity and ends of marriage:

> Dearly beloved friends, we are gathered here in the sight of God, and in the face of his congregation to join together this man and this woman in holy matrimony, which is an honorable estate instituted of God in paradise, in the time of man's innocency, signifying unto us the mystical union that is betwixt Christ and his church: which holy estate Christ adorned and beautified with his presence, and first miracle that he wrought, in Cana of Galilee, and is commended of Saint Paul to be honourable among all men; and therefore is not to be . . . taken in hand . . . lightly . . . but reverently, discreetly, advisedly, soberly, and in the fear of God: duly considering the causes for which matrimony was ordained. One cause was the procreation of children, to be brought up in the fear and nurture of the Lord, and praise of God. Secondly it was ordained for a remedy against sin, and to avoid fornication, that such persons as be married, might live chastely in matrimony, and keep themselves undefiled members of Christ's body. Thirdly for the mutual society, help, and comfort, that the one ought to have of the other, both in prosperity and adversity.

In addition to the familiar elegance of its language, two features of the mini-sermon are noteworthy. First is the emphasis on the dignity of marriage. It was a special concern of a variety of Protestant writers and preachers that marriage had fallen into disrepute since the Reformation began in England. For this they partly blamed themselves since its previous dignity had rested on sacramental status they now denied. Cranmer's service pointedly refers to marriage as an estate (as in The King's Book) or as "God's holy ordinance," and marriage is never called a sacrament. While it is not clear that marriage had suffered in popular fortunes as a result of such shifts, and it is unlikely that this charge can be proven, it is enough that the reformers believed that it had, and that some teaching needed to be undertaken.

The opening exhortation in the marriage service was just a beginning. The gospel appointed for the second Sunday after Epiphany, the story of the marriage at Cana, provided another opportunity to lecture on the dignity and honor of marriage. A sermon by Latimer on that occasion is exemplary. Because Jesus attended the marriage, it was clear that "marriage is a most honourable and acceptable thing in the sight of God." Although the estate brings with it affliction and troubles, Latimer told his hearers:

> [T]hey may comfort themselves with the word of God, and think in their hearts, and say: "O God, thou hast brought us together in the estate of matrimony; it was thy ordinance and pleasure that we should join together: now therefore be merciful unto us; forsake us not, which live in thy ordinance and after thy commandments: pour thy Spirit into our hearts, that we may bear and suffer all these miseries which thou layest upon our necks." And in this manner married folks may comfort themselves with the word of God in all their adversities, because they are sure that marriage is a thing that pleaseth God.[54]

He concluded with an exhortation that couples should turn Godward and, like the couple of Cana, "endeavour yourself so that God may be with you at your marriage, and that Christ be one of the guests; for if he be there you shall have no lack of any thing." Protestant reformers did not, of course, invent the idea of marriage as an honorable estate. Early fifteenth-century humanists in Florence had rejected traditional disparagements of matrimony.[55] Bishop Tunstall had preached extravagantly in praise of matrimony in 1519 on the occasion of the anticipated match of Princess Mary with the Dauphin.[56] What is new to the sixteenth century is the feeling that a diet of this view is not only fit but necessary for mass consumption.

The next striking change of the new service was removing the ring blessing. The ring itself was retained, and a new prayer added which explained that the ring was a token of the vow made, like the jewels exchanged by Isaac and Rebecca. Then the priest joined the right hands of the couple and announced "Those whom God hath joined together let no man put asunder." After a blessing (slightly different in wording from the Sarum rite), the priest and the wedding party moved into the quire, where the priest prayed.

Finally, the Gospel was read, a sermon preached, and the service ended with a note that the newly married couple was to receive communion on that day. (The Sarum rite continued with the Mass of the Trinity.) Since not all priests would be capable of preaching, the Prayer Book included a brief sermon on the duties of husbands and wives towards each other. It consisted entirely of brief excerpts from Paul's epistles to the Ephesians and Colossians, and the epistle of Peter.

The new Prayer Book of 1552 made practically no changes in this service. References to the gold and silver tokens of spousals, given with the ring, were removed, and rubrics for signing with the cross at various points were deleted. In other respects the new service was the same as its predecessor. While Mary scuttled the new liturgy, Elizabeth and her first parliament restored the marriage service of 1552 without alteration and that version remains in use.[57]

Even when the Prayer Book came under attack, especially after 1571, criticisms of the marriage liturgy were few and peripheral, failing to generate anything approximating the unanimous support of puritans. Wedding rings came under attack, notably in the Admonition Controversy, when the ring was named as one of the "corruptions" in the Prayer Book marriage service. Seen as a mere survival of popery with no scriptural warrant, critics argued that the church, for which marriage was no longer a sacrament, still used "a sacramental sign to which they attribute the virtue of wedlock." Whitgift denied this: "I know it is not material whether the ring be used or no: for it is not of the substance of matrimony; neither yet a sacramental sign," and noted Bucer's defense of the ring for its three profitable symbols. When the minister delivered the ring to the bridegroom to give to his bride, it reminded the couple that all they had came from God. Next, placing the ring on the fourth finger of the left hand (believed to contain a vein which came straight from the heart) united their two hearts. Finally, the ring, having no beginning or end, symbolized the perpetual union of matrimony. Cartwright believed that Whitgift either lied or misquoted Bucer, or that "if it be M. Bucer's judgement which is alleged here for the ring, I see that sometimes Homer sleepeth . . . . [S]urely it savoureth not of the learning and sharpness of [his] judgement." The debate shared the peculiar futility of all English debates on adiaphora: Cartwright insisting that nothing omitted from the Bible was allowed and Whitgift that while nothing omitted was essential it was not forbidden.[58] Puritans did not unite in rejecting the ring, however. Richard Greenham, guru of the moderates, for example, used it without objection.[59] As a result, there is little trace of prosecutions for omitting the ring.[60]

The Admonition also argued that the Holy Communion, which accompanied the marriage service, ought to be dropped because it smacked of the popish view that "no holy action may be done without a Mass." Whitgift again cited Bucer: "That is also godly ordained that the new married folks should receive the communion; for Christians ought not to be joined in matrimony but in Christ the Lord."[61] Cartwright, in the very next breath, complained that people did not approach marriage with appropriate solemnity, coming to the church instead with pipers and fiddlers, "whereby they make rather a May-game of marriage than a holy institution of God." It was precisely this reason, the church's campaign to impress upon people the holy and sacred character of marriage, that led to requiring Holy Communion, and Whitgift knew if Cart- wright did not that the elimination of Holy Communion would be counterpro- ductive.

Separatists went even further. If the Bible did not require communion, Henry Barrow pointed out, neither did it require the presence of a minister or the use of an ecclesiastical service:

> I have always found it the parents' office to provide marriages for their children, while they remain in their charge and government; and that the parties themselves affianced and betrothed each other in the fear of God, and the presence of such witnesses as were present, and that in their parents' or other private houses, without running to church to the priest.[62]

In 1587, authorities in London raided a conventicle and arrested twenty-two separatists including John Greenwood, who authorities charged with marrying Christopher Bowman and his wife in the Fleet in a separatist manner.[63] Greenwood said that he had no particular role in this; the couple had acknowledged their consent before the congregation and that, he believed, was sufficient for mar- riage, which was not a minister's duty. Bowman himself was arrested on more than one occasion for his separatist activities, and during examinations in 1593 revealed that he had married a second time, this time in the home of John Penry where a Mr Settel "used prayer" and the couple expressed their consent before the assembly.[64] Other separatists, as examinations revealed, shared this view that marriage was a private matter.[65]

Puritan failure to press vigorously their early complaints against the Prayer Book marriage ceremony surely may be seen as a result of their sensitivity to this mischief which they could inspire. Separatists were undoing centuries of effort by the church to undercut the Alexandrine consent doctrine. While the separatists preferred that marriage be made with the consent of parents, they acknowledged that was an unrealistic hope when the parents were not members of the conventicle. Moreover, while they married with prayer in a meeting of their sect, averring that marriage was not an ecclesiastical matter but was proper to private houses gave a license that no mainstream churchman whatever his views on the surplice or episcopacy could accept. Puritans and their op- ponents consistently found common cause crusading against clandestine marriage.

Indeed, the puritans sought to increase the role of the minister in marriage, even to creating an additional service for betrothal. Richard Greenham defended such a service with the example of Mary and Joseph, and explained that this "standeth with good reason, for that the neglect of it is an occasion that many are disappointed of their purposed marriages, because some of them through inconstancy go back." A betrothal service could be used to lecture the couple on the nature of marriage and their duties to each other and to God. The minister could also inquire whether the parents of the couple consented and whether they had made any prior contract. Barring any intervenient obstacle, they would join hands and recite a promise to be the other's spouse and to confirm that "by public marriage."[66] Greenham implemented such a service in his parish, and refused to marry couples who did not comply.[67]

Thus, by 1603 England had inched well along the theological path taken by the rest of Protestant Europe, and developed a broad consensus favoring a Protestant marriage service. After a stormy, unedifying debate in Henry VIII's reign, marriage had been somewhat uneasily excised from the list of sacraments. The reformers little doubted that there was no scriptural warrant for conjoining marriage with baptism and the Lord's Supper, but their concern for public perceptions sent them searching for a middle ground. The new standardized marriage service was the solution of that greatest of compromisers, Thomas Cranmer. While the language used to describe matrimony was no longer sacramental, the service emphasized the holiness of marriage, and by coupling it with the reception of Holy Communion, must have left the general public, largely ignorant of the theological distinctions between a sacrament and a "holy ordinance" or "estate," thinking of marriage in much the same way as before. In other words, technically things were very different; but was this a difference apparent to any but the theologically savvy?

Also on the reformers' theological agenda was abolishing mandatory clerical celibacy which, in England was, according to its first great modern student, Henry Charles Lea, "a process of far more intricacy than in any other country which adopted the Reformation."[68] Like changing sacramental theology, the process was marked in its earliest stages by vituperative exchanges in print, and shaped both by the quirky conservatism of Henry VIII and the caution of the reformers. Although ultimately made legal, clerical marriage never enjoyed the unalloyed support of the monarchy or the leading clergy. As a result of their reluctance to show the kind of enthusiasm for marriage of the more connubial continental clergy, English clergy did not inspire the sort of sustained revaluation of marriage that took place in German and Swiss reformed polities.

Having said that, it is necessary to add that there are a number of inaccuracies in the standard view of clerical marriage during the reigns of Henry VIII, Edward VI and Elizabeth I.[69] According to historical orthodoxy Henry VIII, acting from his personal conservatism, retained and defended mandatory celibacy in the first stage. Once he died and his leaden foot was removed from the brake, the clergy overwhelmed ineffective conservative opposition in the Edwardian government and rode the cart of legal clerical marriage through the gates. The victory of Edward's reign was reversed in the Marian reaction, and was not reclaimed after Mary's death because of the anticonnubial tastes and religious conservatism of Elizabeth I.[70] Throughout this period, so the story goes, the clergy (a majority of them, at least) struggled to marry legally, only to find royal resistance (except briefly under Edward VI) impossible to overcome.

This traditional outline is misleading in several respects. Elizabeth I's attitude towards clerical marriage is more complex than has been recognized. Regulating such unions, which she did attempt, arose from her desire to establish an ordered church worthy of popular respect and cannot simply be ascribed to a general, almost pathological, personal distaste for marriage or quirky personal religious views. As will be shown, the clergy themselves bear far more responsibility for the grudging and glacially slow recession of the ideal of a celibate clergy in the English church than has been granted. Elizabethan clerical leaders built on an English reformed tradition of ambivalence to a married ministry that can be traced back to Henrician days.

From the outset of the Henrician reformation, clerical marriage was a debated topic. In the earliest stages, however, the king was more concerned to suppress discussions of the subject than its practice, and he banned preaching on a host of contentious issues, including clerical marriage.[71] Favorable preaching continued illegally, however, and the number of married priests began to grow.[72] In November 1536, the king expressed his displeasure that his prohibition had been ineffective and ordered his bishops to conduct secret inquiries to identify married priests in their dioceses, report them to the council or arrest and send them to the king.[73] Some inquiries did take place, but they were not entirely effective. In the Suffolk dissenting stronghold of Mendlesham, the vicar married, and although some local people reportedly were offended, the vicar brazenly claimed that the king knew and did not object and so "men do refrain to do that their hearts would, and as to our ordinary, he dare do nothing."[74]

Although Thomas Cromwell patronized and promoted married priests,[75] and the king was under diplomatic pressure to accept clerical marriage as part of an alliance with Lutheran princes, official government actions were uniformly hostile. A royal proclamation in November 1538 ordered that married priests be deprived and those who presumed to marry after the proclamation be imprisoned at the king's pleasure.[76] This decree moved Philip Melanchthon to write to Cranmer in great despair that the pope had been expelled from England but not his "poison" with him, and the duke of Saxony and Landgrave of Hesse also wrote disapprovingly.[77] Henry refused to accept the suggestion of some of his own divines that he refer the issue to "indifferent judges" at the universities.[78]

Instead, Parliament took up the matter and the result was the Act of Six Articles, a penal statute officially and rather optimistically titled "An act for abolishing diversity in opinions."[79] The act provided that any priest or other person who had freely and maturely vowed chastity but married after 12 July 1539 was guilty of felony and, if convicted, would suffer death for the crime. Marriages that had already taken place were declared void and diocesan ordinaries were to begin formal divorce proceedings. Those who continued to "carnally keep or use any woman" to whom they had been contracted were also adjudged felons, as were any who preached or taught in favor of the marriages of priests or other votaries.[80]

The Act provoked comments from every court.[81] Christopher Mont was optimistic. He told Philip of Hesse that the Act was needed to prevent people being scandalized by sexually active priests and ignoring their preaching, and though he did not know what Henry would do "when the people shall wax stronger and [be] able to eat solid meat," he trusted Henry would act wisely.[82] Chapuys was closer to the truth when reporting to Charles V that Henry had destroyed any hope of an anti-Imperial alliance by his stubbornness on this point. Chapuys believed that Henry's real objection was that "the priests would so increase in numbers by affinity and descent that they would tyrannize over princes themselves."[83] If Henry worried about priests increasing, Bucer feared the opposite: that Henry's decree would empty the kingdom of qualified ministers.[84]

Edward VI's first parliament repealed the Act of Six Articles,[85] but while the taint of criminality was removed from clerical marriage, the question remained whether some positive statement should be made. Convocation debated the subject in December 1547 and, as their votes show, the clergy were deeply and ominously divided.[86] Even a supporter, the influential doctrinal conservative John Redman, couched his support in markedly negative terms.

> I think that although the word of God do exhort and counsel priests to live in chastity, out of the cumber of the flesh and of the world, that they thereby may more wholly attend to their calling, yet the bond of containing from marriage doth only lie upon priests in this realm by reason of canons and constitutions of the church, and not by any precept of God's word. . . . And I think that forasmuch as canons and rules made in this behalf be neither universal nor everlasting . . . the king's majesty and the higher powers of the church may . . . take away the clog of perpetual containing from priests.[87]

Since Convocation lacked authority to provide the desired remedy, parliament had to act. After several delays and revisions, the Commons passed the Lords bill on 26 February 1548.[88]

> Although it were not only better for the estimation of priests and other

ministers in the Church of God to live chaste, sole, and separate from the company of women and the bond of marriage, but also thereby they might better attend to the administration of the Gospel, and be less intricated and troubled with the charge of household, being free and unburdened from the care and cost of finding wife and children, and that it were more to be wished that they would willingly and of their selves endeavour them self to a perpetual chastity and abstinence from the use of women, yet forasmuch as the contrary hath rather been seen, and such uncleanness of living and other great inconveniences, not mete to be rehearsed, have followed of compelled chastity . . . it were better and rather to be suffered in the commonwealth that those which could not contain should after the counsel of Scripture live in holy marriage, than feignedly abuse with worse enormity outward chastity or the single life. . . .[89]

Reflecting Redman's argument, the statute was strikingly halfhearted: clerical marriage was not a positive good; it was simply better than clerical fornication. Chastity was not only praiseworthy but, according to the Bible, preferable to the married state.

Parliament later reenacted the statute with a vigorous denunciation of "uncomely railings . . . and slanderous reproaches" against clerical marriage, and stated explicitly that married priests' children were legitimate.[90] One of the Articles of Religion of 1552 also declared that the single life was not commanded by the word or law of God.[91] Thus matters stood at the death of Edward.

How did the clergy themselves respond to the shifting legal status of their marriages? In the first years of the English Reformation, before the direction of official policy became clear, some clergymen took example from Germany and married, for example John Palmes, who justified his matrimony because the king had "delivered him from the bondage brought into Christ's church by the usurped power of the bishop of Rome,"[92] and the abbot of Walden who married a nun in 1535 to whom he referred, with a Pauline sense of romance, as his "remedy."[93] The vicar of Mendlesham, whose own marriage has been noted above, blessed the marriages of other priests. These are but a few examples.[94]

The Act of Six Articles devastated those priests who had married, especially since it was enforced. William Turner, at that time a deacon, secretly married Joan Alder in late 1540, and when the marriage came to the attention of diocesan authorities, they initiated a divorce trial and Turner left England until after Henry VIII's death.[95] Those without the wherewithal to flee had to throw themselves on the mercy of sympathetic officials. John Foster, who married an ex-nun, wrote to Cromwell that "my disfortune has been to have conceived untruly God's word, and not only with my intellect to have thought it, but externally and really I have fulfilled the same, for I have . . . accomplished marriage." He told Cromwell that once the king's purpose had become clear, he had sent his wife sixty miles away to her family and did not dwell with her.[96]

Better days under Edward saw surprisingly little clerical marriage. Two bishops had married illegally in the previous reign, and others of Edward's first bishops soon joined their number.[97] Records of deprivations under Queen Mary give some idea of numbers of married priests, and that number is not significant. Scholars who have studied the records of the Marian efforts to remove married clergymen report that in Norfolk, Suffolk and Essex, around 25 percent of the clergy were deprived for marriage, while in York, deprivations account for at most 10 percent of an estimated 1,000 diocesan priests. In the city of York, with a clerical population over 260, three vicars choral and one rector married. Three of those renounced their wives and kept their positions; only one was deprived. In Lancashire, the poverty of livings had proved a powerful disincentive to marriage that might have been more important than religious conservatism. Christopher Haigh found only seven married clergy out of 257 in Lancashire. Even a majority of the bishops, who by the end of the reign were a far more overtly Protestant collection than in 1547, remained unmarried.[98]

To what can this hesitation be attributed? Certainly the shifting political climate made caution seem a wise course as late as 1553. The lesson of prosecution and exile of their forward-thinking colleagues after 1539 would not have been lost on the clergy, and the political turmoil of Edward's reign as well as the young king's personal ill health can have done little to encourage the clergy to move quickly even if their impulse was to marry. Mary's reign justified their caution, and they would have carried that with them well past November 1558.

In addition, the English people were often hostile to clerical marriage and clergy wives and children. In spite of its relatively late acceptance in England, by the early sixteenth century popular enthusiasm for clerical celibacy was unmistakable.[99] Clerical wives were derided in ballads, and support of clerical marriage was tainted by its association with Lollardy.[100] The tepid half measures of Edward's parliaments hardly convinced the public to treat the married clergy with respect. Some refused to receive the sacraments from married priests, and midwives refused aid to women married to ministers.[101] John Barbor, curate of Newton, Cambridgeshire, found himself before the bishop of Ely's official accused of marrying in spite of the reclamation of his banns by John Flaxman in 1549. Flaxman had objected at the calling of the banns only because he opposed clerical marriage.[102] In Chester in 1549, Hugh Bunbury contracted marriage with Anne Andrew, but she requested that they delay solemnization until other priests were married, and after his 1549 marriage Robert Wright of Warrington, Lancashire, had to sue a local woman for slanderous remarks.[103]

Bishop Hooper appears to have been the only bishop to use his office, through his visitation articles of 1551/2, to combat this prejudice by teaching the acceptability of clerical marriage. In these articles he announced that since "St Paul doth plainly say that the forbidding of marriage is the doctrine of devils, therefore it is not judged that the marriage of priests, bishops or any other ministers of the church, shall be unlawful, but that the same is both holy and agreeable to God's word."[104]

The more common approach was the learned treatise, targeted to an elite audience – the "opinion-makers" of sixteenth century society. Two features of the writers and their treatises are noteworthy. First, the treatises have virtually nothing positive to say for marriage; it is simply preferable to the clerical fornication that follows hard on the heels of mandatory celibacy. Second, the authors state in print that the Bible says the single life is to be preferred. In their personal lives, they practiced what they wrote.

Robert Barnes, in the first original English treatise devoted entirely to clerical marriage, condemned public attacks on priests who had, following God's law, married out of weakness of nature, while "all the cruelness that could be excogitated against them men thought it too little."[105] Barnes believed that this hostility was based in ignorance of scripture and devotion to old tradition. To the ignorant he revealed, as he saw them, the pope's "false reasons" by use of scripture, the Doctors of the Church, and historical examples.[106] Barnes defended marriage as "an especial and singular medicine" for the disease of fornication, declaring it sinful to reject God's remedy to pursue one's own. Yet he did not reject virginity, and he himself never married and believed, with St Paul, that the single life was good and expedient, though no one could be bound to it who did not have the gift of chastity. Barnes saw papal law as the fulfillment of Paul's prophecy that in the latter days men would forbid marriage, a "doctrine of devils" that burned priests for marrying but not for keeping whores and encouraged people to refuse the company of married priests but not of those who lived in whoredom. Barnes gave no ringing endorsement of marriage except as a physic against fornication. Voluntary celibacy (if it was given by God) was always preferable.[107]

Church Fathers such as Cyprian, Augustine, and Ambrose, and several early councils were also cited against compelled vows of virginity. At the councils, men attacked clerical marriage but "God has always stirred up some good man to resist [them]." One such occasion, cited repeatedly by later authors, was at the Council of Nicaea, at which Paphnutius turned back attempts to forbid married men from becoming priests, which was clearly lawful before the council. Barnes also noted that the decrees of current popes resembled the teachings of the heretic Eustachius condemned at the Council of Gangres. Eustachius taught that priests should forsake their wives and that married priests were unclean and ought to be deprived of their positions.[108]

History demonstrated, said Barnes, that popes forbade marriage not out of principle but out of greed. Peter, the first bishop of Rome, had a wife. In the oriental churches, which "all learned men know . . . receiveth their manners nearer of the Apostles than we," priests still married. Once popes outlawed marriage, they sold dispensations to priests and nuns to marry secretly or to keep whores, proving that they regarded money more highly than chastity.[109] While popes argued that Old Testament priests abstained from their wives during their ministry, and since the priests of the New Testament ministered constantly they must abstain at all times, Barnes responded that it was lawful for priests of the Old Testament to marry and so it must be the same now, while abstaining from their wives was part of the ceremonial law which no longer applied. Finally, papal teaching that chastity could come with prayer and fasting defied reason. God had decreed that marriage was the remedy for fornication, and it was as foolish to reject that as it was to pray and fast to cure a disease rather than using an available physic.[110] For political palatability, Barnes concluded that any man who taught the excellence and greater desirability of chastity was a traitor to the king for such teaching, if heeded, would "within these seven years make the king a lord of a few subjects, or none, and finally none indeed."[111]

This treatise was suppressed by the government, so thoroughly that no copy of the work survives in its original form, but only as part of Barnes's collected works published forty years later. One work which was not suppressed was Richard Taverner's semi-officially sponsored translation of Erasmus's *Praise of Matrimony* (1531).[112] While Taverner prepared it with the intention of refuting the celibate ideal, it went virtually nowhere in that direction. Erasmus had written the piece in 1497 to encourage his patron Lord Mountjoy who was preparing to marry. His intention, in the tradition of civic humanism, was to praise marriage over the life of the single layman but not necessarily over that of the consecrated virgin. He noted that only a few were called to the life of religious chastity and that it would be better if those who vowed chastity and lived debauched lives were allowed to marry,[113] but these remarks were casual and ill-considered. By 1532 Erasmus, under pressure to demonstrate his orthodoxy, had repudiated them.

William Tyndale, to whom More quite inaccurately attributed the view that every priest must marry,[114] was no more advanced than Barnes. While he thought bishops ought to be married because no one should have that kind of authority who had not governed a household, he himself never married, and he expressed a decided preference for the single life in his writings.

After the Act of Six Articles, Miles Coverdale prepared a translation of Heinrich Bullinger's *Der christliche ehestand* which became enormously influential. In the preface, Thomas Becon praised matrimony principally for its procreative dimensions and benefits to the Commonwealth. Marriage, which "maketh the realms to flourish with innumerable thousands of people, whereby the public weal is preserved in safe estate," was contrasted with the single life: celibates were "monsters of nature for their sterility and barrenness [who] die as unprofitable clods of the earth." He blamed the Act of Six Articles for obscuring and nearly extinguishing the glory of matrimony since it exalted whoredom at the expense of wedlock and whores at the expense of virtuous wives: "Honest wives sit at home and almost perish from hunger, but harlots are sumptuously fed with all kinds of dainties." He lamented the failure of England's rulers to abolish "this filthy uncleanness and unclean filthiness." Why, he asked, "do we tumble and bury ourselves in this filthy and stinking puddle of uncleanness and not rather embrace holy wedlock?"[115] This was by far the most enthusiastic treatment of marriage by any Henrician writer, from that rarest of writers on the subject – one who was actually married. Unlike Barnes and Tyndale, who exalted matrimony, did not themselves partake, and believed that while chastity might be a gift from God, a rare gift, it was greatly to be desired and certainly preferred to marriage, Becon lived what he wrote.[116]

George Joye, also in exile, produced a translation of Melanchthon's defense of clerical marriage, which had been written specifically for Henry VIII in 1539. Joye also wrote (under the name James Sawtry) *The defence of the marriage of Priests against Steven Gardiner*, a companion piece to the translation of Melanchthon, which focused on the opponents of marriage in the parliament that passed the Six Articles.[117] Bypassing the doctrinal, scriptural and historical arguments, he focused instead on the players and activity in the parliament which had passed the Act of Six Articles, arguing that the members had been deceived in their "ignorant simplicity" by the spiritualty, of whom he singled out bishops Gardiner and Repps, "the inbringers, authors anew, and maintainers . . . sitting in their profane conjuration house, their hands polluted with blood and fingers embrewed with sin, their lips speaking lies and their tongues painting mischief." Rather than acting in righteousness, "they lean all unto vanity and lies," chief of which was their theology of vows. Since they vowed obedience to the pope and had broken that vow themselves, Joye said that they proved by their own example that ill-advised vows against God's word could be broken. Mandatory clerical celibacy was not God's will, but only "cokatrices eggs lately laid and laterly hatched," leading to lewdness so prodigious that Joye would not repeat it for fear he would "poison the paper and the breath of the reader . . . corrupt the air and infect honest ears."[118]

The true episcopal motive, said Joye, was that they preferred keeping other men's wives: it was cheaper than marriage and brought no responsibilities: "For well know these idle, soft shaven sects what cares, burdens, charges and incommodities there follow and chance to true chaste and honourable wedlock." If burdened with marriage's financial responsibilities, "their jolly peacocks tails [would] be plucked." The spiritualty also chose celibacy because it allowed them to separate themselves from the common people, an attitude which led Joye frequently to label them "the English pharisees."[119]

The bishops were not the only parliamentary foes. The Duke of Norfolk rejected clerical marriage fearing that bishops would marry noble girls and get their lands. Joye's remedy was to require that no priest should marry the daughter of a gentleman without her parents' consent. In fact, he favored apostolic poverty for the clergy. Their wives would then have to satisfy the checklist of qualities set out by St Paul and willingly "wash, wring, spin, card, brew, bake, sweep the house, make ready her husband's dinner, wash the dishes . . . nurse her own children with her own breasts, visit the sick, sore and poor be they never so lothly." Joye chided the nobles that few of their daughters would do these things, while any who would obviously did not care about family wealth and property and would not siphon it away.[120]

Why did the English reformers take such a restrained line toward marriage? In part, their own reluctance to marry might have been a response to the opponents of clerical marriage whose tactic was to assault the morals rather than the scholarship of clerical marriage supporters. Thomas More, as febrile on this subject as on the sacraments, penned two assaults on William Tyndale, *A Dialogue Concerning Heresies* and *The Confutation of Tyndale's Answer*, in which he cited both pagan and Jewish customs to the effect that chastity was the appropriate way of life for the priest, that "only such as be of that sort that are content and minded to live after the cleanness of Christ's holy counsel" should be allowed to minister Christ's sacrament, and he preferred the authority of the past to "such a heretic as Luther and Tyndale, and a better example than the seditious and schismatic priests of Saxony."[121] Generally, More eschewed reasoned theological or historical argument for slander and vulgarity, using Luther's marriage and Tyndale's support of it to discredit the reformers. Rather than disputing scripture and theology (something with which, on this subject at least, More showed little skill) he chose to advertise their behavior and let people draw their own conclusions. Who could put trust in a man who did "not defend it only but commend it also that a nun consecrate unto God should run out of religion, and do foul stinking sacrifice to that filthy idol of Priapus"?[122] Far from exalting marriage, More argued that Luther defiled it by his lechery. Nothing could be farther than "the steps of friar Luther into the nun's bed . . . from the steps that stepped on the mount of Calvary."[123]

The tone of More's defense is not unimportant, for this fear that their personal behavior could undercut the acceptability of the reform might have been a powerful additional motive to men such as Barnes and Tyndale to remain single. Coupled with what appears to have been their genuine personal preference for celibacy, the most articulate and original writers among the English reformers provided no leadership for a rebellion against the celibate ideal.

Shortly before Henry's death, Robert Crowley lamented the impact of royal policy in a piece of genuinely dreadful poetry and prayed for better days:

> God grant we may
> Once see the day,
> Wherein we may be free:
> To lead our lives,
> With honest wives
> And preach Gods verity.
>
> For now he that,
> Containeth not,
> And hath the gift to preach,
> Must either hide,
> That gift or bide,
> Still burning like a wretch.[124]

That day would dawn in 1558. When John Foxe wrote his *Acts and Monuments*, he peppered his narrative with a long historical justification for the marriage of the clergy in the English church, and while his material was familiar from earlier tomes, his tone was not. By 1563, Foxe wrote without defensiveness, for by that date clerical marriage was securely established in the English church and was a clear sign that the Ecclesia Anglicana was faithful to the Gospel and apostolic tradition. How did this happen under the allegedly antimatrimonial Queen Elizabeth?

In the 1559 parliament, Protestants clearly intended, at the very least, to return the English church to its position at the death of King Edward, which meant that clerical marriage should regain the statutory authorization repealed under Mary. The second Supremacy Bill allowed priests to marry,[125] but this was removed from the final bill approved by the queen. A frustrated Edwin Sandys wrote to Matthew Parker: "The Queen's Majesty will wink at [marriage] but not stablish it by law, which is nothing else but to bastard our children."[126] The queen was, in fact, enough of a realist and enough of a Protestant to accept clerical marriage. But while reformers such as Bullinger believed that there was nothing (except "corrupt doctrine") which endangered the church more than immoral clergy, and for that reason they should marry, Elizabeth had cause to believe also that "priests' wives did not often adorn the ministry."[127] The celebrated scandals of her brother's reign had armed the enemies of the church. In 1551 Ponet, the public defender of clerical marriage, then bishop of Winchester, had to be divorced from a woman who was already married to a Nottingham butcher. Ponet paid the butcher damages for committing bigamy with his wife.[128] The Privy Council was also bothered by Anthony Norman demanding similar damages from Archbishop Holgate, who married Barbara Wentworth in 1548. She had been betrothed as a child to Norman. Before her marriage to Holgate she had obtained an ecclesiastical divorce on the grounds that she had been under seven years of age at the time of the espousals and that she had always held that "she could not find in her heart to love the said Anthony nor to use him as her husband." In May 1549, Norman sued for restitution of conjugal rights, but was defeated on proof of the divorce. Ponet's misfortunes seem to have motivated Norman to sue Holgate in 1551, but the council rejected his suit.[129] The queen believed that the church must be protected from further scandal and some control over the choice of clerical marriage partners might serve that end. This resulted in Injunction 29 of the Royal Visitation of 1559.

This text explicitly affirmed the lawfulness of clerical marriage. It noted however that "there hath grown offence and some slander to the church by lack of discreet and sober behaviour in many ministers of the church, both in choosing of their wives and in indiscreet living with them." As a remedy, the Injunction provided

> that no manner of priest or deacon shall hereafter take to his wife any manner of woman without the advice and allowance first had upon good examination by the bishop of the same diocese and two justices of the peace . . . nor without the good will of the parents of the said woman if she have any living, or two of the next of her kinfolks, or . . . of her master or mistress she serveth.

Those who failed to abide by this procedure "shall not be permitted to minister either the word or the sacraments of the church, nor shall they be capable of any ecclesiastical benefice."[130]

This requirement was enforced, at least selectively, right up to 1603.[131] Harsh criticism of Queen Elizabeth and belief in her fundamental hostility toward clerical marriage has been based at least in part on this order. It is, however, unnecessary and unwise to judge her intentions harshly. The injunction contains a clear and unambiguous statement of the legality of clerical marriage – less ambiguous than that of the Edwardian statutes. Elizabeth was, however, deeply agitated by the possibility of scandal in the church. Over the preceding twenty years the church had lurched from one allegiance to another, from one liturgy to another, and from one set of doctrines to another. It was imperative, in the queen's view, that the new church settlement be allowed to establish its credibility with a laity for the most part either hostile to or skeptical of it. Any scandal at the parochial level by the representatives of the Establishment undermined the credibility of the church and the loyalty of the laity to it.[132] Moreover, at a time when the pulpit was used to transmit not only doctrine and ethics but also political ideas and information, undercutting loyalty to the occupant of the pulpit was ultimately undercutting loyalty to the queen herself. This was not a new argument. Christopher Mont suggested it when he reported in 1539 to Philip of Hesse that the cause of the prohibition of clerical marriage was probably that the uneducated "might conceive an opinion of concupiscence in [married priests] and by reason thereof contemn their preachings and the word of God."[133] Elizabeth's attempt to avoid scandal needs to be recognized for what it was, and even though hindsight exposes its failure,[134] it deserves understanding if not sympathy.

If proof is needed that this, and not a pathological dislike for marriage, was behind Elizabeth's policy, it is provided by her reaction to episcopal marriages.[135] Seventy-six bishops were appointed to English and Welsh sees during Elizabeth's reign. Of those, at least fifty-eight (76.3 percent) were married. Fourteen of those married more than once. Since only twenty-three are known to have outlived their first wives, this means that of those who might have married a second time, 61 percent did.[136] Elizabeth's bishops accounted for a total of seventy-four marriages either before or during their episcopacies, but there are only three possible cases of marriage-related troubles with the queen. The case of Tobias Matthew, recommended for promotion by Leicester and Burghley but delayed by the queen because of his youth and marriage, seems to have been invented by Strype.[137] Others involve the second marriages of Richard Cox of Ely and Richard Fletcher of London.

In 1568, Cox married Jane Alder shortly after the death of her first husband, William Turner. This might have aroused scandal since Cox was seventy years old at the time and she was reportedly a good deal younger (though she must have been well into middle age since she had married Turner in 1540).[138] Elizabeth's initial anger quickly subsided since Jane was unquestionably suitable.[139]

Fletcher was not so fortunate, nor did he deserve to be. He apparently first promised the queen that he would not remarry, then broke his promise in a flamboyant way: he married a titled lady (the first bishop to do so) and a member of the queen's household. It was exceedingly unwise to marry one of Elizabeth's ladies without consulting her, as they both should have known. Moreover his marriage into a noble family was considered somewhat inappropriate to his rank and resulted in vicious attacks on his and his wife's characters. He was sequestered and died soon after without being restored.[140]

Both of these cases have one other thing in common. The queen was already furious with both men for resisting her plans for the estates of their sees. Their marriages provided the occasion but not the cause for her outbursts. If the queen had wanted to use marriages against her bishops, she had opportunity in cases far more deserving than those of Cox and Fletcher, but Bishop Thornborough of Limerick received promotions in spite of a scandalous divorce and remarriage.[141] Thomas Cooper, the learned bishop of Lincoln (1571–83) and Winchester (1584–94) married, in 1546, a woman described quite acutely as "both a Xantippe and a Messalina."[142] She was a notorious adulteress long before he was promoted to Lincoln, and on at least one occasion heaved his manuscripts into the fire. Advanced-thinking colleagues at Oxford suggested that he divorce her and marry again, but Cooper refused.[143] Had he done so, that clear violation of canon law would have destroyed his career, but continued marriage to an adulteress and a shrew did not. Bishops of Bath and Wells Thomas Godwin (1584–90) and John Still (1593–1608) both married after becoming bishops, allegedly for money. Both cases were, according to Harington, brought to the attention of the queen.[144] Unlike Fletcher, however, neither bishop had given Elizabeth any other cause for irritation and both were left untroubled.

If the queen had wanted to give some concrete demonstration of her hostility, she had the motive and the opportunity. Many of her bishops suffered severe financial hardships with incomes inadequate for the normal expenses of their office and social position.[145] Such incomes could hardly bear the strain of providing for wives and children, and bishops who tried quickly earned reputations (often well deserved) for greed, nepotism, or both.[146] Just as often, they failed utterly, and the families of deceased and impoverished bishops had to throw themselves on the mercy of the queen.[147] Marriage damned any bishop to spend the rest of his life between the Scylla of his episcopal office and the Charybdis of his familial obligations, and Elizabeth could have used that as the excuse for the appointment of a contingent of celibate bishops.

There was no scriptural warrant that could excuse such a policy, but she had the unmarried personnel from which to choose if she decided to practice *de facto* discrimination. John Jewel, for example, might have been chosen for Canterbury instead of Parker. In the years that followed, some of the most outstanding figures appointed to bishoprics were bachelors: Grindal, Piers, Whitgift, and Bancroft. Unmarried candidates could hardly have fared worse than the long list of married nonentities and catastrophes who were appointed. The fact remains that Elizabeth showed no disposition against married bishops. If anything, she preferred them in numbers higher than the overall percentage of married clergy.

That having been said, it remains to explain the Statute of Ipswich, a royal decree of 9 August 1561 which ordered that no head or member of any college or cathedral church

> shall from the time of the notification hereof in the same college have or be permitted to have within the precinct of any such college his wife or any other woman to abide and dwell in the same or to frequent and haunt any lodging within the same college upon pain that whosoever shall do

to the contrary shall forfeit all ecclesiastical promotions in any cathedral or collegiate church within this realm.[148]

Haugaard argued that this injunction was the fruit of Elizabeth's pent-up resentment against the reformers to whom she had made many concessions and received "great variety in ministration" in return instead of her much-prized uniformity.[149] This had become clear to her during her summer progress through Suffolk and Essex in 1561, and her response to the lack of discipline in the church was this injunction. The authority for this is a letter from Cecil to Parker on 12 August:

> I have had hitherto a troublesome progress, to stay the Queen's Majesty from daily offence against the clergy by reason of the indiscreet behaviour of the readers and ministers in these counties of Suffolk and Essex. Surely here be many slender ministers, and such nakedness of religion as it overthroweth my credit. Her Majesty continueth very evil affected to the state of matrimony in the clergy. And if [I] were not therein very stiff, her Majesty would utterly and openly condemn and forbid it. In the end for her satisfaction, this injunction now sent to your Grace is devised.[150]

Cecil's letter clearly refers to two separate and unrelated issues. The "indiscreet behaviour" of the parochial clergy at which Elizabeth took offense had no logical relationship to the disorders perceived among the cathedral and collegiate clergy. Not even Elizabeth in the grip of her temper could have imagined how the regulation of the latter could affect the former. The wording of the injunction makes no such connection and is designed to address a separate problem.[151]

As in the 1559 injunction, the queen's principal concern must have been decorum and not clerical marriage *per se*. Nothing in the Ipswich injunction suggests that clerical marriage was in itself bad. Under the specific circumstances of colleges and cathedral chapters, the presence of wives and children disrupted study and subverted the communal spirit intended for such places. Bishop Cox, a vigorous supporter of clerical marriage, whose diocese included Cambridge University, conceded as much in a letter to Parker. His only concern was that so many of the cathedral clergy were already nonresident that if the married ones were turned out "owls and doves may dwell there for any continual housekeeping."[152]

Elizabeth did lose her temper on the subject. Parker wrote to Cecil, "I was in horror to hear such words to come from her mild nature and christianly learned conscience as she spoke concerning God's holy ordinance and institution of matrimony." She went so far as to tell Parker that she regretted his appointment, a feeling he likely shared by the end of his meeting with her.[153] When Cecil spoke with her she was still "very evil affected to the state of matrimony in the clergy."[154] But if she ever seriously contemplated banning clerical marriage as a solution to the disruptions – which she knew was as impractical as it was doctrinally insupportable – Cecil calmed her by devising the injunction to address the specific disorders that had provoked her. There is no evidence that it was enforced more than briefly in the royal peculiars of Windsor and Westminster.[155] Nor is there another recorded episode in which the queen raised any objections to clerical marriage. The silence in the sources, especially from men of proven hypersensitivity on the subject, argues the silence of the queen in fact.

As telling as the silence of the queen was the silence of the country at large. In the conservative north, the High Commissioners, whose mandate it was to enforce the religious settlement, considered only four cases over forty-two years in which objection was made to clerical marriage. William Allen, alderman of York, sat through a minster sermon by Ralph Tonstall in favor of clerical marriage after which Allen said in the hearing of the mayor and other aldermen that when Tonstall affirmed that the apostles were married and kept company with their wives, he lied.[156] Ten years later, in 1580, five women were ordered to make public declarations in their parish churches that they were at fault for telling their curate that his marriage was unlawful and his children were bastards.[157] Later, John Stevenson was summoned "for speaking diverse obscene speeches against the ministers of God's word which are married,"[158] and a minister's daughter reported that Robert Swayles referred to her insultingly as a "priest's calf."[159]

Outside of High Commission acta, such cases are equally rare. Dr Haigh reports that the vicar of Ribchester in 1574 presented a parishioner who "cannot suffer or abide a married minister, and hath said that he had rather receive the holy communion at the devil or a dog than at the hands of (him) being a married minister."[160] Bishop Parkhurst was informed of the heretical opinions of Nicholas Stannard, who considered the marriage of priests to be illegal. He also requested his commissary to act against a certain Mr Blake "for saying that all bishops' wives and priests' wives in England were whores."[161]

Given the easy familiarity of sixteenth century folk with sexual defamation, these remarks neither surprise nor suggest deep resentment against clerical marriage. Only in the cases of Allen and Stannard, and in Ribchester, is there any indication that doctrine, and not defamation in the heat of the moment, was involved. The sensitivity of the clergy and their wives and children to this issue makes virtually certain that practically all attacks – the doctrinal or the merely defamatory – would have been presented to the authorities for discipline. In the very complete visitation and instance records for the diocese of Ely there is not even one such case. Not only had the English laity come to tolerate clerical marriage, in some parishes they associated celibacy with heterodoxy.

Hugh Tunckes of Winchester diocese lamented in 1571, "I am called papist and so hooted at that now I am disposed to marry."[162]

A final sign that clerical marriage had ceased to be an issue in the English church is the virtual collapse of the print warfare on the subject, which had raged for nearly thirty years. Parker left a variety of brief essays and collections of sources in favor of clerical marriage among his papers which are of no particular interest or originality and were not intended for publication.[163] In 1562, part of Ponet's rebuttal to Thomas Martin was published posthumously under the title, *A defence of priestes mariage . . . agaynst T. Martin*. This draft had been put aside by Ponet many years before. Its publication was more of a tribute to his work than a part of a vital debate.[164] John Veron wrote a brief dialog between "The True Christian" and "Robin Papist" summarizing the scriptural and historical arguments of the earlier writers, but it pre-dated 1563 because in the earliest days of the new reign, he said, some still "kick against the lawful marriage of the faithful ministers of the church holding still the opinion that it is not lawful for them which are preachers of God's word and do minister the sacraments to be coupled in matrimony."[165] Bishops Pilkington and Jewel defended the English church for allowing clerical marriage in their controversies with Romanists, but their writings on this subject are unoriginal and occupy relatively little space in their defenses.[166]

By 1563, in fact, clerical marriage was a secure and unchallengeable feature of the Elizabethan church. In that year, Convocation established the Articles of Religion that included the following:

> 32. Bishops, priests and deacons are not commanded by God's Law, either to vow the estate of single life, or to abstain from marriage: therefore it is lawful also for them, as for all other Christian men, to marry at their own discretion, as they shall judge the same to serve better to godliness.[167]

Elizabeth resisted authorizing the articles by statute not because she objected to the doctrinal content, but because she opposed any modification of the 1559 settlement, particularly on the initiative of anyone other than herself. In 1566, the Commons passed a bill confirming the articles and because the bishops supported it energetically, the Lords very nearly did as well. The queen was forced to interfere personally to stay the progress of the bill until parliament was dissolved. In 1571, however, the queen did accept the bill for subscription to the articles and thus gave clerical marriage, again and finally, a foundation in statutory law.[168]

Even at this point, however, the successors of England's earliest Protestant controversialists failed to embrace marriage with real enthusiasm, following their esteemed predecessors who had defended clerical marriage with equal parts of scholarship and passion while remaining lifelong celibates with a stated preference for the single life. Much of the leadership of the Elizabethan and early Stuart church was chosen, understandably, from the universities, where fellows were required to remain unmarried. Even those who left university fellowships for pastoral ministry and marriage could not be counted on to encourage a more exalted view of matrimony. Richard Greenham is a case in point.

Greenham was a leader of the Elizabethan moderate puritans at Cambridge University. In the early 1570s, he chose to leave his college and became rector of Dry Drayton, which became a gathering place for young puritan clergymen watching and learning from Greenham. Several of his young apprentices recorded notes of Greenham's advice, and one extended manuscript survives, from which we can see Greenham's perspective on marriage.[169]

Greenham married the widow of Dr Robert Bownde in August 1573 when he was thirty-eight years old and had been at Dry Drayton three years.[170] The marriage was perhaps not a very fulfilling one. In spite of Dry Drayton being a comfortable living, Greenham's charitable impulses left him perpetually short of funds, and the story is told that his wife had to borrow money to bring in the crops from his glebe.[171] Mrs Greenham appears only once in the manuscript mentioned above: a brief note that Greenham "had a fatherly care, not only over the salvation but also over the diet of his wife," constantly urging her to moderation in the things her appetite desired.[172]

Greenham was occasionally asked for advice by people considering marriage. His advice was that no one should "run hastily into that calling." Instead, he recommended a regimen including prayer and fasting to see if one had "the gift of chastity or no." For Greenham, marriage was a last resort in the struggle against concupiscence and little else, and it was that message that the future leaders of the church carried from his little seminary on the edge of the fens.[173]

Even as more and more Protestant English clergymen chose to marry, the celibate ideal survived among the clergy themselves. In the seventeenth century, George Herbert would write: "The country parson considering that virginity is a higher state than matrimony, and that the ministry requires the best and highest things, is rather unmarried, than married."[174] In our own century Bishop Herbert Hensley Henson opined that probably half of "the married clergy of the Church of England . . . were ruined by their wives." As a result, Henson wrote, "I have seen so many clerical careers arrested, and (to all outward seeming) definitely marred, by the clergyman's marriage, that I never hear of a clergyman's becoming 'engaged' without a shiver of anxiety."[175]

Henson's comments, hardly the neo-Roman ravings of an Oxford Movement loony, can thus be seen to be rooted in a venerable tradition of ambivalence to clerical marriage that can be traced to Robert Barnes and the earliest days of the Reformation in England. Because of this ambivalence, as much if not more the product of the clergy than the crown, England did not have the kind of direct, enthusiastic writing on marriage by reformers which was so common in Germany and Switzerland. As a result, the meaning and value of marriage was scarcely examined, and the sorts of changes that developed from that examination elsewhere were absent in England.

4

Canon Law

The ecclesiastical laws of the Roman church received almost universal condemnation from continental Protestant reformers.[1] Martin Luther was typical in demanding: "Let canon law perish in God's name for it arose in the devil's name."[2] Among the most offensive aspects of canon law were the laws governing marriage and divorce,[3] and in the decades after Luther's great treatises of 1520, Europe was alive with proposals to abolish popish canon law in general, and to drive the clergy out of people's bedrooms specifically and back into pulpits where they belonged. City, duchy, principality – as one after another threw off the yoke of Antichrist and embraced the gospel, they joined Luther in heaving (literally or figuratively) the books of canon law onto bonfires like that which he lit in Wittenberg in December 1520. In the place of the old laws and the old courts, the reformed polities set new laws enforced by new courts, but the *Complaynt of Roderick Mors* lamented as late as 1543 that in England "the body and tail of the pope is not banished with his name," defining his tail as "his filthy traditions, wicked laws . . . yea the whole body of his pestiferous canon law."[4] The explanation for this neglect in England can be found in the absence of a constituency with the power or influence to overturn canon law generally or marriage law particularly, especially among those who were the political nation: the crown and parliament.

A wholesale reform of the canons seemed as inevitable as rain to the English in 1534. Since 1529, the Commons had been complaining about the church's independent legislative authority, though Henry VIII had not embraced their complaints.[5] His anger and frustration with the church grew, however, in the early 1530s as difficulties securing his divorce from Katherine of Aragon proved intractable.[6] Although one might expect that this would have given the king a consuming interest in overturning canon law, this proved not to be true.

In 1503, Pope Julius II had dispensed Henry and Katherine, allowing them to marry despite the impediment of affinity created by Katherine's earlier marriage to Henry's brother Arthur, who had died in 1502. Although marriage to one's deceased brother's wife was forbidden in scripture,[7] medieval precedents established that popes could grant dispensations where due cause existed, especially if the marriage was in the interests of peace, as was this diplomatic match.

Early in 1527, Henry expressed doubts that the marriage was valid. For many reasons, Katherine had become a disappointment, but the most compelling was her failure to give Henry a male heir. Although often pregnant during the first nine years of their marriage, only one female child was still alive and it was unlikely she would have another child. Henry noted that the Levitical punishment for a man marrying his brother's wife was childlessness, and having only a daughter was (from Henry's perspective) precisely that. The pope, concluded Henry, while having the power to dispense from man-made laws, must not have been able to so from a biblical proscription.[8] Moreover, since legal consensus held that coitus created affinity, and Katherine had long maintained that Arthur had never known her sexually (and thus her virginity meant that no indispensable bar against marrying Henry existed) Henry adopted a different definition of affinity. According to him, affinity was created not by coitus but by marriage contract. On that basis, Henry sought to have his marriage annulled.

While his frontal assault on papal power made Wolsey anxious and his tactics generally have led some scholars to question his judgement,[9] Henry had no workable alternatives. If coitus created affinity and Katherine had been a virgin as she claimed – and Henry, with his delicate conscience, did not deny it,[10] – the only impediment between them was "public honesty" (or "affinity by contract"), which was not biblical. Pope Julius had not dispensed from it, but ample precedent existed for retroactive dispensations to remedy defects when people married in good faith not intending to break the law.[11] But a new dispensation from "public honesty" would bind him and Katherine more tightly than before and frustrate his hopes for a male heir.

Moreover, Henry's case was soon impelled by his desire to marry Anne Boleyn, which had legal implications of its own. Some years before, Henry had had sexual relations with Anne's sister Mary. If coitus established affinity, the impediment existed between Anne and Henry in precisely the same degree as between Henry and Katherine. How could Henry argue that marriage in the first degree of affinity was forbidden *iure divino* and indispensable in one case and not in the other? First, he noted that while a brother's widow was forbidden in Leviticus, a mistress' sister was not, that is, that the degree was the same but the relationships were not, and only the former was banned.[12] More importantly, he had to argue that contract created affinity, and thus a bond existed between Katherine and Arthur missing between Mary Boleyn and Henry. While he probably knew he would find little canonical support for this argument and heaps of precedent against it, and his narrow interpretation of Leviticus insulted the pope, it did allow Henry to hurl scripture around in court, and the two positions together were the only possible way to free himself from Katherine without torpedoing future Boleyn nuptials.

But the strength of Henry's case is less to the point than is his dogged conviction that he could play within the rules and win. His faith seemed well placed. If history and experience had taught him anything, it was that nearly any papal sentence was available for a price. Humanist and Protestant reformers criticized the great numbers of canonical impediments for making it too difficult to contract a lawful marriage and too easy to annul one once contracted. Papal dispensing power, they alleged, injected a dangerous destabilizing flexibility into marriage. Henry was depending on that flexibility in his own case: that if he made some semblance of a reasonable canonical argument (which he did), an annulment would be his. For centuries, popes had stretched legal points to accommodate Christian monarchs. Henry, whose bitter opposition to Luther seemed to entitle him to some consideration, needed a legitimate male heir to protect England from civil war after his death; Katherine could not provide one. Even if his legal case was not watertight, it was surely sound enough to give some color of justice to his request and he must have been sanguine about his chances with the pope. Ironically, his experience was precisely the opposite from that of the papal critics. If Henry came to share their hatred of papal power, he arrived from the opposite direction, for he never concluded that the fault lay in the law itself (as the Protestants did) but only in the arbitrary and discriminatory application of that law.

In May 1527, Cardinal Wolsey and Archbishop Warham secretly convened a court at Henry's instigation which would charge him with incest, find him guilty and annul the marriage. Realizing that Katherine had the right to appeal a purely English court's decision to the pope, Henry requested a papal commission which would empower Wolsey to judge as papal legate with *plena potestas* as if it were the pope himself judging. Since accepting Henry's case meant acknowledging limitations on his own dispensing power, the pope would naturally be reluctant. Moreover, after imperial troops sacked Rome in May 1527, it was impolitic at least for the pope to aggravate Charles V by ruling against his aunt Katherine. In spite of initial rebuffs, for three years, Henry hoped for relief by playing the game according to the rules.[13]

In November 1529, the first session of a new parliament was held.[14] In his opening speech, the new chancellor Thomas More told the members that they had been summoned because the king recognized "diverse new enormities [had] sprung [up] amongst the people, for which no law was yet made to reform the same." The Commons, considering this a mandate to consider clerical abuses, galloped off in an anticlerical rage. Long simmering anger about probate and mortuary fees, pluralism and nonresidency, and competition from the clergy in agriculture, trade and manufacture resulted in three statutes, all passed over the opposition of the Lords Spiritual.[15] During the debate, a petition appeared which criticized the procedures and fees of ecclesiastical courts, and complained against Convocation's independent legislative powers, which tended to the "demise, diminution, and derogation" of the king's "imperial power, jurisdiction, and prerogative royal."[16]

The petition had no royal support and was easily deflected by the spiritualty, who "frowned and grunted." But Henry was becoming an unreliable ally without their knowing it. Already favorably impressed by William Tyndale's *Obedience of a Christian Man* and Simon Fish's *Supplication for the Beggars*,[17] Henry had now received from his agents the *Collectanea satis copiosa*, a manuscript compilation of ancient sources supporting his divorce case.[18] *Collectanea* suggested that in the past the kings of England had known no earthly superior and had enjoyed great authority over the church. After reading *Collectanea*, Henry pursued an entirely new policy, instructing his ambassadors to tell the pope that Englishmen could not be cited abroad to answer to a foreign jurisdiction and demanding that the pope relinquish his claim to try the divorce case. Until that time, Henry had challenged the theology upon which an individual papal dispensation had been based. Now he challenged the basis of the authority itself while providing a far-reaching alternative. For the next three years, Henry's acknowledgement of papal jurisdiction would be merely tactical: stalling against a decision in Katherine's favor until he had sufficient domestic support for his new claims.[19] On a separate but parallel path, the king also began a crusade to regain legal rights that he now believed were lost by his predecessors and which he had a duty to restore, thus entangling the honor of England with the private business of his own conscience.

Henry's bishops, having successfully resisted the Commons' attempts to clean the ecclesiastical stables in 1529, were blindsided by the king's reaction when the offensive was renewed in 1532.[20] Henry received the Commons' Supplication against the Ordinaries on 18 March, which he passed on to Warham without comment. By April, Gardiner had prepared a reply (presented to Henry on 27 April) which defended the right of Convocation to legislate in matters of "faith and good manners necessary to the soul's health," claiming that in such cases "there needeth not of necessity any temporal power or consent to concur with the same." Gardiner threw Henry's words back in his face, reminding the king that he himself had argued this against Luther, but offering to refrain from passing new laws "except they be such as shall concern the maintenance of the faith and good manners in Christ's church" and to void laws found repugnant to the king which did not fall into those categories.[21] The Lower House of Convocation proposed to abandon their legislative power during Henry's lifetime and to submit existing canons for royal review.[22] Bloated after a hearty meal of doubts about the authority of the clergy, he scorned all proffered compromises and on 10 May, Henry's terms were presented: no new canons were to be adopted without his assent; a royal commission was to review existing canons and have annulled any deemed prejudicial to Henry or onerous to his subjects; existing canons which survived this vetting would stand subject to royal assent.[23] With Gardiner in hiding on one of his estates, a panic-striken rump Convocation unconditionally surrendered on 15 May, recognizing the king to be supreme head of the church in England.[24]

With the ground thus prepared, parliament adopted a statute which used *Collectanea satis copiosa* to justify restraining all appeals to Rome.[25] Cranmer then had the authority to pronounce the marriage of Katherine and Henry null and void which he did on 23 May 1533. Yet the schism was still not complete. Henry continued to pursue a bloodless victory and pressed the pope to ratify his actions. When, and only when, he was threatened with excommunication the final steps were taken to sever the remaining ties with Rome.

In 1534, parliament turned the clergy's submission into an act, giving the king authority to appoint sixteen clergy and sixteen lay members of parliament to "view, search and examine" the existing canon laws and suggest those which ought to be voided. All were to remain in effect until reviewed.[26] (The dispensing power was transferred from Rome to Canterbury by statute.)[27] The potential existed, therefore, to pull down the entire edifice of canon law and make a fresh start of sorts.

Henry never appointed the review committee. Parliament noted this and authorized him to do so again, limiting the authority to three years in a vain attempt to press the king into action.[28] Finally, in 1544, Convocation secretly discussed asking the king to establish ecclesiastical laws and a further bill was introduced in parliament. The new bill provided not only for a review of the old law, but for writing an entirely new code of laws. This innovation resulted in rough sailing in the Lords, but the bill was eventually passed. Henry signed it, but again did nothing.[29]

Throughout this period of royal indolence, men at the highest levels envisioned something more radical than a mere pruning of the existing laws.[30] As early as November 1532, Henry was told that it was his duty to "pluck down the pope and his ministers of law from the high altar . . . and . . . to make that place holy at the altar where the pope's ministers, by his law, judgeth all matters of sin and bawdry."[31] One printed work at this time argued forcefully that the clergy, like the City of London, had no authority to make laws over those "that be not of [their] fellowship and community" and could not "give any punishment or correction to them that be not present at the making of [the] laws nor never consenting unto them."[32] Many shared the belief that legal business was alien to the true vocation of the clergy. A paper of "certain considerations why the spiritual jurisdiction would be abrogate and repealed or at least reformed" submitted in 1534 suggested that all ecclesiastical laws be repealed and replaced by statutes administered by the common law courts. Then the clergy could "better . . . remember their bounden duty to God and the people, which is to edify the people with good preaching and teaching of the true word of God, and then we should shortly have more divines than lawyers where now it is clean contrary."[33]

During the summer of 1535, Thomas Cromwell set his servant Richard Pollard to work. Pollard and others began discussions with civilians from the Arches about precisely what causes should remain with ecclesiastical judges. Pollard favored giving temporal judges jurisdiction over all ecclesiastical matters "and then then there would be but one law in the realm which I think would be better."[34] William Petre suggested that most current business was inappropriate, but matrimonial cases (as they depended on scripture) and the probation of small testaments ("to save expense to the king's subjects") should remain with church courts, but only at the king's sufferance and not by any independent authority.[35]

Meanwhile, Richard Gwent, dean of Arches, and three of his fellows produced a draft for a new code of canon law.[36] Presentation to the king was prevented by an outbreak of plague in 1535, but Cromwell made plans to push the canons through the parliament. He was so confident of their acceptance that he drew up letters for the king to sign ratifying the laws and took the premature step of issuing an injunction to Cambridge against the teaching and public study of and conference of degrees in canon law.[37] The new code was never approved. Cranmer and others were left defending the old laws, trying to secure public compliance in the face of what must have been growing disrespect. In late 1536, Cranmer reported to Henry preaching against "the bishop of Rome his laws" and saying "that many of his laws were contrary to God's laws," but "so many of his laws as were good, men ought not to contemn and despise them, and willfully to break them; for those that be good your grace had received as laws of your realm, until such time as others should be made. And therefore as laws of your realm they must be observed, and not contemned."[38]

If the 1535 draft had been adopted, English marriage law would have been practically unchanged.[39] The draft canons left marriage formation law as it was in Roman canon law. Clandestine marriage prohibitions were trotted out with the same foredoomed approach: while "absolutely forbidden," they were neither void nor voidable. In order to prevent such marriages, banns were to be read three times in the parish church where the wedding would be held. Normally, that would be the home parish of the woman.[40] Solemnization in a parish in which one of the parties had lived for less than a year required permission from the churchwardens of the previous home parish. Priests were to announce the prohibition against clandestine marriages four times per year *in vulgari*, and they would be excommunicated and suspended for three years *ipso facto* for solemnizing them.

The English church would have retained impediments of force, insanity, youth, error of condition, consanguinity and affinity with some changes in definition. Forced marriages had always been ratified by later free consent, which was to be demonstrated if the couple lived together for six months without violence or cries of opposition. The ages beneath which children could not contract marriage were raised: from fourteen to seventeen for men and from twelve to fourteen for women. Affinity would have been legally created by coitus. Finally, the forbidden degrees were set out in some detail. Marriage with anyone in lineal ascent or descent was forbidden; all relationships in the first degree were listed individually and prohibited; all second degree unions fell under a general prohibition and were not listed individually.

Conditional marriages were unaffected, and present tense contracts would still supercede earlier future tense contracts. A party wishing to break a contract *de futuro* against the other party's will could be assessed monetary damages by the ordinary. Deserted spouses (assumed to be women) could not contract again without certain news of the other's death. When someone contracted leprosy (used generally for any extremely serious disease of that sort) after spousals, the healthy party could withdraw from the ill, but not remarry. Medically irreparable impotence nullified a union, allowing the healthy person to marry another, but only if it had been discovered after the contract. If the parties had contracted in full knowledge, nullity was barred.

A series of miscellaneous canons follow. The deaf and mute would be permitted to use signs instead of words to express consent to a marriage. Marriages unchallenged during the life of the parties could not be called into question after their deaths. Suits in ecclesiastical courts have been allowed to proceed even if one party did not appear as long as there had been a thorough search; no more would justice be denied by a defendant's absence, which was frequently the case before. Remarkably, the draft affirmed that mantle children were legitimate and reserved resolving all doubtful legitimacy cases for the church courts.

In many ways the draft is an advance from medieval canon law since it clarified several disputed points. Nonetheless, it is more notable for what it did not say than for what it did. There is no trace whatsoever in it of continental reform influence, no mention of divorce and remarriage, no abolition of spiritual kinship (though perhaps intended by silence), no mention of parental consent being required. Either unwilling to experiment or lacking the imagination to devise new solutions to old problems when offered the opportunity, the conservative civilians at the Arches seemed determined to keep things much as they had been before the break with Rome.

With Bullinger urging Edward, whom he compared to the godly prince Josias, to undertake his duty to reform the church,[41] early in Edward VI's reign, Sir William Paget urged Somerset to appoint "learned men as well for the consideration of the laws, which to be continued and which to be abrogated, as also for the decent orders to be observed in the church," probably a reference to the

Henrician scheme never carried out.[42] Eventually the Commons produced a
bill, amended and passed by the Lords (in spite of near-unanimous opposition
from the bishops) and signed by the king on 1 February 1550. The commission
would have until 4 November 1552 to produce a code, which would be
promulgated by letters patent without parliamentary approval.[43]

The commission was not appointed until October 1551. The original members were eight impeccably Protestant bishops, eight equally reliable divines,
eight civil lawyers and eight common lawyers.[44] The council minutes noted
that out of these men eight should be appointed "to rough hew the canon law,"
presumably in the interests of efficiency.[45]

When Vermigli wrote to Bullinger in Zurich on 8 March 1552, the work was
not completed.[46] Both houses passed bills extending the commission's life, but
parliament was adjourned before the Lords completed the third reading of the
Commons bill.[47] It seemed that law reform would be lost.[48] Somehow the work
was completed, and Cranmer presented a manuscript to the Lords in March
1553, where Northumberland told him bluntly that nothing would come of it.
Apparently the duke was annoyed by increasing opposition to his policies
among the clergy and in an angry outburst he suggested that Cranmer and his
bishops would be better occupied controlling their clergy than in meddling
with the behavior of the laity.[49] Cox had complained to Bullinger that there was
widespread opposition to "Christian discipline" in the country:

> We would be sons and heirs also, but we tremble at the rod. Do pray stir
> us up and our nobility too by the spirit which is given to you to a regard
> for discipline; without which I grieve to say it, the kingdom will be taken
> away from us and given to a nation bringing forth the fruit thereof.[50]

Against the combined opposition of Northumberland and the less fervent
members of both Lords and Commons, Cranmer was helpless, and hopes of
passing the *Reformatio Legum Ecclesiasticarum* died with the king on 6 July 1553.
In the "King's Minutes for His Last Will," he expressed a desire that his
executors "cause godly ecclesiastical laws to be made and set forth," but his
successor assured that that would not be done.[51]

Professor Jordan once praised the *Reformatio Legum*'s "cool and sensible re-
statement of the law of marriage."[52] This is a lengthy portion of the whole:
thirteen chapters on the formation and impediments to marriage; seven chapters on the prohibited degrees; and twenty-one chapters on adultery and divorce.[53]

The marriage section begins with a definition traditional enough to satisfy
any papalist. It was to be contracted by the minister announcing the future
nuptials in the church on three consecutive Sundays or feast days, after which
the couple was to undergo the rites of the church. Each was considered free and

unbound (*liberae solutaeque*) and without power to demand any right of matrimony from the other until they gave and received mutual faith in fixed words in the church. Believing that it was conformable with scripture, piety and justice that no one ought to marry without parental knowledge and consent, without that a marriage was "reduced to nothing" (*ad nihilum recidere*). Permission was expected, and if denied, the couple could go to ecclesiastical judges for a resolution. While proper marriages could be celebrated at any time of the year, they must be in the parish church of either the man or the woman. Priests celebrating marriages in other places incurred excommunication. The minimum marriage ages remained twelve for women and fourteen for men.[54]

Someone who objected in church to a marriage was bound to prove the grounds for objection within a month, or to compensate for the preparations made if his claim was false. Precaution was to be taken that during the period in which the marriage was suspended, neither of the parties contracted another marriage. If one party did, he or she was excommunicated until satisfaction was made to the deserted partner. Impediments included error of person, degree, or status; impotence by nature or maleficium unless both parties were aware of it and consented to marriage in spite of it; and force and fear sufficient to sway a constant man.[55]

The deaf and dumb could marry since they could show consent by signs, but *furiosi* were discouraged from marrying unless the madness was temporary. Christians were discouraged from marrying non-Christians, as were elderly women from marrying young men, in part because they could not have children, and because it was vain and perverse. Finally, brawls and disagreements did not dissolve matrimony.[56]

The second section, *De Gradibus in Matrimonio Prohibitis*, denounced and specified marriages forbidden by God's law, both marriages between those related by generation (*consanguinitas*) and conjunction (*affinitas*). God's law admitted of no human modification or dispensation. As Cranmer had argued earlier, the banned couplings listed in Leviticus were not exclusive. For example, if a son could not marry his mother, then neither could a daughter marry her father. For clarity, all forbidden degrees would be spelled out specifically, those named in scripture and those derived by analogy. What was attributed to the man was held to be equally true of the woman in the same degree, and since man and wife became one flesh, one incurred relationships in affinity in equal degree to the consanguineous relations of the other.[57]

The final section, *De Adulteriis et Divortiis*, established penalties for adultery and provided that the innocent party might contract a fresh marriage. The church preferred forgiveness and reconciliation but recognized that forgiveness could not be legislated. Failing reconciliation, the guilty was still not allowed to remarry. Parties were not to separate on their own, but only by judgement of the ecclesiastical court.[58]

Obstinate desertion was also grounds for divorce. The victim could remarry; the guilty party was to suffer perpetual imprisonment. If a departed spouse did not return for two or three years, and it was impossible to learn if he or she was still alive, the remaining spouse could remarry on condition that if the other spouse returned and proved blameless, they must reunite. Hostility which led to mortal attacks by either spouse or prolonged ill-treatment by a husband beyond that necessary to restrain an obstinate, petulant or evil wife dissolved marriage, but neither did *parvae contentiones*, unless perpetual, nor diseases. The divorce *a mensa et thoro* was abolished as "alien" to scripture and leading to "great perversity."[59]

That the church would even retain jurisdiction over marriage was not inevitable. Many continental reformed churches had not, and Peter Martyr Vermigli and John A Lasco could have urged such a policy, though Bullinger opposed subtracting marriage from ecclesiastical jurisdiction. Panic over supposed decay in discipline argued for urgent royal intervention, and Latimer played Cassandra before the king in 1550, exhorting him "for the love of God, take an order for marriages here in England."[60] Martin Bucer, similarly alarmed, did not preclude transferring marriage to secular courts in his *De Regno Christi*.[61] Historically, pious emperors such as Justinian had provided laws ordering marriage, power usurped fraudulently by "Roman antichrists." With their power in England overthrown, the absence of "just laws" and an "effective plan" had created such confusion, Bucer said, that the king should "assume . . . responsibility for the ordering of marriage," since marriage is *res politica* and "in order that men may rightly contract and enter marriage, observe it reverently, and not dissolve it unless compelled by extreme necessity" the state had always supplied laws.[62] The mere fact that the *Reformatio Legum* did not suggest a jurisdictional transfer argues its conservative side. Of course, it is likely that Cranmer and the other bishops were unwilling further to undermine their crumbling authority by concessions to secular jurisdiction in any form.

Marriage was also defined in a traditional way which did not reflect advanced Protestant thought, current at the time, which made companionship the highest end of matrimony. Bucer, for example, wrote:

> Now the proper and ultimate end of marriage is not copulation or children, for then there was not true matrimony between Joseph and Mary the mother of Christ, nor between many holy persons more; but the full and proper and main end of marriage, is the communicating of all duties, both human and divine, each to other with utmost benevolence and affection.[63]

That traditional impediments were retained is less surprising; reformers were unlikely to applaud forced marriages, for example. According to Latimer this was a serious problem, as "many parents constrain their sons and daughters to marry where they love not, and some are beaten and compulsed."[64]

While possible that marriages without parental consent were to be invalid, imprecise language ("reduced to nothing") makes it impossible to be certain. This was a topic of some concern at the time. Latimer, preaching to Edward in 1549, denounced the state of affairs then current, in which some "inveigle men's daughters, in contempt of their fathers, and go about to marry them without their consent,"[65] and Hooper had enjoined priests not to marry any couple without a careful investigation to determine if the parties had their parents' consent or were not under the power of their parents.[66] This was the most he could do within the law.

Bucer urged the king to reform the law, making the "godless compact of matrimony" without parental consent null and void; papal law was "supremely godless" because it supported contracts made "out of blind love and the desire of the flesh, and for the most part out of the deviousness of seducers and the wantonness of the seduced." On the other hand, parents should not abuse their authority and withhold consent without good cause. If they did, children could enlist the aid of relatives, of presbyters of the church and, as a last resort, of magistrates who would compel the parents to consent if the marriage was not objectionable.[67]

But the *Reformatio Legum* relied instead upon penalties long tried without success, leaving untaken the one useful step of declaring certain unions unambiguously null and void. Cranmer and Peter Martyr, the principal authors, were not canonists and their unconcern with the niceties of legal language might be understandable but it is self-defeating. Judges contending with the law as they wrote it would be left wringing their hands.

De Gradibus also deviated from much continental reformed thought, but it was a real advance and a triumph for the program which Cranmer had been advocating since the 1530s. He had long insisted that the list of forbidden unions in Leviticus was not exclusive, and that to avoid confusion or ambiguity all should be listed. Given the opportunity to write the law, he did.[68]

The section *De Adulteriis et Divortiis* is genuinely radical. Divorce and remarriage in cases of adultery and cruelty was a thorough departure from separation *a mensa et thoro*. Such a provision for desertion is even more surprising, since the Roman church did not have any policy to deal with it. Many Protestant churches allowed remarriage of the innocent party after divorce for adultery basing their permission on scripture. Peter Martyr seemed to have held that scripture permitted remarriage only after adultery though he admitted that the state could extend the grounds for divorce.[69] Bucer, however, recognized divorce for a variety of causes including violating sepulchres, harboring thieves, and witchcraft.[70] Moreover, because he had elevated companionship to the highest position among matrimony's ends, Bucer formulated a bold new understanding of marriage as a covenant which was dissolved whenever companionship left the marriage.[71] Many of his contemporaries felt that he was "more than licentious" in this regard, and the *Reformatio Legum* struck a judicious pose in the middle.[72] If the equity of many of these provisions is beyond dispute to us, in 1552 they required genuine daring. Overall, while attempting a sort of moderation, the *Reformatio Legum* left conservatives horrified and thoroughgoing reformers frustrated. Even had the king lived, one can reasonably doubt that its chances of passage were good.

In 1586, a presbyterian supplication to parliament stated that

> The first [grief] and cause of the rest is, that there is no certain godly law established among us by authority of this honourable house whereby the causes and affairs of the church may be governed, only it is left to be ordered by the canon law, whereby it was ruled in the time of greatest darkness and ignorance that ever was in the church.[73]

Noting that parliament had often previously made reforming canon law a priority, they urged parliament to pursue that goal to its completion.[74] But by 1586, such laments-cum-exhortations had acquired a serio-comic pathetic predictability, for the seeds of such reform had been planted in far more fertile soil and not borne fruit. The Elizabethan regime had proven, in nearly thirty years, to be irredeemably barren soil.

In 1559, a bill to revive the former scheme for appointing the thirty-two-member committee appeared, passed the Commons, and after one reading from the Lords was never seen again.[75] It may have died for much the same reason as the *Reformatio Legum* before it: that "men who could live with the reformation of doctrine and worship were not prepared to accept the reformation of discipline" because of the power over them which it would give to the church.[76] Equally likely, such a proposal enjoyed almost no support in the Lords for other reasons. In 1559, unlike 1552, they were asked only to allow the queen to recreate the machinery to write another code, which Marian bishops would have rejected, while reform-minded peers might have recalled the evil example of Henry VIII who was thrice given the authority to appoint such a committee and never did. There is no evidence that Elizabeth herself raised any objection, probably because in leaving the initiative entirely to her the proposal corresponded nicely to her Erastian views of the prerogative inherent in her supremacy over the church.

In a 1560 letter to Bullinger, Thomas Lever lamented: "No discipline is as yet established by any public authority."[77] The Convocation of 1563 intended to do something about that, and made it one of its highest priorities.[78] The "General notes of matters to be moved by the clergy in the next parliament and synod," which guided the Convocation, resurrected the committee of thirty-two, suggesting that both queen and parliament be requested to appoint such a group with special care taken to have them review the *Reformatio Legum*.[79] From this emerged several sets of articles, including "Articles for government" calling for a new disciplinary code for the clergy and laity. These latter, the closest Convocation actually came itself to providing a new code were "not so allowed" according to Parker's marginal note.[80]

Apparently, Elizabeth would have accepted some adjustments in ecclesiastical discipline in 1562. In his opening speech, Lord Keeper Bacon told parliament that among the causes for which they had been called was "earnestly to think about and consider of the discipline of the Church, as one of the strong pillars of religion" which then suffered from "the imperfection of [its] laws." The bishops, to whom discipline and dogma belonged, were "to confer and consult of these matters, and if in their conference they shall find it behooveful to have any temporal act made for the amendment or reforming of any of these lacks," they were to present the matter to parliament.[81] A bill "for reformation of ecclesiastical laws"[82] which would have revived the committee yet again is quite likely one response, and John Penry suggested in *Reformation no enemy to her majesty and state* that the *Reformatio Legum* was also presented to parliament and committed for translation,[83] though the session's brevity would explain no further mention of either proposal.

In April 1571, Thomas Norton produced a new edition of the *Reformatio Legum Ecclesiasticarum*, published by John Foxe, after a request by William Strickland. A committee was appointed "to have care of that book and to have conference with the bishops therein."[84] Nothing further was heard of the committee or of the *Reformatio Legum* in the parliaments of Elizabeth.[85]

The reform movement's radicalization and the development of presbyterianism changed the nature of the debate about reform so utterly that both the committee of thirty-two and the *Reformatio Legum* became inapposite artifacts of the past. Even had this not happened, the queen would never have bestowed her "La Reyne le veult" upon such a proposal. As Wallace MacCaffrey explains, her hostility was to both the form and the content of such enterprises. In nothing was Elizabeth more her father's daughter than in her passion for religious uniformity. "In 1539," writes MacCaffrey,

> Parliament had, at Henry's irritable bidding, passed a bill hopefully entitled "An act abolishing diversity in opinions." It was an unavailing attempt to restore under royal leadership the kind of uniformity of faith which had hitherto been everywhere the norm of European life. But this particular Humpty Dumpty was not to be set up again in England although the efforts of the king's horses and all the king's men would continue to be engaged at the task.[86]

All the queen's horses and men, too. Elizabeth continued that quixotical struggle, preferring among other things to keep the canon law as it was after the Submission of the Clergy, rather than risk ripping the lid of Pandora's box off its hinges.

The queen was perfectly willing to remedy individual abuses as they arose (or to order the bishops to do so), but she was not willing to have her parliaments tell her uninvited what to do and when to do it. In her dealings with parliament on religion, Elizabeth displayed uncharacteristic political myopia. Her parliaments contained men who cared deeply about religious matters, men driven by conscience and conviction to devote their energies to reshaping the national church in the image and likeness of some scriptural (or Genevan) ideal. The queen never quite grasped the importance of their consciences and convictions as motivations, and her cranky resistance in the face of sincere if tactless attempts to reform the church, and the frustrated realization that any bill passed was fated to disappear forever into the capacious pockets of Elizabeth's skirts, pushed many of these earnest reformers in new directions.

At first employing constitutional strategies, albeit with a radical assumption underpinning their moves, "that religion was a 'commonwealth' rather than a 'state' matter, open to private initiatives and public discussion," they had tried to recruit the bishops to their cause "and to present their proposals as logical and desirable extensions of the reforms already accomplished."[87] But the cloth of alliance between the bishops and the reformers, woven during their exile and the honeymoon period of the new reign, began to stretch under the pressure of the Vestiarian Controversy. It tore with the bishops' refusal to condone the 1571 proposals (and the counterattack mounted by such as Jewel, Horne and Cox with whom the puritans had made common cause in the past) and shredded after the subscription crisis of 1572.[88]

Human reaction to betrayal, real or imagined, is often extreme and unrestrained, and puritans were nothing if not human. While continuing objections to the survival of canon law, they abandoned reasoned political discourse and adopted a tone both of urgency and hysteria. As John Field said: "The wound groweth desperate and the dead flesh hath overgrown all, and therefore the wound had need of a sharp corsive and eating plaster."[89] Although the pope's name was no longer used, "his body, which be the bishops and other shavelings do not only remain, but also his tail, which be . . . his pestiferous canon law." True Christians should go their parishes "and there stand up and say, I believe in God, yet you do but mock with God so long as you walk in those wicked laws."[90]

A vituperative attack on the canons, a mere change of tone, was not the only fruit of lost confidence in episcopacy. From the 1570s, many puritans publicly advocated an entirely new approach to ecclesiastical discipline in England. Under the existing church order, they argued, pastoral care was essentially "the impersonal judicial process of the church courts, where the bishop was represented by officials . . . whose attitude can be described without prejudice as professional rather than evangelical and pastoral."[91] The courts continued to render judgements based on Roman canon law rather than biblical sources, and the bishops continued to make available dispensations and licenses in a manner scarcely distinguishable from that of the pope. For the authors of the *Admonition*, episcopal courts were "the filthy quavmire and poisoned plash of all the abominations that do infect the whole realm."[92]

Presbyterians advocated discipline based exclusively on scriptural principles exercised by the pastor of the individual congregation,[93] and set about putting this into practice. Such endeavors, like the Dedham classis, were foredoomed to very limited success, for their discipline was entirely voluntary.[94]

There was also a well prepared, carefully orchestrated frontal assault on the ecclesiastical polity in parliament in 1586. Among the bills prepared was "An act for the restitution of christian discipline in the Church of England and for the abolishing of the Canon Law in that behalf"[95] which would have required that each parish elect six people from the parish "being known to be the most forward and sound in setting forth the proceeding of the gospel" who would, together with the minister, "hear and examine all causes of offence to the church" within their several parishes. The minister and elders were not to deal with probate, tithes, matrimonial matters ("cases mere civil") nor use censures other than admonition and excommunication.

This was the last serious attempt at constitutional reformation of the church. Measures produced in 1589 were "the mere swell of the sea after the storm had subsided."[96] The ecclesiastical courts and the laws by which they adjudicated were secure after more than half a century of debates and serious challenges.

Absent any whole change in canon law, piecemeal statutory reform remained an option. Cromwell certainly was not satisfied leaving things as they stood, and he devised parliamentary legislation to address some problems, including one "by which young men should be restrained from marriage till they be of potent age, and tall and puissant persons stayed from marriage of old widows."[97] The 1536 succession act enacted the consanguinity rules of the draft code, rejecting the Lutheran principle of barring only pairings mentioned specifically in Leviticus. Cranmer, who carried the day, argued that "By the law of God many persons be prohibited, which be not expressed, but be understood by like prohibition in equal degree," for example a biblical ban of marriage with a brother's wife included the parallel wife's sister.[98] Second, affinity was legally created not by marriage but by carnal knowledge (and therefore Henry, through his carnal knowledge of Mary Boleyn, was in the first degree of affinity with her sister Anne — a case the king now wanted to make).[99] Dispensations against these degrees were impossible, though it remained possible for human law to add further, but dispensable, forbidden relationships.[100]

When Thomas Howard, brother to the Duke of Norfolk, was attainted for marrying Lady Margaret Douglas, legally the highest ranking woman in the kingdom, and preceded in her claim to the English throne only by James V, his traitorous aspirations "to the Dignity of the Imperial Crown of this Realm" resulted in an addendum to his attainder making it high treason in future to espouse or marry the king's children (and those "commonly reputed or taken for his children"), his sisters or aunts, or children of his brothers or sisters without a licence under the Great Seal.[101] Here was the ultimate admission that the principles of papal law were still accepted: even the king, the Supreme Head, could not terminate a marriage by words of present consent without killing the parties. The statute did not alter ecclesiastical law by declaring such marriages void, but could only impose the ultimate penance.

Another statute reforming marriage law is that concerning precontracts and consanguinity of 1540. The preamble rehearsed the bishop of Rome's usurped power and the unquietness caused to the king's subjects by his laws; the impediment of precontract was abolished and kinship prohibitions were restricted to the Levitical degrees. In a session characterized as "the strife of parties," the bill sailed through the Lords without dissent in two days, passing the Commons in another two.[102] Statutory relief against people marrying away from their parish churches without banns in spite of prohibitions or previous contracts was sought but denied.[103]

In Edward's reign, the Henrician statute abolishing divorce for precontract was repealed, because in spite of the nobility of its original stated (not actual) intentions people had abused the law. The bill's authors noted that people were "so set upon sensuality and pleasure, that if after [making a] contract of matrimony they might have whom they more favored and desired they could be contented by lightness of their nature to overturn all that they had done afore . . . more for bodily lusts and carnal knowledge than for surety of faith and truth." After repeal, the law returned to the *status quo ante.*[104]

Bigamy had apparently become something of a problem, at least in the view of the authorities. In 1548, a royal proclamation noted that

> unlearned and evil-disposed persons have not sticked to instill and whisper into men's ears and to persuade abroad evil and perilous opinions against God's law and the good order of the realm, some teaching that a man may forsake his wife and marry another, his first wife yet living, and likewise the wife may do to the husband; other, that a man may have two wives or more at once, and that these things be prohibited not by God's law, but by the Bishop of Rome's law; so that by such evil and fantastical opinions some hath not been afraid indeed to marry and keep two wives.

The proclamation ordered those with ecclesiastical jurisdiction to enforce canon law and punish offenders "with grave and severe punishment." Failing that, JPs or any subjects were to inform the Privy Council so that the king "might see a convenient redress made of such misorder" and also deal with the bishops who were not adequately performing their disciplinary duties.[105]

This must have seemed inadequate since in 1552, the Lords passed a bill providing that no man should put away his wife and marry again unless he be lawfully divorced before competent judges, making a felony of what had only been an ecclesiastical offence. The Commons produced and passed a new bill, which was received by the Lords and given two readings, but fell before the adjournment three days later.[106]

Even before the *Reformatio Legum* proposed remarriage after divorce, a bill to permit it was introduced and had one reading in the House of Commons.[107] A much fuller hearing occurred when it was raised as a matter of personal concern by William Parr, Marquis of Northampton. Parr had married Anne Bourchier, the only child of the Earl of Essex, in 1527. The earl died in 1540 and they were given seisin of his lands.[108] In 1542, Parr separated from his wife for her adultery, and in 1543 secured passage of a private bill bastardizing any children of her adulterous liaison in order to protect Parr's estate.[109] Since at the same time Lord Burgh was pursuing a similar course against his wife, the Lords were roused briefly to consider a bill to deprive women convicted of adultery of their property (possibly the bill for the "true keeping of matrimony" referred to in the same session).

In 1547, Parr informed Edward VI that Henry had intended to appoint commissioners to determine if Parr might "without offence to God, for the avoidance of unlawful life whereunto all flesh is prone, and the procreation of children which he necessarily requireth" marry another woman while Anne lived. He asked the new king to complete what death had stayed his father from doing.[110] He obliged on 19 April 1547.[111] Parr was unwilling to wait for a ruling. Perhaps believing that they would not refuse a Privy Councillor and brother of the dowager queen, he married Elizabeth Cobham sometime in 1547. When the council summoned him to account for his action, he claimed to act in accordance with the word of God, but the council felt "the thing strange normal and against the law whereof being suffered to escape unreformed, namely in a person of such representation, might ensue many and great inconveniences to the whole realm." They were ordered to separate, and Elizabeth was to be sequestered with the dowager queen until the commission gave its decision.[112]

Cranmer's papers contain (in his secretary's writing with additions by Cranmer) a large manuscript entitled "Collections de Divortio."[113] If this collection is related to Parr's divorce,[114] Cranmer had not moved beyond his views expressed to Osiander in 1540. The collected authorities overwhelmingly oppose remarriage.

The argument centered on the interpretation of two virtually identical Matthean texts.[115] Most of the collected patristic and conciliar sources suggest that Jesus's saying implies only a permission, not a requirement, to send away an adulterous spouse; the marriage bond is not absolutely broken by adultery. If the offended party chooses to send away the offender and cannot live unmarried, the Fathers preferred that the couple reconcile, Jesus having given no explicit permission to marry again. In ancient times remarriage occurred only because the adulterer was killed and the first spouse's death freed the innocent party. Remarriage might have been acceptable to the synoptics' Jesus only for that reason.[116]

Attached to this collection were questions and answers. The answers, in unidentified Italian hands,[117] are responses solicited by Cranmer in the same way as he gathered academic opinions for Henry's first divorce. The respondents disagree. Answers favoring remarriage are either ignored or peppered with derisory marginalia in Cranmer's hand: "The answer is not to the purpose," "*Male responsum est*," and so on.

In the first edition of his *Declaration of the Ten Commandments*, Hooper stated that adultery broke marriage bonds and after proof by "lawful testimonies" both parties "may by the authority of God's word, and the ministry of the magistrates' separate and marry again" — a radical view, since no one of Hooper's prominence had suggested that the guilty also might remarry. Probably in response to criticism, the edition of 1550 added several pages of explanation because, Hooper wrote, "Of these few words uncharitably con-strued . . . there is by ignorant and lascivious persons much controversy risen between many men."[118]

By 1552, with Parr's patience surely exhausted and possibly knowing that Peter Martyr was moving Cranmer to accept more liberal views of divorce in the *Reformatio Legum*,[119] a private bill appeared in and passed Lords and Commons. After noting Northampton's divorce from Anne Bourchier for her adultery, it stated that he was thereafter "at liberty by the laws of God to marry" and had done so. To remove doubts about the validity of this marriage or the legitimacy of its future issue, parliament declared it lawful notwithstanding any statute, common or canon law, or custom.[120]

This was not a parliamentary divorce; the divorce had been granted by the ecclesiastical court. This act was designed only to serve the needs of one private (but powerful) individual. Had the act proved successful, there is little doubt that others would have followed suit and parliament might have done on a case-by-case basis what it eschewed on a theoretical one. Equally probable, having taken the finger out of the dike, it might have given way and reformed canon law on this point by statute. But as Northampton (and everyone else) discovered, the disadvantage of relying on parliamentary acts is that what parliament gives, parliament can take away.

Northampton, who remained loyal to Northumberland, was imprisoned when the Grey succession scheme collapsed and his lands were seized by the crown,[121] while a newly-freed Gardiner, embittered by Parr's involvement in his fall and his seizure of Winchester House for his principal London residence, sent the putative marchioness packing.[122] Although his imprisonment was brief, he was restored in blood, his debts to the crown were eventually forgiven, some lands were regranted, and Mary even grudgingly agreed to consider the justice of Elizabeth Cobham's claims on his lands,[123] parliament repealed the act validating his second marriage, declaring it it had proved "an encourage-ment for sensual persons" to find corrupt ways to divorce their wives rather than an "example or godly precedent whereby the people may be induced or stirred to continue with their wives in godly quietness and lawful matrimony."[124] If ever there was a blinding light illumining the dangers of relying upon parlia-ment to solve domestic crises, this was one. The lesson was well learned: a century passed before another such attempt was made.[125]

Elizabeth's parliaments considered, without passing, several bills to end specific abuses emerging from marriage law. These bills, and their fates, pro-vide a small window into grievances of the political elite. The issues addressed were the legitimacy of children born after divorce; bigamy; the legality of marriage during previously forbidden seasons; licenses to marry without banns; abduction and marriage of heiresses; and adultery.

According to canonical precedent, if parents were divorced *a vinculo*, the children were judged bastards unless the parents had married in ignorance of the impediment which resulted in their later divorce. If parents were divorced only *a mensa et thoro*, the children remained legitimate. Children of adulterous liaisons could not be excluded from inheriting using this formula. A 1576 Commons bill proposed that children born after divorce should not inherit unless there was a reconciliation between the parties.[126] This would have excluded an adulterine child if the adultery of the wife, as witnessed by her pregnancy, was the cause of the divorce. It was given one reading and seems to have aroused no particular enthusiasm.

In 1581, a bill making bigamy ("taking a second wife not being lawfully divorced from first, still living") a felony was read twice and committed.[127] A bill eliminating the periods of time during which marriage was forbidden (primarily Advent and Lent) passed the Commons in 1585 but was never read by the Lords,[128] somewhat surprisingly since there was consensus that this prohibition was out of place in a reformed church.[129]

The case of Dinnington who had kidnapped a Devonshire heiress named Alice Stoite and married her against her parents' will provoked some discussion in the parliament of 1597.[130] Dinnington, if the bill which emerged is any indication, used benefit of clergy to secure his acquittal. The Lords passed a bill which would have denied benefit of clergy to violators of the Abduction Act.[131] The furore over Dinnington's case led some members to revive the issue of abusing licenses to marry without banns, since these were often used to circumvent parental disapproval.[132] Here at last was an issue which aroused the genuine interest of a wide circle in the Commons.

Marriage licenses had proved to be something of a running sore on the body of the Elizabethan church. The "General notes" of 1563 and the "Articles for Government" which developed out of them would have eliminated licenses to marry without banns altogether.[133] The ecclesiastical laws drafted for that session were more direct, making such marriages voidable.[134] In 1571 George Carleton produced a bill to reverse the Dispensations Act of 1534 "by which statute the bishop of Canterbury is made as it were a pope."[135] In the long debate which followed, the consensus was that the grievance was genuine but that Carleton's bill was not the solution.[136] It was committed, rewritten, and passed by the Commons, but quietly abandoned in the Lords where it faced the hostility of the bishops.[137]

When Whitgift became archbishop in 1583, he and several bishops proposed a compromise. They noted that "persons of honest worshipful and honourable calling may necessarily and reasonably have occasion sometimes to solemnize marriage by licence [without] the banns asking . . . without any great harm." Rather than abolishing an occasionally useful form, the bishops suggested imposing conditions on issuing future licenses: that there be no matrimonial suit pending against the parties, that they demonstrate parental consent, and that they marry openly in church.[138]

The enforcement of this procedure (incorporated in the canons of 1585 and 1597) would have satisfied those whose concern was to protect patriarchal authority while retaining the right to marry by license if they chose,[139] but grievances against licenses ran far deeper for puritans such as Carleton who objected to them on principle, not because of inconvenient consequences.[140]

The new procedure was not adequately enforced, and in 1597 when the matter was again raised in the Commons, three members were able to produce a lengthy catalog of "divers incestuous and unlawful marriages made by licences by vagrant ministers in lawless peculiars." On November 11, Thomas Cecil moved that a bill be drafted to redress this grievance and he was named to head a committee for that purpose.[141] At this point someone alerted Elizabeth. Determined to prevent the Commons meddling with the church, she resorted to subterfuge, sending a message to the Commons on 14 November expressing her horror at the tales which had come to her ears. She requested that they provide her with a list of abuses so that she could provide some remedy. The committee drafting the bill was expanded and set to work fulfilling the queen's request. The list was completed and sent on to her.[142] Whitgift, however, prepared an aggressive defense of licenses for the queen and reissued the canon of 1585 with additional safeguards, which she gave royal approval.[143] This was enough to strip the extremists of a majority, and a defiant Henry Finch's bill died quietly.[144]

Finally, in the parliament of 1601 a bill was presented which would have punished those convicted of adultery by loss of tenancy by curtesy or dower. Opponents noted that a man without property would not be punished by the bill, making it *"ius inaequale* and not to be admitted." When the Speaker then asked if the bill should be read a second time, the House "gave a monstrous great no."[145]

From either monarch or parliament the monstrous great no had been heard for over seventy years. Why such conservatism from a polity which had thrown over the authority of the pope? First, Henry VIII had a rather personal approach to statute-making. The two acts with any claim at reforming inconveniences in marriage canon law were both passed explicitly to solve Henry's own problems. The Precontract Act was such an obsession that Henry made extensive and often trivial changes in the wording of drafts shown to him, rousing himself to a state of activity for this one bill usually reserved only for hunting and more military pursuits.[146] Luther himself recognized the intimate relation between the king's idiosyncratic designs and the course of events: "What Junker Heinz wills, must be an article of faith . . . for life and death."[147] Other than lack of interest, Henry had a more deliberate reason for fending off legal reform: he had not made himself pope of England to give away his power. The common lawyers, increasingly hard to control, were unlikely to find the king willing to pass ecclesiastical jurisdiction into their hands by parliamentary act. Those who thought otherwise were "Utopian doodlers."[148]

In the confused and occasionally surreal atmosphere of Henry's court, then, the legal reform which took place in Germany was doomed. Ironically, this was no less a magistrates' reformation, in which theologians could have an impact only when, and insofar as, political ambitions of princes and town governments combined to sweep away much in law and theology that was old and replace it either with new ideas, or with the tools to place long dormant ideas and ideals into practice. In England, however, this movement died at birth, strangled by the hamfistedness of Henrician midwifery.

Henry's youngest daughter was no less determined than her father to maintain royal control over the church, and the law as it stood (enforced by her domesticated bench of bishops) offered her a better chance of doing that than the plans envisioned by reformers, now more radical than in her father's day. In between these two cautious conservative monarchs, reform was suffocated in political uncertainty. For while Edward VI would probably personally have favored a radical law reform, he was too young to provide effective leadership. His bishops did not want to hand over traditional church jurisdiction to lay people, and a majority of lay parliamentarians did not want to tighten the church's grip over their private lives. And so matters stayed until 1603.[149]

5

Extraparliamentary Pressure

In arguing that medieval church courts treated canon law as case law, Charles Donahue shows that judges, who viewed their primary responsibility as the settlement of disputes, not the enforcement of a code of laws, left themselves latitude for judicial flexibility.[1] If Donahue is correct, reformers, judges and litigants might have used this flexibility to reform marriage law from the inside out. Did litigants seek, or the courts offer, extraparliamentary relief from the canon law through a sixteenth-century version of judicial activism? This chapter will explore various avenues of extraparliamentary activity in which such challenges and reform might take place, showing that no real reform took place in this way. Although sixteenth-century litigants brought matrimonial cases properly within the jurisdiction of ordinary ecclesiastical courts to Chancery, High Commission and the Privy Council, these bodies turned away such cases, whatever the intentions of the suitors, and lent their authority to a defense of the matrimonial jurisdiction of the church courts and thus also of the law by which they judged.

Litigants in ordinary ecclesiastical courts do not seem to have tried to convince judges there to modify the canons or offer new forms of relief.[2] The Privy Council received some petitions on matrimonial matters. Usually, those cases did not involve them in matters which normally belonged in church courts. Like Chancery, they heard complaints about failures to fulfill the financial side of marriage contracts.[3] Questions of validity usually arose only incidentally and were left to church courts.[4] Only once was a straightforward instance case brought to the Privy Council, a case which involved a couple from Jersey, and came to the council because of the peculiar and confused situation of the Channel Islands after the Reformation. The council referred it immediately to the bishop of Winchester.[5]

As early as Wolsey's years as chancellor, however, people petitioned the Court of Chancery for assistance in matrimonial matters. Most of those petitions requested aid either to secure the return of goods delivered in anticipation of a marriage which did not take place[6] or the delivery of goods promised but withheld after a marriage did take place.[7] In others the petitioner requested the chancellor's aid to overcome some obstacle in pursuing a case in a church court. For example, Roderick Jones asked to be released from prison when his wife, in collusion with another, claimed a precontract at the time of her marriage to Roderick, who feared that he would lose the case (and his wife) if he did not appear to answer the charges.[8] Thomas Patrick's wife asked for relief when her husband deserted her after fifteen years of marriage and began living adulterously with Elizabeth Ronsley, whom he claimed to have married. He had avoided ecclesiastical prosecution by moving, thus being shielded by the statute against summoning a person outside of his diocese.[9] Finally, Thomas Heyward, who contracted marriage with Colchester heiress Marian Barker and was rejected by her in favor of John Daniel, petitioned the chancellor. After Thomas sued her for breach of promise in the bishop's court, she married John secretly and unlawfully in a Tower of London chapel. Knowing that this marriage would eventually be dissolved, John had been selling her inheritance. Thomas knew he would be compelled to marry her after she was destitute, so he requested an injunction against the sale of her property.[10]

Such cases did not threaten the authority of the church courts or the letter of its laws; they merely sought relief where it could provide none. When direct attempts were made to use Chancery to resolve cases undeniably belonging among the instance cases of ecclesiastical courts, these were rebuffed. The principle applied by Chancery was stated most clearly in 1591: such cases were "not to be plucked or drawn from [church courts] by this court, which suffereth all actions to follow their natural course where their ordinary trials lie."[11]

In November 1547, a bill had been introduced in Lords to create a new court of Chancery for ecclesiastical causes, and after a second reading was assigned a distinguished committee.[12] Its composition argues that the bill was taken seriously, though the bill went no further. But in Elizabeth's reign a judicial organ was created which offered a potential locus for reform: the Ecclesiastical Commission. This was not a church court. Composed of both lay and ecclesiastical members, like many of the new courts in Protestant Europe, it was part of ecclesiastical government, yet it derived its authority directly from royal letters patent. Moreover, it could fine and imprison.[13]

Almost immediately after beginning their work in 1561, the northern High Commission was confronted with a matrimonial case, refused on the grounds that it was "mere ecclesiastical."[14] In the next year, the commission refused to meddle in the case of Lord Thomas Langton and his wife, declaring that since the case concerned the bond of matrimony it was the business of the consistory.[15]

Instead of competing or interfering with the normal workings of episcopal courts, the commission carved out for itself an important role as a partner of those courts. Since it had the power to fine and imprison, which church courts did not, bishops turned to the commission for aid in reducing the contemptuous

to conformity when ordinary methods failed. Elizabeth White, the defendant in
a consistory matrimonial suit, was ordered to be sequestered to keep her from
Edward Fawcett. The apparitor of the court was prevented from executing this
order. At that point the commission stepped in. Cowed by the commission's
authority, Elizabeth appeared and was sequestered.[16]

The High Commission continued to act as agent for provincial consistories
throughout Elizabeth's reign. Commissioners sequestered or arrested defendants who refused to appear in consistory or who had been prevented by force
from doing so, and punished those responsible for the prevention.[17] They also
imprisoned those who refused to obey consistory decrees or sequestered them
away from those believed to be dissuading them from compliance.[18] They took
recognizances to comply with court orders or to appear in court to answer suits,
and they imprisoned those who failed to appear.[19] Using their authority to
discipline the clergy, the commissioners also reinforced ordinary marriage law
by imprisoning or suspending clerics who performed illegal marriages.[20]

Their self-imposed limits were occasionally violated, as in the case of Thomas
Standish, which followed closely after the Earl of Westmorland's scandalous
marriage. The earl, who married his deceased wife's sister, defended his deed in
a letter to William Cecil, arguing that since Leviticus did not explicitly
prohibit marrying his wife's sister, he had "done nothing but God's law doth
allow" and that popes had forbidden such marriages only to sell dispensations;
since "the liberty of the gospel [has been] restored, I think I have offended no
law in what I have done."[21] Since his views were deemed to threaten episcopal
teaching authority, he and his wife were prosecuted in the York consistory.[22]
Cecil wrote secretly to Archbishop Young demanding that he "take order . . .
that neither this nor such like disorder be suffered uncorrected."[23] Young, who
was reluctant to dissolve the union, responded, "I think that many lawful
husbands in England be not in such love with their lawful wives."[24] After
Young did as ordered, Westmorland appealed, and the queen appointed a
commission headed by Archbishop Parker to hear the appeal.[25] In October
1562, the similar case of Thomas Standish's marriage was raised, and it by-
passed the consistory, undoubtedly because the issue was considered so politic-
ally sensitive, going directly to the commission. Thus began ten years of
contention, during which Standish consistently rejected the divorce which was
handed down and he was imprisoned in York Castle.[26]

When clergyman Francis Ashburn sought the commission's aid in his suit
against Elizabeth Lacy, whose father was preventing her from appearing in
court, the commissioners showed exceptional interest. Elizabeth was seized on
their orders, but her father arranged her escape, and was arrested himself.[27]
Elizabeth appeared in court and said that she was bound in conscience to marry
Ashburn and wanted to do so. Her father however claimed that Ashburn had
previously promised that he "would not covet his (that is, Lacy's) daughter

against his will." Moreover he reminded the court that "by the Queen's Majesty's Injunctions . . . Francis being within Orders cannot marry his said daughter against his will being her father." The commissioners then took the unusual step of themselves ordering the solemnization of the marriage.[28]

Undoubtedly they did this because Lacy raised the queen's injunctions and therefore the Royal Supremacy which it was their mandate to enforce.[29] By ordering the marriage to be solemnized the commissioners made a significant ruling on the limits of the royal injunctions. Since the old canon law was still in effect, indissoluble marriages still required only the consent of the man and woman. Since Elizabeth was thirty-four years old, her capacity to consent was obvious. For violating the royal decree, Francis was liable to be suspended from his ministry but he and Elizabeth were bound to each other in marriage in the eyes of God and her father had no business to prevent them from solemnizing their union in the church. Neither the royal injunctions nor the authority of the High Commission would be used to modify the canons. At no single point in its history did the Ecclesiastical Commissioners make clearer that they were not, and refused to be, in the business of making new law or meddling with the old.

That being said, the court did appear to create a new and uncanonical form of divorce *a mensa et thoro* for "irreconcilable differences." Rather routinely, they dealt with a handful of cases each year of married couples living apart. The numbers of such cases were too small to suggest any wholesale poaching of business from the consistory,[30] and there is no hint in the terse entries of anything complex or scandalous that required the commission's attention. Possibly these were cases of difficult or stubborn people needing the threat of High Commission's power to fine and imprison to secure their cooperation.

As early as 1566, the commissioners had, rather than issuing the usual cohabitation order, sanctioned a "cooling off period" during which one couple could continue to live apart "trusting that God will so work with them that they shall by both their consent go together again." This was not intended to be a long-term solution however, and when the woman refused even to consider a reconciliation she was excommunicated.[31] In a similar case in 1575 and three more in 1578, due to "divers discords and variances" similar arrangements were allowed, and the women provided with alimony during the separation.[32] Such arrangements were not, strictly speaking, canonical. On the other hand the commissioners stopped well short of creating a new form either of divorce or of permanent legal separation. The probable reason for their involvement was providing alimony: they offered a legally enforceable short-term arrangement that other courts did not.[33] Since this approach was adopted only five times in twenty years, it was clearly undertaken only with reluctance and only when it was the most practical solution.

From 1599 until Elizabeth's death, cases of clandestine or other irregular marriage become a standard feature of commission sessions. While the commissioners had previously punished clergy who participated in such ceremonies, they had not bothered with the principals. The enforcement of canons and synodal statutes against clandestine marriage, marriage without banns, and marriage at certain forbidden times was the bailiwick of the ecclesiastical courts. But the sudden interest shown by the High Commission in these cases did not signal a change in the policy of four decades protecting the jurisdictional integrity of the ordinary courts. Rather, it was part of a change in policy towards Catholic recusants in the north.

In 1599, Thomas Cecil was appointed president of the council and given a direct mandate to crack down on northern Catholics.[34] Burghley may have lacked brother Robert's stomach for politics but he was a zealous Protestant and he undertook his mission with rigor and commitment. He made his mark on the commission's business.[35] Any remotely unconventional marriages raised suspicions of recusancy. But it is important to emphasize that the commissioners were not interested in the marriages *per se*, and said nothing about them. The long lists, filling folio after folio, of couples presented for secret marriages, sandwiched as they are between equally long lists of those noted for being baptized "in a Popish manner" or having "children not lawfully baptized" or simply for recusancy, were clearly compiled in the pursuit of conformity, not reform of marriage law or jurisdictional poaching.[36]

Thus for forty years the Ecclesiastical Commission operated in York with the delegated authority of the Supreme Governor of the Church of England. The commissioners consistently upheld the authority of ordinary ecclesiastical courts to decide matrimonial litigation. As well, they reaffirmed the medieval canons as the basis upon which those cases would be decided, shutting and bolting the door against any possibility that England would reform marriage law by indirection. Indeed so conservative were the Ecclesiastical Commissions that the bishop of Exeter, in 1600, begged Robert Cecil to establish a special commission to put down "intolerable wildness and wickedness" in the diocese, including bigamy and other illegal or irregular marriages.[37]

An additional avenue for reforming marriage law from within the system was the visitation injunction, the orders given to be carried out during mandated regular diocesan visitations. Throughout the sixteenth century, these were used to correct abuses and reform behavior. Although, as Professor Helmholz observes, continuity was more remarkable than reform, bishops undertook some noteworthy initiatives in the many injunctions concerning marriage.[38]

Injunctions survive for six Henrician episcopal visitations. In each, there is some command that ministers preach regularly against privy contracts – a vain hope with a non-preaching clergy – and threaten their congregations with the most extreme penalties for so contracting. Archbishop Lee added that they should preach against marriage without parental consent, and Bonner counselled against solemnizing second marriages without certifying the death of the previous spouse.[39] Edward VI's royal articles for the visitation of 1547 inquired if any lay people were married within the prohibited degrees or were divorced or separated without just cause, if any had made privy contracts or had married without banns.[40] The lack of effective initiative is striking.

Under Elizabeth, more significant lasting measures appear. *An admonition to all such as shall intend hereafter to enter the state of matrimony, godly and agreeable to laws*, better known as Parker's Table of Degrees, is the most important.[41] The exact extent of the relationships within which marriages could be contracted remained unclear in spite of Henrician statutes and *The King's Book*, and it fell to Archbishop Parker to disperse the fog.

While it is possible that Parker was moved by incestuous marriages being all too common at the time, there is very little evidence of that. Consanguinity cases were unimportant in the medieval courts,[42] and that did not change in the years following the Reformation.[43] In fact, Parker was probably prodded into action by the marriage of the Earl of Westmorland to the sister of his deceased wife.[44] Some argued that the Levitical provision forbidding a man from marrying his wife's sister *adhuc illa vivente* was simply against marrying the two women at the same time and that after the first wife had died it was permissible to marry her sister. Others argued that there was no logical reason to assume that, and since a man was forbidden his brother's wife, by analogy a woman must be forbidden her sister's husband. Westmorland's marriage forced the proponents of Cranmer's system of reckoning the forbidden degrees to take some definitive action and, as shown above, William Cecil intervened personally to move Archbishop Young against the earl's marriage, while the earl continued to insist that he had "done nothing but God's law doth allow it . . . whereupon [as I take it] all laws in every Christian commonwealth . . . ought to be grounded."[45] This case, the ten-year struggle over Thomas Standish's marriage[46] and, finally, the 1563 Chafin case in which a man divorced from his sister-in-law by Bishop Jewel appealed to the Court of Delegates, suggested that this particular pairing was a boil in need of lancing.

In 1561, the bishops had already agreed "that all such marriages, as have been contracted within the Levitical degrees, be dissolved, and namely those, who have married two sisters, one after another."[47] This seems to have achieved little and Jewel was so frustrated by Chafin's case that he wrote to Parker, "I would [the Delegates] would decree it were lawful to marry two sisters, so the world be out of doubt."[48]

Doubt was indeed the problem, and while Parker accumulated a small library of dreary unoriginal treatises or memoranda on marriage with deceased wife's sister,[49] he decided that something larger had to be done, for this noisome union was symptomatic of a larger problem, the unresolved question of whether Leviticus was exclusive or illustrative.

Parker had first prepared his *Admonition* in 1560, a hasty effort intended to be provisional. His own copy, included among his papers in the Parker Library, is filled with autograph notes suggesting revisions which needed to be made in future editions. A later edition appeared in 1563, published with royal authority as a broadsheet intended for display in all parish churches.

The text noted that persons in direct line ascendant and descendant were not allowed to marry no matter how far apart in degree they were. It also stated that consanguinity and affinity were created by sexual intercourse, not only by marriage. Although the *Admonition* is best known for its treatment of the forbidden degrees, Parker also used it to admonish against secret contracts without the advice and consent of parents and to issue warnings against a new contract after judicial divorce or separation. The clergy were reminded that they were not to solemnize marriages outside of their own cures, nor in private houses. Banns were to be announced publicly three Sundays or festival days in order for those who could allege some impediment to come forth, while those who made frivolous objections were subject to punishment. Appended to this was a chart listing thirty relatives who were ineligible to be the marriage partners of a man and, in a parallel column, the equivalent thirty for a woman. The list was complete, listing every relationship in the first and second degree of consanguinity and affinity. While nothing in the list was novel, it was a decisive frontal assault on the mischief fostered by thirty years of uncertainty.

How effective was Parker's *Admonition*? Every parish was required to exhibit a copy of it in the church, and visitations regularly took note of those which did not, requiring them to certify acquiring and posting a copy.[50] Grindal tried requiring that the clergy read it twice a year.[51] Although it must have made deadly dull reading from the pulpit, Grindal was being pragmatic. Displaying a copy is one thing. Getting people to read and understand it is another, and getting them to observe its provisions still another. Edward Ward of Langton (Durham) told the consistory after he knowingly married his uncle's widow that "there is divers writing hanging upon the pillars of their church . . . but what they are or to what effect he cannot depose, saying that he and other parishioners . . . is not instruct of any such."[52]

If against such ignorance there was little that church officials could do, it would be unfair to label the *Admonition* a failure. First, there is no way to measure how many marriages were prevented when couples restrained themselves in the face of the prohibitions or because someone in the community intervened at the banns. Presentments in the ecclesiastical courts which give as their proximate cause the scandal of the community suggest that the *Admonition* was not without impact.[53]

Of course, it was not a perfect instrument. Some matters remained unclear, and marriage with deceased wife's sister remained a contentious matter into the twentieth century when efforts to legalize it finally succeeded. First introduced in parliament in 1842, the legislation became an annual event immortalized in Gilbert and Sullivan's *Iolanthe* ("He will prick that annual blister/ Marriage with Deceased Wife's Sister") until passed in 1907.[54] Still, the *Admonition* was undeniably an advance over the muddle of previous years. Some measure of the adequacy with which it filled its appointed task may be found in its durability. It was quoted in the canons of 1603 as the authorized interpretation of the law of God in this matter; it was added to the Prayer Book in 1681 and continued in force until 1940.

In other matters as well the bishops did little more than admonish their flocks to obey the laws which already existed. Visitation injunctions quickly became the hallmark of Elizabethan episcopal administration. The many surviving sets reveal the marriage-related issues of concern to the bishops.[55]

While almost all ritually enjoined enforcement of Parker's *Admonition*, bigamy was of equal concern, especially the illegal remarriage of people who had been divorced *a mensa et thoro* by church courts. In seventeen visitations, bishops demonstrated concerns about precontracts, which could also result in someone having two spouses. Geographical mobility was at the heart of the problem. In 1569, Parkhurst ordered the Norwich diocesan clergy not to marry new arrivals in the diocese without sufficient proof that they were free to marry.[56] Some people did provide certificates to that effect but whether from clerical instigation or their own initiative is unclear.[57] Ultimately, however, Parkhurst's scheme was unenforcable, and bishops who had tried to enforce something like it would only have created another lucrative occupation for unbeneficed and unscrupulous clergy, already running illegal marriage mills, who could begin selling "eligibility to marry" certificates which other clergy would have little choice but to accept as genuine and sincere.

Additional episcopal concerns were a constellation of disorders related to contracting and solemnizing matrimony, most commonly irregularities in the ceremony's time and place. Marriages were not to be solemnized at other than the parish church of at least one of the parties, nor at times (such as before dawn) which precluded public witness.[58] In almost every set was some provision against laity who married without having the banns asked three times as required (or without a license to avoid that requirement), or against clergy who solemnized marriages without properly calling the banns. Others addressed secret betrothals, seeking the people who made them and those in the parish who encouraged them, or ordering clergy actively to discourage them.

These two general problems — irregular betrothals and irregular solemnizations — were two sides of the same coin: almost invariably they were detours around obstacles in the matrimonial road, the most frequent of which (contemporaries believed) was parental consent. Bishop Sandys preached to the parliament of 1585 on this theme: "There is nothing," he said, "more hurtful to the commonwealth than these corner contracts, without consent of parents; contrary to the will of God, the law of nature, the law civil and all right and reason. The inconveniences that follow are not sufferable. . . ."[59] In 1597, Bishop Tobias Matthew of Durham lamented to Burghley that marriage without parental consent was "a great blemish in our reformed church to be no more deeply chastised than it is."[60] The unapproved canons offered in the "General notes" of 1563 proposed the only effective solution: making all such marriages voidable if challenged in court. Since the queen rejected any amendments to the canon law, pastors and preachers had to do their best to change attitudes voluntarily and the visitation was one tool for doing that. In thirty-two sets of printed articles or injunctions which mention matrimonial irregularities, nineteen attached no particular reason to them, but thirteen mentioned failure to obtain parental consent explicitly.

Most striking is that while in the Middle Ages the church was encouraging people to marry in the church rather than privately, by the late sixteenth century that struggle seems to have been won. Fewer than half of the visitation articles and injunctions felt the need to mention privy contracts. Of those, thirteen were in the eighteen sets before 1577; only four were in nineteen that followed.[61] Almost all articles, however, addressed disorderly solemnizations. People were not refusing to make the church part of their marriages; they were misappropriating its authority, and throughout Elizabeth's reign that above all was the most serious concern of the bishops.[62]

Clerical conformity with the Prayer Book's marriage service was apparently of less urgency. Four articles mentioned readers or other nonordained persons solemnizing marriages, three more (the earliest in 1586) popish priests doing so. Only two sounded the tocsin over puritan practices such as omitting the ring and the Holy Communion at marriages.[63] Finally, two visitation articles addressed child-marriages. Both were from northern dioceses (Chester and Durham) which suggests that widespread child-marriage was indeed peculiar to the north.[64]

If these were the issues which concerned church leaders, what agitated the lay leaders of Elizabethan England? The right of parents to consent to marriages was the only issue which seems to have excited any serious or sustained interest on the part of the lay elite. We have already seen how it was a factor in the parliamentary debate over marriage licenses.[65] Yet the gentry and nobility of England never took the line of their counterparts in France, demanding that all marriages made without parental consent be voided. Why this should be so deserves attention.

Since the Middle Ages the church had been urging upon children their duty under the fifth commandment to obtain the advice and consent of their parents before marriage. At the same time parents were admonished not to alienate the affections of their children by making frivolous objections or by stubbornly

withholding their consent without just cause. The historian of marriage needs
to ask two questions about this which can never be answered entirely satisfactorily. First, did children take this duty seriously and believe that it was
improper to marry without consent? Second, did parents themselves believe
that consent was necessary, and if so under what circumstances? For elite
families, the answers to these questions are somewhat different than for the
majority of the population. Here I will address only the elites, for it was these
people who could have led some movement for reform of the relevant laws or
pressured courts for redress.

My difficulty is that which faces any historian of past attitudes and ideas:
ideas cannot be quantified. Differently put, it is impossible to demonstrate that
one attitude was held by more people than another, or that more people
believed a certain position in, for example, 1589 than did so in 1489. Instead,
one treats the public to academic pie-fighting as scholars fling individual
"impressionistic" sources at one another. In this particular case, there is no
alternative.[66]

When children married over strenuous parental objection, parents did not
have legal grounds for invalidating the union, and extralegal parental action
could lead to trouble. The Privy Council intervened when John Stafford, esq.,
spirited away his son Humphrey to break up a marriage of which he did not
approve but which the council was assured was valid "by two very learned in
the ecclesiastical laws."[67] With no apparent appreciation for the irony involved,
the Earl of Hertford (who had been imprisoned in 1562 for marrying Lady
Catherine Grey over Queen Elizabeth's objections)[68] tried to break up the
betrothal of his son Edward to Honor Rogers. He essentially imprisoned his son
to prevent his seeing the woman, and even Walsingham's intervention failed to
move Hertford. Finally, Whitgift investigated the case and ruled that the union
was indissoluble, adding that young Edward could not be excused for matching
himself without his father's consent, but that consent was "*de honestate matrimonii* and not *de necessitate*." The archbishop could only urge Hertford to forgive
his son since there was no undoing what was done and the son was remorseful:
"You know that Christian charity requireth forgiveness even of the greatest
offences if the party offending shall say *peccavi*. God's written law requireth it
in all men, and both the law of nature and the written law also require it in
you."[69]

Since marriages without parental consent were almost always clandestine,
however, the ecclesiastical courts could punish the parties on that account.[70]
Cold comfort for the parents perhaps, but a few weeks in the Kidcote or the
Fleet could provide a salutary example to others. When John Donne clandestinely married Sir George More's daughter in 1601, he was imprisoned by
the High Commission. Donne confessed the illegal marriage to More, admitting as
well that he "knew my present estate less than fit for her [and] I knew . . . that

I stood not right in your opinion." In spite of this he pleaded for More's understanding:

> Sir, I acknowledge my fault to be so great, as I dare scarce offer any other prayer to you in mine own behalf than this, to believe this truth, that I neither had dishonest end nor means. But for her whom I tender much more than my fortunes or life (else I would I might neither joy in this life, nor enjoy the next), I humbly beg of you that she may not to her danger feel the terror of your sudden anger. I know this letter shall find you full of passion, but I know no passion can alter your reason and wisdom, to which I adventure to commend these particulars; that it is irremediably done [and] that my endeavours and industry, if it please you to prosper them, may soon make me somewhat worthier of her.

Instead More had Donne and his associates imprisoned.[71]

If, instead of a clandestine solemnization, the couple had only betrothed themselves, the court might act as arbitrator and do something more to satisfy the father, since betrothal (unlike solemnized marriage) did not require cohabitation of the couple. In 1582, the northern High Commission heard evidence concerning the secret betrothal of William Tattersall to Mary Bell, daughter of Richard Bell, gent. Tattersall confessed the betrothal and was released from prison, but bound under a recognizance of £200 not to have any conversation with Mary for three years without her father's consent. After the three years he was free to solemnize the marriage only if he was worth 200 marks.[72]

How many parents swallowed hard and accepted the unavoidable is impossible to know. Even more impossible to measure is the proportion of children who accepted that they should not marry without parental consent, simply because there is no obvious way in which such beliefs should be manifested. The relative infrequency of cases of conflict between the will of parents and children is suggestive. (Parents who separated their children from spouses risked a suit for restitution in the ecclesiastical courts, and those who interfered with betrothals one of breach of contract.) My case does not rest on negative evidence however.

First, some case studies. Edward Brockton, gentleman of Worcester, turned to Chancery to recover gifts he gave to Dorothy Hering in anticipation of marriage when she refused him due to her mother's objections.[73] Thomas Conge broke up with Elizabeth Patten because of his parents' displeasure, admitting to Elizabeth that in spite of their love, his parents were older and wiser "and do consider more than we are able to know." He wrote to her in some despair when he heard of a rumor that they were secretly contracted:

> I pray you . . . consider every way how I am charged not only by God's

laws which ought to be born in mind but also by the prince's laws which ought to be had in reverence, to be obedient and discharge my duty unto my parents, and what disobedience and undutifulness it is for me to enterprise to have a wife that neither father nor mother nor any friends else will consent unto it. Therefore I pray you seek to bridle and overcome your everlasting affection . . . .

He concluded by begging her to write to his parents and disavow any intention of marriage so that he could have their goodwill again "for they will never believe that I am uncontracted until such time you do write it."[74] A final example: In 1563, William Cecil's cousin the gentleman pensioner Barnaby Googe claimed that he was contracted to Mary Darrell. Her parents disapproved of this match, intending that she marry Sampson Lennard. While there is some evidence that she initially preferred Googe, she wrote to him urging him to withdraw his suit, for

neither presently I have nor I am well assured never shall have the good will or consent of father nor mother to whom I am both by the law of God and nature bound to give honour and obedience, and in no wise willingly grieve or offend them. And do well consider that my chief obedience and duty towards them, is to be bestowed in marriage by their consents and to their good contentation, assuring myself in meditation and thinking hereof that being their obedient child and to them most bounden, in disobeying them therein I shall not only be deprived from that blessing which God hath promised to such as truly honour their parents, but also shall be assured to find and have the like disobedience of my children if ever God shall give me any. . . .[75]

In all of these cases parents felt that they should play a role in the matrimonial choices of their children, who accepted that role. When a reason for this role was indicated, it was economic, not some peculiar or perverse desire to exercise arbitrary power. This was especially the case in the marriages of daughters. Historians like Lawrence Stone who discount parental affection for their children believe that their motivation for interfering in marriage was advancing the wealth and position of their families. The evidence, however, makes it possible to argue that fathers were equally, if not primarily, interested in protecting their daughters from a miserable fate. Because control of a woman's resources passed to her husband at marriage, the danger was ever-present that the husband would not use those resources to support her but would waste them, leaving her destitute. It was this that many fathers and mothers worried about. One Essex esquire, providing in his will for a married daughter, chose not to leave her anything directly because "the same may be taken from her by her husband of whom I have no good opinion." Instead he provided that his wife should make whatever dispositions were best. A Braintree draper provided that if his daughter married "to her utter undoing," rather than receiving a dowry, £60 was to be spent to buy a piece of land from which she would receive the income for life.[76]

Because the average age of first marriage for women in the upper levels of society was significantly lower than for the population as a whole, responsible fathers felt a special sense of urgency: daughters who were going to marry in their late teens or very early twenties might not have the experience or maturity to protect themselves from a wastrel or a fortune-hunter. At a certain age, their judgement might be trusted but before that age, some fathers tried to restrict their freedom of choice.

These very theoretical suggestions can be supported by the evidence from the 512 wills of Essex peers, knights, esquires and gentlemen proved during the reign of Elizabeth.[77] Of those, 169 wills contain provisions for what are clearly never-married daughters. Sixteen of these wills contain bequests conditional on the consent of some third party to the daughter's marriage. Three of those make clear that the girl was not to be restricted after the age of twenty-one. Only 9.4 percent, therefore, tried to insure that unmarried daughters did not marry without consent, and only 7.7 percent extended restrictions into her adulthood.[78]

If the principal concern of fathers was alliance, wealth or status, the marriage of sons should have been of equal concern. It is more difficult to isolate the marital status of males in the Essex wills, but whatever the exact numbers, only three wills restrict grants to sons. One of those uses the sort of tone that the orthodox view supposes:

> Whereas I have given the most part of my manors and goods to my beloved son, hoping that whereby he will bestow himself in some good virtuous house and to maintain the heirs, and for that it should be his quite overthrow to marry any daughters of Cecily North widow for divers reasons to me known and I fear my son may be thereto induced, I do hereby move him to take heed thereof. And if he shall not be hereby admonished I will for a further punishment that the manors and lands and the remain of my goods be distributed equally amongst my daughters. . . .[79]

In one of the other two restrictive wills, only one grant (the lease of a parsonage) is conditional. All other bequests to the son are unrestricted, as are those to his sisters. The third restricts the grants to the daughters as well.

The marriage of sons did not bring with it the same problems as did those of daughters. Were it true that parents were solely concerned with fortune-building then they would have done so. However, parents were concerned with protecting their children from unscrupulous or wastrel spouses. Since sons retained control of their own property and wealth, they did not face the same dangers as did daughters. Moreover, young men married, on average, in their mid- to late-twenties and would thus bring more maturity of judgement to their choice of partner and were less in need of a veto from some third party.

There are three reasons why evidence of desire to veto marriage choices is so rare when matched against the number of potential marriages. First, the church provided assistance in restricting clandestine marriages designed to circumvent parental displeasure. Before dismissing this effort on the part of the church, it is worth considering the case of a Mr Marshall who, in 1582, could not find a priest in Nottinghamshire, Derbyshire or Cheshire who would marry him without banns or license. His friends eventually persuaded him to return to London, in spite of the objections of his intended's father, and be married according to the law.[80] The cumulative effort of the church leaders in canons and visitations, especially with High Commission lurking in the shadows to provide muscle when necessary, had its effect. Moreover, there is no evidence to suggest that the number of children who wished deliberately to exclude their parents from this process or to ignore their advice once given was anything but insignificant. The horror with which such cases were greeted suggests that they were uncommon, and that such examples as there were would have come to some sort of attention. Without evidence to the contrary, it seems that most accepted the Elizabethan view that "children are bound by a natural band of piety to honour and obey their parents to whom . . . both by the law of God and by the light of nature it appertaineth most properly to have care to determine of their children's marriages."[81] One Essex gentleman-testator put it more baldly, urging his children to be ruled by his wife "as they will avoid the plague of God that happeneth to disobedient children."[82] Two Essex testators, both of whom left £2,000 to their daughters, trusted them sufficiently not to restrict these grants but only to urge them to be advised by their mothers in marrying.[83] Finally, in some cases parents simply left the choice of marriage partner to their children because they believed that their views in the matter were at best secondary. When Henry Hudson sued Anne May, daughter of Bishop John May of Carlisle, for breach of contract in 1592, Henry tried to enlist her parents' support. Mrs May rebuffed him, declaring in court that her daughter was free to contract where she liked. "Love," said the bishop's wife, "must be free neither depending upon father's nor mother's mind."[84]

There is no single reason why the English upper classes did not follow the French nobility in demanding reforms which would invalidate marriages made without their consent. In part, they must have felt that if they wished to restrict the marriages of their children they had the tools to do so. Those who might have preferred a change in the law were willing to make do with these. The queen, Hatton and Whitgift had made clear that although the laws against clandestine marriage would be given new force and enforced with greater severity, they would not be changed. Whether people accepted this fatalistically, or whether they actually believed that any change was the thin edge of the wedge with instability and chaos to follow is immaterial, for accept the status quo they did. Neither the obstacles in the way of controlling the marriages of their children nor the hunger to do so was so great as the appetite for stability which the queen promised to satisfy in her own conservative way.

PART III

Marriage and the People

6

Law and Practice in the Formation of Marriage in English Communities

What may anachronistically be called "the political nation," those in a position to reform canon law and the marriage laws, did not use their own power nor successfully apply pressure outside of parliament to do so. Neither was there agitation for reform from the "grass roots," the rest of the nation. The remaining chapters will explore this general silence, proposing both an explanation for the toleration of the marriage laws themselves and widening the discussion substantially, arguing for popular satisfaction with the entire structure of ecclesiastical justice at the time of the English Reformation. I will argue that both the marriage law and the courts which enforced it adequately met the needs and expectations of English villagers. Their satisfaction was such that they were unlikely to take the initiative in agitating for the reform of either.[1]

I share with Martin Ingram the belief that "the role of ecclesiastical justice can be properly understood only through deeper study of the court records, closer reference to the social context, and a more realistic appreciation of what the courts could hope to achieve."[2] In this case, that requires thoroughly understanding the process of courtship, betrothal and marriage in the sixteenth century. While English noble and gentry marriage practices have been studied,[3] we know little about what courtship meant to the less exalted inhabitants in sixteenth-century villages and towns, yet it is these people who accounted for at least 90 percent of all English marriages. Putting together a model of "normal" marriage formation in sixteenth century villages is possible with a careful use of a wide variety of contemporary sources.[4] Examining such a model makes it clear that there were no necessary conflicts between it and church law. In some ways, behavior had been shaped by the church. In others, popular practice and ecclesiastical law coexisted harmoniously. When problems did occur, people well understood that solutions to those problems lay not in amending the law but in adequately enforcing what law there was. The extent to which they failed to resolve certain problems – and fail they certainly did – was dictated by their failure to resolve dilemmas of enforcement that were beyond both the ability and imagination of Tudor society.

The model which this chapter proposes is based on the widest possible variety of sixteenth-century sources: printed books,[5] ballads,[6] church court records,[7] wills,[8] parish registers, and a variety of miscellaneous manuscript sources. Each of these has limitations which need to be respected, but each within its limits can contribute to a credible picture of normative behavior among sixteenth-century villagers.[9]

An anonymous book published in 1616 described the last phase of childhood as beginning at the age of twelve (for girls) or fourteen (for boys) and lasting until twenty-eight *or marriage*.[10] To be fully a member of adult society in early modern England meant to be married, and preparation for adulthood was preparation for marriage.[11] The interim was devoted to acquiring the resources for a self-sufficient household and the serious business of courtship: seeking and finding a spouse. Courtship was the bridge by which young people crossed over into adulthood.

Young people in sixteenth-century England married late, thus delaying and prolonging courtship. Richard Smith calculates that from 1550–99 the average age at which men married for the first time varied from parish to parish within a range of twenty-four to thirty, and the age for women between twenty-two and twenty-seven. The national mean was twenty-seven for men and twenty-five for women.[12] Averages mask a great range of ages at which both men and women married. Since few people married in their natal parishes (as will be seen), and baptismal records are spotty at best until the 1590s, it is rarely possible to trace the baptisms and compute people's ages when they married. In Grantchester parish (Cambs), for example, seventy-four people married for the first time between 1583 and 1603. Of those, only ten can be traced in the baptismal register: six men, who married at ages from twenty to twenty-six, and four women, who married at twenty, twenty-five, twenty-six and thirty-seven. In Dry Drayton from 1583 to 1601, forty-eight married and the ages of eleven can be identified: two men (twenty-four and twenty-nine) and nine women (eighteen to twenty-five, with four marrying at twenty-one). These figures are typical of other parts of England as well. In Shipton (Salop), for example, from 1563 to 1602, a mere fourteen of seventy-six who married can be traced: four men (nineteen, twenty-one, twenty-seven and thirty) and ten women (from twenty to twenty-nine).[13]

In part couples married late because they were expected to have the economic resources to maintain a family before marrying, and needed time to accumulate those resources. "Over hasty marriages and over soon setting up of households" were often identified as principal causes of poverty in England and legal steps were taken to restrict the marriage of apprentices for this reason.[14] The delay was also a result of social pressure, for early modern society saw the young as incapable of stability: "Until a man grow into the age of twenty-four years," wrote one author, "he is wild, without judgement and not of sufficient experience to govern himself."[15]

A preacher named John Stockwood was one of a small minority of writers, whose works were not popular and demonstrably outside of the mainstream, who believed that it was a great vice for children to choose their own spouses. According to Stockwood, God commanded parents to provide marriage partners for their children and at no age could children be considered free from this authority. He modified the severity of his position only by saying that marriages were not to be forced or arranged for money.[16] Charles Gibbon made no such allowances, insisting that children must accept their parents' choices regardless of any attendant inconveniences or apparent evils; parents could even compel their children to marry with the ungodly.[17]

Normally, however, courtship was so much a part of the world of youth that parents did not take an active role in it, except for those parents who preempted the process completely by matching their children while very young, even when still babes in arms, and those who attempted to compel the marriages of older children, but these practices were roundly criticized after the Reformation and were sources of scandal by the end of the century. "Child marriages" were not legal marriages, and by the mid-sixteenth century the church was outspokenly intolerant of them. Protestant controversialists denounced such unions with increasingly uncompromising language. These unions were normally associated with the nobility, as in the popular and influential translation of *Golden booke of Christian Matrimony*, in which Henry Bullinger criticized noblemen who married their children "to such as will give them most money for them" without regard to the potential for perpetual domestic misery. Since the higher duty of parents was to assure their children's happiness, Bullinger concluded by wishing "woe be to that father which had rather satisfy his own covetous affection than to procure a quiet manner of living for his child."[18] In his *Booke of Matrimony*, Thomas Becon excoriated noble parents who treated their children "as the grazier doth his oxen and sheep," marrying them without considering the appropriateness of the match, and he declared that "such parents do greatly abuse their authority, and deserve at the hand of God great plagues and punishments, and before men great ignominy, rebuke, shame and infamy. Neither do the children in this behalf owe such parents any obedience."[19]

These child-marriages were clearly not a peculiarity of the nobility, however. Philip Stubbes made no distinctions of class when he alleged that "much wickedness" sprang from one of the greatest abuses of marriage in England: that "little infants in swaddling clothes are often married by their ambitious parents and friends."[20] Likewise, in *Tell-Trothes New-Yeares Gift*, a treatise on jealousy, the author named as the principal cause of jealousy "ill-assorted unions made up by parents . . . more regarding the linking of wealth and money together than of love with honesty."[21] In actual cases from the diocese of Chester, people of rather low or middling wealth are involved in child-marriages. One male child was later bound apprentice to a shoemaker, for example.[22] And the driving force behind the marriages was clearly money. Elizabeth Hulse, seeking a divorce from the shoemaker's apprentice, said "she was married to him because her friends thought she should have a living by him." Joan Leyland was married to Ralph Whittall "because the said Ralph had about 40s a year of land," and Thomas Fletcher was compelled to marry Anne Whitefield to discharge debts owed by his father.[23]

Scandalous scenes occasionally accompanied child-marriages and must explain, at least in part, why the practice lost whatever respectability it once had. Church court depositions tell frightening stories of fear and brutality. As a child, Joan, the wife of Nicholas Conyers, was so opposed to marrying Nicholas that she refused to put on her wedding clothes or say her part of the ceremony until her father said that if she did not he "would not leave one whole bone of her."[24] Elizabeth Beaumont said that she "had lever leap into a pit ere she would have [John Gomersall] to her husband."[25] Alice Haxtay told her mother that she would never lay with Henry Benson even if they "did draw her with wild horses."[26]

Ballads also denounced parental force in choosing marriage partners. One of the most popular ballads of the century, "The Lamentation of Master Page's wife of Plimmouth, who being enforced by her parents to wed him against her will, did most wickedly consent to his murther, for the love of George Strangwidge; for which fact she suffered death at Barstable in Devonshire. Written by her owne hand, a little before her death." was written in the form of a gallows speech, a popular genre used to teach important moral lessons.[27] The title rather completely describes the plot, but it cannot do justice to the rhetoric, which is unrelentingly critical of the woman's parents:

> In blooming years my Father's greedy mind
> Against my will, a match for me did find;
> Great wealth there was, yea, gold and silver store,
> But yet my heart had chosen long before.
>
> My eye mislikt my Father's liking quite;
> My heart did loath my Parents' fond delight;
> My childish mind and fancy told me
> That with his age my youth could not agree.
>
> On knees I prayed they would not me constrain;
> With tears I cried, their purpose to refrain;
> With sighs and sobs I did them often move
> I might not wed, whereas I could not love.

Her pleas were to no avail and she was forced to forsake Strangwidge and marry
Page, with dire consequences for all concerned:

> You Parents fond, that greedy-minded be,
> And seek to graft upon a golden tree,
> Consider well, and rightful judges be,
> And give your doom twixt Parents' love and me.
>
> I was their child, and bound for to obey,
> Yet not to wed where I no love could lay:
> I married was to muck and endless strife,
> But faith before had made me Strangwidge wife.
>
> Ah, wretched world! which cancred rust doth blind,
> And cursed men, that bear a greedy mind;
> And hapless I, whom Parents did force so
> To end my days in sorrow, shame, and woe!

The ballad concludes with a prayer for God's forgiveness, and a plea that
parents will learn from her example that "the match is marred where minds do
not agree."

As Bullinger had argued, marriages begun in this way were likely to be
unhappy ones, marred by argument and sadness, and often by domestic violence. They divided and disrupted families and communities. As one Cambridgeshire woman said in 1572, "Made marriages never do well!"[28] By the
mid-sixteenth century, child-marriage was a practice exclusive to northern
England, but even there popular sentiment and church hostility combined
virtually to eliminate the practice by century's end.[29]

Parental meddling (short of force) in courtship was not common either. The
mother of Agnes Winter invited Thomas Rich to stay regularly at her house
hoping that "his fancy or love might fall towards Agnes," but such examples are
rare.[30] Parents thought that active intervention was usually inappropriate.
After John Goodrich courted Elizabeth Mason unsuccessfully for seven years, he
sought her parents' support, but they also turned him away.[31] Parental agreement to forward a suit was, in any case, no guarantee of success. John Ingle
obtained support from Isabelle Lister's parents, but Isabelle refused him saying
"he was a stranger to her."[32] So successfully did young people monopolize the
courtship process that parents often did not know it was going on and when
they casually suggested possible suitors to their children, were surprised to hear
that the children were already committed to others.[33]

Where did young people meet those who became the objects of their attention and affection? It was extremely rare for a man to marry a woman from his

natal village. In Dry Drayton, for example, only four of the twenty-four men who married between 1583 and 1601 married a woman born in the parish; in Little Wilbraham, only one of twenty-eight did so from 1586 to 1603.[34] What these figures suggest is that courtship was not a particularly inbred affair with village natives courting and marrying each other.[35] What they do not explain is whether young people married others who lived outside of their own villages or whether, alternatively, their marriage partners were immigrants to the village already living there when the courtship began.

Young people not living in the same village could meet in a variety of settings such as fairs and markets, but the realities of roads and communications would seem to place practical limits on the regular private meetings which courtship entailed. Young people from neighboring villages in densely settled parts of the country would find such meetings feasible, but the geographical range of such contacts would have been limited. In thinly settled districts it must have been even more restricted.

The mobility of young people leaving their natal parishes to take work as servants or learn a craft or trade would logically account for a substantial though incalculable number of marriages between people not born in the parish in which they married.[36] Couples often met while in service, frequently in the same household,[37] as ballads such as "A new mery balad of a maid that wold mary wyth a servyng man" and "The Country-man's Delight; Or, The Happy Wooing, Being the Successful Love of John the Serving-Man, in his courting of Joan the Dary-maid" show.[38] Servants courted each other and only rarely did masters or masters' sons marry their servants.[39]

Once having decided they wanted to court, young people of opposite sexes had enormous freedom to meet in sixteenth century England, both publicly and privately.[40] This can be inferred in part from the great variety of circumstances in which they were alone together for the conversations which led to betrothal. They met in parks, fields, gardens and barns.[41] They also met freely during their daily work. Margaret Tillotson was washing hemp in a brook when her suitor Henry Parker approached her to talk about marriage.[42] In the "Lament of a girl in service," the maid described meeting her beloved Robyn at church, and after church meeting other couples at the alehouse for cakes and ale. She also met him at market and drank wine with him "at the sign of the goose."[43]

Couples also met at family homes commonly enough that the practice might lead to misinterpretation of motives, as in the case of Thomas Grayson who regularly visited the home of Margaret Lawson, but said that it was only "as one neighbour to another's house,"[44] and Robert Brown who frequented Joan Barton's home but always with other young men "to play and make pastime" and was always with her "in the way of honesty and no other."[45]

Such play was taken for granted, and could likewise be viewed as part of courtship. John Coldcote danced with Elizabeth Hogge and talked with her and kissed her "as young folks do," but he denied meaning anything by it.[46] Couples occasionally spent the night together in an inn, but that was rare.[47]

Giving gifts and tokens was an essential element of courtship, as church court records and ballads show. When Henry Best described rural courtship in Yorkshire in 1641, he described gift-giving as very ritualized and formal. According to Best, courtship visits were usually three to four weeks apart. On the third visit, a man gave the first gift: 10 or 20 shillings, or a ring of equal value. On the next (fourth) visit, he would also give 10 shillings. Next, he would give a pair of gloves worth 6s 8d, and at every subsequent visit "some conceited toy or novelty of less value."[48]

According to the evidence in cause papers and ballads, coins, rings and gloves were the most common courtship gifts, but they were not given in the uniform way Best suggests. A variety of very practical gifts of cloth and clothing also appear, as do a dazzling variety of "conceited toys and novelties," available to the sixteenth century consumer at the lowest social and economic level courtesy of petty chapmen.[49]

Ely and York diocesan court papers record the gifts given by 126 men and twenty-five women. Coins, rings and gloves were the most common, given by sixty-seven, fifty-one and forty men respectively. Also popular gifts were girdles, purses, ribbons or laces, kerchiefs, hats, shoes, slippers and hose. More occasional gifts included whistles, crosses, lockets, brooches, pin-cases, knives, spoons, thimbles, frocks, petticoats, and aprons. The most popular gift from women to men was a coin. Ten women gave at least one of those. Six gave kerchiefs, four gave rings, two gave purses and two gave hearts. Gifts given by at least one woman included gloves, hose, a sheet, a looking glass, a cross, a shirt, a towel, a ribbon, a collar, a spoon, and a nutmeg.[50]

In "A New Courtly Sonet of the Lady Greensleeves," the wooer lamented that he had been cast off after showering his lady with gifts: kerchiefs, petticoats, jewels, gilt knives, silk stockings, pumps, a silk smock, a girdle with gold and pearls, a purse, a pincase, a gown with satin sleeves and garters fringed with gold, and a gelding.[51] On a more plebeian level, in the "Lament of a girl in service," a maid recollected the token she received from her Robyn: "a gay girdle like silk and gold," which she believed was a true extravagance costing two pence.[52]

Gifts were intended to win goodwill where none existed, and since women used gifts in this way, it is clear that women could take the initiative in courtship as well as men. Margaret Fornando of London brought a series of gifts to Robert Curtis while he was sick in bed, including money, rings, sugar and marzipan. After he recovered he refused to marry her and she sued him in order to have her goods returned.[53] Margaret Lawson used money, a ring, a sheet and hose when attempting to bribe Peter Gill to marry her after he withdrew his suit on learning that she had an illegitimate child.[54]

Young people also gave gifts such as rings and gloves on special occasions such as New Year's Day, on the occasion of fairs, and on Valentine's Day.[55] It was not always clear whether these gifts were acts of friendship or suggested much more, and donors were rarely careful to make their intentions plain. It was unusual when Richard Clething gave Agnes Hutchinson a handkerchief saying "I will give you this kerchief on this condition that you shall never have other husband while I live but me," or John Rigyall gave Agnes Nelson a pair of gloves saying "These gloves were my mother's, and but that you be now my wife no creature else should have had them."[56]

Entry into and exit from courtship were extremely fluid. It was an experimental venture and no one assumed that courtship would lead automatically to marriage. Long failed courtships were not unknown: John Goodrich pursued Elizabeth Mason for seven years without success.[57] Even when affection or attraction was mutual, there was still no guarantee that marriage would result, since women often had more than one suitor at a time.[58]

Practical considerations or familial pressure could defeat suitors. Ellen Tanfield, a widow, rejected Richard Heslington because remarriage would have meant losing the farm left to her by her late husband.[59] Widows also broke off suits because of pressure from their children, and single women were susceptible to pressure from their families and friends.[60] Men sometimes had good reasons for breaking off, such as Peter Gill had when he discovered the sordid past of Margaret Lawson.[61]

In most cases courtships ended because one or both people lost interest. The "fickle lover" theme is common in sixteenth-century English ballads. In "The Fickleness of Woman", the speaker warns

> Dust is lighter than a feather
> And the wind more light than either
> But a woman's fickle mind
> More light than feather dust or wind.[62]

In ballads, women are portrayed as fickle and unreliable far more frequently than men, in part reflecting the male authorship of ballads, but it must reflect experience as well. Women made up a substantial portion of the market and audience for ballads, and ballad writers were well known for writing on both sides of an issue in order to widen the appeal for their product. Moreover, ballads were commissioned by printers and sellers who often dictated the subject matter to the writer based on their perceptions of the market. If ballads about fickle men would have reflected the experiences of women, they would have been written and sold in greater numbers.

Church court cases confirm that women were more likely to jilt men than the reverse. In the York consistory, male plaintiffs in breach-of-promise cases outnumbered females 275 to 139. During the entire period from 1520–1603 the balance never deviated from roughly a two-to-one ratio. Ely diocesan figures show an even greater proportion of men: 137 men against fifty-four women. If anything, these figures may even overrepresent women. A woman who became pregnant as a result of a relationship was likely to sue rather than passively accept the default of her lover, especially since an unmarried pregnant woman could be whipped as a punishment for fornication. Pregnant plaintiffs account for at least fifty-three of the 139 York cases pressed by women.

The sacrifices men such as Richard Heslington made for love could be substantial. He sold his ship and gave up his trade at the request of Ellen Tanfield and then she refused to marry.[63] Perhaps women enjoyed the sense of implied power that fickleness gave them, or perhaps because they had more to lose from marriage women were more likely to have serious hesitations about proceeding to the point of no return.[64] Whatever the cause, men frequently had reason to "call to mind the instability and frailness of women," as one complainant described it.[65]

Students who based their views of sixteenth century English society exclusively on a reading of contemporary books would be justified in believing that villagers actually debated whether or not they ought to remain single for life. Humanists wrote on both sides of the issue. Those who favored marriage claimed that it was a state created and blessed by God and a duty to the nation.[66] The unmarried were "monsters of nature for their sterility and barrenness [who] die as unprofitable clods of the earth" while married men "maketh the realm to flourish with innumerable thousands of people, whereby the public weal is preserved in safe estate."[67] In his *Commendation of Matrimony*, Agrippa concluded:

> Thou therefore if thou wilt be a man . . . if thou wilt be the lawful son of God, if thou wilt be natural and loving to thy country, to thy family, to the commonwealth, if thou wilt possess and enjoy the earth and deserve heaven, it is necessary that thou enter the lawful bond of matrimony.[68]

The single life, however, had many advantages according to William Perkins, especially that "it frees men from the common cares, molestations and distractions that be in the family," and thus allowed them to meditate uninterrupted on heavenly things.[69] Francis Bacon considered wives and children "impediments to great enterprises" and felt that unmarried men made "the best friends, best masters [and] best servants."[70]

Some divines found such arguments offensive. Bartholomew Batty fumed,

> Such statements as "It is better to bury a wife, than to marry one" or "if

we could be without women, we should be without troubles": These and such like sayings, tending to the dispraise of women, some maliciously, and indiscreetly, do vomit out, contrary to the mind of the Holy Ghost, who saith that she was ordained as a helper, not a hinderer.[71]

Hugh Latimer preached in 1552 on the story of the miracle at Cana, telling his audience that marriage did bring with it "great afflication and tribulation" while assuring them that since marriage was honorable to God, God would provide the grace needed to bear the troubles.[72]

This learned discussion had little relevance to English villagers, for whom marriage was virtually inevitable.[73] The dozens of ballads which praise the bachelor's life do not support the claim that men seriously considered living unmarried out of choice. Rather, as Bernard Capp has explained, "in a period when marriage might well be impossible for a dozen years after the onset of sexual maturity, their message perhaps helped young men to reconcile themselves to a lengthy period of enforced bachelordom."[74] For English villagers, the question was not whether but who and when to marry. Those decisions involved many considerations.

The most important consideration was love. Joan Gipps, the mother of Helen Gipps, recounted that Milo Downham said to her daughter, "Helen, Helen, I do love thee above all women and I love thee as I love mine own body." Her daughter responded, "I cannot tell whether ye think it with your heart that you spoke with your mouth or no," and she demanded further proof, clearly showing that for her at least professions of love should not be mere formula or ritual but be heart-felt.[75] The brother of Thomas Hill organized a dinner party of friends and neighbors for his brother and Margaret Barnard to handfast because he perceived "an earnest love and goodwill grown" between them.[76]

Family and friends often made clear that they agreed with this standard. Katherine Sudbury described how "she never did give any counsel one way or other" to Isabel Ground concerning her marriage "but willed her . . . to take whom she loved."[77] The vicar of Otley counselled Sybil Brodley: "This is a matter that goeth not as friends will. You must lie your own hand upon your heart and tell your own mind therein."[78]

What was it about someone that led to what these people called love? Villagers themselves provide no direct evidence. Ballads give some indication of what true love was and was not founded upon. It was not to be confused with mere physical attraction: "In every face where beauty is/ the heart's not always pure."[79] Thomas Deloney, the most popular Elizabethan ballad writer, wrote in "Salomon's housewife":

> May bachelors of each degree
> In choosing of a beauteous wife

> Remember what is joy to see
> May lead to woefulness and strife;
> Beauty is not a brave outside,
> Beauty within is beauty's pride.[80]

Rather, inner qualities were the basis of love. In "The lament of a girl in service," a maiden reflected on the object of her affections, Robin Brucke-holl, who "hast my heart all others above," and considered "Robin's qualities like me so well/ I must needs love him."[81]

Learned authors described those inner qualities in detail. Bullinger devoted several pages to the choice of a "meet, honest and virtuous mate," telling his readers that their future married lives would reflect the character of the spouse before marriage. "Whose coupleth himself with brawling folks and cometh to disquietness," he warned, "may not complain thereof." He described some of the vices that made someone undesirable: despising God's word, lying, "unshamefastness," serious ill health (that is, "madness, frenzy, the falling sickness, lameness, leprosy, french pox, or such like"), and vanity. He did not condemn beauty as long as it was not considered at the expense of qualities of the mind. Nor did he shun economic considerations, since wealth and poverty could affect one's character. The positive qualities which should be sought were modest language, fear of God, good reputation, modesty in apparel, good choice of companions and virtuous upbringing. Many Elizabethan writers echoed these ideals in their work.[82]

Young people also needed to attend to possible legal obstacles to their marriage. Richard Greenham, who proposed a special betrothal service for the church, suggested that the first question a couple should be asked in the service was whether or not they were related in a way forbidden by God's law.[83] Through Parker's Table of Degrees and episcopal visitations, the church made a sustained effort to inform people which relatives they were not allowed to marry, and these rules were enforced.[84]

The small number of incestuous marriages that the church courts unearthed suggests that its incest taboos were taken seriously in courtship.[85] Nevertheless, Archbishop Parker wrote in 1569 that he was at his wits' end with Gerald Danet and his sister-german who considered themselves man and wife and refused to accept that was sinful: "Thus the devil locketh up men's hearts in outrage. Before God I know not what to do with them and how to deal."[86] In the diocese of Ely, Richard Lawrence and Elizabeth Sybil, his wife's brother's daughter, first came to the attention of the court in 1572. They were assigned a traditional penance to stand at the market cross in Ely for several hours carrying white wands and wearing a penitential white sheet with signs printed front and back reading "for the abominable sin of Incest" in large letters. In July 1574 they were together again. When examined, Lawrence claimed that he could marry her by the law of God and that his conscience was clear. They did not make their final appearance in court until 1584.[87]

Economic circumstances had also to be considered. People might be discouraged from marrying *for* money, but practical considerations made it equally obvious that they not marry *without* it. In "The Highway to the Spital House" (1535), the author engaged in a dialog with a poor-house porter concerning the types of people who ended up there. The porter named

> Young folk who wed or they be wise,
> And alway charges on their hand doth rise,
> House rent and children and every other thing,
> And can do nothing for to get their living,
> And have no friends them for to sustain,
> To come this way at last they must be fain.[88]

Many young people used time in service or apprenticeship to accumulate both money and necessary skills.[89] Others had an inheritance with which they could establish themselves on a sound economic base. If they did not have any resources as yet, young people devised strategies for dealing with suitors. They could postpone or refuse betrothal. In courtship ballads, this theme often recurs. In "A mad kinde of wooing," Nan the Subtle continually refuses Will the Simple until he convinces her that he can maintain her financially.[90] The dialog between John the serving-man and Joan the dairy-maid in "The Country-man's Delight" is similar, with John repeatedly professing his love to Joan while cataloging his goods: a cow, a calf, a house, corn and hay in the barn, three pigs, a mare, a cheese, and three marks tied up in a rag. Joan resists because he is still a servant and might lose his position over her. But John assures her that the job is not important because he has an income guaranteed from his father. At that, Joan relents and they kiss and make plans to go to the parson the next day and "do all things complete."[91]

This mirrors actual practice.[92] Young people made betrothals conditional on a change in economic circumstances, usually on obtaining a house or farm: Agnes Adane told Henry Corbett, "Get you a farm that we dwell not within your mother nor my mother and here is my hand that I will perform all promises made between you and me in the way of marriage." Miles Husband claimed that he told the friends of Joan Wilbore that he was content to marry her, but only as soon as God sent him a farmhold, since until that happened he had nothing to bring her. Robert Pedding and Frances Heslington would marry only after their fathers built them a house.[93] Elizabeth Lister and Francis Hobson handfasted but planned to wait until after his father provided them a house before they married. Francis worked in the cutlery trade, and Elizabeth planned to become an alewife, but she became pregnant and demanded that he marry her right away.[94]

Young people unwilling to delay betrothal until they had the resources to marry undertook long engagements. Anthony Barton handfasted with Elizabeth Sisson before going into service knowing they would have to wait several years.[95] Jane Blitte and William Emberton were betrothed for six years without marrying. They explained that "the want and lack of things necessary was the cause why they married not."[96]

Contemporary writers recognized the ubiquity and also the foolishness of such plans. In *The Passionate Morrice*, the author described several badly matched couples, one of which was an apprentice and a girl tired of a long engagement: "He that will think himself sure to a woman, or she that will build on a man's constancy till the parish priest hath said 'God give ye joy' and the bride's bed hath borne its first night's weight, he is not of honesty's mind . . . ."[97]

Thomas Starkey was one of many who noted that the poverty of apprentices and servants was an obstacle to marriage, which he saw as essential for a necessary increase in population, and he wanted provisions made to enable more people to marry. However, attempts to alleviate economic distress by raising dowries for poor girls through private charity were not successful, and young people were left to solve their economic problems on their own.[98] Ecclesiastical court cases suggest that people generally took the responsibility seriously, and that Philip Stubbes was indulging in polemical hyperbole when he wrote in 1583:

[E]very saucy boy [doth] catch up a woman and marry her . . . without any respect how they may live together with sufficient maintenance for their callings and estate. No, no it maketh no matter for these things, so he have his pretty pussy to huggle withall . . . . Then they build up a cottage, though but of elder poles, in every lane end, almost, where they live as beggars all their life.[99]

Finally, although parents were not to dictate partners for their children, and rarely interfered in courtship, young people were expected to consult them before marrying. The Elizabethan bishop Thomas Cooper, for example, noted that since parental consent before marriage was customary among non-Christians, "much more should that reverence be used among Christians and them that profess the Fear of God."[100]

Writers urging children to consult their parents before marrying often were moved by a belief that without parental assistance, children would make rash decisions which they might later regret. Bullinger wrote that letting children commit themselves to marriage without consultation was "as much to give a mad man a sword."[101] Robert Cleaver taught that children's duties of reverence and obedience, as well as their inability demanded that they "should not so much as give any liking, much less speech of marriage, without the consent of parents." Their wits (particularly those of daughters, "the weaker by nature") were not as sharp as those of their parents, and so children did not always know their own best interests. Parents were not required to consent, according to Cleaver, and he showed examples from the Bible in which parents annulled promises made without their approval.[102] Thomas Becon felt so strongly on this subject that he advocated a change in the law so "that no promise of matrimony might be made of any young persons secretly among themselves, but rather openly in the presence of their elders." Children were not even to accept gifts or risk becoming entangled in any way without parental approval.[103]

Contemporaries recognized that this was a dangerous doctrine since parents might abuse their authority and withhold consent for frivolous or malicious reasons, or in order to avoid paying out portions, and they condemned such abuses.[104] Edmund Bunny considered it a form of murder for parents to restrain their children from marrying those whom they desired. It was the duty of Christian parents, he wrote, to assist their children to marry "where [the children] can best like in the fear of God."[105] Cleaver reminded parents not to abuse their authority and allow their good governance to become tyranny; they did not have an arbitrary rule over their children, but might rule only "under the Lord." Like that of good princes, parental rule should be "mild, gentle and easy to be borne."[106] Parental authority was, therefore, great but limited. At some stage children should seek their consent, but most writers supported an ideal which balanced the freedom of the child with the consent of the parents.

Courtship ballads reflected the popular view that parents who withheld their consent sent their children down a road paved with misery. In "The Marchant's Daughter of Bristow," the merchant and his wife refused consent to their daughter's choice. The suitor left England in despair, going to Padua where he was arrested for his religious beliefs. The merchant's daughter, unwilling to be without him, followed him to Padua, and when she discovered his fate began working for his release. After many struggles she succeeded and the two of them left Italy and returned to Bristol together. There they found that her father had died, and her mother, moved by the story of their adventures and their devotion, relented and gave her blessing.[107]

What role did consent of parents and other relatives and friends play in actual practice? In 1569, Joan Gipps, a sixty-year-old widow, detailed the conversations which preceded the betrothal of her daughter Helen and clergyman Milo Downham. After professions of love from Downham, Helen insisted that he obtain the goodwill of his friends before proceeding any further, for if "they would not be content . . . they shall turn you and so shall I be cast away." He assured her that "to have their goodwill I will be glad, but to go back from my promise I will not, neither for father nor mother." Helen then asked him to ask her mother's goodwill, which he did. Joan replied, "Mr Vicar, if you both be so minded, I will not put you asunder." Turning once again to Helen, Downham asked for her consent and she responded philosophically, "Since I cannot make a man, I shall cast away none," and she added, "I do forsake all other men and only draw unto you as long as my life endureth." The next day they handfasted at her mother's house. In fact, Downham's friends did not approve of his choice and, as Helen had feared, he broke off the relationship.[108] This one case contains within it most of the elements of parental and kin involvement in the sixteenth century: conversations with a parent before handfasting, a parent deferring to the feelings of the couple, bold speeches about defying friends if they do not approve, and the cold reality of their pressure causing a change of mind or heart.

Parental consultation often took place long after courtship had become serious, but before handfasting. When John Wastell asked for the goodwill of Helen Baron's brothers, they played Laban to her Rebecca, deferring to her wishes. Her older brother gave them his blessing, saying that although John was young and had little, "he may do full well as many a one hath done before him."[109] When John Carter asked the father of Beatrice Cambridge for his goodwill, Thomas Cambridge replied that he "did not know his daughter's mind" and would have to learn her feelings first. Later, when all three were together, John and Beatrice told her father they wished to marry. He prayed a blessing on them and gave his goodwill.[110] Nicholas Hitch sent a friend to win William Barons's goodwill, offering a jointure of all his lands to William's daughter. William did not approve of Hitch, but did not forbid Agnes to marry him. He did tell her that she was a fool for considering the match and gave her three days to reconsider, but when her mind was unchanged he simply charged her to make no contract until she had some legal commitment concerning the jointure.[111]

It was not always to parents that suitors turned. When people were in service, masters assumed more importance than parents. Before handfasting with Joan Capper, John Rainold went to Anne Hassell and asked her goodwill since she was Joan's mistress. Like a good parent, Hassell replied that she consented if Joan did. About a week later, Joan's mother was called to Hassell's house and introduced to Rainold as "the man that shall have your daughter." Even when the mother was alive and living nearby, Rainold had considered it proper to go Joan's mistress for goodwill, and her mother was informed only after the fact.[112] Thomas Cottringham secured the consent of Jane Aslaby's brother before handfasting, and told her mother and uncle only after that. It was the consent of her brother that clearly mattered to Thomas.[113]

One compelling reason to meet with parents or a surrogate before handfasting was to arrange for a settlement on the couple. Thomas White claimed to have obtained the consent of Joan Lambard's father. One of his witnesses recounted hearing Joan's father William ask Thomas's sister to buy some of his hemp since he needed to raise money for his daughter to marry Thomas White.[114] John Middlewood's father agreed to enfeoff him in land worth five marks yearly and to make John heir to his land before he was handfasted with **Agnes Warde**.[115] Grace Routh refused to contract with Hugh Atkinson because she feared her father would find out and she would have neither land nor goods from him.[116]

The consent of family, and especially parents, had a value of its own that went beyond economics, as young people's regular refusals to plight their troth without consulting their parents showed. Dorothy Harrison refused to handfast with Gabriel Thwaites, piously declaring that "she would be advised and governed by her father and mother and what they thought was meet for her to do she would do."[117] Katherine Hall's father blocked her courtship with Robert Peacock "until he had further proof of [him]," and Katherine consented, saying "she would never do otherwise in marriage but as my father and mother will."[118] Joan Casson valued parental approval so much that she threatened to drown herself if they refused it.[119] Also, instead of refusing to contract, young people could choose to handfast conditional on the goodwill of parents or friends.[120]

Informing parents and asking approval after a binding contract had been made was at least as common (if not more so) as asking before. Neither approach seems to have been more desirable or appropriate,[121] but an after-the-fact approach had its risks, as people discovered when their parents expressed active disapproval and several breach-of-promise cases originated out of parental disapproval after an allegedly binding contract had been made.[122]

The precise reason for parental disapproval was not always stated. It often appears to be simply personal dislike. William Wrenche's father prevented his marriage to Thomasine Chambers; when the court asked why he would not consent, he said "he will not . . . because he will not," and his wife said she would not because she "will be ruled by her husband,"[123] while Anne Wilberforce told Roger Robinson that he would "never have [her] daughter."[124] Some parents, like Anne Hudson's, objected to a suitor on economic grounds. Although Edward Walker showed that he had saved £10 on his own and would get a good child-portion from his father, even the vicar of Leeds' intervention failed to change their minds.[125] One mother refused her consent to avoid paying a legacy that was due to her daughter upon marriage.[126]

Active parental disapproval was potentially devastating, and desperate young people threatened to kill themselves if thwarted. Broken-hearted suicides appear in ballads,[127] but since one could not sue a dead person for breach-of-promise, it is impossible to know whether this reflects reality or is only dramatic license.[128] The most drastic reaction in court records is that of Richard Clark, who "lost a piece of his wit" when his parents ordered him to stay away from his beloved Margaret Willan. After a time, his parents went to her and asked her help in restoring his mental health. She went to him, he recovered, and then his parents consented to their marriage.[129]

Most couples were more practical when encountering parental objections. If there had not yet been a handfasting, or if it had been conditional, they could accede to the parental demur and break off their relationship.[130] They could also go ahead with their handfasting, hoping that they could sway the parents if they presented them with a *fait accompli*.[131] Although Elizabeth Caillame denied any contract, this is exactly what Robert Peacock claimed happened in their case. He sent several of his friends to her father to get his goodwill and failed but he loved her so much "that he could be content to have her to his wife although her father gave her never a groat to her marriage for [thanks be to God] he found himself able to find them both." He then asked her to promise to marry him "without ifs and ands," which she did, and he gave her a gold ring from his finger which his mother had given to him on the condition that he never give it to anyone except the woman who would be his wife. They then asked their witnesses to keep the matter secret until she could have her brother-in-law "whom she trusted above all others" tell her father. He still refused to consent, but the court decided their contract was binding.[132] Janet Wilkinson admitted to Richard Palliser that her kin were pressuring her not to handfast with him. Nevertheless, she said that "for friend or foe none shall break us" and handfasted with him, planning to go to her mother for her consent afterwards and to "take as much favour as might be gotten."[133]

In the face of continued parental disapproval some tried to back out of promises.[134] Parents also used physical force to separate couples and, when a breach-of-promise suit began, would prevent their child from responding.[135] The northern High Commission used its authority to compel parents to allow their children to appear to answer suits in consistory.[136] Even after sentence was given, some parents did not give up. Philip Pullen of York wrote to Archbishop Sandys complaining that he had contracted with Jane Foster but her father had moved her against him. Pullen turned to the consistory for justice, but when the summoner went to Foster's home, he found that her father had sent her away to avoid appearing in court. Pullen then enlisted the High Commission, which compelled her to appear, and Pullen won his case. Then her father, "to make shipwreck of her soul," had friends convey her away again and kept her in some secret place in contempt of the court.[137]

A couple could choose to elope. Elizabeth Craven handfasted with John Bailey, and her father objected and pressed her to throw over Bailey and contract with Robert Bower. She and Bailey fled instead and her father had her arrested for felony theft, promising to drop the charges if she dropped Bailey, which she refused to do.[138]

The last alternative was for parents or other kin, who could do nothing to frustrate the contract, to retaliate. Elizabeth Barrett's brother, for example, threw her out of their house when he found that she was to marry William Coward, telling a friend that had he known her intentions sooner, he would have had her abducted to prevent it. It was too late for that now, he knew, but he spitefully expressed hope that she would break her neck on her wedding day.[139] Disinheritance was also possible: Eleanor Robson persuaded John Kirkman to marry her after he had gotten her pregnant. When his father learned of this he said to his son "Thou shalt drink as thou hast brewed, for thou shalt never have penny of my goods."[140]

Parents (or other kin) are mentioned in only about 25 percent of court cases. Direct evidence of deceased parents, such as when Alice Hawson testified that she was a "fatherless wench," is very rare.[141] The proportion of cases in which either the man or the woman had at least one parent living who could have been involved in their marriage must have been fairly high. Why are so few parents actually mentioned? Some parents clearly were dead, which can be inferred from the involvement of brothers or uncles functioning as guardians or executors.[142] Widows were free from the authority of their parents and therefore might not consult them before remarriage.[143] Finally, and most importantly, the late average age of marriage implies that parties in matrimonial suits might have been of an age sufficient to be considered independent of their parents, and indeed they were also more likely to be dead by the time their children reached that age.

Reading cause papers, one can find evidence for any view of the role of parents in the final stage of courtship. There are sixteenth century Labans and Bethuels, piously deferring to the preferences of the young people themselves, and there are parents angrily presiding over knife-point handfastings. There are children piously declaring that they would not so much as consider conversation of marriage without consulting their parents, and there are those few who know of their parents' disapproval and proceed with a handfasting. A still smaller number share the view of "A new mery balad of a maid that wold mary with a servyng man," in which she announces her intention to marry a serving man regardless of what her parents advise:

> The sight of serving men doth my heart good
> When I them behold, and wot ye well why?
> Because they be lusty and full of young blood,
> Strong and nimble, and very quick of eye,
> Clean, brave in apparel, and made properly;
> Wherefore let father and mother say what they can,
> I will have to my husband a serving man.
>
> My father and mother giveth me exhortation,
> That if ever their good wills I will have,
> To take a man of some good occupation,
> Or else some rich farmer's son, substance to save.

Thus upon me daily they do crave,
But them both say what they can,
I will have to my husband a serving man.[144]

This variety of responses makes it difficult to generalize the attitudes and behavior of parents and children. Obṭaining parental consent was very important, although there was no consensus about whether it should be obtained before or after handfasting, or what to do if it was refused. That consent was so important that if initially refused, people continued to seek it, trying to change their parents' minds. When parental consent was not sought, it was usually because parents were not there to grant it. Even then, rather than act unilaterally, a couple might seek the approval of a brother, a grandmother, an uncle or an employer. Even the "fatherless wench" mentioned above refused to marry without the counsel of her "friends." Even if handfasting itself was sometimes private, marriage was not entered without consent and support. The marriage law of the church, which so many legal historians claim fostered individualism, seems singularly to have failed to do just that. If parents were not demanding that the "Alexandrine consent doctrine" be discarded by the reformed church in England, it was because experience had given them little cause to feel that their rights and duties as parents were being thwarted by the church's marriage law as it stood.

Betrothal, as shown in chapter 2, required only an exchange of words between a man and woman in which they promised to marry. The words could take three forms. If the couple used words of the present tense (such as "I John take thee Joan.") and there were no impediments, the contract took effect immediately and was binding. If they used future tense words ("I John will take thee Joan.") the contract became binding only after sexual relations or when superceded by another in the present tense. Conditions could be attached to the promise. For example, John could promise to marry Joan only if her father gave them a house. This became binding immediately upon fulfilling the condition. If they had sexual relations, the condition was negated and the contract was considered binding as if it were unconditional. No witnesses were necessary for the contract to bind, but if some dispute arose, the church courts would not consider enforcing the contract without at least two credible first-hand witnesses to the exchange of words; hearsay or "common fame" was not acceptable evidence.

  In practice, if lovers' actions rarely succumbed to the lawyers' tidy-mindedness, neither were they entirely chaotic and insensitive to form. Court records reveal that couples knew what was required of them and often went to a great deal of effort to ensure that their betrothals were according to form and would have the intended impact. They did this by exercising care with the words they used, often refusing to utter them except at church door, and by securing adequate witnesses or refusing to act without them. Those witnesses often included a clergyman, even somewhere other than at church door. While betrothal was far from uniform, couples were not insensitive to the disadvantages and dangers of private espousals.

When Richard Franklin sued Alice Nicholson in the York consistory for breach of promise in 1575, one of Richard's four witnesses told the court that if there was any flaw in the betrothal it was only "in placing of words, for if better words could have been used by [Alice] he saith of his certain knowledge she was fully purposed to have spoken the same." Richard won his case on the strength of his four witnesses and the evidence of intention which regularly had to provide what perfect choice of words did not.[145]

An extraordinary variety of words could be used, especially early in the century. Among the more formal versions is this from 1526: with two witnesses present Nicholas Thompson said to Katherine Pinckney, "Here I take thee Katherine to my handfast wife all other to forsake for love of thee and thereunto I plight thee my troth." She said the same to him (*mutatis mutandis*) and the court judged that he was her lawful husband and ordered them to solemnize the marriage.[146] Some expanded this form, taking each other "for fairer for loather, for better for worse til death us depart."[147] At the other extreme are such simple phrases as "I am content to take thee and thereto I plight my troth."[148] Thomas Shoote won his case against Helen Whitacres with three witnesses who heard her say to him, "So help me God and Holy Dam I take you here to my wedded husband while your life and mine endures."[149]

The advent of the Prayer Book made it much easier for people to be certain that the words they used would be effective.[150] As early as 1551, the Prayer Book was used for the exact words of betrothal when Joan Firth and Robert Romesden were handfast by his father.[151] Later, young people themselves would read from the book; for example, Elizabeth Bore and William Timpsley "being both learned, did themselves read the words out of the *Book of Common Prayer*."[152] The libel produced by William Wright makes clear that use of the Prayer Book was quite practical and not totemic: after privately handfasting with Anne Holmes, "to make more sure" they used the Prayer Book and did it again.[153]

While the Prayer Book was second in private ownership only to the Bible, relatively few couples had access to a copy except in the church itself. They had to rely on some alternative method to insure that their words were sufficient for their intention. A helpful witness might intervene. When Isabel Clark said to William Hosier, "William here I give you my hand and faith of my body to marry you," her kinsman and witness Thomas Sharr said "That binds no matrimony." He told her she must give her faith and troth, which she then did.[154] Her compliance with Sharr's suggestion was later to prove crucial to the court in revealing her mind and thus upholding the union. A most extraordinary option appeared in the 1551 case of Joan Waterhouse and William Oldfield when Edward Fairbank, one of the witnesses, reported that Oldfield came to him to have a schedule of the words of matrimony completed with their names inserted.[155]

Soliciting the aid of an intermediary to say the words was a common device. Since William Stacy and Dorothy Searle "were both ignorant to use and utter the words of contracting matrimony" they asked Thomas Hind "to speak the words of contract" which they would repeat after him.[156] The chosen intermediary was often a local worthy such as Hind (described as a gentleman) or William Lee ("*armiger*") who handfasted John Lindley and Joan Kirby when they came to him in his garden and asked him to do so.[157] Such a choice offered both solemnity to the occasion and additional credibility should the union later be questioned. The choice also fell upon masters, stepmothers and friends.[158] The friends and neighbors chosen were not necessarily of any special status: Francis Cressy and Jane Park were handfasted by a goldsmith; Thomas Pinckney and Janet Roper by a weaver; Robert Hogge and Mary Smith by a husbandman.[159] More important than their status was whether they knew the correct words. John Gammell refused to handfast John Lindley and Cecily Swift because "he did never handfast any afore but his wife."[160] Robert Browne handfasted one couple saying "he had not good knowledge what the words of matrimony were but he should do as well as he could."[161] This might not be enough. William Sidall described how he handfasted Katherine Street and Nicholas Jepson. The words they said were "By my faith and troth I will marry thee in the face of the church when the time shall serve." Sidall reported that "he spake these words, and the said Nicholas followed him, and repeated word by word . . . and so did the same Katherine." When asked "how it chanced that he spake not the words of marriage *de presenti*," Sidall admitted "he was unlearned and knew not those words but . . . if he had known any other words of more effect than the above written were . . . he would have spoken then, for . . . his mind was to have them made as sure as he could."[162]

Finally, clergymen were popular intermediaries.[163] This did not mean that betrothal took place at the church. Richard Bell and Jane Storker were handfasted by the local vicar using the Prayer Book at an alehouse (which happened to be her mother's house),[164] and Robert Ellis and Helen Scott were betrothed "after godly admonitions" by Mr George Still in an inn.[165] Such cases typify the harmony of popular culture and the Reformation in the sixteenth century before it was disrupted by aggressive attempts at "reform." The clergyman with his prayer book and godly admonitions present in the alehouse or inn with a couple and their friends illustrates that marriage was, to the people of the sixteenth century, neither only a secular matter nor a religious one but was both.

Villagers chose a wide variety of locations to speak these words. Over 70 percent of handfastings in Ely diocesan court papers took place in private houses, a pattern matched roughly in York records. The second most popular location was an alehouse or inn.[166] Young people also went off for private conversations that ended in handfasting which took place in fields and stables, in kilns and a buttery.[167] In addition, people appear in court stating that they refused to be handfasted except at the church door. When Alice Pape sued Roger Park for breach of promise in 1544, one of her own witnesses testified that her father had asked Roger why he came to his house so often. Roger replied that he came "for [the] good love and favour" of Alice, and that if he ever married, it would be to her but he would not handfast with her or with anyone until "such time as he came unto the church door."[168] John Dod testified that when Agnes Hullet's mistress demanded to know the nature of his dealings with Agnes, he told her "it is the order and custom where I come from . . . not to make any promise, nor to be sure together before they come to the church door, and no more will I."[169]

Still, cases such as these are vastly outnumbered by those involving betrothals in private houses. That is to be expected, of course, since the latter are those about which disputes over intention and results might more easily arise. Examples of people refusing betrothal except at church door, especially in the presence of witnesses, should be rare in the cause papers because a suit in such circumstances was lost before it began. The practice was certainly much more widespread than the cause papers indicate, and may have been very common since John Dod said that it was "the order and custom," and Matilda Lutton's mother had insisted that Matilda handfast at church door as her mother had done before her.[170]

Those who preferred a contract under the roof of friends, family or the local alehouse would be surrounded by spectators, but even those who exchanged promises under the sky appreciated the value of having more than the clouds as witnesses. In 1561, Thomas Brampton of Little Wilbraham testified that he and William Burgess left the alehouse and began walking through the field when they saw Anthony Foster and Margaret Oliver walking along the foot-path. Foster called them to him, and then told the pair that he and Margaret had just handfasted but "that there should be no mistake they would do it again" for Burgess and Brampton.[171] James Stavely contracted privately with Anne Humble and pressed her to repeat the promise before witnesses. She resisted, declaring "Ye are a marvellous man what need all this! Have I not declared enough to you before this?" Stavely knew his woman. She later tried to back out of the contract, but because he had witnesses, he won his suit.[172] Not everyone planned ahead and some suitors depended on accidental observers. Thomas Scott and James Wells testified to a contract in Robert Palmer's stable only because they had been in the next stable near a breach in the clay wall and had spied through the hole.[173] The convenient unobserved witness was not always genuine, of course. Thomas Halliday's witnesses claimed to have heard his handfasting with Brigit Nettleship while peeking through a hole in the kiln where they made the contract. However, since it would have been impossible to hear from where they stood unless the couple had shouted, Halliday's witnesses eventually admitted that they had been bribed.[174] Other couples who contracted privately might wait until they were with family and then repeat their promises.[175] Over and over, careful securing of witnesses was pivotal in winning a sentence upholding the alleged marriage.[176]

Practically every court session in Ely includes presentments against couples in which one claims a contract but cannot produce witnesses. Several people even initiated instance cases in the Dean of York's court knowing that they had no witnesses and that their only hope was a confession. This happened enough at least to make the gamble worth the effort, though the overwhelming number of these either were dropped or proceeded quickly to an unfavorable sentence.[177] There is obviously no way of knowing how many more people, for whatever reason, never even pressed suits in court. Rather, what these examples of care with words and witnesses are intended to suggest is that knowledge of what was necessary to enforce a matrimonial agreement was widespread. If people found themselves unable to do so, it was their own fault and not that of the church or the law. Lovers may be the least likely people to believe that precautions against each other's bad faith are necessary, and could be offended by the hint that they were, but enough of those who took precautions later had reason to be glad that they had to make care a normal part of betrothal.[178]

Formal betrothal might also involve giving a token, usually a ring or coin.[179] Both John Gillis and Peter Rushton criticize customary gift giving in courtship and betrothal because of the uncertainty that attended the meaning of gifts in litigation.[180] Neither recognized that there were in fact these two different sorts of gifts involved, each of which had a different meaning to the people giving it and later using it as evidence. Courtship gifts were used in evidence to show the seriousness of the suitor and demonstrate the receptivity of the other person to that suit. This aided a circumstantial case in favor of the marriage. While words in the present tense either confessed or witnessed by two credible witnesses were sufficient for a favorable verdict, if there was uncertainty about the meaning of the words, an array of subsidiary evidence such as gifts could be used to demonstrate intent.[181] While no gifts "proved" consent in a legal sense, betrothal tokens were strong circumstantial evidence, for people recognized that such tokens were qualitatively different from mere courtship gifts.[182] When such a ring was given and received there could be little doubt what was intended.

The period between trothplight and solemnization in the church was that which engendered the most confusion and litigation. In part this was due to ambiguities arising from the betrothal itself, but the path to the church was potholed and treacherous. Difficulties arose over the banns; the length of time between betrothal, banns and solemnization; and the sexual activity which was generally acceptable after betrothal. However, what troubles arose were not the fault of church teaching or marriage law but of its execution.

Calling the banns, which was to take place on three separate and consecutive Sundays or holidays,[183] figures prominently in court cases because banns often created the *vox et fama* upon which breach cases were founded.[184] After betrothal, a couple was expected to go to their parson and request that he call the banns of marriage between them.[185] Parsons received a small fee for this service (Frances Heslington insisted that Robert Pedding give the parson 2d even though the fee was half that because "she would be no penny woman").[186] If the man and woman were from different parishes, the banns were to be read in both. Anyone with cause to object could then come forward and show why the marriage should not take place.

Ministers were expected to exercise care before calling the banns. Richard Greenham carefully examined any couple coming before him, assuring that they were legally free to marry and had their parents' consent.[187] Some places required that the minister and churchwardens examine a couple before allowing the banns.[188] If one of the people was a newcomer, some sort of testimonial from their previous home parish might be demanded to show their freedom to marry.[189]

Parsons might refuse to publish the banns for no apparent reason, as Thomas Binks and Elizabeth Warcoppe alleged when they sued the vicar of Rushton, claiming (without proof) that he said to them "I will never ask you, complain thee where thou will for I defy thee and all thy part-takers."[190] More common was a cleric calling the banns without examining the couple even so far as to find out if they were indeed betrothed.[191] Thomas Romont had the banns read for himself and Margery Gotobed and then claimed breach-of-promise against her, though she proved that she did not consent to have the banns asked and never contracted with him.[192] Matilda Carr objected to her banns because the betrothal which led to them had been under compulsion.[193] Individuals used calling the banns to pressure suitors who had rejected their advances[194] and villagers might use banns to pressure a couple involved in sexual activity into marriage.[195]

Although John Gillis alleges that people believed it was bad luck for the couple to hear their banns read,[196] the evidence that they did so is overwhelming. According to the Prayer Book, the banns were to be read after the second lesson. Since church attendance was required by law, everyone should have heard their own banns read. Evidence that they were present and did not object was used against people in breach-of-promise cases.[197] Joan Wigg did not object when her banns were read, but she claimed that her master would not let her go to church to forbid the banns, and that they were asked against her will.[198] Thomas Snelson did not object because he attended a chapel-of-ease four miles from the parish church where the banns were read.[199] Joan Pearson admitted not objecting at first because she was "amazed and altogether astonished" to hear her banns read.[200]

Objections by people other than one of the named parties had to be proven in court. Daniel Large blocked the banns of his son and Margaret Shepherd simply because he did not like her,[201] but this was not typical nor would it be upheld by courts. Most commonly, someone claimed a prior contract with one of the people named in the banns.[202] Also common was objecting that one person already had a spouse who was alive and living somewhere else. If the accused person could produce some evidence of death for the parish, the matter did not need to go to court. Evidence was not always easy to obtain, and some couples chose instead to live together without marriage, or to marry illegally without banns somewhere else, either of which might land them in the church courts.[203] After Robert Hewat's third marriage, High Commission ordered him to prove the deaths of his previous two wives. The first death he proved easily, but his second wife had left him six years before and he had heard "she cut another woman's throat for which he thinketh she is executed." He was not able to prove this, and was not free to marry.[204] The Elizabethan wars exacerbated this issue. Many men died or disappeared in the Netherlands and Ireland, and locating actual witnesses to their deaths was a heavy burden on their widows. The parson refused to marry Henry Johnson and Margaret Potts, whose husband had fought in the Netherlands, and they chose to live together unmarried. Once before the court Potts produced witnesses to her husband's death, and they were then permitted to solemnize.[205]

Once the banns had been read three times without objection, or objections raised had been overcome, there was an unshakeable "common fame" that the couple was betrothed, and they were then expected to solemnize their marriage. It was normal, however, to delay for some time after calling the banns. The length of that gap was not fixed and for reasons of age or economics couples deliberately delayed as long as seven years[206] which might cause concern or irritation among their neighbors.

Bullinger had advocated a church wedding as soon as possible after handfasting "lest any wickedness intervene."[207] Perkins advocated leaving enough time between espousals and solemnization to inquire into impediments.[208] Henry Smith noted that a "stay between the contract and the marriage was the time for their affections to settle in, because the deferring of that which we love, doth kindle the desire which if it came easily and speedily unto us, would make us set less by it."[209]

In practice, local communities decided what they would or would not accept, and those limits were not predictable, and could be quite brief by modern standards. During Archbishop Grindal's visitation of 1575, Thomas Nicholson and Agnes Harrison, and Thomas Pennel and Agnes Jackson were cited by their parish for having banns read six months past "whereat some are displeased thinking they will not marry."[210]

John Gillis claims that people did not see betrothal as an indissoluble contract and that "for many, perhaps the majority, the liminality associated with betrothal, especially the right to a change of mind without loss of status or honour, was its most essential feature." In support, he cites a register entry from Clare, Sussex which he believes shows people could publicly renounce betrothals: "I, Susan Ward of Clare, do resign all my right to John Manson to Susan Frost, so that they may proceed to marriage."[211] Gillis misunderstood his source. If Susan Ward claimed when the banns were read that she had a prior contract with Manson, he and Frost would be ordered not to marry until the matter was settled. Failing to prove her case, the court would declare Manson free of any responsibility to Ward and she would be ordered to trouble him no further.[212] The entry in the Clare parish register represents a formal admission of failure to prove a precontract.

Indeed, popular belief in the indissolubility of betrothal was practically universal and unshakeable in the sixteenth century. Robert Beverly, stepfather of Susan Berwick, described her betrothal with Henry Hancock as "the knot betwixt you with the grace of God that all Englishmen shall not loose."[213] Ely diocese *ex officio* act books contain more than a hundred cases between 1560 and 1600 in which people were accused of contracting (and about half the time of having banns called) but not solemnizing marriage. These are cases in which the complaint comes not from one of the parties to the alleged contract as in the consistory instance cases, but from the community, indicating that binding contracts were viewed seriously by communities and were not to be broken off at the whim of the parties. Even long deferrals were unacceptable since they heightened the risk that the contract would be unfulfilled. That the community considered failing to solemnize to be an offense and a scandal is reinforced by the *obiter dicta* often attached to their presentments: for example, Richard Fuller and Helen Ivat were presented for contracting, having banns asked and not marrying "to the greatest scandal of the parish,"[214] and two couples in 1590 did not solemnize after banns "to the offence of others and the breach of good order".[215] Such *ex officio* breach cases outnumbered the instance cases in Ely diocese; the community was more zealous in enforcing contracts than were the couples themselves. Moreover, testimony and results of the court cases show that the community was accurate in its assessment of when a contract existed. The "conviction rate" in these cases vastly exceeds that of instance cases. Unwitnessed contracts quietly broken might be unenforced unless someone objected at the banns, but even those had a way of coming to light in a small community due to accidental witnesses and conversations among neighbors.

Clearly, if the community knew of (or even suspected) a contract, the couple could not dissolve it at will.[216]

In the sixteenth century, at least, popular acceptance of the indissolubility of betrothals seems to have prevented the later practice of "wife-sale," in which a man would formally transfer his claim over a woman to another man in return for a sum of money.[217] A recusant prisoner in York Castle, George Barnby, offered William Nelson £20 per year for Nelson's wife Frances. Nelson agreed, and a deed was drawn up and signed. Mary Redhead, the gaoler's wife, allowed Frances access to Barnby, claiming to believe that the Nelsons were divorced. Significantly, she did not assert that they were divorced *because* of the deed, which was merely a "wife-lease"; she had simply been informed dishonestly of the divorce by William Nelson and chosen to believe him. Barnby and Nelson must not themselves have thought that a "wife-sale" was viable since their arrangement was for an annual lease only.[218] What often appear as nullifications of betrothals for money are, on closer view, something far less. Elizabeth Midgely offered ten shillings to William Maymond not to escape a betrothal but to be rid of an overpersistent suitor,[219] while John Mudd gave Margaret Glue 40 shillings in 1583 (and promised 20 more) in guilty acknowledgement that he was father to her daughter Dorothy, and she signed a paper promising she would never vex him with any suits or claims. Although Margaret alleged that she was tricked into signing what she thought was a marriage contract, she had no witnesses to support that. It is likely that this claim was intended to prevent her being whipped for fornication, and Mudd's money was indeed child support and no attempt to avoid marriage.[220]

As *Glue* v. *Mudd* suggests, sexual activity after betrothal might not be considered fornication. Since a binding contract in the eyes of church and community began at betrothal, there seemed little reason not to have sexual relations; the man and woman were husband and wife in God's eyes and in law. The church had officially discouraged sex before solemnization throughout the Middle Ages, but without impact on popular practice. In 1528, William Harrington warned that a couple should not "fleshly meddle together" even if betrothed until after solemnization, and "if they do indeed they sin deadly,"[221] but when puritan preachers like Richard Greenham conceded that public solemnization after "an holy and faithful conjunction" in private was not required "for the essence but only for the sanctity of marriage," the old ways were reinforced.[222] Pregnant women were quite common at late sixteenth century altars, accounting for between 20 and 30 percent of all brides.[223]

Pregnant plaintiffs were regular occurrences in marriage cases, since pregnancy made enforcing the contract particularly urgent for economic reasons and to avoid punishment for fornication. Women would claim that sexual relations followed a man's promise of matrimony: Jane Clayborn said that Thomas Hutton promised to marry her and then she "gave him more free liberty than she would [otherwise] have done," and became pregnant, but he married someone else,[224] and witnesses said that Ellen Ricroft was contracted to Thomas Snelson when she conceived, "or else as the voice of the country is, she was so honest, he could not bring his purpose about for after that the banns were asked she took her[self] as his wife and so consented to his folly."[225]

Judicial practice did little to discourage post-betrothal sexual activity. When Thomas Haxby admitting impregnating Dorothy Winterburn, he said he promised "to marry her before he had use of her body and so purposeth in time," and he was not punished.[226] William Allison and Helen Rivell claimed they were man and wife before God and plighted faith and troth, and their penance was deferred pending solemnization.[227]

By century's end, especially after the harvest crisis of the 1590s disrupted many marriage plans, communities began to take a less tolerant attitude toward bridal pregnancy, with the primary intention of preventing the poor from producing children they could not support. Prosecutions for prenuptial fornication, virtually unknown in the 1560s and 1570s in Cambridgeshire, were regular features of sessions in the 1590s,[228] but even then prosecution was selective. Of nine pregnant brides from Grantchester, none were prosecuted; of six from Castle Camps, five from Shudy Camps, and ten from Little Wilbraham, one from each parish came before the courts for fornication.[229] The social status of two of these pregnant brides is uncertain, but their husbands or fathers do not appear as subsidymen in 1597;[230] the Castle Camps defendant Christine Osburne had been deserted by Thomas Rise and next to her name is the memo "*est mendica.*" At the end of Elizabeth's reign this new pattern of prosecution had not been in practice long enough to measure its effect on behavior. That was probably not felt until the 1620s and 1630s.[231]

After the banns were asked and some necessary time had passed, the couple could proceed to solemnize their marriage according to the Prayer Book, although there were a few restrictions over the circumstances in which that could take place. During Advent, Lent and Rogationtide weddings were forbidden by canon law. Although the law was not officially changed and even had the occasional supporter,[232] it was generally rejected by Protestants, and largely ignored in practice by ecclesiastical courts. In Ely diocese, only three couples were presented (all in 1599) for marrying in forbidden seasons.[233] A couple from Great Wilbraham admitted the accusation but was dismissed since everything else had been done properly, while the vicar claimed "he did not know marrying was out" at that time and was dismissed.[234] At St Mary's Ely, the churchwardens were ordered to provided the names of couples married during Lent after an informant complained to the bishop's official. Two couples were excommunicated, but the curate claimed ignorance of the prohibition and was dismissed.[235] While claims of ignorance should usually be received skeptically, these may have been genuine. By 1599, the ban had not been enforced for nearly four decades. Few clergymen in the diocese had any reason even to be dimly aware of it.[236] Advent and Lent continued to be unpopular times for marriages, but for economic and not religious reasons.[237]

Of greater concern than the time of year one married was the time of day. The normal expectation was that as many people from the parish as wanted to be present would be,[238] and the rector of Leverington was presented for locking the church door and conducting a marriage "before day or very early."[239] Even if no objection had been raised at the time of the banns, people had one final opportunity to object at the wedding,[240] and preventing people from attending suggested some intent to deceive or dodge anticipated objections.[241] Requiring that marriages be at a time when the parish could bear witness was only intended to prevent otherwise illegal marriages and was not an end in itself. William and Margaret Pickhaver married in "night season" but explained to the High Commission that their vicar was at a conference of preachers during the day scheduled for their wedding and could not marry them earlier; they were dismissed.[242]

Weddings were to take place in the parish church of one of the marrying parties. If not, the priest performing the marriage was expected to have either a testimonial that the banns had been read properly[243] or a special license, without which all involved were subject to prosecution.[244] Such marriages took place either in another parish or in no church at all. (These latter must be distinguished from legal private handfastings.) Annabel Terrell's witnesses described how they went to an inn called the Lily Pot for breakfast and found Terrell, Peter Wicliffe and Richard Wardroppe, vicar of Shepreth, at one end of the room. Upon hearing some of the words Wardroppe spoke, Robert Bingley said to the inn's owner, "What, have we a marriage here?" He asked if they had a license to marry like that and, when told that they did, objected no further. The marriage continued and the couple received the communion.[245]

These nuptials could be perfectly innocent in intent. When Robert Mason married Margaret Borne in her father's house, the banns had been asked properly, but she was very ill and could not go out of the house without danger. Although the rector who married them was admonished not to marry people contrary to the rules in the future, he was not given a penance.[246] Other extraparochial rites were less innocent. Mabel Turpin's marriage in Whitechester Park, for example, was the result of force.[247] One couple whose parents objected to their union eloped, seeking out an elderly priest, a tenant of one of their relatives. The old man married them, propped up in his bed due to illness.[248] Also, marriages not solemnized in a church often were recusant unions. After Thomas, Lord Burghley, was placed at the head of the government of the north in 1601, he began a campaign against recusants[249] which included a vigorous High Commission assault on "disorderly" or "secret" marriages, such as that of William and Elizabeth King who had been married eight years before by a popish priest in a wood in Lincolnshire and were ordered to solemnize their marriage according to the Prayer Book. Scores of others were caught in the dragnet.[250]

Marriage in a church other than one's parish involved one or more additional violations, such as marrying early in the morning or without banns.[251] The officiating clergyman might claim to have believed that the banns had been asked;[252] the curate of Eltisley, presented for solemnizing matrimony illegally, showed that he had received a certificate (pinned to court's act book) from the vicar of Shepreth testifying that the banns had properly been asked.[253] Usually ministers were paid handsomely to ignore their responsibilities. Lawrence Pasley of Yorkshire married in Derbyshire without banns or license and gave the curate one noble; John Paine and Grace Palmer of Ely diocese paid ten shillings to be married in Lincolnshire.[254] Couples like this, particularly from the Isle of Ely, seem to have had little difficulty finding clergymen in Lincoln diocese who would marry them for a fee. In 1590–1, nine couples were presented for marriages in Stowe-in-Lindsey (one of the illegal marriage mills brought to the queen's attention).[255] Three more couples married in other Lincoln parishes and one each in Derbyshire, Suffolk, Norfolk and Huntingdonshire.[256] The tendency to marry in neighboring counties is understandable; the heavy preference for Lincolnshire might have been due to the poverty of the livings and the susceptibility of the clergy to bribes.[257]

The trouble and expense of travelling outside of the county and bribing a clergyman was a luxury that few could afford. Those who did this were usually trying to put distance between themselves and someone at home, and usually someone with a suit pending in the church courts. Ralph Conyers and Katherine Brakenbury went to Arthuret in Cumbria, "on the farthest part of the west of England" as the act book accurately described it, for their illegal marriage. Edward Salmon had a matrimonial suit pending against Katherine but the solemnized if irregular marriage of Katherine and Ralph was upheld against Salmon's claim, though they were fined £20 and given a penance.[258] Thomas Webster and Margaret Perkin married in Stowe when their minister refused to marry them since one was already contracted.[259]

Practically every such irregular marriage would leave a trace in the court records, either because it would become part of breach-of-promise litigation, or because the local community would demand that couples living as man and wife account for themselves. No parish tolerated couples living together without proof that they were married. If the couple had moved from another parish they could be expected to produce proof of their status from their previous home, and if a native couple married outside of the parish they would have to prove that they were indeed married. Mere words from the couple were hardly adequate: when Richard Mustard and Elizabeth Lamb were presented in 1599, the churchwardens said "they say they are married but we doubt it."[260] Demands from the community for proof of marriage and their intolerance of couples living together without it were unrelenting.[261]

Proof of marriage could be supplied in several ways. Bishop Cox's register and diocesan chancellor Thomas Ithell's formulary book contain examples for marriage licenses. Edward Letheley and Isabelle Ebroll produced a paper from John Baker, curate of St Benet Sherehog (London) which stated that it seemed good "to declare the truth in matters doubtful spiritually where the lack thereof may grow to detriment and hindrance of persons," and confirmed that he had solemnized matrimony between the above named "according to the laws of God and the Queen her majesty's proceedings."[262] Parish registers made the task of confirming marriages much easier and quickly began to appear as evidence in marriage cases, but the curate of Tydd St Giles in the Isle of Ely had to report that he could find no evidence of the marriage of Richard Ellis but suspected that that might be the fault of his predecessor who, the parishioners said, was careless about keeping the register.[263] Fraud was also possible: William Sims wrote a testimonial for two strangers, certifying that they were lawfully married, but the churchwardens proved otherwise.[264]

Parochial suspicions could indeed be well founded and result in inquiries which uncovered wrong-doing, as when the wardens of St Benet Cambridge discovered that John Dent was a bigamist, married in London around 1550 and again in Norwich around 1560.[265] Such irregular marriages were, however, rare. Public morality so strongly reinforced the order of the church that they were not a serious concern, and documented incidents never, in the sixteenth century, were more than a small fraction – perhaps less than one percent – of all marriages.[266] The vast majority of marriages were solemnized, after the banns, in an appropriate parish church according to the lawful form in all respects, with many (if not most) neighbors present.

This model showing how people in the sixteenth century courted and married is not intended to be merely descriptive, though that perhaps is justification enough. Rather, it will serve as a key to unlock a door into the minds of sixteenth century town and village people, to understand why they did not agitate for reform of the marriage law of the church – why there are no petitions, no satirical ballads, no random agitations in the court records. Marriage law was, within the limits of their vision of society and law, serving their needs adequately. What grievances arose were not against the law but against the inadequate enforcement of that law. This can be seen by examining three controversial topics: gifts, impediments, and parental consent.

Peter Rushton, approaching gift-giving as an anthropologist, notes that gifts are normally used as a "medium of social peace" but that in sixteenth century marriage cases they were "as much the subject as the resolution of conflict"; in nineteenth century France, "the language of gifts provided a formal code that substituted for speech, [while] in England it seems to have been the cause of endless, inconclusive, debate."[267] If this were true, one would expect ceaseless agitation for change, but there is none. Rushton has, in fact, misunderstood the role and law of gifts. Gifts were universally understood to be only circumstantial evidence of a contract. Most gifts were only courtship tokens. No one – now or then – would consider such gifts binding, nor would any sensible person wish to change the law or rules of courtship so that they should be.

People wishing to avoid *vox et fama* of a contract could refuse gifts when first offered, or could publicly return the gifts later. Joan Frennell accepted tokens from one Grose and her father was "greatly . . . grieved for her that she would be [his] wife." Upon his urgings, she changed her mind about Grose and returned his gifts, alleging that they had broken off their relationship at that point.[268] If givers wanted gifts back before a contract was made and receivers did not want to return them, a suit in Chancery was possible.[269] Ultimately, it was simply the responsibility of each individual to make intentions clear when giving and receiving gifts. People did not need the church court to assist them in that. Litigation in church courts which involved gifts was not about gifts; it was about words.

Impediments, to Luther, were emblematic: they existed only to make money for the pope through selling dispensations. In England by 1600, although the dispensing power was curtailed, impediments remained essentially intact. This should have made them an even greater source of aggravation than before.

In practice, impediments either ceased to be relevant or played a positive role in society. The impediment of impotence (which Luther found acceptable) remained in force, and English theologians considered producing children so central to the meaning and nature of marriage that they cautioned against marriage with someone who could not produce children.[270] However, there was not a single divorce in sixteenth-century Ely or York dioceses because of it.[271] Impediments of servitude and vows had become irrelevant, and public honesty disappeared after its unhappy history under Henry VIII. The impediment of "crime," which prohibited marriage after a spouse's death to one with whom adultery had been committed during the life of that spouse, might have been at issue in the 1575 case of Anne Webster. She and John Dickson stood accused of adultery, and she was being sued for divorce *a mensa et thoro* because of her adultery when her husband died. Immediately after his death she married Dickson before dawn and without banns, for which she was imprisoned by High Commission. However, she and Dickson were not divorced, nor was the consistory ordered to divorce them, so the old impediment appears not to have been enforced.[272] The impediment of "error of person" was not raised in a divorce case, but it was used to defeat Margaret Walker's breach-of-promise case against Robert Pennyman. Walker claimed to be John Butler's wife and alleged that Butler and Pennyman were the same person; Pennyman denied he was Butler. Proof depended upon the hairiness of Butler's body, and Pennyman stood "ready at any time and place convenient to suffer his body to be seen and viewed," claiming to be hairless on his legs or chest.[273]

Impediments could serve to prevent or undo grave injustices. Force, marriage under the age of consent, and precontract (that is, bigamy) terminated unions which were universally condemned and had evil consequences both for the couples and for society, serving a socially useful purpose which none would have denied except the perpetrators. In a 1601/2 case, the impediment of lunacy prevented a serious injustice. William Wandsford alleged that Cecily Metcalfe (worth less than £30) married his idiot brother Christopher (worth over £1,000) for his money, to which Christopher did not freely consent. Allegedly, she paid John Lofthouse £100 to get Christopher to church where a clergyman of shady reputation was waiting. When Christopher protested that he would marry none but a gentlewoman, her friends persuaded him that she was that, and so he married her. The marriage was annulled on the grounds of the groom's mental incapacity.[274] There are no cases of people tricking poor village idiots (who certainly existed if wills are any indication) into marriage, but one suspects from reading this case that poor idiots stayed unmarried (or married each other) and only the wealthy would have cause to use this particular impediment.

Finally, the Reformation ended the peddling of dispensations for kin-marriage while eliminating many previously forbidden unions from the ban. How important this change was below the nobility is difficult to judge. Since kinship divorces would appear in *ex officio* court books, and those are almost as rare as unicorns for the Middle Ages, before-and-after comparison is impossible. One small part of an *ex officio* act book (from the fourteenth century Rochester diocese), which contains six fornication prosecutions turning at least in part upon consanguinity, does survive. In only one case had the couple married: John Hancock married Maud, daughter of Alice, widow of the smith of Gillingham, but Maud was related to his late wife Joan. Two cases involved couples who made conditional contracts to marry "if we are able to contract by law." Since an impediment of consanguinity was discovered, they were prevented.[275] Since the only couple which actually married had to do so clandestinely, it seems likely that in the other cases people must have called attention to kinship at the banns, implying that people were well aware of the rules and willing to apply them. Second, none of these cases involved people related in degrees later forbidden by Parker's Table of Degrees. Since people knew of, and objected to, attempted marriages with kin in the third and fourth degrees, they must have known about the first and second degrees as well. Since there are no such cases, perhaps non-nobles did avoid marriage with such closely related kin in the Middle Ages.

Parker's Table of Degrees can be seen clearing away the bans responsible for cases in the ecclesiastical courts (in Rochester, at least), sparing people the inconvenience not only of appearing in court but also of having their marriages disrupted. Also, if people had no difficulty in avoiding first and second degree relatives as marriage partners before the Reformation they should have had no difficulty after it, and that seems generally to have been the case. Although disagreement remained in cases such as deceased wife's sister, in defending consanguineous marriages few claimed that what they did was lawful in God's eyes and ought to be accepted by the church. Most unions which came to the courts' attention were the fruits of ignorance or stubbornness, not principled objections to the impediment.

Parental consent remains. After Thomas Becon, no writer specifically demanded changes in the law to require it. Missing in mainstream works is any sense of scandal or outrage, any sense that something was seriously amiss which needed legal redress. Even those writers who said that that consent was necessary were vague about the precise meaning of that word. If they had argued that "necessary" meant "invalid without," the law would have to have been changed, but they did not do this. They perhaps recognized, from experience and from court cases, that parents were as likely to abuse authority as children were to abuse freedom. It must have seemed ill-advised to upset the balance between parental authority and filial freedom by tinkering with the law even in a good cause. Instead, they concentrated their efforts on teaching and hoped for the best.

Parents were no more inclined to agitate for legal reinforcements for their authority than writers were to recommend them. Why? First, parents must have felt that the church was making a conscientious effort to instill in children a spirit of deference to their parents in matters matrimonial. Durham's bishop Richard Barnes, for example, had ordered all parsons in his diocese to preach four times each year "that young folks by the laws of God may not marry without consent of their parents . . . and the offenders are sharply and severely to be punished."[276] Complete compliance with this order was unlikely, but was a push in the right direction. Clergymen like Richard Greenham did preach and teach on this theme, refusing to marry young people who could not demonstrate their parents' consent. Greenham, Henry Smith, Eusebius Paget and John Stockwood, all of whom published works exhorting young people to obtain the consent of their parents, were all preachers and published their sermons. Not all clergymen were preachers nor as conscientious as they might have been, but the godly preaching minister was reaching more and more parishes and with him this message. Furthermore, the canon of 1585 governing the issuance of marriage licenses required proof of parental consent to obtain a license. After 1597, when the queen approved this canon, High Commission used its authority to enforce it. For example, Gilbert Oates, who married Christopher Pibus and

Margaret Harrison, was ordered to declare his offense publicly and not to marry in the future "by virtue of licence without special consent of the parents of both sides by word of mouth to himself."[277]

Parents wishing to guarantee some control over their children's marriages could do so legally by setting conditions upon their inheritances. Of 6,746 wills from Ely diocese (1545–1602), over half made some provisions for children and at least 2,500 for *unmarried* children. Bequests conditional on reaching a specified age are quite common in these wills. Many provide that if the child marries before reaching that age, he or she receives the inheritance upon marriage.[278] A small percentage of wills provide for inheritances to be granted at marriage only, regardless of the beneficiary's age. These testators intended to provide their children a financially independent adulthood with the resources to form a household, but leaving them free to marry as they chose, since the legacy would almost invariably be in the child's possession long before marriage.[279]

Only two Ely wills restrict matrimonial choice. John Hunt left £40 to his daughter Anne at age twenty-four or on her marriage, on condition that she marry with her mother's and uncle's consent. Thomas Wimple left £25 to his daughter Agnes at twenty-one or on her marriage, adding that "I will that my daughter shall not marry with anyone without the consent of her mother, Robert Rimers, Robert Banks, or of two of them at the least."[280] In both wills, the daughters received their legacies at a fixed age whether or not they had married; the fathers restricted their marriages only if the girls chose to marry while they were (by contemporary standards) fairly young. Moreover, both of these testators were wealthy men. Hunt made bequests totalling £140 to four children. Although his will does not state his status or occupation, this places him among the wealthiest yeomen in the county.[281] Thomas Wimple identified himself as a yeoman in his will, and his bequests suggest that his probate inventory would show a total value to justify such a claim. Thus, not only were such conditional bequests both rare and limited, they were chosen only by men among the wealthiest in rural society.[282]

So strongly did Greenham believe that fathers should consent to their daughters' marriages in the presence of the congregation that he suggested they appoint proxies in their wills to perform this duty if any daughters were not yet married.[283] During Greenham's incumbency, seven wills were made in Dry Drayton, and twice he was himself the scribe. Four wills (including both of those which he wrote) made provisions for unmarried daughters, and none of them provide for proxy fathers.

Parents simply did not take advantage of the opportunities available to them to control their children's marriages. The reason why parents did not demand greater legal authority is the same reason why they did not use what they had. Parental consent may have been desirable and may have been sought and received in many cases, but it was not entirely relevant. When children married in their mid-or late-twenties and in parishes other than those in which their families lived, parents were not a vital part of their decision making, nor were the social effects of marriage vast enough to warrant much familial interference.[284]

Finally, since most matrimonial litigation sought to enforce an unsolemnized contract, if the law that allowed such contracts to be considered binding was the source of so much trouble, why not demand that it be changed? Such a question misconceives the church's role in creating the doctrine of matrimony by consent alone. Canon lawyers did not invent the concept. Private marriage contracts antedated western Christianity, and the church had originally tried to demand more than just an exchange of words.[285] This left the lawyers holding theologically untenable positions, so although the church eventually accepted private betrothal, it attempted to Christianize it, campaigning for betrothals publicized at the church door as well as a sacerdotal blessing. Failure to comply with this requirement would not invalidate the betrothal but it would result in punishment. The church largely succeeded as people realized the benefits to be had from publicity and the inconveniences from secrecy. Their role in all of this came to be seen as positive and socially beneficial.[286]

Moreover, people considered any vow or promise which they made to bind them before God. Even if the church had added some requirement of publicity for a valid marriage, people would still have considered themselves bound by promises made before God. To break any vow, not just one of matrimony, was (as litigants noted with impassioned sincerity) to jeopardize one's soul.[287]

Martin Ingram has written that the sixteenth century church was turning away from the old canon law on its own, as favorable verdicts in breach-of-promise cases became more uncommon and courts became increasingly reluctant to enforce private espousals.[288] However, while such verdicts were indeed becoming scarcer, there is another reason for that: as people had learned and understood the necessity for proper words and adequate witnesses, fewer and fewer solid cases were being litigated. The courts were continuing to demand the same high but reasonable standard of proof they always had; fewer could meet it.

Why did people still go to court? First, some people (as we have seen) sued simply out of greed or malice. Pregnant women sued out of desperation. They might harbor some remote hope that the men might marry them, but the real object of such suits was to compel fathers to accept responsibility for children and, if possible, to protect themselves from prosecution for fornication by claiming sexual relations only after betrothal. One woman, citing chapter and verse from Exodus, even urged York consistory to apply Mosaic law and compel the man who deflowered her to marry her, but the court rejected this appeal.[289]

Third, one might try to secure legal assistance removing an obstacle, such as parents, from the matrimonial path. In 1551, Roger Robinson was so clearly winning his case against Margaret Weddell that her mother's second husband refused to continue bearing the charges for the plainly lost case. Her mother was so desperate to prevent the match that she sought friends who would pay the costs, even trying to find someone to abduct Margaret.[290] A court ruling in favor of a union placed the authority of the church behind the couple and against the obstructive parent.

Suits could, finally, be ways of clearing consciences and names. People took seriously the state of their souls, and acted upon those fears. If there were any doubts about whether one was bound to another in the eyes of God and therefore unable to marry anyone else, a suit might settle those doubts while failure to resolve doubts might result in damnation. Moreover, since *ex officio* prosecutions could result from "common fame," a suit could be a way of purging oneself of suspicion in the eyes of the community as well. If the community believed that a person was already bound, when that person tried to marry another someone would prevent it. Leaving the community did not solve that problem since, wherever they went, certification from their previous home that they were free to marry might be demanded. In addition, most people would probably not want to leave. A person with a house and land was rooted in a neighborhood, and a suit in the ecclesiastical courts might be the only way to get his or her affairs ordered satisfactorily.[291]

Much of this is necessarily hypothetical. People with hopeless cases tended not to explain why they brought those cases. While the motives of pregnant women can be inferred, those of the rest must be the subject of speculation. Whatever the motives of litigants, church courts were not changing their attitude towards enforcing the old law. The responsibility for the number of negative verdicts lies with litigants who turned to the courts with inadequate proof.

In 1628, Christopher Sherland spoke these words in the Commons: "I conceive that those constitutions for marriage now on foot are such as ought to be preserved, being counsels of mature deliberation and ancient marks of our church. Therefore, I think we need not esteem ourselves wiser than our fathers, who have not complained to us. . . ."[292] They did not complain because the church's marriage law worked for them. Its requirements were well understood and accepted. The law provided, in many aspects, admirable flexibility well suited to small communities. In some areas there were difficulties, but those too were moving to resolution as the church slowly improved the quality of the clergy[293] and grappled with the problems of enforcement which inflamed all the limbs of the Tudor legal body.[294] The law itself was not a problem, nor was it perceived as such by the people who lived under it.

7

Church Courts and Communities in Reformation England

In the end, the medieval church's marriage law survived so nearly untouched because the courts which enforced it did so. Had the courts themselves collapsed under pressure from critics and reformers, redesigning and rebuilding the ecclesiastical legal system would inevitably have involved wholesale revisions in the law as well. That, unlike in so many other Protestant territories, this did not happen requires explanation, since the survival of these courts might not seem a predictable result.

Literary criticism and satirical attacks on English church courts predate the Reformation by over two centuries. A metrical satire from 1307 complained that women used the courts unfairly to force young men to marry them, clergy too often sided with the women, and court officers (especially the summoners) "misjudg[e] men according to their natural ability." According to the poet, "Herdsmen and all men's servants hate them for they put every parish in pain."[1] In Chaucer's "Friar's Tale," the summoner is a venal miscreant whose attempted extortion earns him a place in hell, "where the summoners have their special shelf."[2]

After the break with Rome, the occasional criticism of the courts tended to be highly personalized, while popular attacks based on principle are virtually unknown.[3] Traditional vexation with court officers who lived off fees, making their livings from the misfortunes of others, continued. Also subject to criticism were parish officers acting (or failing to act) in the line of duty. Such complaints were reactions to particular incidents (usually by someone accused) and neither included nor implied principled opposition to the justice system itself.[4]

On the local level, the church court system as it existed, I will demonstrate below, was so satisfactory as to preclude the alternative of presbyterian discipline, as well as other lesser reforms, It stayed its course through the century because, as in the Middle Ages, it served the needs of its constituents and had earned rather more than their formal allegiance.[5]

In church court records, cases are identified either as instance or *ex officio*.[6] Instance suits, roughly parallel to modern civil litigation, were those in which one individual sued another over defamation, matrimony, wills or tithes.[7] These cases were relatively few in number and affected few people, in part due to the costs of a suit which routinely approached or exceeded one month's wages for an agricultural laborer,[8] and also because they required individual initiative. No one was forced to bring such a suit; the decision to seek a legal separation from a spouse, to dispute the validity of a will, to pursue a reluctant tithe-payer, or to seek redress for opprobrious words always rested with an individual who could choose from a variety of available options instead of litigation. Indeed, although instance cases were normally few in number, their very existence testifies to some satisfaction with the ecclesiastical courts, since each case involved a positive choice to turn to the court for redress.[9]

Ex officio cases usually arose from triennial episcopal (or, as in late sixteenth century Ely, metropolitical *sede vacante*) visitations or quarterly presentments.[10] A wide assortment of activities caused *ex officio* prosecutions. What they had in common, generally speaking, was that rather than a single victim, they offended the entire community.

Many such offenses, for example, took place in or around the church: Thomas Goldsborough disrupted the sermon and annoyed the parishioners by sitting in the womens' pews, poking Anne Addison in the ribs continually "so that she could scant draw wind,"[11] and a Chesterton pew dispute in 1579 had people "heaving and shoving" each other out of the pews "to the great disquieting of the preacher there and the parishioners."[12] A young man playing football in Carlton cum Willingham churchyard accidentally knocked over a pregnant woman and nearly killed her "to the great offence of the honest neighbours,"[13] and Richard Muncke of Littleport "cast a dead hog into the churchyard thereby annoying greatly the inhabitants coming to the church."[14] The behavior of ministers offended communities as well, such as in Sawston where the vicar reportedly was "using the alehouse, which is a great hindrance to him in saying of service."[15]

Matrimonial and sexual offenses engendered the majority of these cases. Oliver and Matilda Browne, although married, were accused of living apart in a disorderly manner, "to the dishonour of God and offence of the whole congregation."[16] Agnes Braken of Cambridge did not live with her husband, which was "an offence to the whole town,"[17] and Joan Gardiner of Leverington, whose husband lived in another county, was "such an evil-disposed woman that all the whole parish is weary of her."[18] In Comberton "much evil rule and incontinent living" was reported in the house of one Skegge, all of whose female servants were pregnant. Skegge was presented because there was a suspicious new woman in the house "and the people being offended do talk very evil upon it because it is reported that she commonly every night scratches his back he being in his bed."[19]

The bishop's official learned of these cases through the parochial churchwardens and questmen, who were expected quarterly to compile a "bill of presentment" listing all violations of church law and breaches of ecclesiastical discipline which had occurred in their parish since the previous bill.[20] Canon law required that there be "common fame," regularly noted in the bill, for a case to be presented. Common fame could be the result of detection by the village constable or night watchman, or of neighborly nosiness. A neighbor saw Edward Spencer follow Isabel Waterhouse into her house and, knowing Spencer to be "of evil demeanour," the witness followed them. He looked through the window and saw Waterhouse in bed with her clothes pulled up and Spencer on top of her.[21] Just as often, however, common fame might be no more than unsubstantiated – though widely credited – rumor.

If churchwardens did not find common fame and refused to present a case to the official, others in the parish might act but they rarely met with success. George Wilson accused a couple in his parish of fornication, but the wardens rejected his demand to present them, insisting that there was no evidence. At the meeting to write the presentment bill the vicar announced that he had received a letter from diocesan officials, to whom Wilson had complained. The wardens "marvelled at this" and confronted Wilson who stubbornly maintained his charges, but the wardens still refused to present the couple, convinced that the charge was malicious, and Wilson was sued for defamation.[22]

Malice often lay behind presentments which made their way to court without the wardens' knowledge or support. Nicholas Serle wrote to the bishop of Ely's official in 1595 supporting one of his neighbors, a penniless widow with small children, who had been called before the judge out of malice and without assent from the wardens. Since she was so poor, this case would be "to her utter undoing" and Serle asked the judge to "do God and the poor town wherein she dwells good service" by releasing her.[23] Indeed, knowing that charges made outside of the normal process tended to be vexatious and intended to cause inconvenience, embarrassment and expense to the accused made courts reluctant to credit them.[24] The Commons' Supplication against the Ordinaries complained that people were being cited "for displeasure, without any provable cause . . . [by] very light and indiscreet persons" and parliament considered a bill in 1532 which would have made illegal summoning anyone not presented in the standard way to answer charges until after an investigation "by honest and discreet persons of the town or parish where the person shall be inhabited."[25]

Even without suggestions of malice, accusations not brought by wardens were viewed skeptically. John Somers was accused of fornication, but the court noted that the matter had been raised not by the wardens but "by one of little credit or none at all" and refused to consider it.[26] Even some of the clergy, presumably not "of little credit," had difficulty gaining a hearing without wardens' endorsement. When William Rutherford of Hinton was presented in

1577 for speaking to the curate "very contemptuously with despiteful words," the churchwardens denied presenting him. Charges were dropped when, after being shown the bill with their marks, they angrily accused the curate, who had written the bill, saying "they were shamefully abused by [him] . . . that he would put any such thing in and let them never know of it, for they say they never heard that matter . . . read to them at the bill making or at the signing of it."[27]

While episcopal officials certainly tried to hold wardens accountable for honoring their oaths of office and demanded that they explain omitting some matters or justify including others, finding actual malfeasance was extremely rare.[28] The record simply will not support the allegations of puritan Edward Hake that "godly parishioners" were being threatened, harassed with suits or beaten for presenting neighbors whose "sins" the churchwardens preferred to conceal.[29] In 1592, the wardens of Castle Camps were called to account for failing to present an adulterous couple which William Greene had allegedly caught in the act, but the wardens had acted appropriately since Greene was the only witness (canon law required two witnesses if there was no admission of guilt) and there was no "common fame."[30] In Linton, neighbors alleged that Agnes Barber's incontinence was commonly known "amongst the better sort of people" and the wardens were summoned to explain why they had not presented her. After they appeared, her accusers were ordered to apologize "for so reporting of her and using such uncharitable words of and against her."[31] Even when the wardens made patently improbable assertions, there was little the courts could or would do. Accused of not collecting fines from those missing church on Sundays, the wardens of Westley Waterless responded "that they could not levy the 12d of any, for that they knew not of any to be absent from church." Although the wardens were ordered to investigate and send the names of nonattenders to the court, they were dismissed finally without having given in the name of a single parishioner.[32]

While an occasional grumpy puritan complained of the "open, known and continual perjury of the churchwardens"[33] the "forward answers" sporadically given by parishioners to their wardens were merely cries of discomfort when the legal shoe began to pinch.[34] Rarely was there just cause to challenge wardenly impartiality. Allegations that Little Abington's vicar did not adequately serve his parish were dismissed when the judge discovered that the presentment was made "upon rancor and stomach born by one Ashby one of the churchwardens" against the vicar, and when Henry Long was charged with causing a disturbance in Dullingham church, he produced witnesses who agreed that he had only asked someone to move who was sitting in his seat, and charges were dismissed. Apparently John Hassell had presented him out of spite, since Long (when a churchwarden) had once presented Hassell.[35] But when a parishioner accused Grantchester wardens of not presenting two people for incontinence, "whereby we think Almighty God to be greatly dishonoured and the congregation grievously offended," the court took no action, preferring the wardens' word when the issue was the mind of the congregation whose elected representatives they were.[36]

Once presented, the accused was summoned to respond. When Stephen Benson was presented in 1601 for Sunday thatching, he confessed and was given a penance which, two weeks later, he certified that he had performed, and he was dismissed.[37] One could claim mitigating circumstances, particularly in cases of sabbath-breaking. This was common in the Cambridgeshire fen parishes, since weather was no respecter of the Sabbath and farmers often had to rush out into the fields to rescue crops before flooding ruined them. If the accused demonstrated that a crisis situation existed and that a serious effort to attend church was made, the case was dismissed.[38] Wardens might not present some violations because mitigating factors averted congregational offense, and they knew that the court would not impose punishment even if the violation had technically occurred. Thomas Webb of Manea, accused by a non-warden of cutting hay on the Sabbath, was not presented by the wardens; the case was dismissed.[39] Other excuses for not attending one's parish church might be passed to the courts for evaluation. John Stavely of Grantchester proved that he attended Barton parish church because he was a shepherd in that parish and he was excused,[40] but Carlton resident John Vale's defense that he attended Brinkley church because it was closer and he was too old to travel the longer distance to his own church was not deemed acceptable.[41] Finally, Lucas Barefoot of Eltisley admitted missing communion but explained that he and his wife, who had two small children at home, took turns minding the children and going to church. While technically the law was being broken, the Barefoots demonstrably intended no contempt for either the church or the law and the judge dismissed the case.[42]

Circumstances might also excuse wives and husbands living apart, which was both illegal (since it meant that the parties were deprived of their conjugal rights) and morally dangerous (since it created opportunities for adultery or bigamy). Since the woman might need poor relief, it could even damage the parish economically. A locally resident husband might be compelled to support her, but if he was away there was little the parish could do except pay the taxes for relief unless his whereabouts were known and she could be sent to him. When a couple living apart claimed that they did not offend anyone by doing so,[43] he was presumably supporting her or had restored her dowry so that she could support herself. While couples might seek and receive divorces *a mensa et thoro* because of cruelty, such suits could be expensive and unnecessary unless there were problems securing alimony.[44] Neighbors found it infinitely preferable to have the parties in a broken marriage apart than to have them forced to live together, disturbing the peace with quarrelling and incommoding passers-by while flinging pots, pans and kitchen knives at each other.

Deserted women could often not in justice be punished for living apart from their husbands. Cecily Sergon of Ely was "a very poor, blind, impotent woman and not able to look for [her husband]"[45] and Marianne Woods claimed that she did not know where to begin looking for her husband but "she uses herself well and honestly there in the town amongst her neighbours."[46] Again, the offense (or lack of it) to the community was pushed to the fore, and these cases were dismissed. Catherine Driver of Linton was deserted by her husband, who was living in Suffolk with another woman. In 1579, the court ordered Catherine either to live with him there or secure his return to her "so to live together as man and wife ought to do," but two years later they were still apart. Charges were dismissed in 1581 when the court accepted her claim that he had made her fear for her life and that she was not at fault since she was always willing to live with him.[47] Helen Dixon, on the other hand, admitted living apart from her husband because he had moved to Norfolk in search of work and she would not follow him "to a strange place and where she had no acquaintance"; she was sent to join him.[48]

This is typical for men apart from their wives; they usually claimed it was for economic reasons. Chesterton parishioners complained to Oakington parish that Robert Bullen's wife and children were living on parish relief in their parish while Bullen was living in the latter. Bullen, who responded that he was willing to live in Chesterton but had unsuccessfully tried to find work there, was ordered to return to Chesterton or move his family to Oakington.[49] Only if the court's orders were not followed might it be necessary to impose some penance.

When a presented person denied guilt, the court might hear witnesses. The churchwardens would serve as adequate canonical eyewitnesses when, for example, the alleged offense had taken place in church. Other cases might involve testimony from a number of witnesses, such as when the events at issue included conversations in the alehouse.[50] More often, especially in cases of alleged illicit sexual activity, a case built on common fame in which the accused denied guilt lacked the canonical two witnesses. While there was occasionally one eyewitness, more often common fame depended on little more than whispers and occasional sightings of people "together . . . at places unseemly, at times unlawful and inconvenient."[51] To clear his or her name, the accused swore an oath of innocence and was ordered to produce a number of compurgators who would swear "to their belief in the trustworthiness of the oath of the accused."[52] Because their responsibility was to address the reliability of the accused only they were usually neighbors and friends.[53]

Compurgators were, in theory, not witnesses and need not know anything about the facts of a case. In practice, however, the Ely court accepted that

compurgators ought to be at least potentially knowledgeable. When Edward
Mason of Chesterton was charged with fornication, he was trapped between
principle and practice. Mason initially purged himself, but Alice Patrick of
Stow cum Quy complained that since his oath-helpers were all from Chesterton,
they could not know how he behaved with her in Stow. He was ordered to
produce compurgators from Stow, but since he was a stranger there he could not
find men who would uphold his oath.[54] A case ended if appropriate compurgators appeared and swore as required. If they were not produced as directed, or if
they refused to uphold the accused's oath, that was considered proof of guilt and
a penance was assigned.[55]

Compurgation has been called "little better than a farce" and "primitive and
unreliable,"[56] and obvious inequities, such as one person admitting fornication
and doing penance while the other denied it and successfully purged, did
occur.[57] However, compurgation was routinely both appropriate and remarkably effective. As Martin Ingram notes, it "was largely confined to cases of
suspected immorality where there was usually no clear-cut evidence and no
individual victim whose interests had to be safeguarded. In these circumstances
it made sense to establish a presumption of guilt or innocence by testing local
opinion."[58]

Compurgation was no mere formality. Judges determined the number
of compurgators necessary in each case, and they could and did use their
discretion to manipulate results. Usually set between four and eight, particularly mistrusted defendants could be ordered to produce a dozen oath-
helpers, a requirement of such difficulty as to virtually assure conviction.[59]
When cases involved parties from more than one village, the court might
require compurgators from all parishes concerned, which made compurgation
more difficult.[60]

Custom also required that the parish be notified formally well in advance of
a compurgation so that anyone who wished to bring evidence against the
accused or challenge the compurgators could do so. After reading the notice
sent to him by the court, the parson had to inform the court that he had done
so.[61] While few objections were raised, they clearly might be. When the vicar
of Dullingham, who was planning to be elsewhere on Sunday, announced an
impending compurgation on Friday, a work day, he outraged the parish,
particularly "those who purposed to object against the same purgation."[62]

Moreover, the conviction rate from compurgation compared favorably with
that of common law jury trials, since as many as half of attempted purgations
failed.[63] This usually occurred when a party could not produce oath-helpers and
instead received a penance. Edward Free's five compurgators appeared, but once
they were told that he had sworn he had not impregnated Alice Kellogg, they
refused to support his oath and he was given a penance.[64]

We might be critical or skeptical of compurgation, but sixteenth century villagers and townspeople were not, because it satisfied a palpable need more successfully than anything else they could imagine. Presentment was based on common fame, and that could get out of hand in small closed communities then as now. Rumors were so dangerous that they destroyed marriages. When Joan and Henry Lawrence were tried for living apart, the judge discovered that the problems between them had arisen from "slanderous rumours and false and ungodly reports of certain evil disposed persons, abhorrers of peace and lovers of strife." Once this was revealed, the couple reconciled.[65]

"Honour and shame," according to J.G. Peristiany, "are the constant pre-occupations of individuals in small scale, exclusive societies where face to face personal, as opposed to anonymous, relations are of paramount importance."[66] In such a setting, purgation provided a ritualized way for people to clear their names.[67] When William Greene accused Thomas Mascall's (unnamed) wife of adultery with Bartholomew Smith but could not prove his case, rather than leave court under a cloud she formally cleared herself with the aid of five neighbors.[68]

Although usually *viva voce* in court, written purgation was also possible, and the chance survival of a purgation certificate highlights its function. After stating that the bearer had been presented for "unlawful dealing" with his maid and had sworn that it was not so, the friends and neighbors whose signatures or marks were affixed averred that he had sworn truly and besought the judge "that this poor man may be restored to the church again that he and we may praise God together."[69] Successful purgation provided the community with a way to heal its (self-inflicted) wounds.

If purgation failed or guilt had been admitted without acceptable mitigating circumstances, what normally followed was a "pious admonition" or a penance. The former was used when a punishment seemed superfluous: Gregory Linton of Landbeach was presented for disorderly behavior in church and when he appeared in the judge's chamber "shed many tears [and] showed himself penitent for this crime," and so received an admonition.[70]

Penances usually involved some form of public humiliation, especially when the crime was a serious one. In 1566, a convicted adulterer was ordered on the following Sunday, when the minister entered the pulpit to read the Gospel, to present himself

and stand before the pulpit with his face towards the people and say with an audible voice as followeth: "Whereas I good people having a wife of mine own which notwithstanding being seduced by the instigation of the devil and not having the fear of God before mine eyes have committed the detestable sin of adultery with one Margaret Grave and gotten a child by her and thereby deserved the indignation of God and given to you all great cause of offence, but now most heartily sorry for these and all my

other offences humbly I desire almighty God for the tender love of Jesus
Christ to have mercy upon me and forgive me."

He was then to ask the parish's forgiveness, warn them to avoid his offense and
lead them in praying the Lord's Prayer for him.[71]

A more elaborate version of this penance used in Ely diocese involved penitents standing at the church porch dressed in floor-length white sheets and
holding white wands while people arrived for morning prayer. They stood there
until the second lesson, asking those entering the church to pray to God for
them and to forgive them. The minister would then fetch them into the church
while the Miserere was read, and place them kneeling in the center aisle until
the Ten Commandments were read, after which the public confession described
above was made.[72] A final variant, probably used only on those of above-average
means, appears in William Grange's case, in which the penitent

> at his own proper cost and charges [must] procure a sermon to be made
> in the parish church . . . wherein the preacher shall inveigh against the
> sin of adultery or fornication, and that the said Grange at the end of the
> said sermon shall openly then and there confess that he hath offended in
> the same offence, desiring God and all the people there present to forgive
> him and to promise them never after to offend in the like by God's help.[73]

Humiliation might be increased by first ordering penitents to stand in the local
market, village square or some other highly visible locale.[74] Elizabeth Hoode
had "to stand at the Bull Ring in Cambridge clothed in a white sheet down to
the ground, holding a white rod or wand in her hand and having a paper written
with great letters pinned upon her breast and the like paper upon her back
declaring her offence."[75] In a bigamy case this bit of doggerel decorated the
paper: "My filthy life I do detest/ that I eight years have lived in./ Alas two
wives I have possessed,/ The Lord forgive my foul sin."[76] Under some circumstances, penances could be performed privately in the presence of the wardens
and minister instead, or a sum given to poor.[77] After the penance was performed, the wardens provided a certificate to the bishop's official and the case
was closed.[78]

Many cases might not move smoothly to a resolution since one or more of the
principals could fail to appear. No contempt for the court was implied when
this proceeded from illness, uncertain road conditions, or misunderstanding the
nature of the summons. While this last claim sounds a bit suspicious, it is
possible to imagine an honest error being made. In 1566, William Line, who
lived with his brother-in-law William Smith, insisted that he "did nothing in
the prejudice or contempt of the bishop of Ely his jurisdiction" and said that he
did not know of any citation fastened to Smith's door by a lawful summoner. A

servant of the apothecary Burwell had "slapped a writing upon the door and there was made such a hurly burly openly in the street that a great number came immediately to that place," but he assumed that the paper had something to do with "blustering, boistering words" spoken by Burwell against him and, not knowing what it said "for he understood not the Latin," he took the paper down. When he discovered what the paper was, and that it was sealed by the bishop's authority, he sought out the bishop's official.[79]

Elizabethan Cambridgeshire had its share of scoff-laws, some of whom abused the churchwardens verbally. William Hevenow used "evil and naughty language" towards his parish's wardens and defied them to present him[80] while a Landbeach resident called the wardens "fools and asses," adding that "there was a scarcity of wise men when [they] were put in office."[81] Others threatened violence.[82] John Cowper was given a penance for allowing his daughter Catherine and William Turner to lie together in his house "and [being] their bawde to cloak their naughtiness," but he refused to perform it. The order was returned endorsed: "He maketh me this answer that if Mr Chancellor or I will deliver to him a white sheet, he will wear it, or else not, with other signs of his contempt, but no token of repentance."[83]

Against such as these, the courts would apply one of two inducements. The mildest was suspension from entry into the church, which was normally enough to overcome simple reluctance to face the public embarrassment of appearing in court. The other was excommunication, the efficacy of which has been the subject of much academic debate.[84] It was certainly useless in many cases: a Catholic recusant, for example, was unmoved by excommunication from a church from which she had removed herself voluntarily. Nor were men and women on the tramp, increasingly numerous by century's end, likely to bother much about it since they would move on to some place where their excommunication was not known. But for regular, integrated members of the village community it was a potent device. Rarely did a villager allow excommunication to continue without doing something to reverse it.

"Aufugit" ("fled") frequently appears next to names in act book marginalia, but those who fled to avoid appearing in court or completing a penance were almost invariably newcomers to the community, people without deep roots who felt they had little (if anything) to lose by moving and starting with a clean copybook somewhere else. The courts made no effort to pursue these people.[85] Death also terminated cases before sentence. Richard Salt of Wisbech failed to appear when accused of bigamy, but he had recently been executed for illegal coining activities.[86] Helen Quilton, accused of fornicating with a servant named John Nicholson, claimed that he had promised to marry her, which if true might reduce or eliminate her penance, but Nicholson could not give evidence since he had been arrested for murdering his master and had died in prison.[87] Less exotic deaths, indicated by a simple *"mortuus est,"* also fill the act

books since diseases and other perils of sixteenth century life were no respecters of litigation.

While critics have been quick to broadcast the occasional inequities and apparent inefficiencies and eccentricities of this system, what they have been less apt to report is that the proverbial dog did not bark in the night-time. In other words, the people who used the ecclesiastical courts did not find them deficient. There are two ways of explaining this. One could believe that these people saw the system's faults but were either irrational or unimaginative not only in retaining it but also in refraining from public criticism. In fact, the church courts satisfied (within the limits of the possible) sixteenth century people, who found them fundamentally neither inequitable nor inefficient.

Perhaps a useful place to begin defending this assertion is with those people who successfully avoided answering charges by flight. Surely it offends against modern notions of order and justice to read such cases. Why were they not hunted down? Such an effort, of course, required communications which Tudor England had not developed. In fact, no one demanded pursuit. Once offending persons removed themselves from offended communities, balance and harmony was restored just as removing a tumor might restore a body to health. Offenders wishing to remain in the community would find reconciliation of some sort was mandatory, but if they chose to remove themselves it was not. Disappearance through flight, therefore, does not necessarily denote failure or inefficiency.

Nor should the large number of people technically guilty of violations but dismissed with no action taken against them be seen as evidence of inconsistency, incompetence or worse. If the measure of guilt was, as so often stated in presentments, offense to the community, the accused might claim that the community was not offended: John and Grace Steward admitted being married but living apart (a violation of church law) but that "there is none in the town that be offended thereat"; the case was dismissed.[88] When Mary Hatley refused to sit in "a very convenient seat in [Harlton] church," instead sitting "among the maidens very undecently being a married wife," she responded that she intended no offense but that there was "not room sufficient for her to kneel" in her assigned place. Since witnesses concurred, she was dismissed.[89] Absence from Sunday church services violated the Act of Uniformity, but rescuing crops in a sodden field or caring for one's children were not culpable actions. A London minister noted in 1580 that when he and the parish officers were ordered to investigate and report those in the parish who did not attend church or receive the communion, "this inquisition [is] not to extend to any others than such as do *obstinately for religion* refuse to come to their parish church and there to receive the communion."[90] In other circumstances, community and church were not offended because the actors in these cases mocked neither the law, nor the values of their neighbors.

When a genuine offense to the community occurred, it desired reconciliation and not revenge or some abstract notion of justice as shown in 1577 when James Pape's wife defamed four men from Bassingbourn, saying that they fornicated with Joyce Brown and two women called Brown "whore" and "bitch." When the judge "heard thoroughly and understood" the matter, he "set them at unity, peace and concord."[91] Anne Greathead of Grantchester admitted slandering her neighbors and apologized, and since "those of the town being present [did] forgive her" she was sent away without a penance.[92] When Annabelle Watson called Gregory Linton of Landbeach a "whoremaster," she was presented but Linton signed a statement for the court saying that he had forgiven her "and [was] content to remit the said injury."[93] Except to the most "precise," *pax* was always preferable to *iudicium*.[94]

Tudor people were not temperamentally litigious; if peace could be restored without going to court so much the better. My research corroborates Susan Amussen's view that village notables preferred to settle as many breaches of law and peace as possible internally.[95] Churchwardens were the elected agents of their parishes, part of an ancient tradition of self-government which considered it a fundamental right for communities to judge themselves or appoint their own judges.[96] It was, therefore, a measure of their adequacy in executing their offices that they correct infractions and heal divisions themselves and they carried out these duties with zeal and some skill.

Many trespasses, therefore, were never listed on quarter bills. Typically, the wardens of Stow did not present John Alee for adultery with a "naughty woman called Singing Jane" because Alee had promised to reconcile with his wife.[97] Though the bishop's official demanded that the wardens be accountable for omitting an offense, what is more to the point is that once the details were explained Alee was not hailed before the court. Private resolution was considered entirely appropriate. Indeed, such conclusions were accepted on the eve of a court appearance. An adulterous Stetchworth couple, "caught in the deed doing," were named in the quarter bill but at the last moment confessed before the churchwardens and minister. The court was notified of this and no further action was deemed appropriate.[98]

Normally "admonition" by churchwardens preceded presentment in hopes that order could be restored without using the courts. In 1584, when Robert Heddley was presented for being "a slack comer to church," the wardens noted that Heddley had first been "sundry times admonished" unsuccessfully.[99] Nicholas Serle, when requesting that the court release a poor widow from his village who was cited "for some slanderous crime," noted that those who presented her (not the churchwardens) did not first "talk with her to admonish her of her fault."[100]

For centuries, parsons had been expected to fill that role, like the priest in *Piers Plowman* proud that he held love-days though unable to read a word of canon law, and Thomas Earl wrote that one of his principal obligations was to "move and keep the parochians to peace and labour to make peace to the uttermost of my powers."[101] An Elizabethan bishop asked churchwardens "whether [their] minister be a peacemaker and exhorter of his parishioners to Christian love and concord, and such a one as is no sower of discord among his neighbours."[102] Residents of Herne (Kent) complained "that Mr Vicar should be a peace maker but is a peace breaker," given to railing against his parishioners.[103] Gilbert Woolward of West Wratting complained that Mr Sykes was "more meet to make an uproar and to set men together by the ears" than to further peace.[104] Moreover, the minister was expected to provide this service *gratis*. Residents of Littleport, whose minister was himself feuding with half the parish (provoking one man to have his servant throw dead animals into the churchyard), complained that Mr Healy held a private court in the parish and took fees to excuse offenses.[105]

When admonition and arbitration were fruitless, presentment became necessary. For example, Joanne Cotteford of Hildersham, presented for showing contempt for the sacrament and slandering the parson, "liveth maliciously against the parish and will not be reconciled."[106] Oliver and Matilda Browne, a married couple, lived apart "to the dishonour of God and the offence of the whole congregation, and both being admonished by the minister, churchwardens and swornmen, they will not be reconciled to live together."[107]

Such cases fit one of a handful of models. Among the most common are those in which the accused were from parishes other than that in which the offense took place, usually adjoining parishes with which there was a good deal of contact. These were understandably more difficult to resolve internally. Also quite common were accusations against strangers, newcomers or vagrants. Villagers were extremely suspicious of strangers of unknown character who might be thieves or vandals. Strange women were particularly vulnerable to mistrust since they might become a burden on the community obliged to provide poor relief and the danger was even greater if they turned out to be pregnant.[108]

Uneasiness was only occasionally the result of crass self-interest. These villagers also had a strict moral code. Their notions of sexual propriety may have been different from the church's but they nonetheless had definite notions of what they would and would not tolerate. Couples who arrived in villages were expected to produce some proof that they were married, and relative newcomers who wished to settle in the parish and marry there would have to produce testimony from their previous homes that they were not already married and were of good character.[109] This was not idle nosiness. As cases of deserted wives suggest, it was a simple enough matter for a man or woman to pack up and move somewhere new where he or she could claim to be unmarried. Suspicious folk unearthed more than a few such cases: John Dent, who paraded around Cambridge market for two hours in a white sheet wearing penitential poetry, had married in London around 1550, moved to Norwich and married again around 1560, and then moved to Cambridge where his past caught up with him.[110]

The poor and dependant also appear in disproportionate numbers, but almost exclusively for sexual offenses. Fornication (even when no pregnancy resulted) led to prosecution because the parish needed to discourage its continuation which likely would lead to pregnancy. Waiting until a poor woman was pregnant was quite literally a case of closing the barn door too late. While communities tended to be tolerant of sexual relations between young men and women who were betrothed, they were less tolerant when the couple was poor. Late in the century, when the resources necessary before marriage became increasingly difficult to procure, there was a near-universal crackdown against previously tolerated pregnant brides. Village officials perceived a danger that betrothed couples might have to abandon or delay their planned marriages when they failed to salt away enough to set up on their own. In the meantime, their sexual relations would lead to children who would burden the parish rate-payers. Discouraging premarital sex by exemplary prosecutions of preg-nant brides went along with a campaign to close the gap in time between betrothal and marriage. When common fame existed of a betrothal and too long a period elapsed with no marriage, the couple would be hauled into court. Frequently, they married before the court met and produced a certificate to that effect. The balance either denied their betrothal or, if they admitted it, were ordered to marry immediately. Thus, community values were not static. In the 1590s, prenuptial fornication had become a threat. When it became necessary, the ecclesiastical courts were used as a tool to teach and enforce new stan-dards.[111]

Finally, there were the insane and incorrigible. A Sawston widow was often presented for not coming to communion; the parish failed to control her because "she is besides her wit."[112] Many parishes also had a resident pain-in-the-neck regularly in their bill of presentment, accused of everything from sexual offenses to snoring during sermons, from dicing and drinking to refusing to pay church rates.[113]

When churchwardens failed to present certain "crimes" it was not due to favoritism, lack of industry or fear of offending their neighbors.[114] When they reported *omnia bene* ("all is well") in quarter bills, as they often did, it did not mean that *omnia* had been *bene* ever since the last bill was sent up, but that what had not been, had been resolved by the community. Harmony and balance were restored without the church courts.[115]

On the other hand, almost all of those whom they did present had this in common: they were not fully integrated members of the community which presented them to the courts. Some did not live in the community at all; others lived, figuratively, on its margins either by fate or design. The presentment system allowed villages to protect the autonomy that they had been developing and protecting for centuries. The church court was the weapon that a community used against those who would not voluntarily submit to its order and show respect for its values. They used it as a last resort. In those twin capacities as protector of local autonomy and weapon of last resort, the court succeeded within the expectations of the people who used it and because of that earned their support and allegiance.

There is no such thing as the "typical" English parish. Only a reckless historian would claim that the experiences of one place might represent all others. That is not the function of local studies. Ideally, the historian studies a local community for the interplay of factors which shaped its unique experience. Competent local studies serve not to typify but to illustrate the range of experiences of English communities in the period under study.

In what remains, relations between the church courts and the people of six Cambridgeshire villages are studied in detail in order to test the argument made above in a more general way.[116] The villages discussed below reasonably sample the variety of experiences in this one county, although Cambridgeshire was not in every respect a typical county. While its agricultural zones are representative of many in the nation as a whole, some are excluded.[117] For example, there are no villages comparable to the sprawling settlements of Yorkshire or the mining districts of Devon. The county was also among the most densely populated and least prosperous of all English counties.[118]

In the 1500s, Cambridgeshire and the diocese of Ely were nearly coterminous.[119] Cambridge University certainly had an impact on its ecclesiastical history. Livings were poor since over 60 percent of them were impropriated, many to colleges, but while other dioceses with poor livings had trouble recruiting graduate clergy, the university's proximity meant that Ely was oversupplied (relative to most parts of England) with preachers. The diocese was also fortunate in its leadership.[120] Bishops Goodrich, Thirlby and Cox were all men of great ability, as were their deputies. Cox was particularly zealous in recruiting clergy and enforcing the Reformation in the diocese.[121] After his death in 1581, although the queen kept the see vacant for the rest of the century in order to add its revenues to the treasury, exceptionally good government continued in the diocese. This influenced relations between villagers and the courts and prevented the deterioration which took place in some dioceses.[122]

The case studies which follow do not pretend to show the "typical" English village. Instead, they claim to represent some of the experiences of sixteenth century English villages. Only future research on other villages in other parts of the country will demonstrate whether the experiences herein described can be matched elsewhere. This project was undertaken with the hope that these would be not the last words, but among the first of many.

Three parishes in northwest Cambridgeshire begin this study. Dry Drayton, about five miles from the university, is average sized for the county (2,389 acres). Its northwestern portion lies in Cambridgeshire's western plateau, an area of boulder clay, deforested long before Domesday Book, better suited for grazing than cereal crops. The village was built at the spring line (c. 200 ft.), as were most villages along the plateau. Spreading out below the village was the main field system: an area of river valley, partly chalk, partly alluvium. Dry Drayton was spared many of the drainage problems of villages on the southern edges of the plateau, hemmed in by Bourn Brook and the River Rhee.

For a village of its size, Dry Drayton was relatively underpopulated in 1500.[123] In the latter half of the fourteenth century, rebellion against conditions of tenure in the village seems to have caused some depopulation. The 1377 poll tax listed 122 people over the age of fourteen, and in 1524, as the English population was recovering from its post-plague lows, Dry Drayton had fewer than thirty-five households, or roughly half the density of 1377.[124] There were only thirty-one households in 1563, but dramatic population growth soon followed. In spite of a mortality crisis in 1570, the surplus of baptisms over burials between 1565 and 1599 was 199 – a staggering potential growth rate. Significant migration out of Dry Drayton ensured that the 1660s population was just over 300, but this still left its real growth rate the highest of any parish in this study.

Heavy clay in the south and the streams which crossed it rendered the parish of Orwell, then a tightly nucleated village with 1,800 acres given over almost entirely to cereal production, badly waterlogged.[125] The 203 counted for the Poll Tax in 1377 meant that Orwell was nearly twice as densely populated as Dry Drayton on more poorly drained soil. Population was still relatively low in 1524 when fifty-one people were assessed, and there were only forty-six households in 1563. Orwell's population stagnated at this level. Although the parish register evidence implies a high growth rate, the number of households in the 1660s was the same as a century before.

The village of Croxton, a 1,900-acre gently sloping outcrop projecting into Huntingdonshire, is built on relatively well-drained heavy clay. While c. 1,300 acres were given over to cereal production, Croxton also had a sizable pasture.[126] In 1377, it had almost exactly half the number of people on roughly the same acreage as Orwell. While thirty-eight people were assessed in 1524, because fifteen were wage-earners, the total number of households was probably closer to twenty-five, the number counted in 1563. Croxton, with well-kept registers from the 1550s, apparently was not badly stricken by the influenza epidemic since it experienced only a small surplus of burials over baptisms from 1555–9.

Modest, manageable growth characterized its next century. From an annual average surplus of one baptism over burial from 1538–64, the surplus rose to three per year from 1565–99, implying a growth rate similar to Orwell's. In fact, Croxton's population grew modestly by 1666.

Even more than Dry Drayton, both Orwell and Croxton kept their numbers under control with significant emigration. Though all three villages experienced potentially damaging population pressures during the century after 1563, only Dry Drayton grew dramatically, but it began at a low enough density level to absorb some increase and carefully enforced stints kept its pasture from being overburdened.[127] Orwell, badly overpopulated already, managed to freeze its population at mid-sixteenth century levels. Soil quality on the western plateau was not of a high enough level to withstand too much additional exploitation, however, so all three villages had to foster emigration to control their populations. Although their rates of growth varied with their potential to absorb increased numbers, all three villages shared this common experience of pressure and response.

In other respects, however, Dry Drayton was very different from its neighbors. Between 1570 and 1591, Richard Greenham established there what has been called "the first model Puritan parish in the country."[128] Greenham was a graduate and fellow of Pembroke Hall who publicly supported Thomas Cartwright after his 1570 lectures on the Acts of the Apostles.[129] Greenham gave up his fellowship for the rectory of Dry Drayton in 1570. His support for Cartwright was no obstacle to the puritan gentleman John Hutton who held the advowson.[130] But in August 1571 he refused to subscribe his support for the Prayer Book, the rules of apparel, and the Articles of Religion.[131] Eventually cited by Cox for nonconformity, he produced a lengthy defense of his beliefs.[132] Cox allowed him to continue unmolested although Greenham never swayed from his opposition to the surplice and willingness to defy the law. "If justice cannot stand except piety fail," he said, "it were better that civil justice should cease than piety be profaned."[133]

Greenham's success with Cox was due to his emphatic belief that the peace of the church was to be sacrificed only in extreme circumstances. He actively discouraged Cambridge students from becoming involved in disruptive controversies[134] and a "godly minister" who sought Greenham's sympathy when his parishioners became outraged over his pulling down "certain painted windows" received a stinging rebuke instead. Greenham said that the minister's first duty was not to destroy but to teach, and that he should first have taught his parishioners and obtained their consent to remove the windows and replace them with "new white glass."[135] In "a mere outward thing" he "would not break the peace of the church," and in "the lesser adjuncts of religion . . . he would not withstand or condemn any but leave them to their own reason, seeing very good men do so disagree in them or change their opinion in them"; only in "the essence of God's worship . . . must we be strict and holy."[136] This irenic disposition earned him the appreciation of Bishop Cox who deliberately overlooked Greenham's disregard for the rules and even employed Greenham to confer with and sway members of the Family of Love in 1580.[137]

The piety and learning which earned his bishop's respect also drew to Greenham several young men who spent some time in Dry Drayton as "clerical apprentices."[138] From their notes of his counsels to them and to his parishioners, it is possible to know a good deal about Greenham's views and his ministry.[139] His parishioners were also well apprised of their minister's views for Greenham was a tireless preacher-catechizer. That "the people might have the better opportunity to attend upon his Ministry" he began his weekday sermons as soon as it was light enough to see, and he preached so enthusiastically that he drenched his clothes with perspiration and had to change after his sermon. Not content with his ministry from the pulpit in the morning, he also went out into the fields to "confer with his neighbours as they were at plough."[140] The reality must have been somewhat more prosaic: the short sober minister with notorious digestive problems up to his ankles in local clay pursuing the muddy farmers who probably wanted simply to finish their work in peace. In his own day, Greenham was famous well beyond his parish for his efforts as a counsellor, and people came from many parts of England seeking solace from him. According to Fuller, "his masterpiece was in comforting wounded consciences [and] God used him herein as an instrument of good to many, who came to him with weeping eyes, and went from him with cheerful souls."[141]

In 1591, Greenham left Dry Drayton ostensibly because of "the untractableness and unteachableness of that people among whom he had taken such exceeding great pains."[142] If that lament, first noted sixty years after Greenham's death, is untrue and his ministry had a positive impact, one might hope to see an increase in fervent, personal professions of faith in will dedicatory clauses, but after examining wills from Cambridgeshire parishes with far less praiseworthy ministers, Margaret Spufford writes that there is "less feeling of convinced Protestantism in the wills of Dry Drayton than any other parish I have examined."[143] Two of the seven Dry Drayton wills from 1570–91 use the simplest form of commendation: "I bequeath my soul to Almighty God."[144] Roger Boyden's will, which bequeathed body and soul to

> the hands of my alone and omnisufficient saviour Jesus Christ who as he hath alonely redeemed me, so do I firmly believe that I shall be saved only by the fruit and mercy of his passion and suffering for my sins, confessing that for my sins I am unworthy of the least of his mercies, yet for Christ's sake that I shall by faith possess and enjoy the kingdom of heaven prepared for all the children of God whereof I am one

was written by Greenham himself and says little of the testator's sentiments since scribes routinely supplied the dedication clause unless the testator specified otherwise.[145] Two other wills begin with very brief, though undeniably Protestant, expressions. John Muns left his soul "to God almighty trusting by the death and passion of his son Jesus Christ my only saviour to receive at the general judgement everlasting life." Greenham witnessed the will of James Hutton, who left his soul "to Christ Jesus in whom only and wholly I by faith do repose my whole salvation." Since this clause is unique, it may be an expression of personal faith (even though Greenham was probably the will's scribe), but given the history of puritan proclivities in the Hutton family it is highly likely that Hutton's strong piety antedated Greenham's arrival in the parish.[146]

Eleven wills from the dozen years following his departure use a variety of the simple dedicatory formula. However, Thomas Giffard left his soul "into the hands of Almighty God my father who created me, second to God the son who redeemed me; thirdly to God the Holy Ghost who sanctified me, and I do believe and confess that these three persons in Trinity do make one god coequal, coeternal, in unity of person." He left his body to be buried in the churchyard "to sleep till the last day when the last trumpet shall blow and the dead in Christ shall arise first and then this my corruptible shall be made like to his glorious body and so shall ever remain with him in his glorious kingdom."[147]

Shortly after Greenham's arrival, Dry Drayton's children began increasingly to receive biblical baptismal names. Of the ten children baptized in 1575, only one received a traditional parish name (Thomas). Instead, there were Peter, Appia, Daniel, Ursula, Nathaniel, Samuel, Josiah and two Sarahs. They were soon joined by several Deborahs and Rebeccas, along with Jehosaphats and Hananiahs, Gemimah, Solomon, Manasses, Moses, Joshua, Eunice, and even Lot and Bathsheba. When Greenham left, the traditional names (William, Henry, John, Elizabeth, Alice and Margaret were the most common in Dry Drayton) returned and biblical names were no longer chosen.[148]

In the church courts during Greenham's incumbency there were two instance cases, a decade apart, involving his parishioners. These figures are not unusual for the shire,[149] but they might be seen as something of a victory for Greenham who was noted as a "promoter of peace and concord amongst his neighbours."[150] Some puritan clergymen based their ministry on the text that Christ came not to bring peace but a sword and made careers out of disrupting communities at peace with their preaching and efforts to discipline the godless. Indeed, George Gifford believed that one indication of true godly preaching was contention, because if the word of God were truly set out, wicked men "would storm and fret against [the preachers]."[151] Greenham, however, was part of the majority which placed a value on harmony second only to that of preaching.[152]

The two instance cases were both suits against people from other parishes, cases in which Greenham could have little impact as a settler of conflict. Defamation cases, which were common among neighbors, did not occur at all. Since it is unlikely that Greenham succeeded in miraculously curbing the tongues of his parishioners, this suggests that tempers were cooled and disputes settled without going to court. Notably absent is tithe litigation, the most common type of suit in the courts. This is striking because Dry Drayton apparently had no glebe land, which made Greenham unusually dependent on tithes,[153] and his heroic charity left the household perpetually short of money.[154]

Ex officio cases tell an interesting tale as well. After Greenham's arrival, there was only one minor matter involving the church: a new Bible was needed in 1584, a fairly common case.[155] Greenham seemingly succeeded not only in establishing harmonious relations with the leaders of the community, but also in moving the community to maintain the church. They even tolerated his nonconformity in apparel. Only shortly after he left did the wardens report that they had no surplice, which suggests that Greenham had thrown it away, had never been turned in, and all concerned had looked the other way for twenty years.[156]

In Greenham's first years, Henry Giffard was accused of withholding money he owed to the town. Attempts to secure it from him by less extreme means failed; he refused even to answer the court and was excommunicated.[157] Alice Steven and Darnegold Newman, both accused of moral offenses, disappeared.[158] Henry Muns turned back fornication charges by producing some of Dry Drayton's leading citizens as his compurgators. Since one of the wardens was a compurgator, this accusation must have been raised outside of the normal presentment procedure.[159] From late 1579 until 1584, not a single disorder was reported to the court.

In 1584 there was a brief flurry of activity. Isabelle Bell, then of Dry Drayton, was accused of bearing an illegitimate child in Madingley before she married and moved to Dry Drayton. The accusation, which she admitted, was raised from Madingley, where she was ordered to do penance.[160] Agnes Wilkinson and Oliver Hinde were accused by the wardens of Great Eversden of fornication with servants of Thomas Leete of that parish. Dry Drayton's wardens accused Leete of pressuring their opposite numbers from his parish.[161] Note that none of these accusations was generated within Dry Drayton itself. There was not another presentment until after Greenham removed to London.

It would, however, be mistaken to imagine that Greenham had succeeded in building a shining city on the clay, a harmonious godly commonwealth in Dry Drayton. In fact, his godly preaching probably made people more aware of the ungodly behavior of their neighbors and themselves. Yet there was no twenty-year flood of presentments. Why?

Before Greenham's tenure, the wardens reported that they had no preaching and no copy of Erasmus' *Paraphrases*, that the rector was nonresident, and that the church was missing some of its windows.[162] In 1568, they presented rector William Fairclough for adultery with Agnes Lakers. Although Fairclough admitted the charge, he was excommunicated when he refused to execute his penance. After several months, he submitted and his penance was commuted in exchange for £6 given to support two poor scholars at Jesus College.[163] Finally, Margaret Giffard and Joan Boyden, both wives of former churchwardens and men of local standing, were named as scolds and later presented for not receiving communion. One admitted the first charge and performed her penance; the other claimed innocence but could not produce four compurgators and did penance also. Joan died before the latter charge was tried; Margaret confessed and was ordered to pay a fine into the poor box.[164]

After Greenham resigned, in addition to noting the absent surplice, five couples, one widow and one single man were presented for not communicating.[165] Two of the couples cannot be traced at all and must have been transients in the parish. Henry Fish (the single man) died in Dry Drayton in 1593, but there is no earlier record of him. The first parish record of Agnes Ducking was in 1583. Her husband died in 1585, and she died in 1599. The other three couples all had children baptized in the parish, but none had been in the parish for more than a few years by 1590.

These cases suggest that with or without Greenham, Dry Drayton was a relatively undisturbed place. This resulted from the fusion of a tradition of self-government with an entrenched parish oligarchy. Self-government was the natural product of the manorial history of Dry Drayton.[166] By the mid-twelfth century, village lordship was highly fragmented and since the principal manors were monastic, the landlords were absentees as well. After the Dissolution, this property was obtained by the Hutton family. Hutton and his descendants lived in the village and shared local offices with the villagers but never achieved any domination over them, except in wealth.[167] After centuries of weak, absentee lordship the practice of self-government was too well established.

The Giffard family, which antedated Domesday Book, dominated Dry Drayton.[168] Giffards headed more than a third of the parish households by Greenham's time, and were connected by marriage to several others. While the family never approached the Huttons' affluence and Giffard men described themselves as husbandmen in their wills, increasingly they monopolized village wealth,[169] and translated this into a stranglehold on parish offices. Scarcely a year went by without one or two Giffards in office, and in 1570, 1573 and 1590 they held three of the four parish offices.

What was not held by the Giffards belonged to a few other important families, of which the most important was the Boydens, with at least five households in the 1570s. Ten other families account for all of the rest of those important enough to tax, and seven of those filled church offices. A similar pattern could be expected in the leet jury.[170]

The parish's uncontentiousness and its internal problem-solving mechanisms can be traced to this long history of self-government and the choke-hold that the principal families maintained over the parish. Absentee landlords created the opportunity for leet juries to undertake virtually all of the business of government. In Dry Drayton, these juries, whose principal duties "grew out of purely local needs for conflict resolution and for the administration of agricultural regulations essential to communities engaged in open-field farming," adopted and enforced by-laws regulating village farming and grazing.[171] Leet juries also controlled residence in villages, and although new families appear without having married into those already resident, most movement in Dry Drayton was out of the parish.

Parochial tranquility certainly benefitted from a minister like Greenham. Greenham's vision of ministry dovetailed nicely with the social vision of his parishioners. He was a gentle man, committed heart and soul to healing, and repelled by division and conflict. It is unsurprising that during his ministry the only presentments from within the parish were against one incorrigible who had put himself outside of the community by refusing to respect its order and two people who had fled the parish and removed themselves from the possibility of peaceful resolution. The others were all the result of problems which occurred outside Dry Drayton before the parties became denizens. The conflict resolution and regulation of behavior which led to infrequent cases in the church courts was not of the minister's creating, but Greenham was able to embrace and baptize so much of the vision and ideal of the community in which he worked that he was able to assist it in maintaining its independence. The church courts as they stood were important to this community because they respected its autonomy and its perceived right to govern itself while providing a forum to resolve conflicts as a last resort.

The village of Croxton was also manorially fragmented before the Reformation, though not so radically as Dry Drayton. The principal manor was passed about as a marriage portion or dower throughout most of the Middle Ages. In 1549, it was sold to Sir Richard Sackville, chancellor of the Court of Augmentations. His son Thomas sold the manor in 1571 to Dr Edward Leeds, Master of Clare and a distinguished civil lawyer, who became the first resident lord in generations (if not centuries). In 1589, the manor passed to his nephew Thomas who lived there until his death in 1622. The remaining village land passed into the hands of established local families during the sixteenth century. A small estate, the manor of Westbury, came under the control of the Cosyns, while 280 acres formerly held by Huntington Priory were sold to William Ratford in 1549 and remained in his family.[172]

As in Dry Drayton, resident lordship followed a long period of absenteeism and powerful local families dominated the parish, but neither the Ratfords nor the Cosyns approached the numbers or influence of the Giffards. In 1524/5, of thirty-eight residents assessed, twenty-three were not wage earners, and Robert Ratford, William Ratford and William Cosyn were three of the wealthiest, all assessed at £10. Three other men were assessed at the same rate, and one at £20, but their families disappeared from the village.[173] Based on later subsidies, Robert and William Ratford and William Cosyn were indisputably the wealthiest men in the village. Two new men with substantial assessments, Thomas King and Edward Bulmer, were probably lessees of the manor.[174] In Elizabethan subsidies, the Ratfords and Cosyns, along with Edward Leeds, and a half-dozen others account for all of Croxton's taxed wealth. Five Cosyns and two Ratfords were taxed in 1597 along with Mr Leeds, Robert Gonnell, William Sutton, John Lawless, William and Robert West, and Ambrose Parnell. These men were all members of families which had regularly been taxed throughout Elizabeth's reign.[175]

Elections to church offices show a similar pattern. In the 1560s and 1570s, only members of the few principal families held office. The Cosyns and Ratfords held office thirteen times, while the other seven families together held office seventeen times. The first "new" name among the officers is that of Edward Reynold, who had lived in the parish more than a decade before election and whose sister married Robert Ratford. Richard Whalley, who married Joan Ratford in 1581, was a warden in 1599. Richard Meade, who moved to Croxton before 1580, was unique. While not connected by marriage to a leading family and never considered wealthy enough to be a subsidyman, he was chosen for parish offices at least twice in the 1590s.

The church courts rarely saw people from Croxton appear as parties to suits, and it was among the three or four parishes most untroubled by suits in the entire diocese. A very involved matrimonial suit brought by Henry Corbett against Agnes Adane in 1539 was probably never resolved since Agnes died in 1540.[176] Two other cases, in 1544 and 1574, concerned disputed tithes. Walter Bire, a defendant in the first case, was apparently one of those local troublemakers who habitually resisted the community's order since William Parnell averred in his deposition that Bire "is a very froward [sic] person and by reason thereof this deponent is moved in his conscience to judge and think that he hath not paid."[177] In the later suit Dr Leeds challenged William Ratford the elder, Croxton's wealthiest resident, over the customary tithe, which Ratford insisted he had paid as required.[178] These cases ably illustrate the function of the court. In the first, a man with a reputation for orneriness was taken to court as a last resort. In the second, the new lord of the manor (who was also the rector) and the village (represented by its chief member) used the court at a moment of transition in lordship to define formally the customary tithe.

Ex officio cases against parish denizens were virtually legal unicorns. Charles Taylor was cited for an unstated cause but never appeared in 1566. Since Taylor does not appear in the parish register, he probably had left town.[179] Richard

Whalley and Joan Ratford were prosecuted for antenuptial fornication.[180] At least two other couples were plainly guilty of this according to the parish registers, but only Joan had delivered her baby before marriage. This was qualitatively different from being pregnant for one's nuptials and required an exemplary penance.

More presentments would certainly not have been surprising, since the parish *après* Leeds was not well served. Rector Francis Alford, a layman residing in London, staffed the parish with a constantly changing cast of curates. After Alford's overdue deprivation, Leeds presented himself to the rectory and served conscientiously until retiring in 1584 when he appointed John Lee, who served until 1609. The ecclesiastical disarray which might have accompanied Alford's nongovernment could not have escaped the careful scrutiny of the new regime but it made not the slightest difference in the number of presentments and amount of litigation, in spite of Edward Leeds being both a dedicated puritan and the presiding officer at most meetings of the episcopal court. Neither his zeal for godly discipline nor his professional interest as a lawyer and judge produced a bumper crop of presentments. Perhaps more than any other example, Croxton's reveals that even to those most self-interested the ecclesiastical courts were a last resort. When there was good government and stability in the parish, as there had been in Croxton for generations with its small and regulated population and strong oligarchy, it was to be expected that disputes would be resolved at home and recourse to the courts would be had only under the exceptional circumstances described above. As lord of the manor and a resident of the community, it was in Dr Leeds's interests to contribute to and support his parish's customary self-government and self-regulation.

Orwell was the most peculiar administratively as well as the most fragmented manorially of all of the parishes in this study. The parish apparently contained two settlements: Orwell proper and what was left of the medieval parish of Malton which was not identified in 1086 but had a separate existence, including a church and separate taxation, by the thirteenth century. Three centuries later, while some testators identified themselves as residents of Malton, both settlements officially were treated as one village.

In Domesday Book, the village was divided seven ways. The largest holding became part of the honor of Gloucester and passed eventually to the Duke of Somerset's daughter Margaret, wife of Edmund Tudor, Earl of Richmond. When she died in 1509 it became a royal manor, administered by a succession of royal bailiffs and stewards and crown tenants. The manor of Malton, acquired by the countess of Richmond and granted to a Cambridge college early in the sixteenth century, was leased to the Sterne family.[181]

Ecclesiastical government did not suffer from these divisions in the sixteenth century. The last rector of Malton was appointed in the 1480s, and when the advowson passed with the manor to Christ's College they did not make any appointments. Most of the small Malton church was pulled down in 1509 and what remained was used as a cowshed.[182]

Early in the fourteenth century, Orwell became a sinecure rectory, and nonresident rectors appointed a vicar or curate to serve the parish which was a relatively poor living.[183] In spite of this, Orwell was well served by its Elizabethan vicars. The first of those, John Relff (c.1561–6) was not a graduate and was not able to preach, but he read the Homilies.[184] Relff never married, and while his will noted that he "trust[ed] to be saved by the merits, death and passion of his son our saviour Jesus Christ, [and] to be an inheritor with all the company of heaven,"[185] this formula was common enough that it might be a scribal provision. Therefore, his personal commitment to the Reformation is unclear. Hugh Roland, a curate about whom nothing is known, served briefly. Roger Davies *alias* Fludd, vicar from 1568 until his death in 1580, was unmarried until 1579, when he married a widow, Grace Barton (nee Caldecot). Davies wrote his own will and in it bequeathed his soul "to Jesus Christ, through faith in whom I hope undoubtedly to be saved."[186]

After Davies, a new phase began. The next three vicars were all graduates, and all were appointed to Orwell immediately after ordination. Unlike their predecessors, they did not die there, but moved to other (presumably more lucrative) livings following internships in Orwell. The first of these, appointed in 1580, was Henry Holland, a disciple of Richard Greenham and editor of his collected works. Holland married Elizabeth Stint of Cambridge in 1585 and in 1591 was suspended for nonconformity, leaving Orwell when he refused to certify his conformity.[187] His replacement was John Money, who married Frances Caldecot in 1593 and transferred to a Norfolk living in 1599. John Bowen served from 1600 to 1611 at which time he took up the living at Warboys (Hunts.) where he remained for thirty-six years.

Like Croxton and Dry Drayton, Orwell had a long tradition of self-government, caused in part by its peculiar divisions and absentee landlords as well as the need for careful regulation of limited meadow and pasture resources. Villagers also relied upon communal action to negotiate leases of additional land from crown tenants.[188] In addition, since Orwell's resources were stretched to their limits, concerted action to regulate the number of households in the village and reverse the consequences of the natural population increase taking place in the sixteenth century was urgently needed if the village were to remain economically viable. Finally, Orwell was undergoing a transformation in the nature of landholding: the disappearance of the small landholder, and an increase in the number of both large landholders and poor cottagers as economic pressures on small farmers, exacerbated by the burden of bequests, made engrossing by wealthier neighbors possible.[189]

Orwell generated the most ecclesiastical court cases of any parish in the district. Even allowing for its larger population, the *per capita* incidence was extremely high. Immorality was the charge in almost all of the cases. In 1579, two male servants of William Sterne were charged with fornication. One murdered Sterne, who was the tenant of Malton manor, and died in prison. Neither the other servant nor the two women ever appeared in court.[190] Thomas and Joanna (Mead) Rowning, William and Avis (Scampion) Rutt, Roger and Margaret Sampfield, and William and Joan (Sampfield) Creswell were presented and admitted to antenuptial fornication and pregnancy. They received and performed penances, except Rowning who paid 10s.[191] What unites these cases is the undoubted poverty of the men accused. Thomas Rowning was a weaver with only four selions of copyhold.[192] William Rutt, a weaver's son, was apparently landless.[193] Roger Sampfield, the son and heir of cottager William Sampfield, was burdened with providing for unmarried siblings out of his limited resources.[194] William Creswell had no house or land, and his marriage to Sampfield's sister brought with it a dowry of 13s 4d, a burden to Roger to pay and little help to the couple.

When John Buttrick and Agnes Fuller were accused in 1597 both of fornication and of not marrying after contracting, he disappeared and she never performed her penance.[195] Giles Peck and his servant Beatrice Gailer were accused of fornication in 1601. She fled; he was dismissed with an admonition after denying his guilt.[196] Edward Jeap never appeared in court after he was accused of adultery with Mary Arthur in 1601. The case went no further, probably because of her mental state.[197] A parishioner accused Margaret Holder of adultery, but she was not troubled after the wardens denied "common fame."[198] None of the accused, except Edward Jeap, were natives of the parish and the readiness with which most of them disappeared suggests that their roots were not deep.

Two marginal members of important families also figure in the presentments: Elizabeth Kettle was presented for fortune-telling but no action against her was recorded and she cannot be traced;[199] Thomas Caldecot was repeatedly presented because he "doth mislike the religion which God be thanked now we have," and he was excommunicated for not appearing in court.[200] Another man accused of recusancy certified that he attended Shepreth parish church and was dismissed; two women accused of scolding were dismissed; Robert Adam admitted carting on the feast of St Peter and was dismissed with an admonition.[201] William Kettle denied that he withheld a legacy due to the parish poor, but witnesses testified that a piece of land which his father purchased from Richard Boston was charged with the legacy and the court ordered a search of Boston's will to resolve the case.[202] Finally, Alice Nostropp was accused in 1601 of allowing the churchyard to be "annoyed with hogs and cattle" by her failure to repair fences. Recently widowed, she had not yet mastered her responsibilities and needed some prodding from the community to do so.[203]

In these suits, two patterns emerge which reflect Orwell's unique experience in the sixteenth century. First, the accused in morality suits (more than half of all suits) were either very poor members of established families or transients. With the position of small landholders deteriorating, the community was extremely sensitive to the behavior of the poor and marginal who they might be forced to support with poor relief. Prosecuting prenuptial pregnancy can be seen as a response to demographic pressure and an attempt to restrict the dangerous natural birth rate.

Second, since some cases arose outside of the presentment process, Orwell was apparently not as tightly controlled as its neighbors. There certainly are no signs of a parish oligarchy in the elections for churchwarden and sidesmen. As the number of wealthy landholders increased during the sixteenth century, too many men and families established some claim on the office. Twenty men with sixteen surnames were taxed in the subsidies of 10 and 14 Elizabeth.[204] Fourteen held parish office after 1567, though none came close to monopolizing elections. William Sterne, tenant of Malton Manor, distanced himself from Orwell matters before his murder. Because records do not survive for all years, and the 1580s are badly served in this regard, it is entirely possible that the other subsidymen served at some point.

The land surveys compiled in the late sixteenth and early seventeenth century further fortify the impression that Orwell had an unusually broad-based leadership because of its high number of major landholders. Those surveys show nineteen men (with fifteen distinct surnames) with combined freehold and copyhold in excess of thirty acres.[205] Except for Robert Sterne of Malton, Matthew Jeap, Richard Skinner, Edward Walter and Thomas Mortlock, they were churchwardens or the heirs of recent churchwardens. Walter and Mortlock were both new to the community. Walter occupied land which had belonged to Robert Adam, and Mortlock had married the widow of Henry Johnson *alias* Butler, who had a life interest in her husband's estates. Jeaps and Skinners alone of the wealthy established families did not hold parish offices. Orwell had too many wealthy families for any one or two to monopolize office in the way the Giffards and Boydens, or the Cosyns and Ratfords, were able to do.

Nor was parish office-holding restricted to these wealthy families. Several times in the 1590s less wealthy members of the parish were elected. Laurence Johnson, a maltster with seven acres of freehold, was a sidesman in 1590.[206] In 1596, Thomas Rutt, a weaver with a cottage and a half-acre was churchwarden, and maltster Thomas Brock was a sidesman.[207]

As with the western plateau villages, the most important factors determining the frequency of suits and presentments in ecclesiastical courts were the demographic regime and the nature of village government. Where population pressure was greatest, use of the courts to regulate poor and marginal people increased. Where communal government was not tightly controlled, whatever the tradition of self-government, the chances that conflicts would spill out into the courts also increased. Most notably absent is the local parson's influence. A respectable and godly minister who fulfilled his duties as peace-maker and mediator might keep some cases out of the courts, but if he was not up to his responsibilities, there were others who might step in. Well-regarded puritans and godly ministers such as Greenham, Leeds and Holland had no more or less success in that role either than the competent, if less distinguished, men or the incompetent wretches who preceded or followed them.

In contrast to the nucleated villages of the northwest, the shire's southeastern zone has a series of long narrow parishes with scattered settlements. Village shape was dictated by topography. A band of heath in the west of this zone was useful for grazing, while heavy clay in the east was suited for pasture also; in between was a wide band of well-drained chalk favorable to cereal production. Long, narrow parishes crossing all three bands favored a mixed and balanced economy. The ground in this part of the county rises steeply from northwest to southeast before descending gradually into the clay. Settlements were built at what would have been the edge of the woods, a point both well drained and well supplied with water, when the villages were peopled.

This pattern caused most of the southeastern settlements to be extremely close together. Each village center is much closer to that of its neighbors than it is to its own eastern or western extremes. This proximity led to remarkable fluidity. People from one village travelled to another to purchase products of local artisans, and to meet at its alehouse.[208] They also moved easily from village to village in the area,[209] and owned land in more than one community.[210] Some villages even had intertwined manorial histories.

Weston Colville, a parish of nearly 3,000 acres, was divided into three manors. Nominal overlordship of the main manor of Colvilles belonged to the Bishop of Ely, but since the twelfth century the manor had been subinfeudated to the Stutvilles and descended through a series of female heirs ultimately to the wife of Sir Thomas Fynderne in 1433. Sir Thomas united the main manor with the two small manors of Moynes and Leverers, but the manors left the direct line when his grandson died without children in 1524. His heir was Sir Thomas Elyot, who also died without issue and left a life interest in the manors to his wife Margaret, who married Sir James Dyer, CJCP. In 1547, John Lennard purchased the reversionary interest and obtained the manors in 1561. His son Sampson inherited the manors when he died in 1591.[211]

Although many of the same people held manors in Carlton cum Willingham, it remained divided among several manors at the end of the century. The two main manors were both held by Lewes priory until its dissolution. Thomas Cromwell sold them to Sir Thomas Elyot. As in Weston Colville, Elyot's manors passed to Richard Puttenham, who granted life interests to Elyot's widow and her husband with remainders divided between Puttenham's brother

George and Margaret Dyer's brother Anthony Aborough. George Puttenham sold his moiety to Hugh Stuckley, who received it upon Dyer's death in 1582 and passed it to his son Thomas in 1589, while Aborough held his moiety at the end of the century.

A small manor came into the hands of Sir Thomas Fynderne in the fifteenth century and descended from him to the Lennards, who called the manor Carlton Parva. It was united manorially to Weston Colville, as was the minor manor of Gatwards. Some land was also held by the Hospitallers until the Dissolution, after which it was purchased by Thomas Barnardiston. His descendants sold it to Sir Stephen Soames of London and his brother-in-law in two sales in 1594 and 1626.[212]

Neither parish was densely populated before 1603. In Weston Colville, twenty-eight residents were assessed in 1524/5. Although fifteen were assessed on only £1, all might have been independent householders since none were taxed on wages.[213] There were twenty-six households in 1563.[214] Settlement density was thus extremely low, with fewer than ten households per 1,000 acres. Moreover, the households were not clustered together. A survey map of 1612 made for Sampson Lennard shows two separate settlements. The original near the church had seven houses and the parsonage, while twenty-six newer houses were arranged around the triangular green.[215] In the 1660s, the number of households had grown to forty-four.[216]

Carlton cum Willingham comprised at least three separate settlements: one in the old parish of Willingham, one near Carlton Parva manor, and another in the center of Carlton proper. In 1524/5, only eight people were assessed, a suspiciously low figure. Two were taxed on £4 and the remainder on £1 in goods.[217] The subsidy assessors had not neglected Willingham, but it is probable that Carlton Parva, which had nine houses in 1612, was already so closely linked with Weston Colville that people with copyhold or leasehold in both, so evident in the 1612 map, were already present and were taxed at their principal residences in Weston. Twenty-two households were recorded in 1563, and by 1674 the total had risen to forty-five.[218] At worst, Carlton cum Willingham had only about ten households per 1,000 acres for most of the sixteenth century.

For those being driven out of clay uplands villages like Orwell, the southeastern parishes were very attractive for two reasons. First, low density and underpopulation meant that immigration would not be restricted. Second, the enormous size of leaseholds opened up the prospect of employment.

When Sampson Lennard mapped his estates in 1612, Weston Colville and Carlton Parva were experiencing enclosure similar to that of other chalk district villages.[219] Both the heath and clay were ideally suited for enclosure and grazing, and enclosure was pronounced by 1612, with several holdings exceeding 100 acres of enclosed land. Margaret Elrington, principal lessee of the

Carlton Parva demesne, had almost 400 acres; the Marshes over 100 acres; and John(?) Vale 121 acres.[220] The middling landholder disappeared in the process of enclosing. By 1612 there were thirty-five landholders, of whom nine held over ninety acres (excluding demesne lessees, who would swell this total), while only three held between forty and ninety acres, and six held between a half and a full yardland. Seventeen people held less than a half-yardland, placing them at or below the "poverty line."[221] Because of the scale of enclosure, common lands were too limited to support supplemental stock raising. In order to survive, many residents must have depended upon wages from working the demesne.

What these factors — short distance between villages and mobility between them, non-nucleated thinly settled communities, high percentages of demesne available for lease and wage labor — suggest is that the villages in the southeast were likely to be socially porous and lack cohesion. This expectation is borne out by subsidy assessments and church officeholding.[222]

Only John Grigg of the eight from Carlton assessed in 1524/5 reappeared in 1547. He was also assessed in 1559, but no Griggs were taxed again until 1598. In addition to Grigg, five other men were assessed in 1547. James Dyer headed the list, as one would expect, and after his death his place was taken by William Lennard. Christopher Amye had the next highest assessment. He died in 1553 and his son Richard took his place in 1559. Since Christopher was buried in Brinkley, he also held land there, which might account for neither Richard nor any other Amye being taxed in Carlton after 1559. Either the family died out or sold its holdings in Carlton and focused on Brinkley.[223] John Dorman, who died without issue in 1557, was succeeded by his brother Giles who was taxed in 1559 and then disappeared.[224] John Harrison was taxed only once and no other Harrisons appeared in an Elizabethan subsidy. Only John Dobido, of those taxed in 1547, can be traced to later subsidies in person or through his heirs. The evidence of continuity in later subsidies is much the same: in 10 and 14 Elizabeth, nine men were assessed, including Lennard and Dobido. Of the remainder, two had heirs taxed in 39 Elizabeth, and the other five names disappeared. In Weston Colville, the discontinuity was even more pronounced.

The population of Carlton was so low that by 1576 the parish elected only one sidesman.[225] Even then, there were few enough men from whom to choose. With the exception the absentee Dyer, the Amyes (who might have spent most of their time in Brinkley) and three widows, those who were taxed in Carlton and were presumably its most prosperous residents, all served in parish office between 1570 and 1599, and in the 1570s most served at least twice. In addition, three men who were not assessed also served, including Richard Owgrave who was relatively poor.[226] In the 1590s, when the impact of immigration would be acutely felt, even more new names appear as parish officers while the old families were pushed aside.

Weston Colville had a similar pattern. In the 1570s, at least fifteen different men shared offices, only six of whom were wealthy enough to be taxed in the parish and included two wage-laborers.[227] In the 1590s, while at least two officers served again, Robert Cockerton, a transplant from Carlton with twenty-four acres in Weston, was elected warden in 1596 soon after moving there. Four other new men were landholders in 1612, but the size of their holding was not a factor in their election. Robert Cooper held ninety-three acres and Peter Kendall fifty acres in 1612, but Thomas Webbe and John Saunder were roughly half-yardlanders.[228] The sidesmen included John Mayles, a blacksmith, and John Chapman, a wage-laborer, neither of whom was from an established family.[229]

The impact of this instability and porosity in the ranks of the prosperous and the parish governors can be seen in the litigation generated by the two parishes, as can the effects of frequent and facile contacts among the parishes in the area. With the exception of one tithe suit from each parish, all of the instance cases with people from Weston or Carlton involved parties from other parishes. Three of those were breach-of-promise cases: Agnes Winter of Dullingham against Thomas Rich *alias* Kellogg of Carlton, Susan Jeniver of Borough Green against John Woolward of Weston Colville, and Marie Teversham who lived with Thomas Heath of Weston Colville (presumably as a servant) against Thomas Westley.[230] Proximity of settlements to one another and frequent contacts must have made communication and courtship between young people of different parishes particularly easy here. The one defamation case was related to an inter-village marriage contract as well. Joan Webbe of Weston Colville accused Beatrice Smith of Whittlesford of defaming her as an "arrant whore" when Smith expressed her objections to her son marrying Webbe. The incident took place in Weston Colville, but the witnesses were all residents of West Wratting who had been in Weston performing errands. While the sentence has not survived, Smith may have been speaking truly since Joan was later accused of fornication with a servant in Whittlesford.[231]

Office cases reveal a good deal of mobility also. Richard Webbe of Carlton was excommunicated for a churchyard quarrel with a man from West Wratting, as was Simon Deekes of Carlton for brawling with William Gyn of Brinkley.[232] Alice Rich *alias* Kellogg of Carlton was accused of fornication with Edward Free of West Wratting. Carlton churchwardens also complained that Alice Davey, a servant in Linton, had been dumped on their parish when she became pregnant and she was living on their alms.[233]

There were also four antenuptial fornication presentments from Carlton: two in 1579, and one in 1599 and 1600. Only two couples married in 1599 and both brides were pregnant – the two presented in 1599 and 1600.[234] There were several other morals cases at the end of the century, including one in which a parish newcomer was suspected of incest.[235] Agnes Mascall, wife of a former churchwarden, used the court to clear her name of a common fame of fornication. This was clearly a case in which the accused welcomed the charge as an opportunity to be formally exonerated.[236]

Churchyard incidents troubled Carlton. Richard Mascall scandalized the parish when he knocked over a pregnant woman while playing football in the churchyard, but since it was an accident, he was dismissed with an admonition.[237] Richard Clark performed a penance for slandering Christopher Marsh in the churchyard.[238] Six men from the parish also admitted involvement in a charivari which ended in the churchyard.[239] Contrary to what is usually assumed about this activity, the participants were not all rowdy youths. Robert Barker was a churchwarden at the time and John Laurence was married and had several children. Finally, in 1600, three men were accused of absence from church and two of working on holidays. John Vale claimed that he went to Brinkley parish church because it was closer to his house (again a feature of the peculiar geography of the area); Edward Carter was never found; Jonas Brice admitted missing church because he was tending sheep. Brice denied killing a sheep on St Bartholomew's Day; Robert Barker admitted carting on St Mark's Day but was dismissed when he demonstrated that it was in "time of need."[240]

In contrast, almost all of Weston Colville's cases centered on Simon Hacksuppe, rector from 1583 to 1605. Hacksuppe, who styled himself "teacher of God's word," was the contentious and divisive sort of puritan hailed by Gifford and scolded by Greenham.[241] Almost immediately after arriving in the parish he was in trouble for not wearing the gown and tippett or the surplice, the last of which he admitted. Worse still, he was constantly involved in bitter rows with members of the parish and took to chiding people during his sermons. He also accused some of his neighbors of railing against him, circumventing the churchwardens to make the accusation. This unedifying feuding continued to his death.[242]

Hacksuppe's influence was probably the headwater of the river of sabbatarian and nonattendance presentments which began to flow out of Weston. In 1591, the wardens were confronted by the court with a list of charges involving five of the leading men of the parish which they were ordered to investigate and present on information from a suspiciously unnamed party. John Woolward was accused of haying on the Sabbath and regularly sleeping during the sermon. Thomas Smith was presented for missing evening prayer, sleeping during the service and working in the pasture on the Sabbath. John Bridge was accused of sleeping during the service. Thomas Vale would not receive communion, and Richard Webbe did not attend church at all.[243]

Aside from the various problems for which Hacksuppe was responsible, either directly or indirectly, very little from Weston Colville came to the court: four fornication presentments and one for a fist fight in the church, which was particularly serious because it was between two of the most prosperous and important men in the village, and was noted to have given great offense to the congregation.[244]

What do the experiences of Carlton cum Willingham and Weston Colville demonstrate about villagers and the courts? First, although the influence of a particularly good rector like Greenham or Leeds might not be apparent in the court records, a catastrophe like Hacksuppe might be. Even then, the damage that Hacksuppe was able to do was severely circumscribed. While he was sowing discord, the village managed its own affairs and did not reap a harvest of litigation except for the suits which Hacksuppe himself caused.

Weston Colville lacked stability in its elite but, unlike any other parish in this study, was assisted by the coherance gained from having been for all practical purposes unimanorial for over a century. Carlton cum Willingham, on the other hand, was spinning out of control. While a divided manorial system had caused villages in the clay uplands to take strong government into their own hands, the effect in a non-nucleated village like Carlton cum Willingham was exactly the opposite. Manorial fragmentation reinforced the scattered settlement pattern of the village, and made it a village with little if any sense of community. This was exacerbated by constant changes in their cast of characters. While southeastern villages were developing dramatic polarities in land distribution, the personnel shifted so that they failed to establish oligarchies or governing castes which reflected that polarization. Litigation and presentments in the ecclesiastical courts bear a direct and clear relationship to the demographic and economic experiences of these two places, as they did in the northwest. While the end results might be very different, it is undeniable that the factors shaping them were the same. The church courts provided a "flexible response" to the pressures and tensions within a village, regardless of their origins.

A final example can be taken from among the villages on the fen edge in northern Cambridgeshire which provide a striking contrast to their southern neighbors.[245] These villages collectively had a different economy, a different demographic experience and, as a consequence, a different way of using the ecclesiastical courts.

Fen-edge village settlements were established with an eye to combining a relatively dry site connected to uplands with easy access to the fens. They are extremely large by county standards. Landbeach, the smallest fen-edge village at 2,500 acres, was still among the largest villages in the county. Its small size was the result of late settlement, having been carved out of Waterbeach some time before 1086. Less than half of its acreage was in open fields. Most of the village was fenland and not arable, but the villagers mastered making a virtue of necessity and used the fens for a variety of resources: fish and water fowl, turves for fuel, reed and sedge for building, willows for traps and weirs, and grasslands for pasturing sheep and cattle. Fen land was common land, which made subsistence easier for landless or near-landless cottagers than in villages dependant on cereal production. The fens also provided work for shepherds and boatmen as well as cheesewrights, fishermen and thatchers.

Protecting these valuable commons required aggressive, vigilant communal government. Fishing and fowling had to be restricted. Safeguards were needed to prevent overdigging of turves. Grasslands had to be guarded against over-stocking, agistment and trespass. The urgency of all of these measures for the economic survival of the villages was undeniable, and court rolls indicate that villagers enforced regulations zealously.

Since the fourteenth century, Cambridge's Corpus Christi College had held the manor of Chamberlains, and the master of the college was Landbeach's rector. The college created small enclosures for sheep and cattle in the fifteenth century, and in the 1540s, Richard Kirby, new lord of Landbeach's other manor, attempted to do the same thing. Kirby, whose father had moved to Landbeach from London, is virtually "the stereotype social villain of the period, the enclosing sheep farmer, newly grown gentleman, destroying his poor tenants' houses and livings, gathering all to himself."[246] While systematically ridding himself of tenants and letting whole blocks of tenements decay, Kirby also began overstocking the commons. The specter of overstocking spurred the residents of Landbeach into action.

When the villagers attempted to avert the approaching crisis with new restrictions in 1548, Kirby ignored them. Seeing the potential for this situation to erupt into Cambridgeshire's version of Ket's rebellion, Matthew Parker (then master of Corpus and rector of Landbeach) intervened, restoring calm by initiating a redefinition of common rights which resulted ultimately in most of the common fen being sheepwalks, divided in four shares. His dramatic inter-vention was prompted by Landbeach's demonstration of the determined spirit of self-regulation typical of all fen-edge communities.

But if the fens provided rich blessings in resources, they were also rich in curses less immediately obvious than the rising waters of the Ouse. This was the most unhealthy part of the shire in which to live. The high death rate in Landbeach had serious consequences for the stability of the community of the village. First, it meant that several families died out after only one or two generations in the village. No family was able to establish itself in the way that families had in the uplands. Second, it meant that fathers frequently died leaving very young children. For stable village government this was a disaster since after the death of a leading member of the community it might be twenty years or more before a son was able to resume his father's place in government. A constant supply of new men, some with very shallow roots in the village, was necessary to fill the offices of both parish and village.

This instability at the upper levels of the village can be demonstrated in several ways. First, it is possible to compare the most prosperous men in the community at several stages in the sixteenth century. Along with subsidy assessments, a detailed survey of landholding prepared during the crisis in 1549 also survives.[247] Comparing the names in these sources reveals a staggering rate of turnover in the village. Thirty-one people were assessed in 1524/5, of whom thirteen were assessed on wages. Only one of these thirteen men occupied land in 1549. While Roger Linton was not assessed later or recorded as holding land, his family continued to live in Landbeach, but none of the Lintons was ever considered prosperous enough to pay the subsidy. For those assessed on lands or goods the survival rate is a bit better but still grim. The Lane family provided five subsidymen in 1524/5, and they were still well represented in 1549, though by different members of the family. The Wards, with two taxed in 1524/5, were also well represented later. Of those assessed for the subsidy, only two others were still in evidence in 1549. Seven families completely disappeared. Taking their places were over a dozen new men and their families. Included were some such as the Gotobeds, Huttons and Thurlows who were prominent for the remainder of the century, but even more of the new families disappeared as quickly as they arrived: of the top thirteen landholders in 1549, only two men and the son of another were taxed in the subsidy two decades later. Hernes, Huttons and Lanes remained in the village, but the other families disappeared without a trace.

Elizabethan subsidy records show a similar pattern. Fifteen men were taxed in 10 Elizabeth, and twenty-five years later, only six of those and the heir of another were taxed again. Seventeen new names appeared on the subsidy roll for 35 Elizabeth, of which fourteen represented families new to the ranks of Landbeach's wealthiest citizens.[248]

This extraordinary turnover is equally pronounced in the ranks of the parish officers. From 1538 to 1544, for which records are particularly complete, eight men from seven families shared the offices of warden and sidesman, usually serving three or four times each during that period. In the 1560s, only one of those families was represented, and six new families had taken their places. Seven more new families produced office-holders in the 1570s, along with two old families which had not previously been represented. Of the eight church-wardens of the 1590s whose names are known, only one had held office before, and six represented families which were demonstrably new to Landbeach.

Even more striking than this fluidity in the ranks of the village governors, is the extent to which the leading members of the community opted out of service in office. Of the thirteen men with the most land in 1549, only four are known to have held parish office. In part this can be explained by their early deaths, since five died by the mid-1550s. Yet even those prosperous families with continuous succession to their properties were noticeably absent from parish office. The two leading families in the parish after mid-century, the Gotobeds and the Huttons, never produced a churchwarden or questman. In the case of the Huttons there is more than a chance that this was because the family was Catholic,[249] but the Gotobeds have no reason for this withdrawal.

Migration into the parish, which provided all of these new families, was well under way by the 1550s as is immediately obvious from the unusually complete parish registers. In 1517, the assessment of "smoke farthings" indicated twenty-six chimneys in Landbeach.[250] In 1524/5, there were thirty-one people taxed, though the high number of wage earners suggests that the number of households was somewhat lower. Since some of the twenty-six chimneys taxed in 1517 must have been in multi-hearth households, it is possible to imagine that there was very little if any growth in Landbeach before 1525, when the population was somewhere between 100 and 125.

Parker's survey book indicates a population rise to over thirty-five households in 1549, suggesting a total increase of at least fifty people. However, the surplus of registered baptisms to burials could not account for an increase of much more than c.25. Thus, immigration must already have been under way, which the evidence of new names would confirm. Some of this migration came from the clay uplands, where population pressure was already stimulating emigration. The prominent and wealthy Huttons, for example, were very likely related to the prosperous Huttons of Dry Drayton.

By 1563, the population of Landbeach was roughly 180.[251] In 1664, there were sixty-four houses in the parish, suggesting a population of 335.[252] This is a modest growth rate, but the parish register indicates a skyrocketing natural growth rate. Without drastic action, Landbeach's population should have topped 400 by 1660, a level which was unsustainable under the best of circumstances.

Dramatic migration had created a Malthusian crisis. The parish was extremely attractive for two different reasons to two different sorts of people. Since wealthy copyholders habitually died without male heirs, the parish provided opportunities for men such as the Gotobeds and Huttons who could afford to buy or lease needed land for their sons. Landbeach, because of the fens, also made subsistence possible on far less land than in other parts of the county. Even a rapid examination of the parish register makes clear the high number of poor landless people who lived a few years and died in Landbeach. While immigration at the upper end of the social scale may have been socially desirable and necessary, migration at the bottom end was a timebomb.

The extreme unhealthiness of the fen-edge was partially a disguised blessing since it prevented a demographic crisis from occurring much earlier. Landbeach and Dry Drayton recorded almost identical numbers of births between 1565 and 1599 (328 and 327), with similar base populations. Dry Drayton, with its more salubrious environment, recorded only 128 burials and was forced to deal with its resultant population pressures rather more urgently. Landbeach, which buried 190 in the same period, was able to absorb more of its own natural growth. Nevertheless, the dramatically-slowed rate by the 1660s indicates that Landbeach either faced a Malthusian check in the early seventeenth century, or reversed its steady influx of migrants.

The effect of the unstable and shifting establishment and population in Landbeach on ecclesiastical court cases is briefly told: By comparison to Landbeach, litigious Carlton was sleepy and Elysian. The church itself provoked very little litigation. Corpus had been very conscientious in providing adequate curates to serve in place of the rector/master. Moreover, in spite of non-residence, the rectors had regularly visited the parish and rooms were kept always ready and waiting in the rectory. After 1569, the parish was served by Henry Clifford who quickly put down deep roots in the parish, where he remained until his death in 1616. His wife bore nine children in Landbeach, and Clifford bought sizable parcels of land for his children, becoming one of the most prosperous members of the community in his own right by the end of the century. Moreover, he did this without any tithe suits against his parishioners.

Before Clifford's advent the church building was spared problems of dilapidation since the college was mindful of its responsibilities. During Clifford's long tenure there were only two minor problems with the building.[253] There were relatively few sabbatarian or attendance problems as well. In addition to recurring presentments of the recusant Roger Hutton, there were seven presentments for nonattendance or for not receiving communion, of which two involved gentlemen.[254] This is unexpected in a parish with a signicant population of transients. Either the parish systematically ignored nonconformity among social marginals, or their attendance was reasonably high. Since sabbatarian presentments were also quite rare,[255] and in the absence of any puritan influence in the parish, it is quite likely that the level of tolerance was fairly high.

What makes Landbeach unique is an exceptionally high number of defamation cases. The six known cases, four of which involve both accused and victim from Landbeach, are indicative of a village with a good deal of unresolved tension.[256] Landbeach is also noteworthy for eight disputed wills and eight matrimonial contract suits.[257] In addition, there is the predictable array of sexual delicts presented, but no cases of antenuptial pregnancy, which suggests that as late as 1600 the parish was not aware of an impending overpopulation crisis.[258] Nor did Landbeach consistently present bastard-bearers. Parents of the three bastards baptized between 1580 and 1583 were not presented.[259]

These cases, along with Landbeach's demonstrated demographic and governmental instability, suggest that this was a village under a great deal of stress in which the mechanisms to resolve conflicts without recourse to the courts had broken down. Under such circumstances, church court intervention was necessary at an unparalled level.

These six case studies have all been a piece of an argument that more present-ments and litigation in the ecclesiastical courts demonstrate neither an efficient justice system nor great popular respect for those courts and their laws. Con-versely, fewer cases imply neither ineffectiveness or disrespect of the presentment system by communities. In the world of sixteenth century litigation, less was more and more was less. More litigation was associated with loosely governed or controlled parishes with weaker internal mechanisms for arbitration and self-regulation, while less litigation implied more control and more effective self-government. Using the number or frequency of cases in the ecclesiastical courts to measure the effectiveness or efficiency of the system shows misunder-standing of the ideals of the people who used those courts. Effectiveness and efficiency were not part of their notions of justice or judgement. In fact, frequent presentments would have been to them the clearest demonstration that their ideal had collapsed.

The presbyterian alternative, vaguely reprehensible to us for its tendency to disrupt communities with its zeal for compelling folk to act in a "godly" way, was in fact far closer to our own twentieth century view of policing and punishing: ideally, all violations of the law should be detected and punished. These were not the goals of sixteenth century villagers who looked to public trial and correction as last recources.

In Edward Evans-Pritchard's classic study of Nuer religion, he writes:

> When a cucumber is used as a sacrificial victim Nuer speak of it as an ox. In doing so they are asserting something rather more than that it takes the place of an ox. They do not of course say that cucumbers are oxen, and in speaking of a particular cucumber as an ox in a sacrificial situation they are only indicating that it may be thought of as an ox in that particular situation; and they act accordingly by performing the sacrificial rites as closely as possible to what happens when the victim is an ox. The resemblance is conceptual not perceptual .... And the expression is asymmetrical, a cucumber is an ox, but an ox is not a cucumber.[260]

The use of a cucumber as symbol for ritual sacrifice in place of an ox may seem quaint and irrational to the modern western mind. Yet in western Chris-tianity, bread and wine serve exactly the same ritual sacrificial role in place of a human sacrifice. Bread and wine would seem as peculiar in that role to the Nuer as the cucumber might to us. Likewise, when we see a legal system four hundred years ago which does not behave in the same way as ours, in which cases are rare and sentences rarer, it is too easy to brand it as quaint, irrational or ineffective. Yet time travellers from sixteenth century Cambridgeshire would feel much the same way about our system – as they might equally have felt, as I have argued, about presbyterian discipline.

Marriage canon law weathered the first seven stormy decades after the Reformation in large measure because the ecclesiastical court system not merely survived but retained the loyalty of English villagers. This is not surprising when it is viewed in the bright light of the legal ideals of the time. The court did for those people what they wished for it to do, and it did not attempt to do more. When it did, a breakdown had occurred.

In the seventeenth century, much would change. Mobility and demographic changes helped contribute to the breakdown of the face-to-face community within which the church courts functioned so well. Moreover, religious nonconformity reached a scale which made nonsense of the sanctions which could be applied by those courts. Finally, religious extremists on both sides who tried to use the courts as a club to bludgeon their visions of godliness through the traditional-minded skulls of their neighbors and countrymen destroyed the influence and effectiveness of those courts. This disruption, combined with dramatic changes in population and its distribution in the seventeenth century, left Humpty-Dumpty's shattered shell unmendable. The English people could restore a king and restore the Church of England, but they were unable to restore the ecclesiastical courts to the position they had once held. That transformation, however, belongs to another century. In the sixteenth century, the English church courts and the English people could still work well together. While this was the case, the courts were insulated from the possibility of drastic reform, and with them the marriage law which they enforced.

Notes

Chapter 1   The European Reformation of Marriage

Please note—References given in these notes appear in full at first instance, and abbreviated thereafter. The note number of first instance is given in brackets, e.g. Spufford, *Contrasting Communities* (n. 116), p. 97.

1   Arthur Conan Doyle, *Memoirs of Sherlock Holmes*, Penguin edn (Harmonds-worth, Middlesex, 1950), p. 28.
2   Sweden alone was like England in this regard, and for reasons similar to some of those applicable to England: Michael Roberts, *The Early Vasas: A History of Sweden, 1523–1611* (Cambridge, 1968), esp. pp. 59–75, 107–24, 167–81.
3   *A Sermon on the Estate of Marriage, 1519*, ed. James Atkinson, in *LW*, vol. 44, pp. 7–14.
4   *The Babylonian Captivity of the Church*, in Martin Luther, *Three Treatises* (Philadelphia, 1970), pp. 220–4.
5   On this topic generally see Steven Ozment, *The Age of Reform 1250–1550* (New Haven, 1980), pp. 381–96, and *When Fathers Ruled: Family Life in Reformation Europe* (Cambridge, Mass., 1983), pp. 3–9.
6   Ronald J. Sider, *Andreas Bodenstein von Karlstadt* (Leiden, 1974), pp. 160–1.
7   G.R. Potter, *Zwingli* (Cambridge, 1976), pp. 79–80.
8   E.H. Dunkley, *The Reformation in Denmark* (London, 1948), pp. 26, 50; Grethe Jacobsen, "Women, marriage, and magisterial reformation: The case of Malmo, Denmark", *Pietas et Societas*, ed. Kyle C. Sessions and Phillip N. Bebb, *Sixteenth Century Essays and Studies* 4 (Kirksville, Missouri, 1984), pp. 62–7.
9   Martin Bucer was married before 1523 when he arrived in Strasbourg, but he was a refugee and excommunicated at that time, not a beneficed clergyman like Firn. See Miriam U. Chrisman, *Strasbourg and the Reformation* (New Haven, 1967), pp. 131–8; idem, "Women and the Reformation in Strasbourg, 1490–1530," *Archiv für Reformationsgeschichte* 63 (1972), 143–67; James Kittelson, *Wolfgang Capito* (Leiden, 1975), pp. 108–9; William S.

Stafford, *Domesticating the Clergy: The Inception of the Reformation in Strasbourg 1522–1524* (Missoula, Montana, 1976), pp. 22–6, 151–9, 210–18.

10 Miriam U. Chrisman, *Lay Culture Learned Culture 1480–1599* (New Haven, 1982), pp. 159–60. Chrisman lists published works from Strasbourg defending clergy marriage in *Bibliography of Strasbourg Imprints 1480–1599* (New Haven, 1982), section P3.7.

11 François Wendel, *Le Mariage à Strasbourg à l'Époque de la Réforme, 1520–1692* (Strasbourg, 1928), pp. 22–3. See also Jean Leclercq, *Monks on Marriage: A Twelfth Century View* (New York, 1982), esp. pp. 27–38.

12 Lorna Jane Abray, *The People's Reformation: Magistrates, Clergy, and Commons in Strasbourg, 1500–1598* (Ithaca, 1985), pp. 216–17.

13 *To the Christian Nobility of the German Nation*, in *Three Treatises* (n. 4), pp. 95–6.

14 Scott Hendrix, *Luther and the Papacy* (Philadelphia, 1981), pp. 117–18.

15 Stafford, *Domesticating the Clergy* (n. 9), pp. 9–11.

16 *The Estate of Marriage*, ed. Walther I. Brandt, in *LW*, vol. 45, p. 17.

17 *Babylonian Captivity* (n. 4), p. 226.

18 *Estate of Marriage* (n. 16), pp. 22–30; *Babylonian Captivity* (n. 4), pp. 224–36. See Steven Ozment, "Luther and the Family," *Harvard Library Bulletin* 32 (1984), 36–53; idem, *Protestants: The Birth of a Revolution* (New York, 1992), pp. 151–68.

19 Ozment, *When Fathers Ruled* (n. 5), pp. 27–9.

20 Lyndal Roper, " 'Going to Church and Street': Weddings in Reformation Augsburg," *Past and Present* 106 (1985), p. 96; idem, *The Holy Household* (Oxford, 1989), chap. 4.

21 Detailed studies of the marriage laws after the Reformation are: Hartweg Dieterich, *Das Protestantische Eherecht in Deutschland bis zur Mitte des 17. Jahrhundert* (Munich, 1970); Judith Harvey, "The influence of the Reformation on Nuremberg marriage laws, 1520–1535," The Ohio State University Ph.D., 1972; Walther Köhler, *Zürcher Ehegericht und Genfer Konsistorium*, 2 vols (Leipzig, 1932, 1942); Adrian Staehelin, *Die Einführung der Ehescheidung in Basel zur Zeit der Reformation* (Basel, 1957); Wendel, *Le Mariage à Strasbourg* (n. 11). See summaries in Ozment, *When Fathers Ruled* (n. 9), chap. 1, and Thomas Max Safley, *Let No Man Put Asunder. The Control of Marriage in the German Southwest: A Comparative Study, 1550–1600, Sixteenth Century Essays and Studies* 2 (Kirksville, Missouri, 1984), chap. 2.

22 Thomas Robisheaux, *Rural Society and the Search for Order in Early Modern Germany* (Cambridge, 1989), chap. 4, esp. pp. 102–3.

23 Protestants were not alone in grappling with the wishes of the laity in this regard. In France, pressure was so intense that in 1556 the king approved a law giving fathers the right to disinherit their children if they married

without consent. The aristocracy had wanted a law that went further, but Henri II refused to go against church law, leaving the matter to the Council of Trent. Since Trent also resisted French pressure and did not require parental consent for valid marriages, French law became stricter. The edict of Blois (1579) established punishments for priests who officiated at marriages without parental consent, and decreed the death penalty for inducing a minor to marry without consent. See Barbara Diefendorf, *Paris City Councillors in the Sixteenth Century: The Politics of Patrimony* (Princeton, 1983), pp. 156–65. Rabelais had Gargantua deliver to Pantagruel a blistering denunciation of the law of "molecatchers" which permitted children to marry without the consent of their parents: François Rabelais, *The Histories of Gargantua and Pantagruel*, trans. J.M. Cohen (Harmondsworth, Middlesex, 1955), pp. 417–21.

24 For examples see Gerald Strauss, ed. *Manifestations of Discontent in Germany on the Eve of the Reformation* (Bloomington, Indiana, 1971).

25 Miriam U. Chrisman, "Lay response to the Protestant Reformation in Germany, 1520–1528," *Reformation Principle and Practice*, ed. Peter Newman Brooks (London, 1980), p. 39.

26 *Table Talk*, ed. Theodore G. Tappert, *LW*, vol. 54, p. 194; see pp. 305, 363.

27 J. Wayne Baker, "Church and magistracy, 1532–1535: Heinrich Bullinger, Leo Jud, and Casper Schwenckfeld," unpublished Sixteenth Century Studies Conference paper, October 1986, p. 2. (Paper provided by the author.) For views of Johannes Brenz, see J.M. Estes, *Christian Magistrate and State Church* (Toronto, 1982).

28 Robert Kingdon, "The control of morals in Calvin's Geneva," *The Social History of the Reformation*, ed. Lawrence P. Buck and Jonathan W. Zophy (Columbus, Ohio, 1972), 1–14; E. William Monter, "The Consistory of Geneva, 1559–1569," *Bibliotheque d'Humanisme et Renaissance* 38 (1976), 467–84.

29 Ozment, *When Fathers Ruled* (n. 5), p. 30.

Chapter 2   Church, Crown, Lordship and Marriage in Medieval England

1 R.H. Helmholz, *Marriage Litigation in Medieval England* (Cambridge, 1974), p. 3.

2 Georges Duby has described what he views as two competing models of marriage, the royal secular and the ecclesiastical, during the period before matrimonial jurisdiction was taken over by the court: *Medieval Marriage: Two Models from Twelfth-Century France*, trans. Elborg Forster (Baltimore, 1978); *The Knight, the Lady and the Priest: The Making of Modern Marriage*

in Medieval France, trans. Barbara Bray (New York, 1983). I am concerned with the period *after* the "takeover," when I believe that what took place was not the simple victory of one model over another, but eventually (at least in England) the forging of a system which harmonized both models. See also Christopher Brooke, *The Medieval Idea of Marriage* (Oxford, 1989), chap. 6.

3   See *MER*, pp. 17–31.

4   On the Anglo-Saxon church and its relations with both papacy and royal government, see Margaret Deanesly, "The Anglo-Saxon church and the papacy," *The English Church and the Papacy in the Middle Ages*, ed. C.H. Lawrence (New York, 1965), pp. 29–62, and Frank Barlow, *The English Church, 1000–1066* (London, 1963). For the texts, see *English Historical Documents, I: c.500–1042*, ed. Dorothy Whitelock (London, 1955) pp. 746, 810, 813; *The Laws of the Kings of England from Edmund to Henry I*, ed. A.J. Robertson (Cambridge, 1925), pp. 95, 163. Resistance may have followed from the peculiar Anglo-Saxon kinship structure, which did not give specific terms for various sorts of cousins. Anglo-Saxons were not concerned to make the kinds of distinctions among lateral relations which were necessary to avoid violations of church law: Lorraine Lancaster, "Kinship in Anglo-Saxon society," *British Journal of Sociology* 9 (1958), 230–50; David Herlihy, *Medieval Households* (Cambridge, Mass., 1985), pp. 29–55.

5   Robertson, *Laws* (n. 4), pp. 85, 211, 213.

6   Deanesly, "Anglo-Saxon church (n. 4)," pp. 57–62; D.C. Douglas, *William the Conqueror* (Berkeley, 1964), pp. 105–32, 187–8, 317–45, and Charles Duggan, "From the Conquest to the death of John," *English Church*, ed. Lawrence (n. 4), pp. 65–115. See also Z.N. Brooke, *The English Church and the Papacy* (Oxford, 1931); H.G. Richardson and G.O. Sayles, *The Governance of Mediaeval England from the Conquest to Magna Carta* (Edinburgh, 1963), pp. 285–320; Margaret Gibson, *Lanfranc of Bec* (Oxford, 1978); *The Letters of Lanfranc Archbishop of Canterbury*, ed. and trans. Helen Clover and Margaret Gibson (Oxford, 1979).

7   *English Historical Documents, II: 1042–1189*, ed. D.C. Douglas and G.W. Greenaway (London, 1953), p. 647. See Colin Morris, "William I and the church courts," *English Historical Review* 82 (1967), 449–63. This edict was designed to prevent episcopal jurisdiction from being usurped by Hundred courts; the development of a separate court as an institution was completed in the next century, the crucial period being from 1135 to 1200: *Select Cases from the Ecclesiastical Courts of the Province of Canterbury c.1200–1301*, ed. Norma Adams and Charles Donahue, Selden Society 95 (1981), shows that evidence from the late years of archbishop Hubert Walter (d. 1205) indicates an informal court, with incomplete use of the latest procedures, but well on the way to being the formal court in place by the 1270s.

8   W.L. Warren, *Henry II* (Berkeley, 1973), p. 404.

9   Uta-Renate Blumenthal, *The Investiture Controversy: Church and Monarchy from the Ninth to the Twelfth Century* (Philadelphia, 1988); Norman Cantor, *Church, Kingship, and Lay Investiture in England 1089–1135* (Princeton, 1958); A. Fliche, *La Reforme Gregorienne* (Paris, 1946); Gerd Tellenbach, *Church, State and Christian Society at the Time of the Investiture Contest*, trans. R.F. Bennett (Oxford, 1948); Brian Tierney, *The Crisis of Church and State 1050–1300* (Englewood Cliffs, NJ, 1964); Walter Ullmann, *The Growth of Papal Government in the Middle Ages* (London, 1955).

10 Tierney, *Crisis* (n. 9), p. 87.

11 Although Gregory VII admitted that William did not always behave as he might wish, the king's general concern for peace, justice and the church's good, and his support for such papal pet causes as clerical celibacy, moved the pope to call William a "jewel among princes" in 1080: Douglas, *William the Conqueror* (n. 6), p. 341.

12 On the church under William II and Anselm, see Frank Barlow, *William Rufus* (Berkeley, 1983); Brooke, *English Church* (n. 6), chap. 10; Cantor, *Church, Kingship and Lay Investiture* (n. 9), pp. 42–130; Emma Mason, "William Rufus: myth and reality," *Journal of Medieval History* 3 (1977), 1–20; A.L. Poole, *From Domesday Book to Magna Carta 1087–1216* (Oxford, 1955), pp. 100–4, 172–7; R.W. Southern, *St. Anselm and His Biographer* (Cambridge, 1966), pp. 150–63; Sally Vaughn, "St. Anselm of Canterbury: the philosopher-saint as politician," *Journal of Medieval History* 1 (1975), 279–306 and *Anselm of Bec and Robert of Meulan: The Innocence of the Dove and the Wisdom of the Serpent* (Berkeley, 1987).

13 For the church under Henry I, see Martin Brett, *The English Church under Henry I* (Oxford, 1975); Cantor, *Church, Kingship and Lay Investiture* (n. 9), pp. 131–320.

14 *Leges Henrici Primi*, ed. and trans. L.J. Downer (Oxford, 1972).

15 Ibid., cap. 7.

16 Ibid., cap. 11, esp. § 2–5, 10, 13.

17 Brett, *English Church under Henry I* (n. 13), pp. 148–50.

18 Cantor, *Church, Kingship and Lay Investiture* (n. 9), p. 320.

19 Brett, *English Church under Henry I* (n. 13), p. 51.

20 Ibid., pp. 53–5.

21 Ibid., p. 62.

22 Warren, *Henry II* (n. 8), pp. 409–11.

23 For Stephen, see R.H.C. Davis, *King Stephen* (3d edn., London, 1990). See also Brooke, *English Church* (n. 6), chap. 12; H.A. Cronne, *The Reign of King Stephen 1135–54: Anarchy in England* (London, 1970), chap. 4; Edward J. Kealey, *Roger of Salisbury* (Berkeley, 1972); Avrom Saltman, *Theobald Archbishop of Canterbury* (London, 1956); L. Voss, *Heinrich von Blois Bischof von Winchester (1129–1171)* (Berlin, 1932).

24 Davis, *King Stephen* (n. 23), pp. 17-18.

25 Jane Sayers, *Papal Judges Delegate in the Province of Canterbury 1198-1254* (Oxford, 1971), p. 4; Duggan (n. 6), "From the Conquest," p. 85. Second-hand evidence in the course of a suit (1158-63) between Richard Anstey and Mabel de Francheville to determine the rightful heir of William de Sackville suggests that Innocent II wrote to Henry of Winchester in 1139 charging him with the divorce case pending between William de Sackville and Adelicia de Vere: C.R. Cheney, *From Becket to Langton: English Church Government 1170-1213* (Manchester, 1956), pp. 54-5.

26 Tierney, *Church and State* (n. 9), pp. 53-73.

27 Ibid., p. 97; Cheney, *From Becket to Langton* (n. 25), pp. 42-3.

28 The decretal as defined by Stephen of Tournai (mid 12th-century) was "a papal rescript sent to any bishop or ecclesiastical judge on some doubtful point of law when the Roman Church had been consulted." Such letters were considered absolutely authoratative *"tanquam ipsius divini Petri voce firmatae"* unless in conflict with church teaching: Dist. XIX, c. 2; Dist. XIX, dict. post c. 7. For a survey of the development of church law in the years before Gregory VII: *The New Catholic Encyclopedia*, vol. 3, pp. 34-45.

29 W.L. Warren, *Henry II* (n. 8), p. 418.

30 See Stephan Kuttner, *Harmony from Dissonance: An Interpretation of Medieval Canon Law* (Latrobe, PA, 1960), and *New Catholic Encyclopedia*, vol. 6, pp. 706-9.

31 Stanley Chodorow, *Christian Political Theory and Church Politics in the Mid-Twelfth Century* (Berkeley, 1972) argues that this was a deliberate policy on Gratian's part. While not always convincing, the book is an excellent survey of the material. See review by Robert L. Benson in *Speculum* 50 (1975), 97-106.

32 Sayers, *Papal Judges Delegate* (n. 25), pp. 1-41.

33 Cheney, *From Becket to Langton* (n. 25), pp. 44-5.

34 Stephan Kuttner and Eleanor Rathbone, "Anglo-Norman canonists of the twelfth century," *Traditio* 7 (1949-51), 279-358; Jane Sayers, *Papal Government and England During the Pontificate of Honorius III (1216-1227)* (Cambridge, 1984). See *New Catholic Encyclopedia*, vol. 12, p. 31, sub *Quinque Compilationes Antiquae*.

35 In 1582, the *Corpus Iuris Canonici* was formed by joining the *Decretals* with Gratian's *Decretum*, the *Liber Sextus* of Boniface VIII (1298), and the *Clementinae* of John XXII (1317).

36 *Report of the Commissioners into the Constitution and Working of the Ecclesiastical Courts* (n.p., 1883), vol. I, p. xviii.

37 F.W. Maitland, *Roman Canon Law in the Church of England* (London, 1898), esp. chap. 2. C.R. Cheney has argued most persuasively that the native English legislation existed *"de corrigendis excessibus et moribus reformandis,"* as

necessary for particular needs and interests of the time and place: "Legislation of the Medieval English Church," *English Historical Review* 50 (1935), 193–224, 385–417; idem, *Medieval Texts and Studies* (Oxford, 1973), pp. 138–57, 185–202; M.M. Sheehan, "Marriage theory and practice in the conciliar legislation and diocesan statutes of medieval England," *Mediaeval Studies* 40 (1978), 408–60.

38 For the debate from Stubbs and Maitland to more recent times, see *MER*, pp. 37–54; Mary Cheney, "The Compromise of Avranches of 1172 and the spread of canon law in England," *English Historical Review* 56 (1941), 177–97; idem, *Roger, Bishop of Worcester 1164–1179* (Cambridge, 1980); Charles Duggan, "The Becket Dispute and the criminous clerks," *Bulletin of the Institute of Historical Research* 35 (1962), 1–28; Adrian Morey, *Bartholomew of Exeter* (Cambridge, 1937). English judges and lawyers were exceptionally sensitive to papal authority and wrote often for help filling gaps in the law. A staggering number of private collections of decretal letters were made in England, many of which are responsible for the survival of decretals which would otherwise have been lost: *Papal Decretals relating to the Diocese of Lincoln in the Twelfth Century*, eds Walther Holtzmann and Eric Kemp, Lincoln Record Society 47 (1954); Charles Duggan, *Twelfth-Century Decretal Collections and their Importance in English History* (London, 1963); Kuttner and Rathbone, "Anglo-Norman canonists (n. 34)."

39 J.W. Gray, "Canon law in England: some reflections on the Stubbs-Maitland controversy," *Studies in Church History* 3 (1966), 48–68, calls attention to the recurring problem of pluralists as an example.

40 Charles Donahue, Jr., "Proof by witnesses in the church courts of medieval England: An imperfect reception of the learned law," *On the Laws and Customs of England: Essays in Honor of Samuel E. Thorne*, ed. Morris S. Arnold, et al. (Chapel Hill, 1981), 127–58.

41 "Roman canon law in the medieval English church: Stubbs vs. Maitland re-examined after 75 years in the light of some records from the church courts," *Michigan Law Review* 72 (1974), 647–716, esp. pp. 674–8, 684–99.

42 Ibid., p. 706.

43 See esp. Warren, *Henry II*; also Frank Barlow, *Thomas Becket* (Berkeley, 1986); Brooke, *English Church* (n. 6), chap. 9; Cheney, *Roger of Worcester*, pp. 17–55; David Knowles, *The Episcopal Colleagues of Archbishop Thomas Becket* (Cambridge, 1951); idem, *Thomas Becket* (Stanford, 1971); Morey, *Bartholomew of Exeter* (n. 38); Morey and C.N.L. Brooke, *Gilbert Foliot and his Letters* (Cambridge, 1965).

44 See, e.g., *The Chronicle of Battle Abbey*, ed. and trans. Eleanor Searle (Oxford, 1980); idem, "Battle Abbey and exemption: the forged charters," *English Historical Review* 83 (1968), 449–80.

45 The famous case of *Anstey* v. *Francheville* is a clear example to the contrary. In 1158, Richard of Anstey sued in the king's court to prove his claim as heir of his uncle William of Sackville, claiming that Mabel of Francheville was illegitimate and incapable of inheriting. Henry's court referred the case to the church for assistance. Richard was unable to reach a satisfactory solution in the archbishop's court and, with Henry's approval, appealed to Rome which referred the case back to judges delegate in April 1161. The case was finally settled in Richard's favor in December 1162 and the desired information relayed to the royal court. While Henry was consulted for permission as a matter of prudence, he did not object; in fact, his courts created the situation which made the Roman appeal necessary: Cheney, *From Becket to Langton* (n. 25), pp. 54–8; P.M. Barnes, "The Anstey case," *Medieval Miscellany for Doris Mary Stenton*, ed. P.M. Barnes and C.F. Slade, Pipe Roll Society new ser., vol. 36 (1960), 1–24. For other English appeals see: Cheney, *From Becket to Langton* (n. 25), pp. 58–9; C.N.L. Brooke, "Marriage and society in the central Middle Ages," *Marriage and Society: Studies in the Social History of Marriage*, ed. R.B. Outhwaite (London, 1981), pp. 31–2.

46 Warren, *Henry II* (n. 8), pp. 427–46.

47 *English Historical Documents* (n. 7), vol. 2, pp. 718–22.

48 Warren, *Henry II* (n. 8), pp. 518ff.

49 J.W. Gray, "The *ius praesentandi* in England from the Constitutions of Clarendon to Bracton," *English Historical Review* 67 (1952), 481–509; Cheney, *From Becket to Langton* (n. 25), pp. 110–17. Alexander's ban is *Quanto te* (X.2.1.3). For the text of the writ of prohibition, see *The Treatise on the Laws and Customs of the Realm of England Commonly Called Glanvill*, ed. G.D.G. Hall (London, 1965), §IV.14.

50 See Norma Adams, "The writ of prohibition to court christian," *Minnesota Law Review* 20 (1936), 272–93; G. Flahiff, "The use of prohibitions by clerics against ecclesiastical courts in England," *Mediaeval Studies* 3 (1941), 101–16; idem, "The writ of prohibition to court christian in the thirteenth century," ibid., 6 (1944), 261–313 and 7 (1945), 229–90; Richard Helmholz, "The writ of prohibition to court christian before 1500," ibid., 43 (1981), 297–314; idem, "Writs of prohibition and ecclesiastical sanctions in the English courts christian," *Minnesota Law Review* 60 (1976), 1011–33.

51 Donahue estimates that 40% of cases heard in the fourteenth century York consistory could have been stopped and were not. If both parties were satisfied to have the case heard in the ecclesiastical court, it would proceed; the writ could only be used if one of the parties requested it: "Roman canon law (n. 41)," pp. 546–8.

52 Warren, *Henry II* (n. 8), pp. 548–9.

53 I am not convinced by the argument that the writ *Circumspecte agatis* (1286)

was the resolution of an attack by Edward I and his father on church jurisdiction, which they intended to reduce to matrimonial and testamentary matters only: David Millon, *"Circumspecte Agatis* revisited," *Law and History Review* 2 (1984), 105–23. I also find Henry III an unlikely character to attack the liberties of the church, since he owed his throne to the papacy and demonstrated his devotion to the church by plunging into financial and political disaster in support of it. Although the rebel barons were associated in a general way with many leading churchmen, there is no evidence that those churchmen traded their support for promises to remedy specific grievances. The barons made only general promises to reform the church, and while an argument from silence should be viewed with caution, it is improbable that the higher clergy would not take advantage of such a situation to extract specific concessions if the king were poaching in their property: F.M. Powicke, *King Henry III and the Lord Edward* (Oxford, 1947), pp. 259–89, 357, 371–2; *Documents of the Baronial Movement of Reform and Rebellion 1258–1267*, ed. R.E. Treharne and I.J. Sanders (Oxford, 1973), pp. 107, 321; W.E. Lunt, *Financial Relations of the Papacy with England to 1327* (Cambridge, Mass., 1939).

54 W.R. Jones, "Relations of the two jurisdictions: Conflict and cooperation in England during the thirteenth and fourteenth centuries," *Studies in Medieval and Renaissance History* 7 (1970), pp. 106–15, 132–8, discusses some new writs employed by the royal courts. These writs were virtually never used, from which Jones concludes that church courts had surrendered, making the use of the writs unnecessary. This conclusion was made without looking at church court records, however, and the research of Helmholz and Donahue (cited above) suggests that Jones's argument is probably untrue.

55 Jones, "Relations," pp. 209–10, stresses that in a stare-down the church courts would always have to blink first, which is convincing, in spite of the suggestion by Helmholz in *Canon Law and Common Law* (London, 1983) that the church had the means to fight back.

56 For example, *Select Cases from Canterbury* (n. 7), A.1, D.17.

57 Customary law varied: on the manor of Wakefield, children born after trothplight but before marriage were legitimate which reinforced the need to publicize a betrothal: *Borough Customs*, ed. Mary Bateson, Selden Society, vol. 21 (1906), pp. 135–6.

58 X.4.17.7.

59 *BNB*, pp. 104–7.

60 F.D. Logan, *Excommunication and the Secular Arm in Medieval England* (Toronto, 1968).

61 J.H. Denton, *Robert Winchelsey and the Crown 1294–1313* (Cambridge, 1980), points out that the conflict between church and state at the end of

the century was over taxation, and not jurisdiction. That set the pattern for later church-state conflicts: idem, "Canterbury episcopal appointments: the case of Walter Reynolds," *Journal of Medieval History* 1 (1975), 317–28 and "Walter Reynolds and ecclesiastical politics, 1313–1316," *Church and Government in the Middle Ages*, ed. C.N.L. Brooke, et al. (Cambridge, 1976), pp. 247–74. See also J. Robert Wright, *The Church and the English Crown 1305–1334* (Toronto, 1980). The Statutes of Provisors and Praemunire are placed in their correct context in May McKisack, *The Fourteenth Century 1307–1399* (Oxford, 1959), pp. 272–83.

62   Duby, *Knight, Lady and Priest* (n. 2), pp. 29, 33–4.

63   Ibid., p. 153.

64   Ibid., p. 120.

65   Ibid., chaps 2–3, esp. pp. 65–74.

66   Cheney, *From Becket to Langton* (n. 25), p. 54.

67   The marriage sections of the *Corpus Iuris Canonici* are *Causae* 27–36 of the *Pars secunda* of Gratian, and Book IV of the *Decretals*. The absence of gaps is highlighted by the local legislation which touched on marriage, discussed by Sheehan, "Marriage Theory and Practice (n. 37)." The legislation can be found in *Councils and Synods with other documents relating to the English Church, II. AD 1205–1313*, ed. F.M. Powicke and C.R. Cheney (Oxford, 1964), with some material of interest in *Councils and Synods, I*, ed. Dorothy Whitelock, Martin Brett, and C.N.L. Brooke (Oxford, 1981).

68   The following discussion is drawn from the texts themselves, emphasizing those relevant to the practice of the English courts. A fuller discussion of the subject can be found in J. Dauvillier, *Le Mariage dans le droit Classique de l'Eglise* (Paris, 1933) and A. Esmein, *Le Mariage en Droit Canonique*, 2 vols, (Paris, 1891). The historical development is treated in James A. Brundage, *Law, Sex, and Christian Society in Medieval Europe* (Chicago, 1987).

69   For example, "*Hic accipio te Elizabet in uxorem meam fidelem coniugatam, tenendam et habendam usque ad finem vite mee et ad hoc do tibi fidem meam*": BI, CP.E.18 (quoted in Helmholz, *Matrimonial Litigation* (n. 1), p. 194). The deaf and mute were allowed to demonstrate consent with a sign: X.4.1.25.

70   "*Matrimonio solo consensu contrahitur*": X.4.1.1.

71   "*{U}bi non est consensus utriusque non est coniugium*": C.30 q.2 c.1.

72   C.30 q.5 c.1. Gratian also cited Pope Hormisdas ("*Nullius fidelis, cuiuscumque condicionis sit, occulte nuptias faciat, sed benedictione accepta a sacerdote publice nubat in Domino.*") and the Council of Arles ("*Nullum sine dote fiat coniugium; iuxta possibilitatem fiat dos nec sine publicis nuptiis quisquam nubere vel uxorem ducere presumat.*") to the same effect: C.30 q.5 cc.2, 6.

73   C.30 q.5 c.3 and dictum post c.6.

74   "*Coniugia que clam contrahuntur, non negantur esse coniugia, nec iubenter dissolvi si utriusque confessione probari poterunt*": C.30 q.5 dictum post c.9.

75 *"Sciendum est quod coniugium desponsatione initiatur, commixtione perficitur."*:
   C.27 q.2 dictum ad c.34.

76 X.4.3.1.

77 X.4.3.2.

78 This is made clear by the number of cases in which marriage banns were
   blocked because of an alleged prior contract: see *Registrum Hamonis Hethe,
   Diocesis Roffensis A.D. 1319–1352*, vol. 2, ed. Charles Johnson, Canterbury
   and York Society, vol. 49 (1948), pp. 979–80, 984, 990–1, 1016, 1031,
   1039.

79 *CPPR*, vol. 3, p. 456; vol. 4, p. 441.

80 M.M. Sheehan, "Choice of marriage partner in the Middle Ages: Development and mode of application of a theory of marriage," *Studies in Medieval
   and Renaissance History*, new ser. 1 (1978), p. 23.

81 X.4.3.3.

82 H.A. Kelly, *Love and Marriage in the Age of Chaucer* (Ithaca, N.Y., 1975),
   p. 169; M.M. Sheehan, "The formation and stability of marriage in fourteenth-century England: Evidence of an Ely Register," *Mediaeval Studies* 33
   (1971), 228–63.

83 In *Councils and Synods II* (n. 67), see Salisbury I (1217X19) c. 85; Durham
   Peculiars (c.1228) c. 52; *Constitutiones Cuiusdam Episcopi* (1225–30) c. 59;
   Lincoln (1239?) c. 42; Norwich (1240X43) c. 39; Chichester I (1245–52)
   cc. 27–8.

84 Kelly, *Love and Marriage* (n. 82), p. 172.

85 Kelly, *Love and Marriage* (n. 82), pp. 170–1.

86 Helmholz, *Marriage Litigation* (n. 1), pp. 29–30. Ignorance of the law was
   not completely eliminated: in *CPPR*, vol. 6, p. 135, the pope absolved a
   priest from *ipso facto* excommunication incurred under the canon in 1408
   because of ignorance; see ibid., vol. 8, p. 56. Archbishop Bourchier was
   trying to improve the situation in 1455–60 by increasing the standards of
   proof in the courts and tightening up the requirement for banns: *Registrum
   Thome Bourgchier*, ed. F.R.H. DuBoulay, Canterbury and York Society,
   vol. 54 (1957), pp. 20–5, 92.

87 Duby, *Knight, Lady and Priest* (n. 2), pp. 171, 182. Gratian had attempted
   to extricate himself from the difficulty by saying that Mary and Joseph had
   "marital affection" but this was rejected by canonists as too difficult to
   prove. See John Noonan, "Marital affection in the canonists," *Studia Gratiana: Collectanea Stephan Kuttner* 12 (1967), 489–509.

88 *Liber IV Sententiarum*, book IV, dist. 26–36.

89 X.4.1.30. In *Reg. Hethe* a couple admitted fornication; he admitted a
   contract *de futuro*; she had him declared her husband as a result: vol. 2,
   p. 950.

90 X.4.1.31.

91 X.4.1.10 & 17, discussed in Anne Lefebvre-Teillard, "*Ad matrimonium contrahere compellitur*," *Revue de Droit Canonique* 28 (1978), 210–17.

92 Helmholz, *Marriage Litigation* (n. 1), pp. 35–6.

93 F. Pollock and F.W. Maitland, *The History of English Law*, (2nd edn, Cambridge, 1968) vol. 2, pp. 368–9.

94 Helmholz, *Marriage Litigation* (n. 1), pp. 36–7. Witnesses were not always clear on the words used: in *Select Cases from Canterbury* (n. 7) C. 6 (1271–2) three witnesses testified to a contract. Two claimed the words used were "*habebo te*" and one "*accipio te.*" The court ruled against the contract because of this confusion.

95 Helmholz, *Marriage Litigation* (n. 1), pp. 47–57. See X.4.5.

96 P.E. Corbett, *The Roman Law of Marriage* (Oxford, 1930), pp. 24–53; Susan Treggiari, *Roman Marriage: Iusti Coniuges from the Time of Cicero to the Time of Ulpian* (Oxford, 1991).

97 Helmholz, *Marriage Litigation* (n. 1), pp. 57–66, 76–7; Sheehan, "Ely Register (n. 82)," pp. 251–3. *Select Cases from Canterbury* (n. 7) C.3, D.1; *Reg. Hethe*, vol. 1, pp. 457–8; vol. 2, pp. 924–5, 937–8, 946–7, 956, 985, 993, 998–9.

98 X.4.14. Dispensations before marriage were usually based only on exceptional circumstances such as settling feuds, or cementing peace between nations. Retroactive dispensations were given to avoid the scandal of a divorce, particularly when there were children, or to avoid family violence. If a couple married knowing of a kinship impediment and sought a dispensation, they were also given a penance and first made to separate.

99 Helmholz, *Marriage Litigation* (n. 1), pp. 98–9; X.4.2; cf. X.4.1.25. Divorces granted on the grounds of contract *infra annos nubiles* were often also on grounds of force by parents: *CPPR*, vol. 3, p. 164; vol. 13, pp. 503–4; *The Register of Roger Martival, Bishop of Salisbury 1315–1330*, ed. K. Edwards, C.R. Elrington and D.M. Owen, Canterbury and York Society, vols 55–59, 68 (1959–75), vol. 68, pp. 24–31; *Act Book of the Ecclesiastical Court of Whalley 1510–1538*, ed. Alice M. Cook, Chetham Society, new ser. vol. 44 (1901), no. 12.

100 Helmholz, *Marriage Litigation* (n. 1), pp. 87–90; X.4.15. See Corbett, *Roman Law* (n. 96), p. 53; P.A. D'Avack, "*Il problema dell'Impotenza nel matrimonio canonico*," *Revue de Droit Canonique* 28 (1978), 123–9; Jacqueline Murray, "On the origins and role of 'wise women' in causes for annulment on the grounds of male impotence," *Journal of Medieval History* 16 (1990), 235–49. See *CPPR*, vol. 13, pp. 487–8.

101 Genuine fear of disinheritance was acceptable as well.

102 Helmholz, *Marriage Litigation* (n. 1), pp. 90–4; C.31 q.2; John Noonan, "Power to choose," *Viator* 4 (1973), 419–34. See *CPPR*, vol. 5, pp. 532–3; vol. 8, p. 519; vol. 9, pp. 179–180; vol. 12, p. 435; vol. 13, pp. 627, 797; vol. 15, no. 762, no. 819; *Whalley Act Book* (n. 99), no. 5.

103 Helmholz, *Marriage Litigation* (n. 1), pp. 94–8; X.4.7; *CPPR*, vol. 12, p. 715; vol. 13, p. 237.

104 This was not an idle concern. In *CPPR*, vol. 8, p. 601, a couple married secretly because of unequal condition and fear of their families' reactions. In *The Register of Edmund Lacy, Bishop of Exeter, 1420–1455*, ed. G.R. Dunstan, Canterbury and York Society, vols 60–63, 66 (1963–1972), vol. 62, pp. 217, 219–20, the abbot of Tavistock was charged with wastage on Werrington manor on the grounds that he had manumitted too many female villeins, leaving the men without an adequate supply of potential brides.

105 Helmholz, *Marriage Litigation* (n. 1), p. 100.

106 C.L. Powell, *English Domestic Relations* (New York, 1917), p. 9.

107 In addition to work of Helmholz, Sheehan, et al. for England, Anne Lefebvre-Teillard has surveyed French medieval divorces and concludes ("*Regle et realite: Les nullites de mariage a la fin du moyen age,*" *Revue de Droit Canonique* 32 [1982], 145–55) that the three causes for actual suits were, in order of importance, "self-divorce" (i.e., pre-contract and bigamy), impotence, and consanguinity.

108 X.4.19.2, 5 and 7. *Saevitia* does not appear in the canons but was a later development. Helmholz, *Marriage Litigation* (n. 1), pp. 100–1.

109 J. Goody, *The Development of the Family and Marriage in Europe* (Cambridge, 1983).

110 Duby, *Medieval Marriage* (n. 2), p. 3.

111 Charles Donahue, Jr., "The policy of Alexander the Third's consent theory of marriage," in *Proceedings of the Fourth International Congress of Medieval Canon Law*, ed. Stephan Kuttner (Monumenta Iuris Canonici, C:5, 1976), 251–81, esp. pp. 251–3, 275; idem, "The canon law on the formation of marriage and social practice in the later Middle Ages," *Journal of Family History* 8 (1983), 144–158; Michael M. Sheehan, "Choice (n. 80)," pp. 12–16; idem. "Theory and practice: Marriage of the unfree and the poor in medieval society," *Medieval Studies* 50 (1988), 457–87; Noonan, "Power to choose (n. 102)", pp. 430–1.

112 Especially since the "model marriages" were those of Adam and Eve in paradise and that of Christ with the church: see Duby, *Knight, Lady and Priest* (n. 2), pp. 178ff.

113 Corbett, *Roman Law* (n. 96), pp. 71–8, 90–6. *Patria potestas* could be ended with increasing ease: Barry Nicholas, *An Introduction to Roman Law* (Cambridge, 1962), pp. 76–80. The principle (Digest 35, 1, 15) was *Consensus non concubitus nuptias facit*.

114 Suzanne Fonay Wemple, *Women in Frankish Society: Marriage and the Cloister 500 to 900* (Philadelphia, 1981), pp. 34–6.

115 Ibid. pp. 75–123.

116 C.30 q.5 c.3 and C.32 q.2 dictum post c.12.

117 X.4.16.2.

118 Helmholz, *Marriage Litigation* (n. 1), p. 4.

119 *CRR*, vol. 8, p. 244.

120 *CRR*, vol. 11, no. 2271. See *Rolls of the Justices in Eyre for Gloucestershire, Warwickshire and Staffordshire*, ed. D.M. Stenton, Selden Society, vol. 59 (1940), p. 390: a knight Warin who had made a habit of robbery during wars found after they stopped in Henry II's reign that he could not break old habits. He stole a woman, married her, and had a child by her. After he died, she returned home, married again and had another child. Who was her heir? The jury could not decide if Warin's child was legitimate, but his wife's cohabitation with him until his death raised the possibility that she ultimately consented and that the marriage was valid.

121 "*{M}ulier, nubens infra annum lugubrem, infamiam non incurrit*": X.4.21.4–5, in response to the suggestion that infamy was attached: Gratian in C.2 q.3 dictum ad c.7.

122 "*Nulla vidua distringatur ad se maritandum dum voluerit vivere sine marito, ita tamen quod securitatem fecit quod se non maritabit sine assensu nostro, si de nobis tenuerit, vel sine assensu domini sui de quo tenuerit, si de alio tenuerit*": Magna Carta, c. 8.

123 Sue Sheridan Walker, "Feudal constraint and free consent in the making of marriages in medieval England: Widows in the king's gift," *Historical Papers* (1979), 97–110.

124 A.L. Poole, *Obligations of Society in the XII and XIII Centuries* (Oxford, 1946), pp. 98–9.

125 *CPR Edward II, 1313–1317*, pp. 303, 551, 552, 646; *CPR Edward II, 1318–1321*, pp. 47, 49, 241, 387, 598. See Walker, "Widows (n. 123)," pp. 101–2.

126 *CPR Edward II, 1324–1327*, p. 153.

127 *CRR*, vol. 5, p. 75; vol. 14, no. 445. Ox. Bod., Ashmolian MS 1115, f. 245: in the Duchy of Lancaster office, *temp.* Henry VII, it was noted "Licences of marriage of the king's widows be fineable after the rate of the value of their dower, that is to say, they shall pay for these licences the third part of the yearly value of the dower. Also they shall pay for their pardon in the case after the marriage the whole yearly value of the dower."

128 *Novae Narrationes*, ed. Elsie Shanks and S.F.C. Milsom, Selden Society, vol. 80 (1963) C.228.

129 *Glanvill* (n. 49), § VII, 12.

130 *BNB* nos 965, 1098; *CRR*, vol. 3, 257; vol. 15, no. 1932; Walker, "Widows (n. 123)," p. 99.

131 *SR*, vol. 1, p. 226.

132 Emma Mason, "The resources of the earldom of Warwick in the thirteenth century," *Midland History* 3 (1975), pp. 69–70.

133 P. Landau, *"Hadrians Dekretale 'Dignum est'* (X.4.9.1.) *und die Eheschliessung Unfreier in der Diskussion von Kanonisten und Theologen des 12. und 13. Jahrhunderts,"* *Studia Gratiana* 12 (1967), 513–53; Charles Verlinden, *"Le 'mariage' des esclaves,"* *Il Matrimonio Nella Societa Altomedievale, Settimane di studio del centro Italiano di studi sull'alto medioevo,* 24 (1977), 569–93; Sheehan, "Marriage of the unfree (n. 111)." Slaves did not have *conubium* in Rome: Corbett, *Roman Law* (n. 96), p. 30.

134 Paul Hyams, *Kings, Lords and Peasants in Medieval England: the Common Law of Villeinage in the Twelfth and Thirteenth Centuries* (Oxford, 1980).

135 Eleanor Searle, "Seigneurial control of women's marriage: The antecedents and functions of merchet in medieval England," *Past and Present* 82 (1979), p. 11.

136 R.M. Smith, "Some thoughts on 'hereditary' and 'proprietary' rights in land under customary law in thirteenth and early fourteenth century England", *Law and History Review* 1 (1983), pp. 123–6.

137 *Court Rolls of the Abbey of Ramsey and of the Honor of Clare*, ed. Warren Ault (New Haven, 1978), pp. 195, 211.

138 *Court Rolls of the Manor of Wakefield*, ed. William Paley Baildon, et al., 5 vols to date, Yorkshire Archaeological Society, vols 29, 36, 58, 78 (1901–), *passim*.

139 *Wakefield Court Rolls* (n. 138), vol. 3, p. 123.

140 *Ramsey Court Rolls*, p. 211; *CRR*, vol. 15, no. 1932; *Court Rolls of the Manor of Hales, 1220–1307*, ed. John Amphlett, Worcestershire Historical Society (1912), vol. 1, pp. 268, 273.

141 *CRR*, vol. 9, p. 128.

142 Walker, "Widows (n. 123)," p. 109.

143 Margaret Ruth Kittel, "Married women in thirteenth century England: A study in common law," (University of California, Berkeley, Ph.D., 1973), asserts that widows did not have their canonical freedom. This is not true: they just had to pay for it.

144 *English Historical Documents* (n. 4), vol. 2, no. 19.

145 *Glanvill* (n. 49), § VII, 12.

146 *CRR*, vol. 7, p. 225.

147 For examples see, generally, *Wakefield Court Rolls* (n. 138), vol. 4; compare *Select Pleas in Manorial and other Seignorial Courts*, ed. F.W. Maitland, Selden Society, vol. 2 (1889) pp. 27, 29; *Ramsey Court Rolls* (n. 137), pp. 184, 192, 203, 207, 211, 217, 239, 241, 247, 258; *Hales Court Rolls* (n. 137), vol. 1, pp. 16–17; vol 2, pp. 36, 48, 57, 146, 147, 153, 188; *Court Roll of Chalgrave Manor, 1278–1313*, ed. Marian K. Dale, Bedfordshire Historical Record Society, vol. 28 (1948) pp. 2, 38, 44, 53, 54, 55, 58, 59, 63; *CRR*, vol. 15, no. 137.

148 Sue Sheridan Walker, "Free consent and marriage of feudal wards in medieval England," *Journal of Medieval History* 8 (1982), 123–34.

149 *SR*, vol. 1, pp. 1–4 (cc. 6–7), 26–39 (c. 22).

150 Henry de Bracton, *Bracton on the Laws and Customs of England*, ed. Samuel E. Thorne, 4 vols (Cambridge, Mass., 1968–75), vol. 2, pp. 256–7; *Readings and Moots at the Inns of Court in the Fifteenth Century*, ed. Samuel E. Thorne, Selden Society, vol. 71 (1952), p. 108. A ward fined: *CRR*, vol. 16, no. 596; disseised: ibid., nos. 1203, 1331, 1429.

151 *Yearbooks of Edward II, vol. iv. 3 & 4 Edward II. AD. 1309–1311*, ed. F.W. Maitland and G.J. Turner, Selden Society, vol. 22 (1907), pp. 8–10; *Yearbooks of Edward II, vol. xi. 5 Edward II. AD. 1311–1312*, ed. W.C. Bolland, Selden Society, vol. 31 (1915), pp. 216–19. A lord could also put his ward in a convent in an attempt to keep her lands. Maud, ward of Saher, Earl of Winchester, seduced John of Marston while on the way to the convent and got him to marry her. Saher was awarded compensation for the loss of her marriage: *Select Pleas of the Crown*, ed. F.W. Maitland, Selden Society, vol. 1 (1888), no. 202.

152 Gratian (C.31 q.2) assumed that the threat would come from the family. One case in which force by a feudal lord was alleged was that of John de Warenne, Earl of Surrey. He was a ward of Edward I almost from his birth, and was betrothed to another royal ward, Joan, daughter of Henry, Count of Bar and Eleanor, the king's daughter. The wards were married in 1306, but by 1313 John actively sought a divorce. Archbishop Greenfield investigated the case which alleged that the marriage was within the forbidden degrees of consanguinity and was contracted by force and fear sufficient to sway constant people; he dispensed from consanguinity, but made no mention of force. John then alleged a precontract with his true love, Maud Narford; this suit was rejected. He continued to live with Maud and have children with her, but Joan remained his legal wife. As a result, he died without legitimate heirs. *Papers and Letters from the Northern Registers*, ed. James Raine, Rolls Series, vol. 61 (1873) pp. 228–30; F. Royston Fairbanks, "The last Earl of Warenne and Surrey," *Yorkshire Archaeological Journal* 19 (1907), 193–264.

153 Sue Sheridan Walker, "Common law juries and feudal marriage customs in medieval England: The pleas of ravishment," *University of Illinois Law Review* (1984), 705–18; J.A. Brundage, "Rape and marriage in the medieval canon law," *Revue de Droit Canonique* 28 (1978), pp. 74–5. Walker argues that ravishment was rarely used to get wives – there were easier ways – but to steal wards. It represented competition between guardians.

154 For example, *CCR Henry III*, vol. 5, pp. 498–500; see *BNB* no. 1090; *CRR*, vol. 2, pp. 63, 92; vol. 6, pp. 74, 156; *Year Books of Edward II, vol. xix,*

9 *Edward II, A.D. 1315–1316*, ed. G.J. Turner and W.C. Bolland, Selden Society, vol. 45 (1929), pp. 28–33; *Wakefield Court Rolls*, vol. 4, p. 93.

155 Walker, "Wards (n. 148)," pp. 126–7; *Yearbook 3 Edward II*, pp. 21–2; *CPR Edward II*, vol. 2, p. 553; vol. 3, p. 43. See *CCR Henry III*, vol. 4, p. 408; *CRR*, vol. 10, p. 159; vol 15, no. 1284.

156 *Civil Pleas of the Wiltshire Eyre, 1249*, ed. M.T. Clanchy, Wiltshire Record Society, vol. 26 (1971), p. 464. Exception of "no marriage" in dower cases: *CRR*, vol. 16, no. 934, 1063, 1674, 2086, 2134; inquisition in ecclesiastical court in which the woman proves marriage: *Select Cases from Canterbury* (n. 7), A.6; a case before the pope, *CPPR*, vol. 4, pp. 44–5; certificates by bishop: *The Register of John le Romeyn Lord Archbishop of York*, Surtees Society, vol. 123 (1913), p. 54; *Registrum Henrici Woodlock Diocesis Wintoniensis AD 1305–1316*, ed. A.W. Goodman, Canterbury and York Society, vols. 43–4 (1940–1), pp. 378–9, 411; *Reg, Lacy* (n. 104), p. 200.

157 *BNB*, no. 291.

158 Maitland suggested that while such an unsolemnized marriage defeated a possessory action, if William had used a writ of right instead the issue would have been referred to the ecclesiastical court, which would have declared the marriage of his parents valid and he would have been able to inherit. Precedent suggests this is not true: in the 1270s, William sued a writ of right against John, and when John excepted that William had no right because his parents were not married at church door, the inquest agreed that the marriage was *in lecto mortali* and not solemnized at church door and William's claim was rejected. The church's reluctance to bind the dead also stands against Maitland's theory. The validity of John and Katherine's marriage depended on their consent, and after the death of John there was no unimpeachable way to prove his consent to the marriage. Pollock and Maitland, *History of English Law* (n. 93), vol. 2, pp. 383–4; *Casus Placitorum and Reports of Cases in the King's Courts 1272–1278*, ed. W.H. Dunham, Selden Society, vol. 69 (1952), p. 43. See ibid., pp. 72–7.

159 Pollock and Maitland, *History of English Law* (n. 93), vol. 2, p. 374.

160 *Casus Placitorum* (n. 158), pp. 3, 34: if a woman claims dower and her adversary objects that there was no marriage, she gets a writ to the bishop to prove the marriage; if he objects that her husband was not seised of the land on the day of the marriage, she gets a writ to the sheriff for inquiry into seisin.

161 Dower denied: *Gloucester Eyre* (n. 120), no. 1163; *BNB*, nos. 1669, 1875; *CRR*, vol. 9, p. 190; vol. 11, no. 2032; vol. 12, nos. 705, 2000, 2077; vol. 13, no. 1829. When the ecclesiastical court decreed that such a marriage was valid, it still gave no dower rights: *Civil Pleas* (n. 156),

p. 109. After defeating a putative widow's suit in court, one heir recognized his moral obligation and made a small cash settlement to her: *CRR*, vol. 12, no. 1829.

162 *Glanvill* (n. 49), § VII, 14. See N. Adams, *"Nullius filius*: A study of the exception of bastardy in the law courts of medieval England," *University of Toronto Law Journal* 6 (1946), 361–84; R.H. Helmholz, "Bastardy litigation in medieval England," *American Journal of Legal History* 13 (1969), 360–83; J.L. Barton, "Nullity of marriage and illegitimacy in the England of the middle ages," *Legal History Studies 1972*, ed. Dafydd Jenkins (Cardiff, 1975), pp. 28–49.

163 *CRR*, vol. 12, no. 1691. See also, *CRR*, vol. 14, nos. 237, 460; Adams, *"Nullius filius* (n. 162)," p. 365 n. 12. In *CRR*, vol. 15, no. 1793, the exception seems to have been rejected by the court without a hearing and the claimant recovered seisin.

164 *Casus Placitorum* (n. 158), pp. 72–7.

165 *"Tanta est vis matrimonii, ut qui antea sunt geniti post contractum matrimonium legitimi habeantur"*: X.4.17.6.

166 *CCR, Henry III, 1231–1234*, pp. 598–9. The situation leading to this writ is described in *CRR*, vol. 15, no. 1178 and *BNB*, no. 1117.

167 p. 17.

168 As early as 1237, the bishop of Carlisle used it to his advantage in a disseisin case, *Rex* v. *Wigenhall*, *BNB*, no. 1175, 1181; *CRR*, vol. 15, no. 1882.

169 *Glanvill* (n. 49), § VII, 13.

170 X.4.17.2; X.4.17.14–15.

171 Pollock and Maitland, *History of English Law* (n. 93), vol. 2, pp. 376–7.

172 *Glanvill* (n. 49), § VI, 17; *Bracton* (n. 150), vol. 2, p. 185.

173 In the case of the heirs of William de Cardunville, the contestants were two boys called Richard. One was born of William's wife Alice, who was divorced from him in 1253 on the grounds of his precontract to one Joan. The other son was the child of Joan and William born *c.*1230, long before his divorce from Alice and the solemnization of his union with Joan. The court preferred Joan's son, even though he was a mantle-child. Maitland (*History of English Law* (n. 93), vol. 2, pp. 379–80) misrepresents this case in two ways when he says "they preferred the unsolemnized to the solemnized marriage." Joan and William were solemnly married after the divorce; William and Alice were null and void from the start, and therefore there was no marriage in their case. The court preferred a late, solemnized marriage to none at all.

174 Ibid., p. 377; Adams, *"Nullius filius* (n. 162)," p. 363, n. 6; and Helmholz, "Bastardy litigation (n. 162)," p. 371 all disagree. Maitland's cited case from *CPPR*, vol. 1, pp. 254–5 is not on point: the child, Thomas,

who is allegedly a bastard is not the child of divorced parents, and good
faith is not raised.

175 *Glanvill* (n. 49), § VII, 18.

176 *The Court Baron*, ed. F.W. Maitland and W.P. Baildon, Selden Society,
vol. 4 (1891), p. 129. See also M. Clare Coleman, *Downham-in-the-Isle*
(Woodbridge, Suffolk, 1984), p. 41: *Adam Buk* v. *William de Stoneye* for
36s 8d due for Adam's marriage to William's daughter.

177 M.M. Sheehan, "The influence of canon law on the property rights of
married women in England," *Mediaeval Studies* 25 (1963), pp. 115–16;
Registrum Roberti Winchelsey, Cantuariensis Archiepiscopi AD 1294–1313,
ed. Rose Graham, Canterbury and York Society, vols 51–2 (1952),
pp. 163–4; *Reg. Woodlock*, pp. 556–7; *CPPR*, vol 11, p. 319.

178 For example, *CRR*, vol. 2, pp. 267, 298; vol. 5, p. 251; vol. 14, no. 1387.

179 *CRR*, vol. 14, no. 575: *"cognitio de maritagio pertinet ad forum ecclesiasticum
de denariis."*

180 See J.H. Baker, *An Introduction to English Legal History* (2d ed., London,
1979), pp. 263–87; idem, *The Reports of Sir John Spelman*, Selden Society,
vol. 94 (1978), pp. 255–98; M. Blatcher, *The Court of King's Bench
1450–1550* (London, 1978); M. Hastings, *The Court of Common Pleas*
(Ithaca, N.Y., 1947).

181 PRO, KB 27/979 m.71v.

182 PRO, C1/782/36. (No sentence survives.)

183 PRO, C1/780/18. (No sentence survives.)

184 PRO, C1/867/69. (No sentence survives.)

185 R.M. Smith, "Some reflections on the evidence for the origins of the
European marriage pattern in England," in *The Sociology of the Family*, ed.
C. Harris, Sociological Review Monograph 28 (1979), p. 98.

186 Pollock and Maitland, *History of English Law* (n. 93), vol. 2, p. 375.

Chapter 3   *Theology, Ritual and Clerical Marriage*

1 Carl S. Meyer, "Henry VIII burns Luther's books, 12 May 1521," *Journal
of Ecclesiastical History* 9 (1958), 173–87.

2 *LP*, vol. 3, pt. 1, nos. 1220, 1233.

3 Henry VIII, *Assertio Septem Sacramentorum*, trans. T.W. (London, 1766),
p. 53.

4 *Assertio* (n. 3), p. 148.

5 Richard Marius points out Henry's lavish praise of marriage in the
Assertio which contrasted to the views of Thomas More (who is often
supposed to be the actual author). Virginity was praised more highly by
More, who asserted it was heresy to believe that the married state was as

pleasing to God: "Henry VIII, Thomas More and the Bishop of Rome," *Quincentennial Essays on St Thomas More*, ed. Michael J. Moore (Boone, N.C., 1978), 89–107.

6 Luther was quoted by More: *Responsio ad Lutherum*, ed. J.M. Headley; trans. Sister Scholastica Mandeville, *CW More*, vol. 5 (New Haven, 1969), p. 671. Luther actually disagreed with Erasmus on Eph. 5:32. Erasmus said in a note that while no one could prove from Scripture that marriage was a sacrament, the church was within its authority to name it so, though he rather adroitly dodged the controversy by declining to say whether he himself thought it was: *In Laud and Praise of Matrimony*, trans. Richard Taverner (London, 1531), esp. A5v–8v. G. Krodel points out that although it was rumored that Erasmus wrote the *Assertio* the theology of marriage is ample proof that he did not: "Luther, Erasmus and Henry VIII," *Archiv für Reformationsgeschichte* 53 (1962), 60–78. The rumor sprang from Erasmus's attempts to distance himself from Luther after 1520 and reflected his consequent loss of credibility for many reformers. After some urging by the Danish king, Luther apologized insincerely to Henry for his tone, claiming never to have believed that Henry had written the *Assertio*, which was the work of "some crafty sophist" abusing Henry's name; Henry rejected the apology: *LP*, vol. 4, nos. 1614, 2446.

7 *Responsio* (n. 6), p. 671.

8 *Responsio* (n. 6), p. 91.

9 *Responsio* (n. 6), p. 213.

10 *Responsio* (n. 6), p. 219–21.

11 William Clebsch, *England's Earliest Protestants, 1520–1535* (New Haven, 1964), pp. 19–23.

12 *LP*, vol. 4, no. 40.

13 *LP*, vol. 4, nos 995, 2607. On the situation in London, see Susan Brigden, *London and the Reformation* (Oxford, 1989), esp. pp. 155–60. Language assured these works small audiences anyway, and only one of Luther's treatises on marriage was published in translation, a 1523 commentary on 1 Corin. 7. In 1529, William Roy tried to avoid the ban on Luther's works by fobbing it off as a work of Erasmus, but few were fooled. It quickly entered the forbidden books list, was rounded up and destroyed. The loss is trivial; the piece hardly deserved publication, being singularly tedious and far inferior to Luther's earlier *Vom ehelichen leben*: Clebsch, "The earliest translations of Luther into English," *Harvard Theological Review* 56 (1963), 77–81; *Earliest Protestants* (n. 11), pp. 229–40.

14 *LP*, vol. 4, no. 6738.

15 *LP*, vol. 5, no. 618.

16 *Doctrinal Treatises . . . by William Tyndale*, ed. Henry Walter (Cambridge, 1848), p. 254.

17 Regular burnings marked the anti-New Testament crusade of late 1525 through mid-1527. Cardinal Campeggio said of them "No holocaust could be more pleasing to God." See *LP*, vol. 4, nos 1803, 2648, 2652, 2677, 2721, 2797, 2903, 3132. The king's hostility to Bible translations was known: Vives reported to Erasmus in 1524 that the king opposed common people showing "immoderate curiosity as to Divine mysteries": ibid., no. 828.

18 R.B. Merriman, *Life and Letters of Thomas Cromwell* (Oxford, 1902), pp. 336–7; cf. Clebsch, *Earliest Protestants* (n. 11), pp. 137–204. Tyndale, called by Clebsch the "elusive grand prize of heretic hunts," was caught by imperial agents and killed in 1536.

19 *The Confutation of Tyndale's Answer*, ed. Louis A. Schuster, Richard C. Marius, James P. Lusardi, and Richard J. Schoeck, *CW More*, vol. 8 (New Haven, 1973); see also R. Marius, *Thomas More* (London, 1984) pp. 424–8, 432–3.

20 *Confutation* (n. 19), p. 254; cf. pp. 645, 704.

21 *Confutation* (n. 19), pp. 85–7.

22 Harrington's book was written *c.*1513 but not published until 1528. See Ralph Houlbrooke, *The English Family 1450–1700* (London, 1984), p. 93; Kathleen Davies, "Continuity and change in literary advice on marriage," in *Marriage and Society*, ed. R.B. Outhwaite (London, 1981), p. 61. John K. Yost misrepresents him as moving from a legal to a modern pastoral approach: "The development of a reformist approach to marriage and celibacy in early English humanism," *Nederlands Archief voor Kerkgeschiedenis*, new ser. 57 (1976), 1–15.

23 Sig. Ei. After its first edition, there were at least eight more by 1537. See Glanmor Williams, "Two neglected London-Welsh clerics: Richard Whitford and Richard Gwent," *The Transactions of the Honourable Society of Cymmrodorion* (1961), 23–32.

24 The literature on this subject is extensive. A.G. Dickens, *Lollards and Protestants in the Diocese of York, 1509–1558* (Oxford, 1959) describes the principal Lollard concerns as criticism of pilgrimages and saints, and of the sacrament of the altar, a generalized anti-clericalism, and support for individual study of the translated Bible. He describes heresy cases in the north as looking more like Lollardy than foreign Protestantism. This view is supported by John F. Davis, *Heresy and Reformation in the South-East of England, 1520–1559* (London, 1983), pp. 41–65, who finds similiar concerns in the 1520s. Luther is mentioned in heresy accusations but only peripherally; people are vaguely familiar with his ideas but not influenced by them. See also John Fines, "Heresy trials in the diocese of Coventry and Lichfield, 1511–12," *Journal of Ecclesiastical History* 14 (1963), 160–74, and Margaret Aston, "Lollardy and the Reformation: Survival or revival?" *History* 49 (1964), 149–70.

25 *The Register of Richard Mayhew, Bishop of Hereford*, ed. A.T. Bannister, Canterbury and York Society, vol. 27 (1921) p. 66.

26 R.L. Williams, "Aspects of heresy and Reformation in England 1515–1540" (Cambridge University Ph.D., 1976), p. 95. Harman was a figure of some importance. He fled England and took up residence in Antwerp, where he became a burgess before 1528. John Hackett succeeded in having the authorities in Antwerp arrest Harman in late 1528 and hold him without charges pending a bill of particulars to be supplied by Wolsey. In spite of Hackett's repeated pleas Wolsey failed to produce the bill and the Council in Antwerp was forced to release him in April 1529, and Hackett faced the threat of having to pay damages for false arrest: *LP*, vol 4, nos. 4511, 4569, 4580, 4693–4, 4714, 4746, 5078, 5461–2. Another Cranbrook resident Agnes Grebell was suspected of Lollard-type beliefs as well as heterodox views on marriage in 1511, but no details were given: *LP*, vol. 1, no. 752.

27 Brigden, *London and the Reformation* (n. 13), p. 53.

28 *LP*, vol. 5, no. 583.

29 Brigden, *London and the Reformation* (n. 13), esp. pp. 179–87.

30 A.W. Reed, "The regulation of the book trade before the Proclamation of 1538," *Transactions of the Bibliographical Society* 15 (1917–19), 157–84; cf. *LP*, vol. 4, no. 2607.

31 Ibid., no. 995.

32 Ibid., nos 2721, 3132.

33 Jennifer Loach, "Pamphlets and politics, 1553–8," *Bulletin of the Institute of Historical Research* 48 (1975), 31–44.

34 *LP*, vol. 4, no. 4073; cf. nos 4004, 4030. Forman also had support in high places: Brigden, *London and the Reformation* (n. 13), pp. 113–15, 128, 161, 178, 184, 221.

35 *LP*, vol. 4, no. 4030.

36 Ibid., nos 4330, 4407; cf. nos 4260, 4282.

37 David M. Loades, "The press under the early Tudors," *Transactions of the Cambridge Bibliographical Society* 4 (1964), 29–50; idem, "The theory and practice of censorship in sixteenth century England," *Transactions of the Royal Historical Society* 5th ser., 24 (1974), 141–57.

38 J.A. Guy, *The Public Career of Sir Thomas More* (New Haven, 1980), pp. 171–4; G.R. Elton, *Policy and Police* (Cambridge, 1972) pp. 218–21, 255–6; *TRP*, vol. 1, pp. 181–6, 193–7.

39 *TRP*, vol. 1, pp. 270–6, 373–6; 34/5 Henry VIII c. 1; Stanford E. Lehmberg, *The Later Parliaments of Henry VIII 1536–1547* (Cambridge, 1977), pp. 186–7.

40 PRO, SP 6/13/10, ff. 123–7.

41 PRO, SP 6/8/2, 6/8/8. Richard Moryson also denounced the contentions

and prepared a statement on the dignity of matrimony: SP 6/2/19, ff. 150–1.

42 *The Institution of a Christian Man* (London, 1537), f. 53v.

43 PRO, SP 6/3/2, ff. 5–9, esp. 5v–6. Henry's corrections on marriage itself are limited to a couple of technical word changes and a suggestion that the forbidden degrees of consanguinity be spelled out more completely: BL, Royal MS 17.C.XXX, ff. 29–30.

44 PRO, SP 6/6/2.

45 BL, Royal MS 7.C.XVI, f. 205v; Royal MS App. 78, f. 21. Entries in Cranmer's commonplace book (Royal MS 7.B.XI, ff. 168–77v) show that he gave the matter continued thought, but cannot be dated.

46 BL, Cotton MS Cleopatra E.V, ff. 39–47, 56–9, 121; Lambeth MS 1108, ff. 69–73v, 77, 94, 115–15v.

47 *A Necessary Doctrine and Erudition for any Christian Man* (London, 1543), ff. K3v–4v. Marriage was, in fact, called an "estate," the first time to my knowledge that this very Lutheran usage was employed in official statements in England. I am grateful to Professor Sir Geoffrey Elton for raising this observation in a private conversation.

48 28 Henry VIII, c. 7; Lehmberg, *Later Parliaments* (n. 39), pp. 20–4. For the Privy Council, see especially Dale E. Hoak, *The King's Council in the Reign of Edward VI* (Cambridge, 1976). The bibliography on Henry's will has become rather extensive, but Hoak has argued persuasively that the will was the conscious work of the king, not the product of plotters acting against the king's personal wishes, as suggested by Starkey: D. Hoak, "Henry VIII's last will and testament: New evidence and a fresh interpretation," paper delivered at NACBS meeting, 16 October 1987 (cited with permission). Hoak's views will be developed at length in *War, Reformation, and Rebellion: Politics, Government and Religion in England, 1540–53* (Cambridge, forthcoming). I am very grateful to Professor Hoak for his assistance on this topic. Other major views of the will are: Helen Miller, "Henry VIII's unwritten will," *Wealth and Power in Tudor England*, ed. E.W. Ives, et al. (London, 1978); J.J. Scarisbrick, *Henry VIII* (Berkeley, 1968), pp. 488–95; Lacey Baldwin Smith, *Henry VIII: The Mask of Royalty* (Chicago, 1982), esp. pp. 306–13, and idem, "The last will and testament of Henry VIII: A question of perspective," *Journal of British Studies* 2 (1962); David Starkey, *The Reign of Henry VIII: Personalities and Politics* (London, 1985), chap. 8.

49 W.K. Jordan, *Edward VI: The Young King* (Cambridge, Mass., 1968), pp. 40–5; Lacey Baldwin Smith, "Henry VIII and the Protestant triumph," *American Historical Review* 71 (1966), 1237–64.

50 Jordan, *Young King* (n. 49), pp. 47–50.

51 Jordan, *Young King* (n. 49), pp. 130–54, 230–304; Hoak, *King's Council* (n. 48), pp. 172–4. See also Glyn Redworth, *In Defence of the Church*

    Catholic: The Life of Stephen Gardiner (Blackwell, 1990); T.F. Shirley, *Thomas Thirlby, Tudor Bishop* (London, 1964); Charles Sturge, *Cuthbert Tunstal* (London, 1938).

52   See *Manuale et processionale ad usum insignis ecclesiae Eboracensis*, Surtees Society, 63 (1875) pp. 24–40, 17*–26*.

53   *The Sarum Missal in English*, trans. F.E. Warren, Alcuin Coll., vol. 11 (1913), pp. 143–61; *The Two Liturgies . . . of King Edward VI*, ed. Rev. J. Ketley (Cambridge, 1844), pp. 127–34. Although substantial portions of the medieval rites were in "the vulgar tongue," regional dialect was responsible for some variations smoothed out by Cranmer's text. See J.H. Blunt, ed., *The Annotated Book of Common Prayer* (London, 1872), pp. 267–8. The new marriage service and its critics receive only glancing notice in Horton Davies, *Worship and Theology in England: From Cranmer to Hooker, 1534–1603* (Princeton, 1970).

54   Hugh Latimer, *Sermons by Hugh Latimer*, ed. G.E. Corrie, 2 vols (Cambridge, 1844–5), vol. 2, pp. 160–6.

55   David Herlihy and Christiane Klapisch-Zuber, *Tuscans and their Families* (New Haven, 1985), pp. 228–31.

56   *Cuthberti Tonstalli in laudem matrimonii oratio . . .* (London, 1519).

57   For the decision to readopt the 1552 Prayer Book, see N.L. Jones, *Faith by Statute: Parliament and the Settlement of Religion 1559* (London, 1982).

58   *The Works of John Whitgift*, ed. John Ayre, 3 vols (Cambridge, 1851–53), vol. 3, pp. 353–5. See *The Seconde Parte of a Register*, ed. A. Peel, 2 vols (London, 1915), vol. 1, pp. 124–5, 127, 201, 259, 300; *The Folger Library Edition of The Works of Richard Hooker*, ed. W. Speed Hill, 4 vols (Cambridge, Mass., 1977–82), vol. 2, p. 404.

59   John Rylands Library, English MS 524, f. 45; Henry Smith, *A Preparative to Marriage* (London, 1591), p. 24. The puritan laity in the diocese of Chester were not as interested in the ring as in the surplice or the crossing in baptism: R.C. Richardson, *Puritanism in Northwest England* (Manchester, 1972), p. 26.

60   Cases from 1573 and 1586 in *Seconde Parte* (n. 58), vol. 1, p. 124; vol. 2, p. 38. There are only two cases in the abundant Ely records. In one (1599), John Smith, vicar of Haslingfield, resigned rather than conform, but he was troubled for more than refusing to use the ring: he refused the surplice, churching of women, and the sign of the cross in baptism: EDR, B2/17 f. 19v–20, 75. While few prosecutions under the tolerant Cox would be expected, only one during eighteen years of Whitgift's metropolitical jurisdiction argues the insignificance of the issue.

61   Whitgift, *Works* (n. 58), vol. 3, pp. 353, 356–7.

62   "A brief discoverie of the false church" (1590), in *The Writings of Henry Barrow 1590–1591*, ed. Leland H. Carlson, Elizabethan Non-Conformist Texts, vol. 5 (London, 1966), pp. 454–5.

63 *The Writings of John Greenwood 1587–1590*, ed. Leland H. Carlson, Elizabethan Non-Conformist Texts, vol. 4 (London, 1962), pp. 24–5.

64 *The Writings of John Greenwood and Henry Barrow*, ed. Leland H. Carlson, Elizabethan Non-Conformist Texts, vol. 6 (London, 1968), p. 338.

65 Ibid., pp. 299, 304, 353.

66 *The Works . . . of Richard Greenham* (1599), pp. 288–99.

67 Rylands MS 524, f. 43, 51v. Cartwright used such a ritual: *Cartwrightiana*, ed. A. Peel and Leland H. Carlson (London, 1951), pp. 180–91; *A directory of church government, Anciently contested for, and as farre as the Times would suffer, practised by the first Non-conformists in the daies of Queen Elizabeth* (1644), f. B3.

68 H.C. Lea, *History of Sacerdotal Celibacy in the Christian Church*, 2 vols (London, 1907), vol. 2, p. 77.

69 Some of this discussion has previously appeared in Eric Josef Carlson, "Clerical marriage and the English Reformation," *Journal of British Studies* 31 (1992), 1–31, © by The North American Conference on British Studies. All rights reserved.

70 This view has endured for over a century of modern scholarly historical writing on Elizabeth. James A. Froude wrote, "Marriage, under all forms, was disagreeable to her; the marriage of the clergy was detestable; the marriage, and especially re-marriage of her prelates, approached incest": *History of England from the Fall of Wolsey to the Death of Elizabeth*, 12 vols (New York, 1870), vol. 9, p. 383. Sir John Neale wrote: "There can be no doubt that Elizabeth was strongly, nay bitterly, opposed to marriage of the clergy": *Essays in Elizabethan History* (New York, 1958), p. 101. Richard Spielmann assumed that Elizabeth "detested clerical marriage almost as much as her half-sister Mary": "The beginning of clerical marriage in the English Reformation: The reign of Edward and Mary," *Anglican and Episcopal History* 56 (1987), p. 251.

71 BL, Cotton MS Cleopatra E.V, f. 294v.

72 *LP*, vol. 9, no. 812; vol. 10, no. 82; vol. 12, pt 2, no. 450.

73 BL, Cotton MS Cleopatra E.V, f. 299.

74 BL, Cotton MS Cleopatra E.IV, f. 151; Diarmaid MacCulloch, *Suffolk and the Tudors. Politics and Religion in an English County, 1500–1600* (Oxford, 1986), pp. 178–9.

75 *LP*, vol 13, pt 1, no. 147.

76 *TRP*, no. 186. The original draft was altered by Henry to add references from Scripture and the Fathers on clerical marriage: BL, Cotton MS Cleopatra E.V, f. 382.

77 *LP*, vol. 14, pt 1, nos 631, 666, 698.

78 BL, Cotton MS Cleopatra E.V, ff. 53–4.

79 31 Henry VIII, c. 14 (1539).

80 *SR*, vol. 3, pp. 739–41, modified by 32 Henry VIII, c. 10, reducing penalties for incontinence from death (considered "very sore and too much extreme") to forfeiture of benefices or life imprisonment (for a third offense). See G.R. Elton, "Thomas Cromwell's decline and fall" in *Studies in Tudor and Stuart Politics and Government*, 3 vols (Cambridge, 1974–83), vol. 1, pp. 206–11; Lehmberg, *Later Parliaments* (n. 39), pp. 65–74, 119; Glyn Redworth, "A study in the formulation of policy: The genesis and evolution of the Act of Six Articles," *Journal of Ecclesiastical History* 37 (1986), 42–67. See also *LP*, vol. 14, pt 1, nos 971, 1068; PRO, SP 1/210, ff. 22–5.

81 *LP*, vol. 14, pt 1, nos 1091–2, 1108, 1207; vol. 16, no. 737.

82 *LP*, vol. 14, pt 1, no. 844.

83 *LP*, vol. 16, no. 733. In reality, clerical incomes were so low that they lacked the means to make themselves into a hereditary caste, they could not afford to prepare their children for the job, and the life was rarely attractive to most of the children. See J.H. Pruett, *The Parish Clergy under the Later Stuarts: The Leicestershire Experience* (Urbana, Ill., 1978), pp. 32–7.

84 *LP*, vol. 14, pt 2, no. 413; reactions of other reformers in vol. 14, pt 1, no. 1278; vol. 14, pt 2, nos 379, 444; vol. 15, nos 310, 509.

85 1 Edward VI, c. 12.

86 Jordan, *Young King* (n. 49), p. 309, reports a vote of 53–22 in Convocation in 1547. In 1548, the motion passed 32–14 according to the list of voters: CCCC, MS. 113.

87 CCCC, MS. 113, pp. 170–1.

88 *CJ*, vol. 1, pp. 3–5, 8; *LJ*, vol 1, pp. 311, 323, 326, 339, 342–3.

89 2/3 Edward VI, c. 21.

90 5/6 Edward VI, c. 12.

91 *Synodalia*, ed. E. Cardwell (Oxford, 1842), pp. 29–30.

92 He was cited by the bishop of Winchester to answer charges against him for marrying and then deprived: *LP*, vol. 14, pt 1, nos 120, 206, 890.

93 *LP*, vol. 9, no. 661, cited in Geoffrey Baskerville, *English Monks and the Suppression of the Monasteries* (London, 1937), p. 138; Charles Wriothesley, *A Chronicle of England during the Reigns of the Tudors, From A.D.1485 to 1559*, ed. W.D. Hamilton, Camden Society, new ser., vol. 11 (London, 1875), p. 63. See also *LP*, vol. 4, no. 6473: the confession of John Lawrence, servant, to a robbery committed with a priest named Richard, "a sanctuary man of St. Martin's or else falsely professing priesthood," who married a woman called Charity.

94 See Ralph A. Houlbrooke, *Church Courts and the People during the English Reformation, 1520–1570* (Oxford, 1979), pp. 180–1.

95 Eric Josef Carlson, "The marriage of William Turner," *Historical Research* 65 (1992), 336–9. See also Whitney R.D. Jones, *William Turner, Tudor Naturalist, Physician and Divine* (London, 1988).

96 BL, Cotton MS Cleopatra E.IV, f. 116.

97 See Mary Prior, "Reviled and crucified marriages: The position of Tudor bishops' wives," *Women in English Society, 1500–1800*, ed. Mary Prior (London, 1985), p. 122. Bishops Holbeach, Ferrar, and Bird all married, probably in Edward's reign. Archbishop Holgate married in 1549. His protests that he married only under pressure to prove his loyalty to Protestantism should not be taken seriously. His "Apology" was written in 1554, and he had every reason under the circumstances to protect himself. A.G. Dickens, "Archbishop Holgate's Apology", *Reformation Studies* (London, 1982), pp. 353–63 (the text is PRO, SP 11/6/84) argues the contrary; see also his "Robert Holgate, Archbishop of York and President of the King's Council in the North" (ibid., pp. 344–6). The best evidence to the contrary is published by Dickens himself ("Two Marian petitions," ibid., pp. 83–5, 89). John Houseman (PRO, SP 15/7/8) claimed that Holgate refused him holy orders in 1550 because he opposed clerical marriage. The tone of the petition suggests a zeal on Holgate's part unlikely in one who married reluctantly.

98 Any figures based solely on deprivations will be low, since some of the married clergy fled abroad with their wives and some who remained probably escaped detection. Spielmann ("Beginnings [n. 70]," p. 259) estimates that the total must have been roughly 1,500, and that seems somewhat high since some parts of the country had so few. See Geoffrey Baskerville, "Married clergy and pensioned religious in Norwich Diocese, 1555," *English Historical Review* 48 (1933), 43–64; H.E.P. Grieve, "The deprived Marian clergy in Essex, 1553–61," *Transactions of the Royal Historical Society* 4th ser., vol. 22 (London, 1940), pp. 142–3; A.G. Dickens, "The Marian reaction in the Diocese of York: Part I, The Clergy," *Reformation Studies*, pp. 93–130, esp. pp. 104, 112–21; Claire Cross, "Priests into ministers: The establishment of Protestant practice in the city of York, 1530–1630," *Reformation Principle and Practice*, ed. Peter Newman Brooks (London, 1980), 203–25, esp. p. 216; Christopher Haigh, *Reformation and Resistance in Tudor Lancashire* (Cambridge, 1975), pp. 153, 179–81.

99 Anne Llewellyn Barstow, *Married Priests and the Reforming Papacy: the Eleventh-Century Debates* (New York, 1982), pp. 87–96. See also C.N.L. Brooke, "Gregorian reform in action: Clerical marriage in England, 1050–1200," *Cambridge Historical Journal* 12 (1956); Charles A. Frazee, "The origins of clerical celibacy in the Western church", *Church History* 41 (1972), 149–67.

100 "A godly saying" in *Ballads from Manuscripts*, ed. F.J. Furnivall, 2 vols (Ballad Society, 1868–72), vol. 1, pp. 314–15; see the alleged Lollard John Tyball, who confessed in April 1528 that "on Paul's authority . . . every priest and bishop ought to have a wife" (*LP*, vol. 4, no. 4218).

101   *Visitation Articles and Injunctions*, ed. W.H. Frere, Alcuin Club, vol. 15 (1910), pp. 189, 292–3.

102   EDR, B/2/3, p. 41.

103   Haigh, *Reformation and Resistance* (n. 98), p. 182.

104   *Visitation Articles* (n. 101), p. 274; "A brief and clean confession of the Christian faith" (1550) in *Later Writings of Bishop Hooper*, ed. Charles Nevinson (Cambridge, 1852), pp. 55–6.

105   Robert Barnes, "That by God's word it is lawful for Priests that hath not the gift of chastity to marry Wives," in *The whole works of W. Tyndall, Iohn Frith, and Doct. Barnes* (London, 1573), pt 2, pp. 303–39, esp. p. 309. See also J. Yost, "The Reformation defense of clerical marriage in the reigns of Henry VIII and Edward VI," *Church History* 50 (1981), pp. 155–8; W.D.J. Cargill Thompson, "The sixteenth-century editions of a supplication unto King Henry the Eighth by Robert Barnes, D.D.: A footnote to the history of the Royal Supremacy," *Transactions of the Cambridge Bibliographical Society* 3 (1960), 133–42; J.P. Lusardi's biography of Barnes in *CW More*, vol. 8, pt 3; Clebsch, *Earliest Protestants* (n. 11), pp. 58–77.

106   Barnes, "That by God's word (n. 105)," pp. 309–10.

107   Ibid., pp. 311–16.

108   Ibid., pp. 318–22.

109   Ibid., pp. 325–30.

110   Ibid., pp. 333–9.

111   Ibid., p. 339. This theme, that marriage was desirable for the commonwealth because it increased population, was repeated by most Henrician and Edwardian humanist writers.

112   On which, see J. Yost, "Taverner's use of Erasmus and the Protestantization of English humanism," *Renaissance Quarterly* 23 (1970), 266–76; idem, "German Protestant humanism and the early English Reformation: Richard Taverner and official translations," *Bibliotheque D'Humanisme et Renaissance* 32 (1970), 613–25; Albert Hyma, "Erasmus and the sacrament of matrimony," *Archiv für Reformationsgeschicte* 48 (1957), 145–64.

113   Desiderius Erasmus, *A right fruitful epistle devised by the most excellent clerk Erasmus in laude and praise of matrimony*, trans. Richard Taverner (London, 1531), sig. B8v–C2v.

114   Thomas More, *A Dialogue Concerning Heresies*, ed. Thomas M.C. Lawler, Germain Marc'hadour, and Richard C. Marius, *CW More*, vol. 6, bk 3, chap. 13, esp. pp. 303–9.

115   [Heinrich Bullinger,] *The golden booke of Christian matrimony, most necessary and profitable for all them that intend to live quietly and godly in the Christian State of holy wedlock* (London, 1542), sig. A3–6.

116   I am grateful to Dr Seymour House of Otago University for his assistance

on Becon and for correcting my error regarding his marital status in "Clerical marriage (n. 69)," p. 9.

117 Charles C. Butterworth and Allan G. Chester, *George Joye 1495?–1533* (Philadelphia, 1962); Yost, "Defence (n. 105)," pp. 158–62.

118 James Sawtry/George Joye, *The defence of the marriage of Priests against Steven Gardiner* (1541), sig. A5–7, B1–2.

119 Ibid., sig. B8v–C1.

120 Ibid., sig. C2. This is not an exhaustive treatment of promarriage treatises. William Turner is actually an exception to the rule I have noted: a married deacon who wrote in defense of clerical marriage also, but his discussion of the subject is brief and buried in his two treatises against Stephen Gardiner, written while he was in exile: *The huntyng and fyndyng out of the Romishe fox* (1543), and *The seconde course of the hunter at the Romishe fox* (1545). They are discussed in Celia Hughes, "Two six-teenth–century northern Protestants: John Bradford and William Tur-ner," *Bulletin of the John Rylands Library* 66 (1983), 122–38; and Jones, *William Turner* (n. 95), pp. 150–65. In 1549, the future bishop John Ponet published *A defence for mariage of priestes by scripture and aunciente wryters*, which was also largely concerned with the fornication that re-sulted from mandatory celibacy.

121 More, *Dialogue* (n. 114), pp. 312–13.

122 More, *Confutation* (n. 19), p. 207.

123 Ibid., p. 726.

124 Although written in 1546, this was not published until 1567. Robert Crowley, *The opening of the wordes of the Prophet Joell, in his second and third Chapters, rehersed by Christ in Mathewe, xxiiii, Marke, xiii, Luke, xxi, and by Peter Actes, ii, concerning the Signes of the last day* (1567), sig. F8.

125 Jones, *Faith by Statute* (n. 57), p. 98.

126 *Correspondence of Matthew Parker*, ed. J. Bruce and T.T. Perowne (Cam-bridge, 1853), no. 49.

127 *The Decades of Henry Bullinger*, ed. Thomas Harding, 4 vols (Cambridge, 1849), vol. 1, p. 402; William P. Haugaard, *Elizabeth and the English Reformation* (Cambridge, 1968), pp. 200–1.

128 Winthrop S. Hudson, *John Ponet (1516?–1556) Advocate of Limited Mon-archy* (Chicago, 1942), pp. 94–5.

129 Dickens ("Holgate (n. 97)," pp. 345–6), discusses the marriage, though he is incorrect in thinking that the material in BI, CP. G. 404 is from the divorce suit. From internal evidence, the divorce was in the past, and this is a separate suit, most likely for restitution. For the later suit, see *APC*, vol. 3, pp. 421, 427.

130 *TRP*, no. 460. Note that this procedure was not necessary for a valid marriage; marriages without proper license were punishable but not voidable.

131 Carlson "Clerical marriage (n. 69)," pp. 13–20.

132 John Veron addressed this in his contemporaneous work, *A stronge defence of the maryage of pryestes agaynste the pope Eustachians made dialogue wise* (Pre-1563). He said that ministers without the gift of chastity ought to marry, and that if they did not, "Godly magistrates ought to compel them . . . lest by their incontinent living they be an offence and stumbling block unto the church and a slander unto the doctrine that they have taught and set forth." (sig. C2). See also Francis Trigge, *A Touchstone, whereby may easilie be discerned which is the true Catholike faith, of all them that professe the name of Catholiques in the Church of Englande, that they bee not deceived* (London, 1599), pp. 235–8: clergy wives brought them into disrepute, and if the clergy expected anyone to listen, they had best put their own houses in order first. If the clergy had virtuous wives, he concluded, no one would speak ill of clerical marriage. In a letter to Robert Cecil, Archbishop Hutton noted that "the common cause of religion . . . hath received some disgrace" from the marital problems of the Archbishop of Limerick: PRO, SP 12/270/75.

133 *LP*, vol. 14, pt. 1, no. 844. One of Mont's great skills was convincing the Germans that Protestantism had a future in England: Esther Hildebrandt, "Christopher Mont, Anglo-German Diplomat" *Sixteenth Century Journal* 15 (1984), p. 287.

134 Carlson, "Clerical marriage (n. 69)," pp. 17–20.

135 Based on: Joel Berlatsky, "Marriage and family in a Tudor elite: Familial patterns of Elizabethan bishops," *Journal of Family History* 3 (1978), 6–22; Prior, "Tudor bishops' wives (n. 97)," pp. 118–48; F.O. White, *Lives of the Elizabethan Bishops* (London, 1898).

136 Barnes, Blethin, N. Bullingham, H. Cotton, Cox, Fletcher, Godwin, Middleton, Overton, Sandys, Still and Young married twice; Goldsborough and Hutton three times: Prior, "Tudor bishops' wives (n. 97)', pp. 135, 147 n. 100.

137 Strype, *Annals*, vol. 2, pt 1, p. 515.

138 Carlson, "Marriage of William Turner (n. 95)."

139 Cox wrote a passionate defense to Cecil of his wife's character and his need to marry: PRO, SP 12/48/64.

140 His cringing protest to Robert Cecil (*HMC, Salisbury*, vol. 2, pp. 106–7) is in sharp contrast to the tone of Cox's to Cecil's father. A scathing poem, "On the marriage of Lady Mary Baker to Richard Fletcher, Bishop of London" has recently been attributed to Sir John Davies (*The Poems of Sir John Davies*, ed. Robert Krueger [Oxford, 1975], pp. 177–9).

141 Hutton had been ordered by the queen to dispense Thornborough to marry again. He wrote to Cecil that although he believed that the law of God allowed *pars innocens* to marry again, it was "flat contrary to Her

Majesty's ecclesiastical laws of this land and much misliked by most of the clergy of this realm": PRO, SP 12/270/75. See A.L. Rowse, "Bishop Thornborough: A clerical careerist," in *For Veronica Wedgwood These*, ed. R. Ollard and P. Tudor-Craig (London, 1986), pp. 89–108.

142 White, *Elizabethan Bishops* (n. 135), p. 189.

143 *Athenae Oxoniensis*, ed. Philip Bliss, 2 vols (Oxford, 1813–15), vol. 1, p. 611.

144 Sir John Harington, *A Supplie or Addicion to the Catalogue of Bishops to the Yeare 1608*, ed. R.H. Miller (Potomac, Md., 1979), pp. 117, 123. This book is better known by the title under which it was posthumously published in 1653, *A Briefe View of the State of the Church of England*. I am grateful to Professor Miller for providing me with a copy of his edition. Harington is responsible for the anecdote most often quoted to display the queen's antipathy to episcopal marriage. When taking her leave from Archbishop and Mrs Parker after being their guest for a meal, Elizabeth "gave him very special thanks, with gracious and honourable terms, and then looking on his wife, and you (saith she) Madam I may not call you, and Mrs I am ashamed to call you but yet I do thank you" (ibid., p. 35). The story is suspect. Harington wrote for James I's son Henry around 1608 intending to ridicule and slander bishops. He repeated every vicious or embarrassing bit of gossip he could find to advance this cause and, as Neale said, "was too much the established wit to look closely at a good story": *Essays in Elizabethan History* (n. 70), p. 101.

145 Patrick Collinson, *The Religion of Protestants* (Oxford, 1982), pp. 70–9; Felicity Heal, *Of Prelates and Princes* (Cambridge, 1980), pp. 203–327.

146 See Sandy's lavish provisions for his children, e.g., BL, Lansdowne MS 50.34. Another complaint was that they ignored their traditional responsibilities, "And . . . it is thought that divers of the clergy, now being married and having wives and children do overmuch alienate their minds from the honest and careful duty which they ought to bear towards the maintenance of good hospitality": PRO, SP 15/24/8. On the expectation of hospitality, see Felicity Heal, "Hospitality in early modern England," *Past and Present*, no. 102 (1984), pp. 66–93, and *Hospitality in Early Modern England* (Oxford, 1990).

147 PRO, SP 12/259/47: "To move her majesty's compassion towards the poor orphans of the late bishop of London." See also BL, Additional MS 33410, f. 13, a letter from the Privy Council to the Archbishop of Canterbury in 1591 in favor of the wife and children of the queen's chaplain, Dr Tomson, who pursued the "advancement of the Gospel" at the expense of his material advancement "so as thereby his wife and poor children are left in distressed estate" with £300 debts and no provision. The Privy Council asked Whitgift to provide for them.

148   Inner Temple, Petyt MS 47, f. 373.

149   Haugaard, *Elizabeth* (n. 127), p. 203.

150   Inner Temple, Petyt MS 47, f. 372.

151   The dean and chapter of Worcester were reportedly melting down the organ to provide dishes and bedsteads for the prebendaries' wives: A.L. Barstow, "The first generation of Anglican clergy wives: Heroines or whores?" *Historical Magazine of the Protestant Episcopal Church* 52 (1983), p. 11. This quixotic crusade was clearly not entirely, if at all, her own idea. In July 1561, Elizabeth was petitioned to take even more drastic action than she did: PRO, SP 15/11/24. See also BL, Lansdowne MS 487/7.

152   Inner Temple, Petyt MS 47, f. 378. In a ballad from the same period, a Cambridge student lamented that love and marriage had ruined his university life, and as he prepared to leave, he prayed that his fellows might be kept safe from beauty "whose bait hath brought me to my bain, and caught me from my books": Clement Robinson, *A Handefull of Pleasant Delites*, ed. Arnold Kershaw (London, 1926), pp. 21–4.

153   Inner Temple, Petyt MS 47, f. 374.

154   Inner Temple, Petyt MS 47, f. 372.

155   Haugaard, *Elizabeth* (n. 127), p. 204. Archbishop Young enjoined obedience to the order in his visitation of the cathedral in 1563: Ox. Bod., Ashmole MS 862, pp. 198–9. It cannot have been observed. One of the minster clergy, Anthony Blake, had been married since the reign of Edward and was a residentiary canon from 1565 to 1570. Thomas Atkinson, another of the minster clergy, was also married during his tenure: *York Clergy Wills 1520–1600: I, Minster Clergy*, ed. Claire Cross, Borthwick Texts and Calendars, vol. 10 (York, 1984), pp. 110, 112. See also Cross, "Priests into ministers (n. 98)," pp. 203–25.

156   BI, HC.AB.5, f. 190.

157   BI, HC.AB.10, f. 54.

158   BI, HC.AB.11, f. 51.

159   BI, HC.AB.13, f. 231v; see the 1586 case of Anne Grecyan, cited in Dickens, *Lollards and Protestants* (n. 24), p. 187.

160   Haigh, *Reformation and Resistance* (n. 98), p. 221.

161   *The Letter Book of John Parkhurst*, ed. Ralph Houlbrooke, Norfolk Record Society, vol. 43 (1974), nos 73, 249. For a few additional cases, see Christopher Haigh, "The Church of England, the Catholics and the people," in *The Reign of Elizabeth I*, ed. Haigh (London, 1984), p. 216; Collinson, *Religion of Protestants* (n. 145), p. 106.

162   *Winchester Consistory Court Depositions 1561–1602*, ed. A.J. Willis, (Lyminge, Kent, 1960), pp. 4–11.

163   CCCC, MSS. 101, 110, 113.

164 Hudson, *Ponet* (n. 128), pp. 80–9.

165 Veron, dedicatory letter.

166 John Jewel, *A Defence of the Apologie of the Church of England* (1567), in *The Works of John Jewel, Bishop of Salisbury*, ed. John Ayre (Cambridge, 1848), vol. 3, pp. 385–429; James Pilkington, "The Burning of St Pauls," in *The Works of Bishop Pilkington*, ed. J. Scholefield (Cambridge, 1842), pp. 564–78.

167 Up to the colon, the wording is that of Article 31 of the Edwardian 42 Articles: *Synodalia* (n. 91), pp. 29–30.

168 13 Eliz., c. 12. See J.E. Neale, *Elizabeth I and her Parliaments 1559–1581* (London, 1953), pp. 166–8, 203–7.

169 The manuscript, Rylands English MS 524, has been edited for publication by Kenneth L. Parker. We are jointly preparing a larger work on Greenham incorporating this text.

170 CRO, Dry Drayton original parish register; *DNB*, s. v. Greenham, Richard, vol. 8, p. 528.

171 Samuel Clarke, *The Lives of Thirty-Two English Divines*, 3d ed (London, 1677), p. 13.

172 Rylands MS 524, f. 38.

173 Rylands MS 524, f. 16v. To avoid concupiscence, Greenham suggested "a continual examination of yourselves by the law; a reverent and daily meditating of the word; a painful walking in our honest calling; an holy shaming of ourselves, and fearing of ourselves before our friends; a continual temperance in diet, sleep and apparel; a careful watching over our eyes and other parts of our bodies; a zealous jealousy to avoid all occasions of persons, times and places which might nourish in us concupiscence; a godly frequenting of times, persons, and places which breed in us mortification, together with an humbling of ourselves, with the shame of sins past, with the grief of sins present, and with the fear of sins to come. Lastly, a careful use of fasting, prayer and watching . . . are means to come to mortification herein, which being wisely and some convenient time used, with a moderate motion and exercise of the body, if they do not prevail, it is like the lord doth call a man to the holy use of marriage" (f. 21v). For Greenham's pastoral counselling activities, see Eric Josef Carlson, "Pastoral ministry in Elizabethan Cambridgeshire" (forthcoming).

174 George Herbert, *A Priest to the Temple, or The Countrey Parson His Character, and Rule of Holy Life*, in *The Works of George Herbert*, ed. F.E. Hutchinson (Oxford, 1941), chap. 9.

175 Henson's letters quoted in Susan Howatch, *Glittering Images* (paperback edn, New York, 1987), pp. 23, 41.

Chapter 4   Canon Law

1   Some of this material previously appeared in Eric Josef Carlson, "Marriage reform and the Elizabethan High Commission," *Sixteenth Century Journal* 21 (1990), 437–51, and is used by permission of its publisher.

2   *To the Christian Nobility of the German Nation Concerning the Reform of the Christian Estate*, ed. J. Atkinson, in *LW*, vol. 44, p. 203.

3   See Steven Ozment, *When Fathers Ruled: Family Life in Reformation Europe* (Cambridge, Mass., 1983), chap. 1.

4   Henry Brinkelow, *The Complaynt of Roderick Mors*, ed. J.M. Cowper, Early English Text Society, extra ser., vol. 22 (1874), pp. 56–7.

5   *The Reformation of the Ecclesiastical Laws of England, 1552*, ed. James C. Spalding, Sixteenth Century Essays and Studies, vol. 19 (Kirksville, Missouri, 1992), pp. 1–57, surveys attempts at canon law reform under the Tudors, but Spalding has not used much recent scholarship and does not know of important manuscripts which would significantly alter his narrative.

6   For a more detailed treatment of this topic, see Eric Josef Carlson, "Royal divorce" in *Historical Dictionary of Tudor England, 1485–1603*, ed. R.H. Fritze (Westport, Conn., 1991), pp. 146–9; H.A. Kelly, *The Matrimonial Trials of Henry VIII* (Stanford, 1976); J.J. Scarisbrick, *Henry VIII* (Berkeley and Los Angeles, 1968), pp. 163–97; *The Divorce Tracts of Henry VIII*, ed. Edward Surtz, S.J., and Virginia Murphy (Angers, 1988), pp. i–xliv.

7   Leviticus 18:16, 20:21. Deuteronomy 25:5 permitted it if the first union was childless, but a decretal of Innocent III established the principle applied in 1503: potentially valid marriage to a brother's childless widow required papal dispensation from the Levitical ban (X.4.19.9).

8   Henry's knowledge of scripture and theology, if eccentric, was adequate for him to reach these conclusions on his own. His position required that he gloss away Deuteronomy 25:5, which he did in two ways. First, he said it was part of the ceremonial law of the Jews which did not bind Christians. Second, he argued from the examples cited in scripture that marriage to a brother's widow required a direct mandate from God, which he did not have. Henry also attacked the specific dispensation he received on technical grounds, but it was the argument from Leviticus which dominated: Scarisbrick, *Henry VIII*, pp. 163–77, 180–83.

9   Ibid., pp. 183–97.

10 Only several years later were Arthur's wedding-night boasts about his sexual conquest of Katherine published: Steven W. Haas, "Henry VIII's *Glasse of Truthe*," *History* 64 (1980), 353–62.

11 Dispensations appear regularly in every volume of *CPPR*.

12 Scarisbrick, *Henry VIII* (n. 6), p. 161.

13 Ibid., chaps. 8–9.

14 Stanford E. Lehmberg, *The Reformation Parliament, 1529–1536* (Cambridge, 1970), pp. 1–7, 76–104.

15 21 Henry VIII cc. 5, 6, 13.

16 Susan Brigden notes that these complaints represent something new, in that they can be seen as attacks on jurisdiction, and not merely greed: *London and the Reformation* (Oxford, 1989), pp. 174–9.

17 Scarisbrick, *Henry VIII* (n. 6), pp. 247–8.

18 Graham Nicholson, "The Act of Appeals and the English Reformation," in *Law and Government under the Tudors*, ed. Claire Cross, David Loades, and J.J. Scarisbrick (Cambridge, 1988), pp. 19–30.

19 Scarisbrick, *Henry VIII* (n. 6), pp. 289–93.

20 On the Commons' Supplication and Submission of the Clergy, see G.R. Elton, "The Commons Supplication of 1532: parliamentary manoeuvres in the reign of Henry VIII," *English Historical Review* 66 (1951), 507–34; J.P. Cooper, "The Supplication against the Ordinaries reconsidered," ibid. 72 (1957), 616–41; John Guy, *The Public Career of Sir Thomas More* (New Haven, 1980), pp. 187–9; Michael Kelly, "The Submission of the Clergy," *Transactions of the Royal Historical Society*, 5th ser., vol. 15 (1965), 97–119.

21 BL, Cotton MS Cleopatra F.I, ff. 104v, 105v, 106–6v. See Glyn Redworth, *In Defence of the Church Catholic: The Life of Stephen Gardiner* (Oxford, 1990), pp. 35–8.

22 BL, Cotton MS Cleopatra F.I, ff. 101–1v.

23 A draft act was prepared, probably for the current session of parliament, which gave the review authority to a "great standing council": PRO, SP 6/7/14, f. 29.

24 *Documents Illustrative of English Church History*, ed. Henry Gee and W.J. Hardy (London, 1896), pp. 176–8.

25 24 Henry VIII, c. 12. Lehmberg, *Reformation Parliament* (n. 14), pp. 163–9, 174–6.

26 25 Henry VIII, c. 19.

27 25 Henry VIII, c. 21.

28 27 Henry VIII, c. 15.

29 35 Henry VIII, c. 16. See *LJ*, vol. 1, pp. 238–40, 244, 250, 254.

30 G.R. Elton, *Reform and Renewal: Thomas Cromwell and the Common Weal* (Cambridge, 1973), pp. 129–38.

31 BL, Lansdowne MS. 97, ff. 148–53.

32 Anon., *A dyaloge betwene one Clemente a clerke of the Convocacyuon, and one Bernarde, a burges of the parlyament, dysputynge betwene them what auctoryte the clergye have to make lawes. And howe farre and where theyr power dothe extende* (n.d.), sig. B6–8v, cited in Harry C. Porter, "Hooker, the Tudor Constitution,

and the *Via Media*," in *Studies in Richard Hooker*, ed. W. Speed Hill (Cleveland, Ohio, 1972), pp. 86–8.

33 BL, Cotton MS Cleopatra F. II, f. 241.

34 *LP*, vol. 9, no. 119; cf. ibid., no. 1065 which, echoing the complaint that the clergy were neglecting their true duties because of the canon law, said that since the clergy were not "preaching, teaching and good example giving," the king should remove almost all of their jurisdiction and teach them that what remained did so at the sufferance of king and parliament and not by "any right that they may claim therein by the laws of God or by any other way." *A Supplycacion to our moste Soveraigne Lorde Kynge Henry the Eyght* (1544), p. 48, listed the business of the courts and said "not one belongs to [the bishop's] office and vocation appointed by God's word."

35 PRO, SP 1/99 f. 231; Elton, *Reform and Renewal* (n. 30), p. 134. See *LP*, vol. 5, no. 805: Chapuys reports that the Duke of Norfolk suggested that matrimonial causes belonged to the temporal sword, but apparently no one agreed. See also SP 6/5, ff. 2–31.

36 BL, Additional MS 48040, ff. 69v–76v. See Donald Logan, "The Henrician Canons," *Bulletin of the Institute of Historical Research* 48 (1974), 99–103.

37 *LP*, vol. 9, nos 549, 615(2), 690, 1069; BL, Cotton MS Titus B.I.160. Studying canon law "engendereth a popish heart": *Supplycacion to our moste Soveraigne Lorde* (n. 34), p. 46. Although university study ceased, private study did not. William Cecil had Thomas Windebank buying canon law books for him in France in 1562: PRO, SP 12/22/9.

38 BL, Cotton MS Cleopatra E. VI, f. 232.

39 BL, Add. MS 48040, ff. 69v–76v.

40 A "home parish" was one in which a person had resided for the previous year.

41 *The Decades of Henry Bullinger*, ed. Thomas Harding, 4 vols (Cambridge, 1849), vol. 3, pp. 119–21.

42 Dale Hoak, *The King's Council in the Reign of Edward VI* (Cambridge, 1976), p. 176.

43 *CJ*, vol. 1, pp. 14–16; *LJ*, vol. 1, pp. 367, 369, 371, 384, 387; 3/4 Edward VI, c. 11. Of the eleven bishops voting, only Barlow voted aye; opponents included reformers Cranmer, Goodrich and Ridley and conservatives Tunstall, Thirlby and Health. The bishops felt that the committee was a stalling tactic and preferred the bill "touching ecclesiastical jurisdiction," a reaction to the decay of ecclesiastical discipline since the Submission of the Clergy, which gave bishops extensive power to imprison and excommunicate. It had been sent to the Commons and buried there. See J.C. Spalding, "The Reformatio Legum Ecclesiasticarum of 1552 and the furthering of discipline in England," *Church History* 39 (1970), 162–71.

44 *APC*, vol. 3, p. 382; see *Reformation of the Ecclesiastical Laws* (n. 44), ed. Spalding, pp. 37–9, for the membership.

45 *CPR, Edward VI, 1550–53*, pp. 114, 354; *APC* vol. 3, p. 410.

46 *Original Letters Relative to the English Reformation*, ed. H. Robinson, 2 vols (Cambridge, 1846–7), vol. 2, p. 503.

47 *LJ*, vol. 1, pp. 419, 428.

48 Martin Micronius blamed Ridley and Goodrich for delaying the business "with their worldly policy": *Original Letters* (n. 46), vol. 2, p. 580.

49 This is suggested in Scheyfve's memo of 10 April 1553: *CSP Span.*, vol. 11, pp. 32–4.

50 *Original Letters* (n. 46), vol. 1, p. 123.

51 *Literary Remains of King Edward the Sixth*, ed. J.G. Nichols (London, 1857), p. 574. A proclamation of 1554 ordered that the old canon law be restored "with all speed and diligence": *TRP*, no. 407. The experience in these years suggests that Joan Kent's argument ("Attitudes of members of the House of Commons to the regulation of 'personal conduct' in late Elizabethan and early Stuart England," *Bulletin of the Institute of Historical Research* 46 [1973], 41–71) applies equally well to the 1540–50s.

52 W.K. Jordan, *Edward VI: The Threshold of Power* (Cambridge, Mass., 1970), p. 360.

53 I have made my translation from Matthew Parker's copy of the 1571 edition of the *Reformatio Legum Ecclesiasticarum*: CCCC, MS 431, ff. 19–28. This has been checked against the text published by Spalding (*Reformation of the Ecclesiastical Laws* (n. 5), pp. 91–106), which appeared after this chapter was completed.

54 This summarizes caps 1–2, 4–5. Cap. 3 orders men to marry women whom they have abused as whores; if they do not, judges were to appraise their goods and give the woman one-third. At very least, the man was to support his children by her.

55 Caps 6–7, 12.

56 Caps 8–9, 11. Cap. 10 banned polygamy, and cap. 13 said that mothers ought to breast-feed their own children.

57 Forbidden kin are listed in *Reformation of the Ecclesiastical Laws* (n. 5), ed. Spalding, p. 98. Illicit unions were included, e.g. a father's concubine was forbidden just as was a father's wife. Death had no impact: a brother's wife was forbidden even after the death of the brother. *Cognatio spiritualis*, the relationship created by godparenthood or confirmation sponsorship, was not scriptural, and ceased to bar marriage.

58 Caps 1–7, 16–18.

59 Caps 8–13, 19.

60 *Sermons by Hugh Latimer*, ed. G.E. Corrie, 2 vols (Cambridge, 1844), vol. 1, p. 243.

61 The section is Book 2, chaps 15–47, in *Melancthon and Bucer*, trans. Wilhelm Pauck, Library of Christian Classics, XIX (Philadelphia, 1969);

John Milton, *The Judgement of Martin Bucer Concerning Divorce* (London 1644). Bucer's teaching is discussed in Pauck, *De Regno Christi: Das Reich Gottes Auf Erden* (Berlin and Leipzig, 1928).

62 Bucer also proposed that each parish have lay "guardians of matrimony" who would watch and investigate all marriages. If anything was amiss they would try to resolve it, admonishing the couple, and only failing that would they turn to civil magistrates: Bucer, *De Regno Christi* (n. 61), cap. 21.

63 Bucer, *De Regno Christi* (n. 61), cap. 38; see *Bullinger's Decades* (n. 41), vol. 1, pp. 397–8.

64 Latimer, *Sermons* (n. 60), vol. 1, p. 170.

65 Ibid., p. 169.

66 Visitation article no. 32 (1551/2): *Later Writings of Bishop Hooper*, ed. Charles Nevinson (Cambridge, 1852), p. 126.

67 Bucer, *De Regno Christi* (n. 61), cap. 18. See Bucer's letter to John Haddon, CCCC, MS 113, pp. 21–3 (22 May 1550) which makes a similar point based on Roman law precedents, which was adequate precedent for him because he considered marriage a civil matter. Bullinger (*Decades* (n. 63), vol. 1, pp. 395, 403–4) agrees that parents are to be honored, but not to the point of allowing them to sever couples.

68 C. Hopf, *Martin Bucer and the English Reformation* (Oxford, 1946), pp. 107–15 unjustifiably gives Bucer credit for this. Cranmer had held the position long before he was in contact with Bucer, and it was Cranmer, not Bucer, who was on the committee.

69 J.P. Donnelly, "The social and ethical thought of Peter Martyr Vermigli," in *Peter Martyr Vermigli and Italian Reform*, ed. J.C. McLelland (Waterloo, Ont., 1980), pp. 114–15.

70 Bucer, *De Regno Christi* (n. 61), cap. 36.

71 Ibid., cap. 38. See James Turner Johnson, *A Society Ordained By God* (New York, 1970).

72 Burcher to Bullinger, 8 June 1550, *Original Letters* (n. 46), vol. 2, p. 665; see L.T. Dibdin, *English Church Law and Divorce* (London, 1912), p. 25.

73 *The Seconde Parte of a Register*, ed. Albert Peel, 2 vols (London, 1915), vol. 2, p. 72.

74 Ibid., p. 73.

75 *CJ*, vol. 1, pp. 55–6, 58; *LJ*, vol. 1, pp. 566, 568.

76 Norman L. Jones, *Faith by Statute: Parliament and the Settlement of Religion 1559* (London, 1982), p. 99.

77 *Zurich Letters, 1558–1602*, ed. H. Robinson, 2 vols (Cambridge, 1845), vol. 1, p. 85.

78 William Haugaard, *Elizabeth and the English Reformation* (Cambridge, 1968), pp. 169–76, 342–56.

79   Bishop Sandys made a similar suggestion: Strype, *Annals*, vol. 1, pt 1, pp. 475–6, 500.

80   Ibid., pp. 502–6, 508–12; CCCC, MS 121, pp. 267–355.

81   *Proceedings in the Parliaments of Elizabeth I, Volume I: 1558–1581*, ed. T.E. Hartley (Leicester, 1981), pp. 81–2.

82   Huntington Library, Hastings Religious Papers, Box 1 (unnumbered). I am grateful to Norman Jones for calling my attention to this text, now printed in "An Elizabethan bill for the reformation of the ecclesiastical law," *Parliamentary History* 4 (1985), pp. 184–6, though I dispute his dating.

83   Jones, "Elizabethan bill (n. 82)," pp. 179–80.

84   Hartley, *Proceedings* (n. 81), pp. 200–1.

85   See G.R. Elton, *The Parliament of England 1559–1581* (Cambridge, 1986), pp. 207–9.

86   Wallace T. MacCaffrey, *The Shaping of the Elizabethan Regime* (Princeton, 1968), pp. 11–12, 406–7.

87   Wallace T. MacCaffrey, *Queen Elizabeth and the Making of Policy, 1572–1588* (Princeton, 1981), p. 64.

88   See Patrick Collinson, *The Elizabethan Puritan Movement* (London, 1967), pp. 109–21.

89   *Seconde Parte* (n. 73), vol. 1, p. 89.

90   Ibid., p. 58.

91   Collinson, *Puritan Movement* (n. 88), p. 38.

92   Donald McGinn, *The Admonition Controversy* (New Brunswick, NJ, 1949), p. 339.

93   *Seconde Parte* (n. 73), p. 150, for example.

94   Collinson, *Puritan Movement* (n. 88), pp. 222–39.

95   *Seconde Parte* (n. 73), vol. 2, pp. 1–4.

96   MacCaffrey, *Making of Policy* (n. 87), p. 117.

97   BL, Cotton MS Titus B.I, f. 160. Possibly the bill became the (unsuccessful) bill to prevent the marriage of minors without parental consent which was part of a flood of legal reform in 1539–40. The bill passed the Lords but disappeared.

98   28 Henry c. 7, § 7; BL, Cotton MS Cleopatra E.V., f. 102. Wriostheley reported in March 1536 that Lutherans married wives' sisters, and abolished spiritual cognition: *LP*, vol. 10, no. 586. Cranmer may have been influenced by Osiander: PRO, SP 6/9/1.

99   Cranmer seemed to reject this principle when he refused to allow Henry Reppes of Suffolk to marry his nephew's widow; she claimed that she had not had sexual relations with her first husband. Reppes had married her after receiving the favorable advice of Ridley, Hooper and a Lasco: Ralph Houlbrooke, *Church Courts and the People during the English Reformation 1520–1570* (Oxford, 1979), p. 75.

100 Later, 28 Henry VIII c. 26, § 2 sorted out marriages made by Roman dispensations before 3 November 1534: unless forbidden by God's law, scripture, or the Act of Succession, they were upheld.

101 28 Henry VIII, c. 24; Stanford E. Lehmberg, *The Later Parliaments of Henry VIII 1536–1547* (Cambridge, 1977), pp. 34–6; David Head, " 'Beyng Ledde and Seduced by the Devyll': The attainder of Lord Thomas Howard and the Tudor law of treason," *Sixteenth Century Journal* 13 (1982), pp. 3–16.

102 32 Henry VIII, c. 38; *LJ*, vol. 1, pp. 150–2; Lehmberg, *Later Parliaments* (n. 101), p. 101; BL, Cotton MS Cleopatra E.V, ff. 112–18.

103 *LP*, vol. 14, pt. 1, no. 870; vol. 18, no. 167. Apparently clergymen used Bethlehem Hospital in London to marry in violation of the Six Articles: *LP*, vol. 14, pt 1, no. 896; EDR, D/2/3, ff. 15, 19; F/5/35, ff. 133–35; G/1/8, ff. 6–7. See Eric Josef Carlson, "The marriage of William Turner," *Historical Research* 65 (1992), 336–9.

104 2/3 Edward VI, c. 23. For passage: *LJ*, vol. 1, p. 333; *CJ*, vol. 1, p. 7.

105 *TRP*, no. 303, pp. 422–3.

106 *LJ*, vol. 1, pp. 413, 425; *CJ*, vol. 1, pp. 22–3.

107 *CJ*, vol. 1, pp. 6, 9.

108 *LP*, vol. 16, no. 878(26). For the extent of the Bourchier lands, see Eric Josef Carlson, "The Bourchiers," U.C.L.A. Department of History M.A. paper, 1978.

109 HLRO, 34/5 Henry VIII, O.A. 39. The text is badly damaged. A fair copy used in a debate of 1659 can fill the gaps: Ox. Bod., MS Rawlinson A. 112, ff. 66–7. See *LJ*, vol. 1, pp. 215, 217–18, 221, 224, 232.

110 PRO, SP 10/2/32, undated, 1547.

111 *CPR, Edward VI*, vol. 1, p. 137. One change in membership was made 7 May: ibid., p. 261.

112 *APC*, vol. 2, pp. 164–5. It is possible that Parr's actions were in part behind the proclamation of 1548 and the proposed bigamy act described above, but the extreme language of these instruments makes it seem unlikely to me that they were aimed at only one person's example.

113 Lambeth MS. 1108, ff. 144–81v.

114 There is no direct evidence for this, though the tradition is strong.

115 Matthew 19:9 (". . . *quicumque dimiserit uxorem suam, nisi ob fornicationem, et aliam duxerit, moechatur*"); and 5:32 (". . . *excepta fornicationis causa, facit eam moechari*"); cf. Mark 10:11, Luke 16:18.

116 Jesus let an adulterous woman go unpunished in John 8:1–11, and in that gospel, Jesus says nothing about divorce.

117 Dibdin, *Church Law and Divorce* (n. 72), App. E.

118 *Early Writings of John Hooper*, ed. S. Carr (Cambridge, 1843), p. 379. Hooper sent what he had written to Bucer so that he could judge Hooper

for himself in light of *"multis et falsis calumnii"* levelled against him: BL, Add. MS. 28571, f. 24.

119 Internal evidence suggests that *De Matrimonio* and *De Gradibus* were Cranmer's, and *De Adulteriis* Vermigli's work, since the former includes issues long of concern to Cranmer, and the latter radical continental theology which Cranmer rejected two years before. Arguments based on language in different sections of law codes are too hazardous to accept: see Bruce W. Frier, "Law on the installment plan", *Michigan Law Review* 82 (1984), 856–68. On authorship of *De Adulteriis*, see R. Haw, *The State of Matrimony* (London, 1952), pp. 81–7.

120 HLRO, 5 Edward VI, O.A. no. 30; *LJ*, vol. 1, pp. 408–9; *CJ*, vol. 1, pp. 20–1.

121 David Loades, *The Reign of Mary Tudor* (London, 1979), pp. 71–2, 206.

122 J.A. Muller, *Stephen Gardiner and the Tudor Reaction* (New York, 1926), pp. 187, 217.

123 Loades, *Reign of Mary* (n. 121), p. 137; 1 Mary, st. 3 c. 47; *CPR 1553–4*, p. 213 (13 January 1554); *CPR 1557–8*, pp. 376, 382 (6 & 8 August 1558); PRO, SP 11/12/47.

124 HLRO, 1 Mary session 2, O.A. no. 30; *CJ*, vol 1, pp. 30–1.

125 A few patchwork canons in 1585 and 1597, never knit together into anything resembling a code of laws, were adopted. They lacked coherance and completeness, as well as parliamentary ratification, which was their undoing. Collinson noted, "Their capacity to excite the loyalty and obedience of clergy and laity was not great.": *Puritan Movement* (n. 88), p. 39; Canons printed in *Synodalia*, ed. E. Cardwell (Oxford, 1842).

126 *Proceedings* (n. 81), ed. Hartley, p. 477; *CJ*, vol. 1, pp. 104, 106.

127 *Proceedings* (n. 81), ed. Hartley, pp. 529–30; *CJ*, vol. 1, p. 120. Such a bill did pass in 1604: 1 James I, c. 12.

128 *LJ*, vol. 2, p. 99; Simonds D'Ewes, *A Compleat Journal of the Votes, Speeches and Debates both of the House of Lords and House of Commons Throughout the Whole Reign of Queen Elizabeth of Glorious Memory* (London, 1594), pp. 360–3, 367.

129 When Cartwright raised objections to selling dispensations to marry during these times, Whitgift admitted that he too "misliked that there should be any time forbidden to marry in": *The Works of John Whitgift*, ed. John Ayre, 3 vols (Cambridge, 1851–3), vol. 3, pp. 276–8. However when this bill was proposed, Whitgift complained to the queen that the bill slandered the church by suggesting that it had maintained an error: John Strype, *The Life and Acts of John Whitgift, D.D.*, 3 vols (London, 1718; repr. Oxford, 1822), vol. 1, p. 391. Admittedly, the prohibitions were ignored in practice: see chap. 6.

130 *APC*, vol. 27, pp. 201–3; A.F. Pollard and Marjorie Blatcher, "Hayward

Townsend's Journals," *Bulletin of the Institute of Historical Research* 12 (1934), p. 12. See also E.W. Ives, "Agaynst taking awaye of Women: the inception and operation of the Abduction Act of 1487," in *Wealth and Power in Tudor England*, ed. E.W. Ives, et al. (London, 1978), 21–44.

131 *LJ*, vol. 2, pp. 195, 197.

132 If the abduction was collusive and the couple wanted to avoid her parents, they would obtain a license to marry away from either of their parishes and without banns. While they might find a minister who would marry them without a license, that was more trouble than securing the license. See Patrick McGrath, "Notes on the history of marriage licences," in *Gloucestershire Marriage Allegations 1637–1680*, ed. B. Frith, Bristol and Gloucestershire Archaeological Society, Record Section, 2 (1954). A survey of cases from the Act Books of the northern High Commission suggests that the causes of such marriages were about equally divided between dodging parental disapproval and marrying to frustrate a matrimonial suit in progress against one of the parties: BI, HC.AB.1–14, passim.

133 Strype, *Annals*, vol. 1, pt 1, p. 475; pt 2, pp. 563–4.

134 Strype, *Annals*, vol. 1, pt 1, p. 484. They were voidable only if the parents chose to file suit, not *ipso facto*.

135 *Proceedings* (n. 81), ed. Hartley, p. 222.

136 D'Ewes, *Journal* (n. 128), pp. 167, 222–3.

137 *CJ*, vol. 1, pp. 84, 87–8; D'Ewes, *Journal* (n. 128), pp. 180–2.

138 Ox. Bod., Ashmole MS 1792, ff. 4v–5; PRO, SP 12/163/31.

139 The Canon of 1597 reinforced parental authority even more, establishing additional safeguards to insure that people did not fraudulently demonstrate consent with forged documents or other devices: *Synodalia* (n. 125), vol. 1, pp. 143, 152–3, 161–3.

140 *Seconde Parte* (n. 73), vol. 1, pp. 182, 190, 194.

141 D'Ewes, *Journal* (n. 128), pp. 555–6.

142 Ibid., pp. 556, 558; Inner Temple, Petyt MS 538; BL, Cotton MS Cleopatra F. 2, ff. 232–3.

143 BL, Cotton MS Cleopatra F. 2, f. 228.

144 D'Ewes, *Journal* (n. 128), pp. 561–2.

145 Ibid., p. 641; BL, Stowe MS 362, ff. 114v–15.

146 His changes are apparent in the manuscript: BL, Cotton MS Cleopatra E.V, ff. 112–18.

147 *LP*, vol. 16, no. 106.

148 Elton, *Reform and Renewal* (n. 30), p. 140. Henry probably did not even see their reform treatises: Cranmer to Capito: Henry "has not the patience to read [treatises] himself" but farmed them out: *Miscellaneous Writings and Letters of Thomas Cranmer*, ed. J.E. Cox (Cambridge, 1846), no. 192.

149 For the fate of canon law study, see R.H. Helmholz, *Roman Canon Law in Reformation England* (Cambridge, 1990), pp. 121–57. Helmholz's book, which appeared after this chapter was completed, discusses changes in marriage and divorce law (pp. 69–79) which largely harmonize with the discussion above.

Chapter 5   Extraparliamentary Pressure

1 Charles Donahue, "Roman canon law in the medieval English church: Stubbs vs. Maitland re-examined after 75 years in the light of some records from the church courts," *Michigan Law Review* 72 (1974), 647–716.

2 This statement is based upon my study of the consistory in the dioceses of Ely and York, and the court of the Dean of York, as well as the material surveyed by Ralph Houlbrooke, *Church Courts and the People during the English Reformation 1520–1570* (Oxford, 1979).

3 *APC*, vol. 19, p. 148; vol. 20, pp. 167–8, 242–3; vol. 21, pp. 102–3; vol. 22, p. 259; vol. 24, p. 283.

4 *APC*, vol. 17, pp. 286–7; vol. 18, pp. 18–19; vol. 25, pp. 211–12.

5 *APC*, vol. 13, pp. 104–5; J.H. LePatourel, *The Medieval Administration of the Channel Islands, 1199–1399* (London, 1937); A.J. Eagleston, *The Channel Islands under Tudor Government, 1485–1642: A Study in Administrative History* (Cambridge, 1949).

6 For example, PRO, C1/1108/34: Edward Brockton contracted marriage with Dorothy Herring. Although her mother initially consented, after Edward gave Dorothy money for clothes and jewels, the mother convinced Dorothy to refuse marriage. He requested aid in recovering his expenses. See also C1/780/18, C1/867/69, C1/1150/79.

7 For example, PRO, C1/1150/65: John Polleckson complained that Harry Cantrell promised him, before witnesses, white tin worth £4 if he married Joan Maynard. John married Joan but Harry refused to fulfill his promise and since John did not have a common law remedy, he asked the Chancellor's aid. See also C1/782/33, 36; C1/808/61; C1/1133/1, 13, 78–9.

8 PRO, C1/832/49.

9 PRO, C1/867/12.

10 PRO, C1/703/2. Records of action have not survived for any of these cited petitions.

11 *Acta Cancellariae*, ed. Cecil Munro (London, 1847), p. 9.

12 *LJ*, vol. 1, pp. 300–1. The committee included Archbishop Cranmer; the bishops of London, Durham, Ely, and Coventry and Lichfield; the earls of Arundel and Southampton; Lord Cobham; and others *"a consiliis jurisperitis."*

13 Philip Tyler, "The significance of the ecclesiastical commission of York," *Northern History* 2 (1967), 27–44. The southern Ecclesiastical Commission's records do not survive. This study is based on the Borthwick Institute's fourteen act books (a complete run) of the northern Commission, created in 1561. Much of what follows has appeared previously in Eric Josef Carlson, "Marriage reform and the Elizabethan High Commission," *Sixteenth Century Journal* 21 (1990), 437–51, and is used here with permission of its publisher.

14 BI, HC. AB. 1, f. 18.

15 BI, HC.AB.1, f. 92.

16 BI, HC.AB.1, ff. 9v–10. See also the case of Ralph Conyers, who married Katherine Brakenbury without banns knowing that there was a matrimonial suit pending against her and refused to separate from her. The commissioners had him imprisoned for his contempt. He was fined £20 on top of his penance for marrying without banns: HC.AB.1, ff. 113, 115v–116, 157, 164, 167v.

17 BI, HC.AB.6, ff. 103v, 150v–1, 159; HC.AB.7, ff. 50–1, 66v, 77, 79v.

18 BI, HC.AB.7, f. 191v; HC.AB.8, ff. 6, 13; HC.AB.7, ff. 192, 195; HC.AB.8, ff. 5, 13.

19 BI, HC.AB.8, ff. 43v, 77, 80, 94, 148; HC.AB.9, ff. 18, 27v, 32, 43, 52, 54, 65, 72v, 76–77, 85v, 175v, 234.

20 BI, HC.AB.2, f. 93; HC.AB.3 ff. 140v–1, 148.

21 PRO, SP 12/12/154.

22 BI, CP.G.863, 1033; CCCC, MS. 105, pp. 195–7.

23 PRO, SP 12/19/25.

24 PRO, SP 12/20/22.

25 *CPR, Eliz, I. 1560–63*, pp. 336–7; CCCC, MSS. 105, 113.

26 HC.AB.1, ff. 34v–35; HC.AB.7, ff. 121–2v. The commission's attitude towards incest cases was somewhat unpredictable: see Carlson, "Marriage reform (n. 13)," p. 446.

27 HC.AB.7, ff. 50–51.

28 HC.AB.7, ff. 66v, 77.

29 For the Injunction, see p. 59 above.

30 They refused to hear some such cases: HC.AB.10, f. 180v.

31 HC.AB.2, ff. 80v, 82–83v, 84v–86.

32 HC.AB.8, ff. 119v, 141, 146; HC.AB.9, ff. 154, 161.

33 R.H. Helmholz, *Roman Canon Law in Reformation England* (Cambridge, 1990), pp. 77–9.

34 PRO, SP 12/271/144, 145; SP 12/272/7.

35 HC.AB.14, ff. 191v–192v.

36 For example, HC.AB.14, ff. 230v, 238, 242.

37 *HMC, Salisbury*, vol. 11, p. 26.

38 Helmholz, *Roman Canon Law* (n. 33), p. 69.

39 Printed in *Visitation Articles and Injunctions*, ed. W.H. Frere and W.P.M. Kennedy, Alcuin Club, vols 14–16 (1910).

40 Ibid., vol. 2, pp. 111–12.

41 CCCC, MS. 113, used here, contains various editions with Parker's personal notations. The text is printed in *Documentary Annals of the Reformed Church of England*, ed. E. Cardwell, 2 vols (Oxford, 1844), vol. 1, pp. 316–20.

42 R.H. Helmholz, *Marriage Litigation in Medieval England* (Cambridge, 1974), pp. 77–87.

43 Based on the records of the consistory courts of York and Ely for the years 1530–1558. There are no cases from Ely nor in any of the cause papers for York. Parker's register notes one case in 1560 of a man who married his wife's sister's daughter: *Registrum Matthei Parker*, ed. E. Margaret Thompson, Canterbury and York Society, vols 35, 36, 39 (1928), vol. 1, p. 667.

44 See above, p. 90.

45 PRO, SP 12/12/54. See also PRO, SP 12/19/25, 12/19/53, 12/20/22; BI, CP. G. 1033; *CPR, Eliz. I, 1560–63*, pp. 336–7.

46 BI, HC.AB.1, ff. 34v–35; HC.AB.7, ff. 121–122v.

47 *Documentary Annals* (n. 41), vol. 1, p. 301.

48 *Correspondence of Matthew Parker*, ed. J. Bruce and T.T. Perowne (Cambridge, 1853), pp. 176–7.

49 CCCC, MS.105, pp. 123–97; MS. 113, pp. 411–22.

50 See Visitation *Articles and Injunctions* (n. 39).

51 *Visitation Articles and Injunctions* (n. 39), vol. 3, p. 277.

52 *Depositions and Other Ecclesiastical Proceedings from the Courts of Durham*, ed. James Raine, Surtees Society, vol. 21 (1845), p. 59.

53 See below, chap. 7.

54 Nancy F. Anderson, "The 'Marriage with a Deceased Wife's Sister Bill' controversy: Incest anxiety and the defense of family purity in Victorian England," *Journal of British Studies* 21 (1982), 67–86. See Helmholz, *Roman Canon Law* (n. 33), pp. 75–6.

55 Based on *Visitation Articles and Injunctions* (n. 39); and *Elizabethan Episcopal Administration*, ed. W.P.M. Kennedy, Alcuin Club, vols 25–7 (London, 1924).

56 *Visitation Articles and Injunctions* (n. 39), vol. 3, p. 208.

57 See below, chap. 7.

58 The old taboo against marriage during certain seasons of the year was mentioned only twice in thirty-seven sets of articles and injunctions, apparently being allowed officially to fall into desuetude.

59 *The Sermons of Edwin Sandys DD*, ed. James Ayre (Cambridge, 1841), pp. 50–1.

60 *HMC, Salisbury*, vol. 7, p. 453.

61 Helmholz (*Roman Canon Law* [n. 33], pp. 71–2) notes that the church began *ex officio* prosecutions against lay people who were present at - clandestine marriages which, he believes, "must have worked to discourage" them. People would now either be unwilling to witness such a contract, or would be reluctant to appear in court to uphold it since that would be self-incriminating.

62 Interestingly, this was not the subject of an official homily. Instead, there is only a homily (written by Thomas Becon) on fornication and adultery: *Certain Sermons or Homilies (1547)*, ed. Ronald B. Bond (Toronto, 1987), pp. 174–86. See Bond, " 'Dark deeds darkly answered': Thomas Becon's homily against whoredom and adultery, its contexts, and its affiliations with three Shakespeare plays," *Sixteenth Century Journal* 16 (1985), 191–205.

63 See chap. 3. The one visitation article which inquired if ministers married couples without the Lord's Supper was from Chichester in 1586 (*Elizabethan Episcopal Administration* [n. 55], vol. 3, p. 213) which could reflect the durable classical movement in Sussex: Roger Manning, *Religion and Society in Elizabethan Sussex* (Leicester, 1979).

64 Christopher Haigh, *Reformation and Resistance in Tudor Lancashire* (Cambridge, 1976), pp. 48–9, where he disputes Peter Laslett, *The World We Have Lost* (London, 1983), pp. 81–90.

65 See pp. 85–6

66 This subject has also been taken up by Lawrence Stone, *The Crisis of the Aristocracy 1558–1641* (Oxford, 1965), pp. 594–611, and *The Family, Sex and Marriage in England 1500–1800* (New York, 1977).

67 *APC*, vol. 15, pp. 31–2.

68 The Grey-Hertford marriage and its aftermath is discussed in detail in *MER*, pp. 282–8. I hope soon to address these events in an article on marriage and the Royal Supremacy.

69 *HMC, Bath*, vol. 4, pp. 155–6, 190–3, 199; BL, Add. MS 38139, ff. 251v–2; Add. MS 32092, f. 52.

70 BI, HC.AB.10, f. 126.

71 *The Loseley Manuscripts*, ed. Alfred Kempe (London, 1836), pp. 329–33, 336–8.

72 BI, HC.AB.10, ff. 182v–3.

73 PRO, C1/1108/34.

74 PRO, SP 46/24/128–9.

75 BL, Lansdowne MS 7/38–41; PRO, SP 12/31/1–2; John Strype, *The Life and Acts of Matthew Parker*, 3 vols (London, 1711; repr. Oxford, 1821) vol. 1, pp. 286–9.

76 F.G. Emmison, *Elizabethan Life: Wills of Essex Gentry and Merchants* (Chelmsford, 1978), pp. 85, 319.

77 Based on ibid., and Emmison, *Elizabethan Life: Wills of Essex Gentry and Yeomen* (Chelmsford, 1980).
78 Stone suggests that such restrictions became less common over time, but he gives no evidence: *Crisis* (n. 66), pp. 597–8. The Essex wills with restrictions are very evenly distributed, arguing against Stone's view.
79 *Wills of Essex Gentry and Merchants* (n. 76), p. 123.
80 PRO, SP 12/154/47.
81 Quoted in Stone, *Crisis* (n. 66), pp. 596–7.
82 *Wills of Essex Gentry and Merchants* (n. 76), p. 216.
83 Ibid., pp. 8, 211.
84 BI, CP.G.2668–9.

Chapter 6   *Law and Practice in the Formation of Marriage in English Communities*

1 For a similar argument, see Martin Ingram, *Church Courts, Sex and Marriage in England, 1570–1640* (Cambridge, 1987), with whom I agree, though with differences in emphasis and focus.
2 Ibid., p. 15.
3 Vivienne Larminie, "Marriage and the family: The example of the seventeenth-century Newdigates," *Midland History* 11 (1984), 1–22; Miriam Slater, *Family Life in the Seventeenth Century: The Verneys of Claydon House* (London, 1984); Lawrence Stone, *The Crisis of the Aristocracy 1558–1641* (Oxford, 1965); idem, *The Family, Sex and Marriage in England 1500–1800* (New York, 1977).
4 While similar models have been developed in earlier studies, none has attempted to combine sources synthetically in this way, or focused exclusively on the sixteenth century before the Canons of 1603 significantly altered the playing field. See Susan Dwyer Amussen, *An Ordered Society: Gender and Class in Early Modern England* (Oxford, 1988); Ralph A. Houlbrooke, *The English Family 1450–1700* (London, 1984), chap. 4; and Keith Wrightson, *English Society 1580–1680* (New Brunswick, NJ, 1982), chap. 3. John Gillis, *For Better, For Worse: British Marriages 1600 to the Present* (New York, 1985), pp. 11–105, reads back from much later material, producing serious distortions of early modern practices.
5 See Kathleen M. Davies, "Continuity and change in literary advice on marriage," *Marriage and Society: Studies in the Social History of Marriage*, ed. R.B. Outhwaite (London, 1981), pp. 58–80; and Chilton Latham Powell, *English Domestic Relations 1487–1653* (New York, 1917). James Turner Johnson, *A Society Ordained by God* (New York, 1970) and Margo Todd, *Christian Humanism and the Puritan Social Order* (Cambridge, 1987), chap. 4, are limited in focus but useful. Louis B. Wright, *Middle-Class Culture in*

Elizabethan England (Chapel Hill, N.C. 1935), pp. 201–27, is valuable for its description of the contents of Elizabethan books, although his use of the category "middle-class" is not: J.H. Hexter, "The myth of the middle class in Tudor England," *Reappraisals in History* (Evanston, Ill., 1961), pp. 71–116. Richard L. Greaves, *Society and Religion in Elizabethan England* (Minneapolis, 1981), pp. 115–99, makes often arbitrary and uncritical attempts to classify books as either "anglican" or "puritan"; Lu Emily Pearson, *Elizabethans at Home* (Stanford, 1957), chap. 5, uncritically mixes material from both centuries to describe "Elizabethan" life.

6   See Bernard Capp, "Popular literature," *Popular Culture in Seventeenth Century England*, ed. Barry Reay (London, 1985), 198–243; Hyder E. Rollins, "The black-letter broadside ballad," *Proceedings of the Modern Language Association* 34 (1919), pp. 258–339; Tessa Watt, *Cheap Print and Popular Piety, 1550–1640* (Cambridge, 1991); and Natascha Würzbach, *The Rise of the English Street Ballad 1550–1650* (Cambridge, 1990). Excellent though limited to the seventeenth century are: Martin Ingram, "The reform of popular culture? Sex and marriage in early modern England," *Popular Culture*, ed. Reay, pp. 129–65; J.A. Sharpe, "Plebeian marriage in Stuart England: Some evidence from popular literature," *Transactions of the Royal Historical Society*, 5th ser., vol. 36 (1986), 69–90; and Margaret Spufford, *Small Books and Pleasant Histories: Popular Fiction and Its Readership in Seventeenth Century England* (London, 1981), pp. 156–93. See also Joy Wiltenburg, *Disorderly Women and Female Power in the Street Literature of Early Modern England and Germany*, (Charlottesville, Va., 1992).

7   See Ralph A. Houlbrooke, *Church Courts and the People during the English Reformation 1520–1570* (Oxford, 1979); idem, "The making of marriage in mid-Tudor England: Evidence from the records of matrimonial contract litigation," *Journal of Family History* 10 (1985), 339–51; Ingram, *Church Courts* (n. 1), chap. 4; and Diana O'Hara, " 'Ruled by my friends': Aspects of marriage in the diocese of Canterbury, *c*.1540–1570," *Continuity and Change* 6 (1991), 9–41.

8   See Eric Josef Carlson, "The historical value of the Ely consistory probate records," in *Index of the Probate Records of the Consistory Court of Ely 1449–1858*, ed. Elisabeth Leedham-Green, 3 vols (London, forthcoming), vol. 1, pp. xvii ff.

9   For the sources and their uses, see *MER*, pp. 324–41.

10 *The Office of Christian Parents: Shewing how children are to be governed throughout all ages and times of their lives* (Cambridge, 1616), p. 134. (My emphasis.) See Erik Dal and Povl Skårup, *The Ages of Man and the Months of the Year: Poetry, Prose and Pictures Outlining the Douze mois figures Motif Mainly Found in Shepherds' Calendars in the Livres d'Heures (14th to 17th Century)*, Historisk-filosofiske Skrifter 9:3 (Copenhagen, 1980).

11 In twelfth century France, a man would not be considered a *vir* until he had children; married men without children were called youths, regardless of chronological age: Georges Duby, "Youth in aristocratic society: Northwestern France in the twelfth century," in *The Chivalrous Society*, trans. Cynthia Postan (Berkeley, 1977), pp. 112–13. Sir Thomas Smith wrote that in England no one could be called a "yeoman" until he was married and had children and had some authority among his neighbors: *De Republica Anglorum*, ed. Mary Dewar (Cambridge, 1982), p. 76.

12 Richard M. Smith, "Population and its geography in England 1500–1730," *An Historical Geography of England and Wales*, ed. R.A. Dodgshon and R.A. Butlin, (London, 1978), 199–237; idem, "Some reflections on the evidence for the origins of the European marriage pattern in England," *The Sociology of the Family*, ed. C. Harris, Sociological Review Monograph 28 (London, 1979), 49–73. See also John Hajnal, "European marriage patterns in perspective," *Population in History*, ed. D.V. Glass and D.E.C. Eversley, (Chicago, 1965), 101–36; R.B. Outhwaite, "Age at marriage in England from the seventeenth to the nineteenth centuries," *Transactions of the Royal Historical Society*, 5th ser., vol. 23 (1973), 55–70; and E.A. Wrigley and R.S. Schofield, *The Population History of England 1541–1871* (Cambridge, Mass., 1981), pp. 257–65, 423–4.

13 CRO, original registers of Grantchester, Dry Drayton; *The Registers of Shipton*, Shropshire Parish Registers, Diocese of Hereford, vol. 1 (1900); Ingram, *Church Courts* (n. 1), pp. 129–30.

14 Susan Brigden, "Youth and the English Reformation," in *Rebellion, Popular Protest and the Social Order in Early Modern England*, ed. Paul Slack (Cambridge, 1984), pp. 77–80, 86.

15 Quoted in Keith Thomas, "Age and authority in early modern England," *Proceedings of the British Academy* 62 (1976), p. 217.

16 John Stockwood, *A Bartholmew Fairing for Parentes, to bestow upon their sonnes and daughters, and for one friend to give unto another: shewing that children are not to marry without the consent of their parents, in whose power and choise it lieth to provide wives and husbandes for their sonnes and daughters* (London, 1589), pp. 10–11, 34–5, 80–4.

17 Charles Gibbon, *A Work worth the Reading, Wherein is Contayned five profitable and pithy Questions, very expedient, as well for Parents to perceive howe to bestowe their Children in marriage, and to dispose their goods at their death; as for all other Persons to receive great profit by the rest of the matters herein expressed* (London, 1591), pp. 2–16.

18 [H. Bullinger,] *The golden booke of Christian matrimony, most necessary and profitable for all them that intend to live quietly and godly in the Christian state of holy wedlock*, trans. Miles Coverdale, (London, 1542), sig. B1v–3; *The*

Decades of Henry Bullinger, ed. Thomas Harding, 4 vols (Cambridge, 1849), vol. 1, pp. 395, 403–4.

19 Thomas Becon, *The booke of Matrimony both profitable and comfortable for all them, that entende quietly and godly to lyve in the holy state of honourable wedlock*, in *The worckes of Thomas Becon*, 3 vols (London, 1564), vol. 1, f. 610.

20 Philip Stubbes, *The Anatomie of Abuses* (London, 1583), sig. V5.

21 *Tell-Trothes New-Yeares Gift*, ed. F.J. Furnivall, New Shakespeare Society, ser. 6, vol. 2 (London, 1876), p. 5. William Vaughan said one of the principal duties of parents was that they "not mar their children by marrying them during their minorities": *The Golden-grove, moralized in three Bookes: A worke very necessary for all such, as would know how to govern themselves, their houses, or their countrey* (London, 1600).

22 *Child-Marriages, Divorces, and Ratifications, etc. In the Diocese of Chester, A.D. 1561–6*, ed. F.J. Furnivall, Early English Text Society, vol. 108 (London, 1897), p. 4.

23 *Child-Marriages* (n. 22), ed. Furnivall, pp. 4, 10, 12, 23, 32.

24 PRO, C1/1412/55.

25 BI, CP.G.163.

26 BI, D/C.CP.1536/1.

27 See J.A. Sharpe, "Last dying speeches: Religion, ideology and public execution in seventeenth century England," *Past and Present* 107 (1985), 144–67. The ballad text is in *RB*, vol. 1, pp. 555–8.

28 EDR, D/2/7, f. 221.

29 See Peter Laslett, *The World We Have Lost*, (3d edn, London, 1983), pp. 86–7; Christopher Haigh, *Reformation and Resistance in Tudor Lancashire* (Cambridge, 1975), pp. 48–9; *MER*, pp. 343–50.

30 EDR, D/2/11, ff. 202–3; see BI, CP.G.1337, 1358.

31 BI, TRANS.CP.1564/1; BI, CP.G.779. See also BI, CP.G.1733, 1746; CP.G.2668–9.

32 BI, CP.G.1330.

33 BI, CP.G.167, 756.

34 CRO, Original Registers of Dry Drayton, Little Wilbraham.

35 David Hey, however, calculates that 41.4% of marriages in Myddle between 1541 and 1599 involved two people from the parish. Another 54.4% involved at least one person from Myddle. He does not explain how he arrives at the decision that someone is "from" Myddle, and these figures are extremely suspect given the very low rates in nearby parishes: *An English Rural Community: Myddle under the Tudors and Stuarts* (Leicester, 1974), p. 201.

36 Ann Kussmaul, *Servants in Husbandry in Early Modern England* (Cambridge, 1981); Ilana Krausman Ben-Amos, "Service and the coming of age of young men in seventeenth-century England," *Continuity and Change* 3

(1988), 41–64; Steven R. Smith, "The London apprentices as seventeenth-century adolescents," in *Rebellion, Popular Protest and the Social Order* (n. 14), pp. 219–31.

37 BI, D/C.CP.1534/1; D/C.AB.7, ff. 405–6; CP.G. 174, 311, 834, 1004, 1008, 1512, 2394; EDR, D/2/2, ff. 35–7v; D/2/7, f. 247; D/2/11, ff. 105, 202–6v.

38 *Old Ballads from Early Printed Copies of the Utmost Rarity*, ed. J.P. Collier (Percy Society, 1840), pp. 21–5; *RB*, vol. 3, pp. 593–6. See also *Songs and Ballads . . . Chiefly of the Reign of Philip and Mary*, ed. Thomas Wright (London, 1860), pp. 133–6.

39 BI, D/C.CP.1589/6; CP.G.1782; EDR, D/2/2, f. 47v; D/2/7, f. 221; D/2/8, f. 42v.

40 Spufford, *Small Books* (n. 6), pp. 161–8.

41 BI, CP.G.167, 213, 351, 1067, 1956, 2859; EDR, D/2/2, ff. 15v, 38.

42 BI, CP.G.174; see a similar Leicestershire case in A. Perceval Moore, "Marriage contracts or espousals in the reign of Queen Elizabeth," *Associated Architectural Societies' Reports and Papers* 30 (1909), pp. 297–8.

43 Wright, *Songs and Ballads* (n. 38), pp. 134–5. While young people made up an important part of the clientele of alehouses, single women did not go there alone, but would go with their boyfriends or in groups of friends: Peter Clark, *The English Alehouse* (London, 1983), pp. 127, 131. Cause papers confirm that view: BI, CP.G.1330, 1590, 1894.

44 BI, CP.G.1012.

45 EDR, D/2/11, f. 215.

46 BI, HC.CP.1589/11.

47 For example, BI, CP.G.399. I have found no examples of the courtship practice of "bundling," i.e. laying in bed together without sexual intercourse, discussed by W.A. Champion, "A case of 'bundling' in late-sixteenth century Shropshire," *Local Population Studies* 35 (Autumn, 1985), p. 52.

48 *The Farming and Memorandum Books of Henry Best of Elmswell, 1642*, ed. Donald Woodward (London, 1984), pp. 122–3.

49 Margaret Spufford, *The Great Reclothing of Rural England: Petty Chapmen and their Wares in the Seventeenth Century* (London, 1984).

50 Peter Rushton found similar gifts in Durham diocesan cause papers: "The testament of gifts: Marriage tokens and disputed contracts in north-east England, 1560–1630," *Folk Life* 24 (1985–6), 25–31.

51 Clement Robinson, et al., *A Handefull of Pleasant Delites (1584)*, ed. Arnold Kershaw (1926), pp. 37–41.

52 Wright *Songs and Ballads*, (n. 38), p. 135. In the seventeenth century, Margaret Spufford finds the same sorts of gifts in chapbook courtship stories: bracelets, gloves, handkerchiefs, looking glasses, scarves, ribbons, thimbles, and bodkins: *Small Books* (n. 6), p. 169.

53 PRO, C1/699/19; see also BI, CP.G.2356.

54 EDR, D/2/7, f. 276. For gifts forced on unwilling recipients, see BI, CP.G.1425; EDR, D/2/7, f. 141; D/2/11, f. 58.

55 EDR, D/2/3, f. 98; D/2/7, ff. 41v, 164, 318; D/2/11, f. 12.

56 BI, CP.G.149, 224.

57 BI, CP.G.1733, 1746.

58 BI, CP.G.1002, 2614.

59 This was a regular provision of wills. It was not meant to prevent widows from remarrying however. Rather, since a woman's property passed to her husband upon marriage, such provisions were designed to protect a man's property from passing away from his own family to the family of his wife's future husband.

60 For example, BI, CP.G.543, 548.

61 See above, p. 111.

62 *A Collection of Seventy-Nine Black-Letter Ballads and Broadsides, Printed . . . Between . . . 1559 and 1597*, ed. Thomas Wright and J.O. Halliwell (London, 1867), p. 193.

63 BI, CP.G.2657.

64 See Eric Josef Carlson, " 'The Fickleness of Woman'? Church courts and popular culture in Reformation England," Sixteenth Century Studies Conference paper, October 1991, which I hope to expand in print soon.

65 EDR, D/2/4, f. 13.

66 H.C. Agrippa, *The commendation of matrimony*, trans. David Clapham (London, 1540), sig. B1; William Harrington, *In this boke are conteyned the comendacions of matrymony, the maner and fourme of contractyng, solempnysynge and lyving in the same With declaracyon of all suche impedimentes as dothe let matrimony to be made. And also certeyne other thynges whiche curates be bounden by the lawe to declare oftentymes to theyr paryshe* (London, 1528), sig. A2v–3; Desiderius Erasmus, *A right fruitful epistle devised by the most excellent clerk Erasmus in laude and praise of matrimony*, trans. Richard Taverner (London, 1531), sig. A4v–8v; Bullinger, *Golden booke* (n. 18), sig. A3v–4; Becon, *Booke of Matrimony* (n. 19), pp. 567–72.

67 Bullinger *Golden booke*, (n. 18), sig. A3. See also Thomas Starkey, *A Dialogue Between Reginald Pole and Thomas Lupset*, ed. Kathleen M. Burton (London, 1948), p. 138.

68 Agrippa, *Commendation* (n. 66), sig. D3.

69 William Perkins, *Christian oeconomie: or, a short survey of the right manner of ordering a familie, according to the Scriptures*, trans. Thomas Pickering (London, 1609), p. 12; idem, *A Reformed Catholike* (London, 1619) [wr. 1597], p. 147.

70 Francis Bacon, *Essays, Civil and Moral* (New York, 1909), p. 22.

71 Bartholomew Batty, *The Christian mans Closet*, trans. William Lowth (London, 1581), f. 156: quoted in Todd, *Christian Humanism* (n. 5), p. 114.

72 Hugh Latimer, *Sermons*, ed. George Elwes Corrie (Cambridge, 1844), pp. 161–2.

73 The percentage of people never marrying varied from decade to decade, but it is unlikely that it ever exceeded 9% in the sixteenth century, and could have been as low as 4% at times: Wrigley and Schofield, *Population History* (n. 12), pp. 257–65; David R. Weir, "Rather never than late: Celibacy and age of marriage in English cohort fertility, 1541–1871," *Journal of Family History* 9 (1984), 340–55; R.S. Schofield, "English marriage patterns revisited," ibid. 10 (1985), 2–21.

74 Capp, "Popular literature (n. 6)," p. 214.

75 EDR, D/2/7, ff. 74v–75v.

76 EDR, D/2/4, f. 13.

77 EDR, D/2/6, f. 68v.

78 BI, CP.G.537.

79 "An hundred godly lessons" (*c.*1590), in *RB*, vol. 1, p. 432.

80 Collier, *Old Ballads* (n. 38), p. 95.

81 Wright, *Songs and Ballads* (n. 38), pp. 133–4.

82 Bullinger, *Golden Booke* (n. 18), sig. G7, G8v, H2v. Thomas Becon wrote in *Sick Man's Salve* (in *Worckes* [n. 19], vol. 3, p. 133): "And when the ripeness of thy age doth require thee to marry, take heed whom thou choosest to be thy yoke-fellow. Follow not the corrupt manners of the wicked wordlings, which in choosing their wives have their principal respect unto the worthiness of the stock, unto the wealthiness of the friends, unto riches, beauty, and such other worldly vanities. Consider thou rather the godliness than the worthiness of the maid's parents; the honest and virtuous bringing up of her; her chaste and sober behavior; her christian and godly manners; her modesty, gravity, sobriety, and womanliness; her faith, obedience, humility, silence, quietness, honesty, housewifeliness, and such other fruits of God's Spirit." See Henry Smith, *A Preparative to Marriage* (London, 1591), pp. 20–1, 23–4, 27–33; Robert Cleaver, *A Godly Forme of Houshold Government for the ordering of private families, according to the direction of Gods Word* (London, 1598), sig. G3. All of these works were extremely popular and went into multiple editions. See also Edmund Leites, "The duty to desire: Love, friendship, and sexuality in some puritan theories of marriage," *Journal of Social History* 15 (1979), 383–408.

83 John Rylands Library, English MS 524, f. 43; see also [Robert Allen,] *A Treasurie of Catechisme, or Christian Instruction* (London, 1600), p. 182; Cleaver, *Godly Forme* (n. 82), sig. G2, I1; *Cartwrightiana*, ed. A. Peel and Leland H. Carlson (London, 1951), p. 183; *A directory of church-government. Anciently contested for, and as farre as the Times would suffer, practised by the first Non-conformists in the daies of Queen Elizabeth* (London, 1644), sig. B3; Perkins, *Christian oeconomie* (n. 69), pp. 25–50.

84 See pp. 93–5. Visitation records suggest that the Table was, as required, "placed or fixed . . . in a convenient place" in nearly every parish church in England. In the diocese of Ely, a careful survey of all parishes in 1570 found only six parishes without a copy of Parker's Table: EDR, D/2/8, ff. 78v, 88, 88v, 96v, 99v, 109v, 111v, 124v. In an extensive 1597 survey of Norwich diocese, less than 10% of the parishes lacked the Table: *Bishop Redman's Visitation, 1597*, ed. J.F. Williams, Norfolk Record Society, vol. 18 (1946). These parishes may have had copies at one time. The Table was extremely perishable: a single sheet of paper hanging on the damp wall of a damp church could not expect a long life.

85 BI, HC.CP 1579/1; HC.AB.8, ff. 108, 114, 121, 122; HC.AB.11, f. 139v; HC.AB.12, ff. 95v, 105v, 117, 125, 132v, 143, 274, 276v; HC.AB.13, f. 274v; HC.AB.14, ff. 186v, 285v; CP.H.5; *Redman's Visitation* (n. 84), pp. 58, 118; *Archbishop Grindal's Visitation 1575: Comperta and Detecta Book*, ed. W.J. Sheils, Borthwick Texts and Calendars: Records of the Northern Province, vol. 4 (York, 1977), pp. 14, 29, 38. Alan Macfarlane may be correct in believing that people did not much care about incest. One of the couples divorced by the High Commission had been together twenty-six years, and a couple divorced in the consistory in 1600 had four children which implies that they had been together several years at least. But this needs to be said: some people must have cared, because couples were being reported to the courts, and in the case of the Lawrences (above, pp. 115–16), reported over and over again. Cases which did appear tended to involve people as distant as possible within the limits of the Table. The courts were not finding evidence of extremely close kin marrying. The only problems were on the frontiers of the forbidden zones – areas uncertain enough that even Cambridge divines of the reputations of Overall and Playfair were willing to defend the unions. See: BI, HC.AB.14, ff. 127v, 134; CP.H.1.

86 BL, Lansdowne MS 11/62.

87 EDR, D/2/9, ff. 31v, 44v, 113v, 151v; B/2/10, f. 10; D/2/14, f. 48. This was the only case in Ely with any proceedings; two presentments in 1600 had no action taken: EDR, B/2/17, f. 188; B/2/18, f. 6v.

88 *The Elizabethan Underworld*, ed. A. V. Judges, (London, 1965), p. 25.

89 Charles Phythian-Adams, *Desolation of a City: Coventry and the Urban Crisis of the Late Middle Ages* (Cambridge, 1979), pp. 84–5.

90 *RB*, vol. 2, p. 121.

91 *RB*, vol. 3, pp. 593–6.

92 See also Amussen, *Ordered Society* (n. 4), pp. 70–6.

93 EDR, D/2/2 ff. 38, 39A–40A; BI, D/C.CP 1557/3. See also BI, CP.G.256, 531, 708, 2976; D/C.CP 1544/6. One lad made his promise conditional on the death of his mother, presumably because he would then inherit the resources to marry: CP.G.1574. Joan Hundley made her promise to Arthur

Chamberlain conditional on her liking his stock of cattle: EDR, D/2/7, f. 69v; D/C.CP 1596/4; D/C, AB.8 ff. 81v–82v.

94 BI, CP.H.82.

95 BI, CP.G.540; see also EDR, D/2/8, f. 77; BI, CP.G.1476, 1486.

96 EDR, D/2/10, ff. 39v, 50, 83. See also EDR D/2/10a, f. 80.

97 Anon., *The Passionate Morrice (1593)*, ed. F.J. Furnivall (London, 1876), pp. 87, 90.

98 Starkey, *Dialogue* (n. 67), pp. 138–41; W.K. Jordan, *Philanthropy in England 1480–1660* (London, 1959), pp. 222, 274, 370–1. Greenham complained about a man piping in the church and did not believe his claim that he was raising money for dowries. He found this even more offensive than the money changers criticized by Jesus. At least, said Greenham, they plied their trade outside the door of the temple: Rylands MS 524, ff. 26v–27.

99 Stubbes, *Anatomie* (n. 20), sig. V5.

100 Thomas Cooper, *A briefe exposition of such chapters of the olde testament as usually are redde in the Church at common praier on the Sundayes, set forth for the better helpe and instruction of the unlearned* (London, 1573), p. 132.

101 Bullinger, *Golden Booke* (n. 18), sig. D5, D6v, E2v–3v.

102 Cleaver, *Godly Forme* (n. 82), sig. I2, I4, V4v–6, Y6v–Z1.

103 Becon, *Booke of Matrimony* (n. 19), pp. 618–19, 623–4; *Catechism* (n. 83), pp. 371–2.

104 *The Sermons of Edwin Sandys*, ed. John Ayre (Cambridge, 1841), pp. 326–7; George Estey, *Certaine Godly and Learned Expositions upon divers parts of Scripture* (London, 1603), f. 68v; Eusebius Pagit, *A Godly Sermon: Preached at Detford in Kent, on Monday the ix. of Iune, in Anno. 1572.* (London, 1586), sig. B8–C1; Richard Rogers, *Seven Treatises, containing such direction as is gathered out of the Holie Scriptures, leading and guiding to true happines, both in this life, and in the life to come: and may be called the practise of Christianitie* (London, 1603), pp. 169–70.

105 Edmund Bunny, *The whole Summe of Christian Religion* (London, 1576), ff. 61v, 63v.

106 Cleaver, *Godly forme* (n. 82).

107 *RB*, vol. 2, pp. 86–95.

108 EDR, D/2/7, ff. 74v–75v, 126.

109 EDR, D/2/11, ff. 97–102v.

110 EDR, D/2/11, f. 13.

111 EDR, D/2/3, ff. 4v–5; see also BI, CP.G.1354.

112 EDR, D/2/2, ff. 35v–36; see also Marjorie K. McIntosh, "Servants and the household unit in an Elizabethan English Community," *Journal of Family History* 9 (1984), p. 21.

113 BI, CP.G.819.

114   EDR, D/2/2. f. 42.

115   BI, CP.G.647; see also CP.G.1354, 1700.

116   BI, CP.G.729.

117   BI, CP.G.2866.

118   BI, CP.G.1246, 1288, 1289.

119   BI, CP.G.939.

120   BI, CP.G.340, 582; EDR, D/2/3, f. 11; D/2/18, ff. 23v, 45v; B/2/11, f. 219; B/2/12, ff. 9v–10v; B/2/16, f. 134v.

121   For example, BI, D/C.CP 1596/4.

122   See also Amussen, *Ordered Society* (n. 4), pp. 104–7.

123   EDR, B/2/18, f. 50.

124   BI, CP.G.483; see CP.G.135.

125   BI, CP.G.988.

126   EDR, D/2/7, f. 19; see also BI, HC.CP 1596/1.

127   "The repentant song of Sara Hill," in *RB*, vol. 4, p. 422.

128   See Michael MacDonald and Terence Murphy, *Sleepless Souls: Suicide in Early Modern England* (Oxford, 1990) and Murphy's " 'Woful Childe of Parents Rage': Suicide of children and adolescents in early modern England, 1507–1710," *Sixteenth Century Journal* 17 (1986), 259–70.

129   BI, CP.G.1984.

130   EDR, B/2/14, f. 162Av; D/2/7, ff. 64v–65v, 67–69.

131   BI, CP.G.135.

132   BI, D/C.CP 1572/2; D/C.AB.6, f. 89v.

133   BI, CP.G.543, 548.

134   *Winchester Consistory Court Depositions 1561–1602*, ed. A.J. Willis (Lyminge, Kent, 1960), pp. 37–8; BI, D/C.CP 1587/2; D/C.AB.7, f. 303v.

135   BI, CP.G.411, 483.

136   For example, HC.AB.8, f. 148; HC.AB.11, f. 175v; HC.CP 1597/6.

137   BI, HC.CP 1589/7. See also *Grace King* v. *Richard, Margaret and George King*, which ran over two years in HC.AB.3–5. In the first final decree, the commissioners ruled that Grace and George were man and wife and should be living together. This went unheeded, and in the second ruling, his parents were forced to enter a recognizance for £40 to stop keeping them apart: HC.AB.4, f. 123; HC.AB.5, ff. 206v–207.

138   BI, CP.G.2173.

139   EDR, D/2/4, f. 26v.

140   BI, CP.G.248.

141   BI, CP.G.3530; see D/C.CP 1596/4, 1597/2. Keith Wrightson estimates that roughly half of those marrying in the village of Terling had lost at least one parent: Keith Wrightson and David Levine, *Poverty and Piety in an English Village: Terling, 1525–1700* (London, 1979), p. 131.

142   BI, HC.CP 1596/1, 1596/4.

143 Jane Radcliffe, who had been widowed at least once before contracting with Thomas Molyneaux, was still under her father's control. However her example is unrepresentative since the families involved were upper-class: BI, CP.G.1005.

144 Collier, *Old Ballads* (n. 38), pp. 21–2.

145 BI, CP.G.1741.

146 BI, CP.G.180; see also CP.G.97.

147 BI, CP.G.164; CP.G.454. See also CP.G.410: "I Christopher take thee Jane to my wedded wife to have and to hold from this day forward and all other women's company to refuse and only to thee to draw so long as my life endure and there I plight thee my troth."

148 BI, CP.G.311; CP.G.127; BI.D/C.CP 1533/1.

149 BI, CP.G.138.

150 John Gillis (*For Better For Worse* [n. 4], p. 44) alleges that its use in betrothals was totemic, citing a Chester case in which a witness reported that he held a book which John Botherton had taken out of his hose, while John said to Alice Ince, "Here I take thee Alice to my wife before all other women, so help me God and Holy Dam and by this book." The witness admitted that he did not know what the book was since he did not open it, though he assumed it was a "psalter book." Swearing on a book was customarily part of Cheshire handfastings, however, and there is no reason to assume that the Prayer Book was being given any sort of magical role. See *Child-Marriages*, ed. Furnivall (n. 22), pp. 68–9, 186–7, 198.

151 BI, CP.G.504, 521, 556.

152 BI, CP.G.2143; see also CP.G.1906, 2873. One witness described a contract as "in very truth by the words used in the Book of Common Prayer": HC.CP 1597/6.

153 BI, CP.G.2829.

154 BI, CP.G.3491.

155 BI, CP.G.477.

156 EDR, D/2/11, ff. 378–80v.

157 BI, CP.G.213.

158 BI, CP.G.1004, 1804, 3548; D/C. CP 1566/1; EDR, D/2/2, ff. 15v, 19.

159 BI, CP.G.1002, 2972–5; D/C.CP 1558/2.

160 BI, CP.G.213.

161 BI, D/C.CP 1566/1.

162 *Child-Marriages* ed. Furnivall, (n. 22), p. 186.

163 For example, BI, CP.G.537, 3484; D/C.CP 1597/2; EDR, D/2/4, ff. 12–14, 41–3.

164 BI, CP.G.2671–1A.

165   EDR, D/2/11. ff. 65–66.

166   EDR, D/2/7, ff. 81–4v; D/2/11, ff. 65–6; BI, CP.G.1590, 1894, 2326, 2671–1A.

167   EDR, D/2/2. ff. 15v–16, 38–40A; D/2/4, f. 43; BI, CP.G.174, 351, 611, 1067, 1956; D/C.CP 1573/1.

168   BI, D/C.CP 1544/6.

169   EDR, D/2/7, f. 179v. For similar examples, see BI, CP.G.320, 640, 1005, 1008, 1354, 2321.

170   BI, CP.G.32O.

171   EDR, D/2/4, f. 43.

172   BI, CP.G.756. See also CP.G.174.

173   EDR, D/2/2, f. 16. See also BI, CP.G.138.

174   BI, D/C.CP 1573/1.

175   BI, CP.G.220, 631, 636.

176   BI, CP.G.1067, 1894, 3491.

177   For confessions, see BI, D/C.AB.6, ff. 44, 249v; D/C.AB.7, ff. 198v, 200–200v. No witnesses, suit dropped: D/C.AB.4, ff. 11–13, 114v–15; D/C.AB.6, ff. 251v, 255v–6; D/C.AB.7, ff. 33v, 351v–2, 353, 354v, 357v, 358v; D/C.CP 1568/5. No witnesses, sentence against: D/C.CP 1544/7, 1569/3, 1581/4, 1600/2; D/C.AB.5, ff. 78v–90v; D/C.AB.6, ff. 92v–110. John Holme had no witnesses against Agnes Hebblethwaite and when sentence was given against him he announced his intention to appeal: D/C.CP 1567/2; D/C.AB.5, ff. 22, 23.

178   John Gillis (*For Better, For Worse* [n. 4], p. 44) observes that "couples made their vows first in the presence of friends, not parents or kindred." This claim is unsubstantiated and the cause papers of the Dean of York's court suggests otherwise. In fifteen cases, there are clearly identifiable witnesses to an actual handfasting (not a vague conversation or hearsay); witnesses in seven include relatives (including four parents) and others: BI, D/C.CP 1534/1, 1536/3, 1544/1, 1546/4, 1557/1, 1596/4, 1600/3. In another, only kin gave evidence (D/C.CP 1603/1), while in the remaining seven, none of the witnesses were kin. Since one of these betrothals (D/C.CP 1597/2) took place in the woman's brother's house, however, he was probably present. At the very most, only a third of these sample couples made their vows without some parents or other kinsmen present: D/C.CP 1543/3, 1546/3, 1554/3, 1566/3, 1572/2. Moreover, since kin were considered biased witnesses, and were frequently challenged by the party against whom they testified (for example EDR, D/2/7, f. 171), a claimant with sufficient non-kin witnesses might choose not to produce challengable evidence from relatives present at the handfasting, thus creating an "optical illusion" in the sources. Since parents and kin were regularly involved in discussions surrounding betrothal, it is inconceiv-

able that they were regularly excluded from the handfasting itself in favor of other witnesses.

179 Rings: BI, CP.G.138, 531, 631, 636, 2612, 2614; coins (rare after 1560): CP.G.311, 320, 322, 531, 543, 548; both: CP.G.1406.

180 Gillis, *For Better, For Worse* (n. 4), pp. 31–4; Rushton, "Testament of gifts (n. 50)."

181 Others were claims that the defendant publicly admitted the contract explicitly or indirectly such as in calling the plaintiff's parents "mother" and "father," or that there was *"vox et fama"* in the local community that they were married. None of these, separately or collectively, proved marriage without words of the present tense (or future tense with sexual relations) but they helped create the presumption of marriage if that was necessary.

182 These rings are specifically called a "trothplight" and later a "wedding ring": BI, CP.G.225, 3412; D/C.CP 1543/3.

183 In other words, a couple normally could legally solemnize a marriage no less than three weeks after betrothal, unless there was a holiday between two of the Sundays: Geoffrey Geffrason and Mary Rialles handfasted on 25 January and solemnized on 11 February: BI, CP.G. 1337.

184 For example, EDR, D/2/4, ff. 39, 44–7; BI, CP.G.146.

185 For example, EDR, D/2/4, f. 12v. It is not clear what length of time intervened between betrothal and banns. Normally it seems to have been a matter of days, but one case mentions a delay of six months without criticism, while in another a gap of three months was considered scanda-lous: EDR, D/2/10a, f. 13v; BI, CP.G.985. A ballad couple went the day after handfasting to ask for the banns: *RB*, vol. 3, p. 596.

186 BI, D/C.CP 1596/4.

187 Rylands MS 524, f. 43.

188 EDR, D/2/14, f. 8. When Great Shelford's vicar complied, refusing to call the banns without examining a couple, one parishioner called him a "dolt," for which he was punished by the court: EDR, D/2/10, ff. 229v–30.

189 *LP*, vol. 4, no. 4351; EDR, D/2/18, f. 96v.

190 BI, CP.G.304; see also EDR, B/2/13, f. 85v.

191 Robert Hutchinson claimed that he had no choice but to read the banns of couples whose names were given to him unless he was ordered other-wise by his ordinary: BI, CP.G.3510.

192 EDR, D/2/5, ff. 41v, 60v, 63v, 65v–6, 75v, 82v. There are many cases in which people objected to their own banns, asked without their consent: BI, CP.G.798, 2003, 2169; EDR, D/2/7, f. 144; D/2/7, ff. 236, 275–6.

193 BI, CP.G.985.

194 EDR, D/2/9, ff. 144, 154v, 160v.

195   EDR, D/2/7, f. 79. Only once in the Ely records was someone punished for procuring banns without the parties' consent: EDR, D/2/18, f. 32v.
196   *For Better, For Worse* (n. 4), p. 52.
197   BI, CP.G.874; EDR, D/2/6, ff. 80–2.
198   EDR, D/2/4, ff. 39, 44–7.
199   BI, TRANS.CP 1564/1.
200   EDR, D/2/7, ff. 136v–7.
201   EDR, B/2/21, f. 118v.
202   EDR, B/2/11, ff. 190, 200; B/2/12, ff. 89, 96v–7, 133; B/2/18, ff. 156, 168v; BI, D/C.AB.3, ff. 212, 274–8, 287, 290–90v; PRO, C1/898/48.
203   BI, HC.AB.1, f. 200; HC.AB.6, f. 102; HC.AB.7, ff. 27, 118v.
204   BI, HC.AB.7, ff. 70, 144v. See also HC.AB.6, ff. 30, 52; HC.AB.7, ff. 70v, 152v; HC.AB.8, ff. 72v, 129, 165v; HC.AB.9, ff. 3v, 22, 28v, 44; HC.AB.13, ff. 178v, 180v; EDR, D/2/10, f. 128.
205   EDR, B/2/14, f. 150. For a soldier who died in Ireland, see BI, HC.AB.14, ff. 134, 138, 141v. Margaret Hardyman married Nicholas Palmer believing that her first husband died in Wales, as did her community which supported her marriage. When a witness appeared claiming to have met her husband in Wales three months before, she was not punished for bigamy since she had acted in good faith: EDR, D/2/9, ff. 138v, 139v; see also D/2/11, ff. 191–2.
206   BI, D/C.CP 1557/3; CP.G.540, 1476, 1486, 2834; CP.H.82; EDR, D/2/7, f. 167; D/2/10, ff. 39v, 50; D/2/10a, f. 80. Delays of between two and four years (with no excuse): EDR, D/2/10a, f. 43; B/2/16, f. 106v; BI, HC.AB.10, f. 64v.; D/C.CP 1554/5.
207   Bullinger, *Golden booke* (n. 18), sig. H8.
208   Perkins, *Christian oeconomie* (n. 69), p. 19.
209   Smith, *Preparative* (n. 83), pp. 1–2.
210   *Grindal's Visitation* (n. 85), ed. Sheils, p. 36.
211   Gillis, *For Better, For Worse* (n. 4), p. 50.
212   See, for example, BI, CP.G.200, 220, 224, 534–5, 791, 925, 1023, 1113, 1643, 1665, 1679, 1728, 1797, 1894, 1902; EDR, B/2/18, ff. 156, 168v.
213   BI, CP.G.2326.
214   EDR, B/2/5, p. 76.
215   EDR, D/2/18, f. 39.
216   Based on forty-six cases from 1568–1583 in EDR D/2/8, D/2/9, D/2/10, D/2/10a, B/2/10.
217   Samuel P. Menafee, *Wives for Sale: An Ethnographic Study of British Popular Divorce* (New York, 1981). An example of attempted "husband-sale" pre-dates any known "wife-sale." Anthony Barton and Elizabeth Sisson handfasted before he went into service, and she promised to wait seven years for him, during which time her parents pressed her to marry

William Birdsall, which she was willing to do. When Barton returned she offered him 13s 6d to release her; he refused: BI, CP.G.540; see TRANS.CP 1564/11. For Essex "wife-sales" in 1585, see *A Series of Precedents and Proceedings in Criminal Causes, 1475–1640, from the Act Books of the Ecclesiastical Courts of the Diocese of London*, ed. W.H. Hale (London, 1847), p. 186. In 1583, a woman in the archdeaconry of Leicester was accused of volunteering to abandon her claim for £7, but the court ruled that her claim was not valid: Moore, "Marriage contracts (n. 42)," pp. 283–6.

218 Redhead and William Nelson were found guilty of bawdry; Barnby and Frances Nelson of adultery: BI, HC.AB.13, ff. 214v, 236–7, 239v–40, 248v–52v.
219 BI, CP.G.296.
220 BI, D/C.CP 1583/4.
221 Harrington, *Commendations* (n. 66), sig. A4v.
222 Rylands MS 524, f. 30v.
223 P.E.H. Hair, "Bridal pregnancy in rural England in earlier centuries," *Population Studies* 20 (1966), 233–43; idem, "Bridal pregnancy in earlier rural England further examined," ibid., 24 (1970), 59–70. See *MER*, p. 448; Ingram, *Church Courts* (n. 1), esp. pp. 219–37; Wrightson and Levine, *Poverty and Piety* (n. 141), p. 132.
224 PRO, C1/1419/36; see also BI, CP.G.779; HC.CP 1590/9.
225 BI, TRANS.CP 1564/1.
226 BI, HC.AB.10, f. 142.
227 EDR, D/2/10, f. 68v. This practice of withholding a penance or penalty if the couple married probably originated in medieval manorial courts which did not assess leyrwite in cases of subsequent marriage: "*Et si idem cum quo ipsa prius fornicata fuerit eam postea desponsaverit tunc quietus erit de gersuma*": BL, Cotton MS Claudius.C.xi, f. 117v, quoted in Richard Smith, "Marriage processes in the English past: Some continuities," in *The World We Have Gained*, ed. Lloyd Bonfield (Oxford, 1986). Tim North has shown ("Legerwite in the thirteenth and fourteenth centuries," *Past and Present* 111 [1986], 3–16) that leyrwite was not a fine for sexual misconduct *per se* but for alienating a lord's property which occurred when a fine was paid to the church for fornication. If the church courts did not punish couples who married subsequent to the fornication, then neither would the lord have to punish for alienation. Church court records lead me to prefer this view of leyrwite to that in Zvi Razi, *Life, Marriage and Death in a Medieval Parish: Economy, Society and Demography in Halesowen 1270–1400* (Cambridge, 1980), and Margaret Spufford, "Puritanism and social control?" in *Order and Disorder in Early Modern England*, ed. Anthony Fletcher and John Stevenson (Cambridge, 1985),

41–57. See also Richard M. Smith and Larry Poos, "Legal windows onto historical populations? Recent research on demography and the manor court in medieval England," *Law and History Review* 2 (1984), 128–52.

228 EDR, B/2/12–14, 16–28.

229 EDR, B/2/12, ff. 51v, 110; EDR B/2/17, f. 92v.

230 PRO, E179/83/307.

231 Wrightson and Levine, *Poverty and Piety* (n. 141), pp. 131–3.

232 John Cosin, *A Collection of Private Devotions* (London, 1627), preface.

233 In a sample from Cambridgeshire parish registers, March and December (months which normally fell within Lent and Advent, respectively) were virtually free of marriages, but none of those that took place were prosecuted.

234 EDR, B/2/17, f. 7v.

235 EDR, B/2/14, ff. 165v–6, 166A; see *Proceedings*, ed. Hale (n. 217), pp. 190–1; *The Archdeacon's Court: Liber Actorum, 1584*, ed. E.R. Brinksworth, Oxford Record Society, vols 23–24 (1942), pp. 50, 57, 64.

236 On the other hand, the original Little Wilbraham register shows that when the rector Robert Willan married in December, he did so three days before Advent started. Perhaps this is coincidental.

237 David Cressy, "The seasonality of marriage in old and new England," *Journal of Interdisciplinary History* 16 (1985), pp. 1–21 (figures based on Wrigley and Schofield, *Population History*, app. 2). See also Ann Kussmaul, "Time and space, hoofs and grains: The seasonality of marriage in England," *Journal of Interdisciplinary History* 15 (1985), pp. 755–79. Jeremy Boulton "Economy of time? Wedding days and the working week in the past," *Local Population Studies* 43 (1989), 28–46 explores the question of the days of the week on which people married, but notes that for rural parishes there were so few marriages each year that it is difficult to arrive at meaningful patterns.

238 For example, BI. CP.G.3317.

239 EDR, B/2/15, ff. 172v–3.

240 EDR, D/2/6, f. 69.

241 BI, CP.G.1461, 3318.

242 BI, HC.AB.14, f. 178. For night-marriages with no excuse: HC.AB.13, ff. 320v. 327; HC.AB.14, ff. 179v, 182, 203, 220v.

243 BI, CP.G.3317; HC.AB.2, f. 93; HC.AB.3, ff. 140v–1.

244 BI, HC.AB.12, f. 182v; HC.AB.13, f. 202; HC.AB.14, ff. 66v, 125, 202v, 206, 255v–6, 262v; CP.G.2848.

245 EDR, D/2/7, ff. 160–2, 240 (no sentence survives); see also BI, CP.G.2344.

246 *Proceedings* ed. Hale, (n. 217), p. 192.

247 BI, CP.G.1273.

248 *Child-Marriages* ed. Furnivall, (n. 22), pp. 65–7.

249 BI, HC.AB.14, ff. 191v–2v; see Eric Josef Carlson, "Marriage reform and the Elizabethan High Commission," *Sixteenth Century Journal* 21 (1990), pp. 448–50.

250 BI, HC.AB.14, ff. 230v, 232, 238, 239v, 242, 242v, 243–4, 253v. See Hugh Aveling, "The marriage of Catholic recusants 1559–1642," *Journal of Ecclesiastical History* 14 (1963), 68–83.

251 For example, EDR, D/2/14, f. 32v; BI.CP.G.3318.

252 BI, CP.G.3317.

253 EDR, B/2/11, f. 207v.

254 BI, HC.AB.14, f. 143v; EDR, D/2/18, f. 406.

255 EDR, D/2/18, ff. 63, 64, 65, 111v, 123, 203, 205v; BL, Cotton MS Cleopatra F.2, f. 232.

256 EDR, B/2/10, ff. 23, 70v, 72v; B/2/16, f. 159v; D/2/18, ff. 20v, 150v.

257 See Margaret Bowker, *The Henrician Reformation: The Diocese of Lincoln under John Longland, 1521–1547* (Cambridge, 1981), pp. 133–5. Two successive curates in Colne ran illegal marriage mills to supplement a stipend of only £4: Haigh, *Reformation and Resistance* (n. 29), pp. 238–9.

258 BI, HC.AB.1, ff. 113, 115v–16, 157, 164, 167v.

259 EDR, D/2/18, f. 203. See also BI, HC.AB.8, ff. 142, 148, 154, 158v; HC.AB.9, ff. 4, 6, 137v; HC.AB.10, f. 193v, 208v, 229A; HC.CP 1590/16; HC.AB.11, ff. 263v, 271v; CP.G.576, 3318. These *durante lite* cases appear on the surface to suggest that people married believing that a solemnized if irregular marriage would be upheld over an unsolemnized private contract, and the court upheld that. However, in none of the cases in which the court upheld the illegal solemnized union did the plaintiff in the matrimonial case have the evidence to win. If the alleged betrothals had been attested properly, they would have been upheld and the solemnized unions would have been declared bigamous and voided. Essentially, they represented a misunderstanding of the law. That there were any at all was because they appeared to achieve the desired goal of frustrating the suit, but that there were so few compared to the number of breach suits is perhaps because most people understood the way the law worked.

260 EDR, B/2/17, f. 81.

261 EDR, B/2/13, f. 187v; *Proceedings* ed. Hale, (n. 217), p. 185.

262 EDR, G/1/8, f. 52v; F/5/35, f. 160; see also D/2/5, f. 36; G/1/8, ff. 181v–2. The bailiffs of Colchester certificate said "nothing is more commendable or acceptable than that a perfect truth may appear in things doubtful": BI, CP.G.1342.

263 ULC, Add. MS 6605(AA), f. 251.

264 EDR, D/2/18, f. 260v; B/2/14, ff. 4, 36.

265 EDR, D/2/5, f. 8.

266 Irregular marriages were so unusual that they did not appear in ballads (private communication from Bernard Capp). This rarity is not true for the seventeenth century: John Gillis, "Conjugal settlements: Resort to clandestine and common law marriage in England and Wales, 1650–1850," in *Disputes and Settlements: Law and Human Relations in the West*, ed. John Bossy (Cambridge, 1983), 261–86, and Roger Lee Brown, "The rise and fall of the Fleet marriages," in *Marriage and Society*, ed. Outhwaite (n. 5), 117–36.

267 Rushton, "Testament of gifts (n. 50)," p. 30.

268 *Winchester Depositions*, ed. Willis (n. 134), pp. 37–8.

269 See pp. 31–2. Chancery, an equity court, was used because its evidentiary rules did not require written instruments, such as receipts, which lovers were unlikely to exchange.

270 Cleaver, *Godly Form* (n. 82), sig. I1; Perkins, *Christian oeconomie* (n. 69), p. 54; Allen, *Catechisme* (n. 83), p. 182.

271 Two Essex cases are unclear: F.G. Emmison, *Elizabethan Life: Morals and the Church Courts* (Chelmsford, 1973), pp. 165–6.

272 BI, HC.AB.8, f. 161.

273 BI, CP.G.1095, 1102, 1222.

274 BI, CP.H.112.

275 *Registrum Hamonis de Hethe*, ed. C. Johnson, Canterbury and York Society, vols 48–9 (1948), vol. 1, pp. 206–7; vol. 2, pp. 924, 939, 940, 951, 964, 1039.

276 *The Injunctions and other Ecclesiastical Proceedings of Richard Barnes, Bishop of Durham 1575–1587*, ed. James Raine, Surtees Society, vol. 22 (1850), p. 22.

277 BI, HC.AB.14, ff. 138v, 201, 208v.

278 Testators assumed that marriage would not normally precede the specified age of inheritance, which is not surprising, since the average age of marriage was over twenty-four.

279 See Margaret Spufford, "Peasant inheritance customs and land distribution in Cambridgeshire from the sixteenth to the eighteenth centuries," in *Family and Inheritance: Rural Society in Western Europe 1200–1800*, ed. Jack Goody, Joan Thirsk, and E.P. Thompson (Cambridge, 1976), 156–76.

280 EPR, AW1586 (Hunt); CW1589 (Wimple).

281 According to Margaret Spufford, the median value of the probate inventory of a seventeenth century yeoman was £149 in Lincolnshire and £58 in Cambridgeshire: "The limitations of the probate inventory," in *English Rural Society, 1500–1800: Essays in Honor of Joan Thirsk*, ed. John Chartres and David Hey (Cambridge, 1990), 139–74; idem, *Contrasting Communities* (Cambridge, 1974), pp. 37–8; idem, "The significance of the Cambridgeshire Hearth Tax," *Proceedings of the Cambridgeshire Antiquarian*

Society, 55 (1962), 53–64. (An unpublished chart based on this article has been supplied by Dr Spufford.) Values are unlikely to be significantly different in the 1580s than early in the next century, but this can't be tested because only a handful of Cambridgeshire inventories survive from the sixteenth century. I assume that the total of bequests will be less than that of the probate inventory; only one sixteenth century Cambridgeshire testator is known to have misjudged his net worth, and he did not miss by much.

282 Two York diocese cases (*Parker* v. *Tillotson* in 1575 and *Hogge* v. *Smith* in 1596) confirm that these devices were employed only by the very wealthy. Both women claimed that the men were fortune-hunters – Parker a poor lead miner, and Hogge an unthrifty haunter of alehouses – and both said that they would receive sizable amounts (£40 for Tillotson and £100 for Smith) if they married with consent: BI, CP.G.1750, 2974.

283 Rylands MS 524, ff. 49v–50.

284 On medieval marriages and parental interference, see Judith M. Bennett, *Women in the Medieval English Countryside* (Oxford, 1987), p. 96.

285 For what follows, see chap. 2

286 Arguably, the church's laws on binding marriage promises could be seen, by extension, to support Philippe Ariès's view that rural communities saw stable relationships, especially marriage, as the foundation of stable communities and therefore embraced indissoluble marriage: Ariès, "The indissoluble marriage," in *Western Sexuality: Practice and Precept in Past and Present Times*, ed. Philippe Ariès and André Béjin (Oxford, 1985), 140–57.

287 For example, BI, HC.CP 1589/7; *Child-Marriages*, ed. Furnivall (n. 22), pp. 187–96.

288 Martin Ingram, "Spousals Litigation in the English Ecclesiastical Courts, *c.* 1350–1640," in *Marriage and Society*, ed. Outhwaite (n. 5), p. 53.

289 BI, CP.G.1082. Something like this had been done in the past but abandoned when judges realized it caused more unhappiness than it relieved: R.H. Helmholz, *Marriage Litigation in Medieval England* (Cambridge, 1974), pp. 172–81.

290 BI, CP.G.483.

291 A related option was to raise a defamation suit against one who spread rumours of a contract in order to prevent presentment on "common fame": see C.A. Haigh, "Slander and the church courts in the sixteenth century," *Transactions of the Lancashire and Cheshire Antiquarian Society* 78 (1975), 1–13.

292 *Commons' Debates in 1628*, ed. Robert C. Johnson, Mary Freer Keeler, Maija Jannson Cole, and William B. Bidwell, 3 vols (New Haven, 1977), vol. 3, p. 26.

293 Patrick Collinson, *The Religion of Protestants* (Oxford, 1982), chap. 3.

294 Noteworthy is the High Commission's crusade against clergy who
     allowed the banns to be abused or avoided. Christopher Wilkinson, an
     "old and simple" curate who admitted marrying a Lincolnshire couple
     without banns, was only "enjoined . . . to confess his fault" in the church.
     Other clergy did not find the commissioners "dealing gently" with them;
     suspension or prison were the usual reward for breaking the rules on
     banns: BI, HC.AB.2, f. 93; HC.AB.3, ff. 140–1, 148; HC.AB.11, ff. 37,
     179; HC.AB.12, ff. 168, 181–2v, 256v. The combination of exemplary
     punishments and improving standards among the clergy was the only
     practical solution to the abuse of banns, not another law.

Chapter 7   Church Courts and Communities in Reformation England

1 *Historical Poems of the XIV and XV Centuries*, ed. R.H. Robbins (New York,
   1959), pp. 24–7; translation from Margaret Spufford, "Puritanism and
   social control?" in *Order and Disorder in Early Modern England*, ed. Anthony
   Fletcher and John Stevenson (Cambridge, 1985), pp. 51–2.
2 Geoffrey Chaucer, *The Canterbury Tales*, trans. Nevill Coghill (Harmonds-
   worth, Middlesex, 1960), pp. 310–21.
3 In this way, criticism resembles anticlericalism, which was almost largely
   ad hominem: C. Haigh, "Anticlericalism and the English Reformation,"
   History 68 (1983), 391–407. The courts are not criticized or satirized in
   Reformation or "condition of England" ballads. (Private communication
   from Dr Tessa Watt.) "A new ballad of the parator and the Devil" (*temp.*
   Charles I), apparently the earliest to return to this topic, virtually pla-
   giarized Chaucer, though this summoner even attempted to extort money
   from the Devil: quoted in C.H. Firth, "The reign of Charles I," *Transactions
   of the Royal Historical Society*, 3d ser., vol. 6 (1912), pp. 39–40.
4 Attacks on the principle of ecclesiastical discipline and its specific courts,
   such as those which appear in the *Admonition to Parliament* and the ensuing
   debate between Cartwright and Whitgift (Donald McGinn, *The Admonition Controversy* [New Brunswick, NJ, 1949], pp. 339–40, 346–7, 510–37)
   leave no traces in the local communities which I have studied.
5 I am in agreement with Martin Ingram, who makes a similar argument in
   Church Courts, Sex and Marriage in England, 1570–1640 (Cambridge,
   1987), chap. 11. I also believe there is continuity with previous centuries
   in the "corporate" nature of local communities rather than a shift to
   "individualism": R.M. Smith, " 'Modernization' and the corporate medieval village community in England: Some sceptical reflections," in *Explorations in Historical Geography: Interpretive Essays*, ed. Alan R.H. Baker and
   Derek Gregory (Cambridge, 1984), pp. 140–79.

6 Dorothy M. Owen, "Ecclesiastical jurisdiction in England 1300–1550: The records and their interpretation," *Studies in Church History* 11 (1975), 199–221.

7 My discussion of court procedure, based on original research, differs only in minor details from previous studies. See esp. Ralph Houlbrooke, *Church Courts and the People during the English Reformation 1520–1570* (Oxford, 1979), pp. 21–54, and Ingram, *Church Courts* (n. 5), pp. 27–69. See also R.A. Marchant, *The Church Under the Law: Justice, Administration and Discipline in the Diocese of York 1560–1649* (Cambridge, 1969); Richard M. Wunderli, *London Church Courts and Society on the Eve of the Reformation* (Cambridge, Mass., 1981).

8 A relatively straightforward suit would cost around 14s (*c*.1550–70), but costs regularly exceeded that by 40s or more. Costs included the proctor's *per diem* (4d) and masses of required paperwork such as libels (3s 4d), document copies (1s), examination of witnesses (2s), and sentences (6s): EDR, D/2/11, f. 129v; see also Ingram, *Church Courts* (n. 5), p. 56; Christopher Haigh, *Reformation and Resistance in Tudor Lancashire* (Cambridge, 1975), pp. 225–9. The average daily wage for agricultural labor was between 6d and 8d: *The Agrarian History of England and Wales, Volume IV: 1500–1640*, ed. Joan Thirsk (Cambridge, 1967), p. 864.

9 R.H. Helmholz notes that although litigation dropped and self-confidence and standards of record keeping declined temporarily, they show recovery after 1570. People chose to use the court, showing confidence in its ability to give them what they wanted, "a jurisdiction worth invoking": *Roman Canon Law in Reformation England* (Cambridge, 1990), pp. 28–54, esp. p. 44.

10 Dorothy M. Owen, "Episcopal Visitation Books," *History* 49 (1964), 185–8; Helmholz, *Roman Canon Law* (n. 9), pp. 104–19.

11 EDR, B/2/17, f. 88v.

12 EDR, D/2/10, f. 132.

13 EDR, B/2/12, f. 26v.

14 Muncke escaped punishment because he proved he did so under orders from his master: EDR, D/2/9, f. 152.

15 EDR, D/2/17a, f. 48v.

16 EDR, B/2/15, f. 105v.

17 EDR, D/2/10, f. 28.

18 EDR, D/2/10a, f. 32v.

19 One of the servants was pregnant by William Clark who said that he would thrust a pitchfork in her belly rather than be blamed for the pregnancy: EDR, B/2/3, pp. 53–4.

20 EDR, D/2/14, f. 52v, includes a copy of the order to the churchwardens to appear, as well as a "A good form of making a bill"; for a quarter bill, see

ULC, Add. MS 6605, #96; EDR, B/9/1. Episcopal visitation articles (for example, in *Elizabethan Episcopal Administration*, ed. W.P.M. Kennedy, Alcuin Club vols 25–7 [1924]) also instructed churchwardens on matters requiring presentment.

21 BI, CP.G.1387. See F.G. Emmison, *Elizabethan Life: Morals and the Church Courts* (Chelmsford, 1973), pp. 8–10; Joan R. Kent, *The English Village Constable 1580–1642: A Social and Adminstrative Study* (Oxford, 1986), pp. 25–39; Wunderli, *London Church Courts* (n. 7), p. 39. A foreign visitor was "told that in England every citizen is bound by oath to keep a sharp eye on his neighbor's house, as to whether the married people live in harmony": "Diary of the journey of the most illustrious Philip Julius, Duke of Stettin-Pomerania through England, 1602," *Transactions of the Royal Historical Society*, new ser., 6 (1892), p. 65.

22 EDR, D/2/6, ff. 126v–31, 132v–3v; D/2/7, f. 9.

23 ULC, Add. MS 6605, #177.

24 Alice Cooke and John Capit were accused of fornication but wardens said the charge was groundless and made maliciously, and it was dismissed: EDR, D/2/18, f. 38v.

25 *English Historical Documents, V: 1485–1558*, ed. C.H. Williams (London, 1967), p. 733; PRO, SP 2/M/42. For the bishops' response and an evaluation, see Margaret Bowker, "The Commons Supplication Against the Ordinaries in the light of some archidiaconal acta," *Transactions of the Royal Historical Society*, 5th ser., 21 (1971), p. 76.

26 EDR, D/2/10, f. 78.

27 EDR, D/2/10, ff. 67v–8.

28 Helmholz (*Roman Canon Law* (n. 9), pp. 106–9) takes a rather more sanguine view of these efforts than my reading of the act books permits.

29 Edward Hake, *A Touchestone for this time present, expresly declaring such ruines, enormities, and abuses as trouble the Churche of God and our Christian common wealth at this day* (1574), sig. C2v–3.

30 EDR, B/2/12, ff. 26v, 39, 44.

31 EDR, B/2/31, ff. 81v–4.

32 EDR, D/2/10, ff. 9, 16v; see also St Benet Cambridge, ibid., f. 28; and Barton quarter bill, EDR, B/9/1.

33 Anthony Gilby, *A dialogue between a soldier of Barwick and an English chaplain* (Middelburg?, 1581), sig. M2. I am grateful to John Craig for this reference. The Admonition to Parliament contrasted wardens (among others) to a proper "lawful and godly seigniory," and some in the Dedham classis questioned "whether [wardens] and their offices were lawful" but the majority apparently preferred to baptize the office and use it to further godly parochial discipline: McGinn, *Admonition Controversy* (n. 4), p. 470;

The Presbyterian Movement in the Reign of Queen Elizabeth I, ed. R.G. Usher, Camden Society, 3d ser., vol. 8 (1905), pp. 73, 99.

34 EDR, D/2/10, f. 176.
35 EDR, D/2/10, f. 105, 226. Matthew Sanders of Ely accused the wardens of leading a faction, but this did not result in any action: D/2/8, f. 141v.
36 EDR, B/2/12, ff. 90v–1; see also B/2/11, f. 127; B/2/16, f. 32.
37 EDR, B/2/18, f. 33.
38 EDR, D/2/9, f. 90; D/2/10, f. 28v; B/2/14, ff. 138–9.
39 EDR, D/2/18, f. 31v.
40 EDR, B/2/11, ff. 127v, 138v.
41 EDR, B/2/17, f. 212.
42 EDR, D/2/8, f. 124v. Another excuse occasionally used was that one could not attend church without being arrested for debt: ULC, Add. MS 6605, #126.
43 Above, chap. 6.
44 BI, CP.G.2235, 3036, 3082, 3401. Cruelty was the most common cause of divorce in early modern Andalusia, and evidence from that region supports my argument: James Casey, "Household disputes and the law in early modern Andalusia," in *Disputes and Settlements: Law and Human Relations in the West*, ed. John Bossy (Cambridge, 1983), 187–217.
45 EDR, D/2/10a, ff. 6, 54v.
46 EDR, D/2/10a, f. 25.
47 EDR, D/2/10, ff. 138v, 242.
48 EDR, D/2/10a, f. 7v.
49 EDR, D/2/10, f. 211v. Virtually identical is the case from Girton of John Lambe, a tailor, whose wife was in Durham: D/2/14, f. 45.
50 See case against Thomas Harrington, EDR, K11/25, 25a, 68–9.
51 EDR, B/2/12, ff. 26v, 39, 44.
52 R.H. Helmholz, "Crime, compurgation and the courts of the medieval church," *Canon Law and the Law of England* (London, 1987), 119–44, esp. pp. 131–6.
53 An exception was made with clergy. When William Holdsworth, vicar of Linton, was accused of fornicating with his servant, he was ordered to produce four clergymen and two laymen as compurgators: EDR, B/2/18, f. 57v.
54 EDR, B/2/13, ff. 118v, 129.
55 For example EDR, D/2/10, ff. 24, 34, 38v.
56 Helmholz, "Compurgation (n. 52)," p. 136; Houlbrooke, *Church Courts* (n. 7), p. 46.
57 EDR, B/2/13, f. 146v. When John Gibson successfully purged himself of adultery charges and was dismissed, Alice Disborough argued that she

logically should be exempted from producing her own compurgators; the court agreed: D/2/10, ff. 227–7v. See also D/2/23, f. 182.

58 Ingram, *Church Courts* (n. 5), pp. 331–2.

59 EDR, D/2/10, ff. 69, 73, 84, 90v.

60 Edward Free of West Wratting was ordered to produce six men from Carlton cum Willingham, West Wratting and Weston Colville: EDR, D/2/8, f. 82; see B/2/13, ff. 118v, 129.

61 Formal notifications: ULC, Add. MS 6605, #162, 176, 187, 221, 253, 287, etc.

62 EDR, B/2/12, f. 18v.

63 Ingram, *Church Courts* (n. 5), pp. 333–4. Medieval numbers are somewhat lower: Helmholz, "Compurgation (n. 52)," pp. 136–8. It was less successful in London: Wunderli, *London Church Courts* (n. 7), pp. 47–9. I have not been able to provide precise numbers for Ely diocese to 1603, but my evidence generally supports Ingram's figures.

64 EDR, D/2/8, f. 87.

65 EDR, B/2/5, pp. 90–2.

66 Cited in J.A. Sharpe, *Defamation and Sexual Slander in Early Modern England: The Church Courts at York*, Borthwick Papers, 58 (York, 1980), p. 18.

67 Helmholz, "Compurgation (n. 52)," p. 139.

68 EDR, B/2/12, ff. 26v, 39, 44.

69 EDR, B/2/21, f. 18v. On the connection between formal harmony and worship, see David Sabean, *Power in the Blood: Popular Culture and Village Discourse in Early Modern Germany* (Cambridge, 1984), pp. 37–60; Susan Brigden, "Religion and social obligation in early sixteenth-century London," *Past and Present* 103 (1984), pp. 79–80.

70 EDR, B/2/11, f. 151.

71 BI, HC.AB.2, f. 89.

72 ULC, Add. MS 6605, #246. Many penances formulas are included in that volume. It should be noted that this did not always come off smoothly. Edmund Spicer was given a penance for using abusive language against Nicholas Tabraw in 1595, but at the time when he was to make his penitential speech he became disorderly and offended the congregation by his speech: ULC, Add. MS 6605, #209–10.

73 EDR, D/2/10, f. 90v.

74 In addition to her parish church (Little Abington), Alice Smith was ordered to do penance in both Cambridge and Linton markets: EDR, B/2/11, ff. 213v–14.

75 After doing this from 10 a.m. until 2 p.m. on a Saturday, she was to do the same at her parish church on three consecutive Sundays: EDR, D/2/10, ff. 83, 86, 90v, 96.

76 EDR, B/2/5, p. 171. For other examples, see Hubert Hall, "Some Eliza-

bethan penances in the diocese of Ely," *Transactions of the Royal Historical Society*, 3rd ser., 1 (1907), 263–77.

77 ULC, Add. MS 6605, #305; EDR, D/2/8, f. 96v.
78 Provision of this certificate is regularly note in the court books, e.g. in Hoode's case above. For examples of the certificates: ULC, Add. MS 6605, #21–2, 40, 201, 223, 228.
79 EDR, D/2/7, ff. 29v–30.
80 EDR, D/2/9, f. 29v.
81 EDR, B/2/11, f. 151v.
82 EDR, D/2/10, f. 124v.
83 ULC, Add. MS 6605, #271.
84 Mervyn James believes that excommunication was efficacious when the magical powers of the eucharist were an item of faith, but the Reformation undercut this sanction when it stripped the sacrament of magical trappings: *Family, Lineage and Civil Society* (Oxford, 1974), pp. 54–5. For a discussion of the efficacy of excommunication, the most complete and convincing discussion is Ingram, *Church Courts* (n. 5), pp. 340–61. See also R. Hill, "The theory and practice of excommunication in medieval England," *History* 42 (1957), 1–11; Houlbrooke, *Church Courts* (n. 7), pp. 48–50; Marchant, *Church Under the Law* (n. 7); F.D. Price, "The abuses of excommunication and the decline of ecclesiastical discipline under Queen Elizabeth," *English Historical Review* 57 (1942), 106–115; Elisabeth Vodola, *Excommunication in the Middle Ages* (Berkeley and Los Angeles, 1987).
85 It is perhaps reasonable to question how literally "*aufugit*" ought to be taken, since it reflects the inferences of the courts and might not be based on any evidence. Given the people so designated, it is possible that their moves were only obliquely related to pending court action.
86 EDR, D/2/9, ff. 47, 57.
87 EDR, D/2/10, ff. 164v, 166, 169–70.
88 EDR, D/2/10, f. 57v.
89 EDR, B/2/18, f. 18v.
90 ULC, MS Mm.1.29, ff. 36v, 40 (emphasis mine).
91 EDR, D/2/10, f. 55.
92 EDR, D/2/10, f. 167v.
93 EDR, B/2/16, f. 147.
94 Hake, *Touchestone* (n. 29), C2v–3; Michael Clanchy, "Law and love in the Middle Ages," *Disputes and Settlements* (n. 44), pp. 47–68.
95 Susan Dwyer Amussen, *An Ordered Society: Gender and Class in Early Modern England* (Oxford, 1988), pp. 173–4; Keith Wrightson, "Two concepts of order: Justices, constables and jurymen in seventeenth-century England," in *An Ungovernable People: The English and Their Law in the Seventeenth and Eighteenth Centuries*, ed. John Brewer and John Styles (New Brunswick, NJ,

1980), pp. 21–46. I differ with Dr Amussen only in that by referring to "elites," I believe she somewhat understates her case. The office-holding pool in Elizabethan villages was fairly large; the "elites" usually included at least half of the adult males. The "reluctance of village notables to turn to outside institutions" to which Amussen refers was shared by the overwhelming majority of villagers.

96 Susan Reynolds, *Kingdoms and Communities in Western Europe 900–1300* (Oxford, 1984), p. 58. For a thorough discussion of the elections and responsibilities of churchwardens, see Eric Josef Carlson, "The churchwardens of rural Cambridgeshire," in *The World of Rural Dissent, 1520–1700*, ed. Margaret Spufford (Cambridge, 1994).

97 EDR, B/2/13, ff. 73, 84.

98 EDR, B/2/16, ff. 166v–7.

99 EDR, D/2/16, f. 59; see also B/2/10, f. 109v.

100 ULC, Add. MS 6605, #177.

101 ULC, MS Mm.1.29, f. 50v. See Michael Clanchy, "Law and love in the Middle Ages," in *Disputes and Settlements* (n. 44), ed. Bossy, pp. 47–67; H.G. Richardson, "The parish clergy of the thirteenth and fourteenth centuries," *Transactions of the Royal Historical Society*, 3d ser., 6 (1912), 89–128; Edward Powell, "Arbitration and the law in England in the late Middle Ages," *Transactions of the Royal Historical Society*, 5th ser., 33 (1983), 49–67; idem, "Settlement of disputes by arbitration in fifteenth-century England," *Law and History Review* 2 (1984), 21–43.

102 *Elizabethan Episcopal Adminstration* (n. 25), ed. Kennedy, p. 56.

103 "Visitations of the Archdeacon of Canterbury," ed. Arthur Hussey, *Archaeologia Cantiana* 25 (1902), p. 26.

104 EDR, B/2/11, f. 146v; see also ibid., f. 205; B/2/10, ff. 58v–59; D/2/10, f. 24.

105 EDR, D/2/18, f. 175.

106 EDR, D/2/10, f. 24.

107 EDR, B/2/15, f. 105v. Such language was not unique to church courts. In 1391, a serf in Hemingsford was "in rebellion against his neighbors and will not submit to the judgement of his fellows, to the injury of the community": W.O. Ault, "Village assemblies in Medieval England," *Album Helen Maud Cam: Studies presented to the International Commission for the History of Representative and Parliamentary Institutions*, 23 (Paris and Louvain, 1960), p. 23.

108 EDR, D/2/9, f. 180; D/2/10, f. 33.

109 Above, chap. 6.

110 EDR, D/2/5, f. 8.

111 See Ingram, *Church Courts* (n. 5), chap. 7. Ingram notes (p. 231) that Ely diocese undertook this crusade earlier than others.

112 EDR, D/2/10, f. 154v.

113 For example, William Acres of Leverington: EDR, B/2/10, ff. 5v, 78v. He had a remarkable conversion by the end of his life, leaving one of the most genuinely "godly" of more than 6,000 Ely diocese wills in the sixteenth century: EPR, CW1590.

114 Sir Owen Hopton moved in the 1571 parliament that presenting for not attending church not be left to churchwardens, "who being simple men and fearing to offend would rather incur the danger of perjury than displease some of their neighbours": *Proceedings in the Parliaments of Elizabeth I, Volume I: 1558–1581*, ed. T.E. Hartley (Leicester, 1981), p. 202.

115 In the seventeenth century *"omnia bene"* came to be used as a deliberate act of rebellion against Laud and his supporters in their pursuit of nonconformity: Margaret Spufford, "The quest for the heretical laity in the visitation records of Ely in the late sixteenth and early seventeenth centuries," *Studies in Church History* 9 (1972), 223–30. This contempt for episcopal authority cannot be read back to the earlier period. It should also be noted that bills often reported defects in the parson or the fabric of the church, e.g. EDR, B/9/1. Since these were unrelated to the behavior of lay parishioners, the wardens were not held equally responsible for resolving them outside of the courts.

116 This comparative method was introduced in place of the single village study by Margaret Spufford (*Contrasting Communities: English Villagers in the Sixteenth and Seventeenth Centuries* [Cambridge, 1974]), and has also been used by Martin Ingram (*Church Courts*). In choosing villages, I have been sensitive to Keith Wrightson's list of "required" sources for adequate local studies ("Villages, villagers, and village studies," *Historical Journal* 18 [1975], pp. 638–9) and the need for secondary material to provide background information. For sources and methodology, see *MER*, pp. 520–30.

117 On the settlement and rural economy of Cambridgeshire, see: H.C. Darby, *The Domesday Geography of Eastern England* (Cambridge, 1952), pp. 264–314; John Jones, *A Human Geography of Cambridgeshire* (London, 1924); Spufford, *Contrasting Communities* (n. 116), chap. 1; idem, "General view of the rural economy of the county of Cambridge," (typescript); idem, "Rural Cambridgeshire 1520–1680," (Leicester Univ. M.A., 1962); and Charles Vancouver, *General View of the Agriculture in the County of Cambridge* (1794).

118 Spufford, *Contrasting Communities* (n. 116), chap. 1; Robin Glasscock, "The distribution of lay wealth in south-east England in the early fourteenth century," (Univ. of London Ph.D., 1962); Roger Schofield, "The geographical distribution of wealth in England, 1334–1649," *Economic*

History Review, 2d. ser., 18 (1965), 483–510; John Sheail, "The distribution of taxable population and wealth in England during the early sixteenth century," *Transactions of the Institute of British Geographers* 55 (1972), 111–26; idem, "The regional distribution of wealth in England as indicated in the 1524/5 lay subsidy returns," (Univ. of London Ph.D., 1968).

119   The diocese did not include two eastern hundreds (Staploe and Cheveley). See D.M. Owen, "Ely diocesan records," *Studies in Church History* 1 (1964), 176–83; idem, *Ely Records: A Handlist of the Records of the Bishops and Archdeacon of Ely* (1971).

120   See Felicity Heal, "The bishops of Ely and their diocese during the Reformation," (Univ. of Cambridge Ph.D., 1972); G.L. Blackman, "The career and influence of Bishop Richard Cox 1547–1581," (Univ. of Cambridge Ph.D., 1953).

121   D.M. Owen, "The enforcement of the Reformation in the diocese of Ely," *Miscellanea Historiae Ecclesiasticae* 3 (Louvain, 1970), 167–74; Heal, "Bishops of Ely (n. 120)," pp. 106–31.

122   F.D. Price, "Gloucester diocese under Bishop Hooper 1551–3," *Bristol and Gloucestershire Archaeological Society Transactions* 60 (1938), 51–151; idem, "An Elizabethan church official: Thomas Powell chancellor of Gloucester diocese," *Church Quarterly Review* 128 (1939), 94–112; idem, "Elizabethan apparitors in the diocese of Gloucester," *Church Quarterly Review* 134 (1942), 37–55; idem, "Bishop Bullingham and Chancellor Blackleech: a diocese divided," *Bristol and Gloucestershire Archaeological Society Transactions* 91 (1972), 175–98.

123   *VCH, Cambs.*, vol. 9, pp. 71, 77–81. Poll tax figures from *Cambridgeshire Subsidy Rolls, 1250–1695*, ed. W.M. Palmer (Norwich, 1912); 1524–5 subsidy from PRO, E179/81/126, /130, /161, /163; 1563 survey from BL, Harl. MS 594, ff. 198–200v; baptisms and burials from original registers in CRO; hearth taxes from PRO, E179/84/436–7 and E179/244/22–3. On using these sources, see M.W. Beresford, "The poll taxes of 1377, 1379, and 1381," *The Amateur Historian* 3 (1958), p. 275 and Larry R. Poos, "The rural population in Essex in the later Middle Ages," *Economic History Review*, 2d ser., 38 (1985), pp. 527–8; Roger Schofield, "Parliamentary lay taxation, 1485–1547," (Univ. of Cambridge Ph.D., 1963); D.M. Palliser and L.J. Jones, "The diocesan population returns for 1563 and 1603," *Local Population Studies* 30 (1983), 55–8; Margaret Spufford, "The significance of the Cambridgeshire hearth tax," *Proceedings of the Cambridge Antiquarian Society* 55 (1962), 53–64. Julian Cornwall ("English population in the early sixteenth century," *Economic History Review*, 2d ser., 33 [1970], 32–44) believes subsidies included the better-off but only enough others to make the assessment look realistic;

by comparing subsidies to the 1522 Muster Returns, Bruce M.S. Campbell ("The population of early Tudor England: A reevaluation of the 1522 muster returns and 1524 and 1525 lay subsidies," *Journal of Historical Geography* 7 [1981], 145–54) argues that they give a fairly accurate count of adult males. Poos ("Rural Population (n. 123)," p. 529) is probably correct that accuracy depends on the parish. To convert from assessments to total population, mean household size is taken to be 4.75 (J. Krause, "The medieval household: Large or small?" *Economic History Review*, 2d ser., 9 [1957], 420–32; Peter Laslett, "Mean household size in England since the sixteenth century," and Richard Wall, "Mean household size in England from printed sources," both in *Household and Family in Past Time*, ed. Laslett and Wall [Cambridge, 1972], 125–58, 159–203). While many wage-earners did not head independent households, and some who did were poor enough to be omitted entirely, I believe Cornwall exaggerated the need to adjust the base figure and multiplier. M. Zell ("Families and households in Staplehurst, 1563–4," *Local Population Studies* 33 [1984], 54–7) convincingly argues that the 1563 count is useful for village population, though masking mid-century growth since it was made after the influenza epidemic of the late 1550s (F.J. Fisher, "Influenza and inflation in Tudor England," *Economic History Review* 2d ser., 18 [1965], 120–9; D.M. Palliser, "Dearth and disease in Staffordshire, 1540–1670," in *Rural Change and Urban Growth 1500–1800*, ed. C.W. Chalkin and M.A. Havinden [London, 1974], pp. 54–75). Towns are not as well-served, according to Nigel Goose ("The ecclesiastical returns of 1563: A cautionary note," *Local Population Studies* 34 [1985], 46–7; idem, "Household size and structure in early Stuart Cambridge," *Social History* 5 [1980], 347–85).

124 Chesterton Hundred subsidies are misleading since the first (E179/81/126) names far fewer wage-earners in many parishes than does the second. Since nothing which occurred would account for many new wage-earners entering the parish in one year, the difference must be due to more thorough assessment. While the more thorough count makes the second subsidy more credible, it also renders comparison with parishes in other hundreds problematic. For example, wage-earners account for 50% of the Dry Drayton list but only 29% in Orwell. The additional wage-earners are probably the poorer ones, and less likely to be independent householders. Thus, to compare Dry Drayton to other villages, I have used the lower total as a base.

125 *VCH, Cambs.*, vol. 5, pp. 241, 245; Spufford, *Contrasting Communities* (n. 116), pp. 22–8, 94–119.

126 *VCH, Cambs.*, vol. 5, pp. 36, 40.

127 *VCH, Cambs.*, vol. 9, p. 81.

128 Spufford, *Contrasting Communities* (n. 116), p. 327.

129 A.F. Scott Pearson, *Thomas Cartwright and Elizabethan Puritanism 1535–1603* (Cambridge, 1925), App. III, VI.

130 *VCH, Cambs.*, vol. 9, p. 86; *The House of Commons 1558–1603*, ed. P.W. Hasler, 3 vols (London, 1981), vol. 2, p. 359.

131 EDR, B/2/6, pp. 198–202.

132 *A parte of a register . . .* (Middleburg, 1593), pp. 86–93.

133 John Rylands Library, English MS 524, ff. 47v–8.

134 George Downame, *Two Sermons* (London, 1608), dedic. epis.

135 Ibid., ff. 36v–7.

136 Ibid., ff. 54v–5.

137 Gonville and Caius College, Cambridge, MS 53/30, ff. 126v–9; Christopher W. Marsh, *The Family of Love in English Society, 1550–1630* (Cambridge, 1993).

138 Patrick Collinson, *The Religion of Protestants* (Oxford, 1982), p. 119. Robert Browne lived there briefly but decided that the Cambridge puritans were not earnest enough.

139 Rylands MS 524. Patrick Collinson (" 'A Magazine of religious patterns'. An Erasmian topic transposed in English Protestantism," in *Godly People* [London, 1983], p. 508) first called attention to this text, which Kenneth Parker and I are editing for publication.

140 Samuel Clarke, *The Lives of Thirty-Two English Divines*, (3rd edn, London, 1677), pp. 12–15.

141 Thomas Fuller, *The Church History of Britain from the Birth of Jesus Christ until the Year M.DC.XLVIII.* (London, 1655), p. 219.

142 Clarke, *English Divines* (n. 140), p. 15; Fuller, *Church History* (n. 141), p. 219. He settled in London, and preached regularly at Christ Church parish until his death in April 1594: Guildhall Library, London, MS 9163, ff. 305, 320v.

143 Spufford, *Contrasting Communities* (n. 116), p. 328. For wills as evidence of piety, Christopher Marsh, "In the name of God? Will-making and faith in early modern England," in *The Records of the Nation*, ed. G.H. Martin and Peter Spufford (Woodbridge, Sussex, 1990), 215–49; Spufford, *Contrasting Communities* (n. 116), pp. 320–44. For a lengthy bibliography and discussion of this topic, see Eric Josef Carlson, "The historical value of Ely consistory probate records," in *Index of the Probate Records of the Consistory Court of Ely 1449–1858*, ed. Elisabeth Leedham-Green, 3 vols (London, forthcoming), vol. 1, pp. xvii ff.

144 EPR, CW1573 (Barbour); EPR, CW1585 (Wrattam).

145 EPR, CW1571. Dry Drayton schoolmaster William Helsbie used an identical clause in a later will: EPR, CW1580 (Ivatt).

146 EPR, CW1582 (Hutton); CW1588 (Muns). The seventh will has no dedicatory clause: EPR, CW1570 (Bennett).

147 EPR, CW 1597. According to a handwritten memo in a 1655 copy of
Fuller's *Church History* (n. 141), Greenham told his successor (who told
the annotator's father) "I perceive no good wrought by my ministry
on any but one family": transcribed by C.F.S. Warren, *Notes and Queries*,
6th ser., 7 (12 May 1883), p. 366. Perhaps Thomas Giffard's was that one
family.

148 The fashion for naming children with pious ejaculations, used by Dudley
Fenner in Cranbrook, did not penetrate much beyond East Sussex
and the Kentish weald, but the Hebraicization demonstrated in Dry
Drayton's register was more widespread beginning in the 1560s. See
Nicholas Tyacke, "Popular puritan mentality in late Elizabethan
England," in *The English Commonwealth*, ed. Peter Clark (Leicester, 1974),
77–92.

149 For comparison, figures from some sample parishes during the same
years: columns A–D are the major instance suits (tithe, testamentary,
defamation and matrimonial); E gives the number of households in 1563,
and F the density per thousand acres.

	A	B	C	D	E	F
Dry Drayton	0	1	0	1	31	13.0
Abingdon Parva	2	0	1	1	15	13.0
Bassingbourn	4	0	0	2	90	27.5
Carlton cum Willingham	2	0	0	0	22	10.0
Castle Camps	1	0	0	0	37	14.0
Croxton	1	0	0	0	25	13.0
Landbeach	0	3	2	0	36	14.5
Orwell	1	0	1	0	46	25.0
Shudy Camps	0	0	0	0	30	13.0
Weston Colville	3	2	0	0	26	9.0
Willingham	5	3	1	0	105	27.0

150 Clarke, *English Divines* (n. 140), p. 13.

151 George Gifford, *A briefe discourse of certaine points of the religion, which is
among the common sort of Christians, which may bee termed the Countrie
Divinitie. With a manifest confutation of the same, after the order of a Dialogue*
(London, 1582), ff. 47v–8.

152 Collinson, *Religion of Protestants* (n. 138), pp. 108–11.

153 EDR, H/1/3; *VCH, Cambs.*, vol. 9, p. 85. Clarke (*English Divines* [n. 140],
p. 13), however, speaks of Mrs Greenham being forced to borrow money
"to get in his [Greenham's] harvest."

154   Clarke, *English Divines* (n. 140), pp. 12–13.

155   EDR, D/2/17a, f. 41v.

156   EDR, B/2/11, f. 89v. See Paul S. Seaver, "Community control and puritan politics in Elizabethan Suffolk," *Albion* 9 (1977), 297–315.

157   EDR, D/2/10, f. 57.

158   EDR, D/2/8, ff. 117, 131v.

159   EDR, D/2/10, f. 132v.

160   EDR, D/2/14, f. 44.

161   EDR, D/2/17a, f. 1; D/2/16, pp. 35, 101–3.

162   EDR, B/2/3, p. 128.

163   EDR, D/2/10, f. 57.

164   EDR, D/2/8, ff. 117, 131v.

165   EDR, B/2/11, ff. 89v, 150v–1, 152, 161v–2v, 196.

166   D. and S. Lysons, *Magna Britannia*, (Cambridge, 1808), vol. 2, pt. 1, p. 179; *VCH, Cambs.*, vol. 9, pp. 74–7; Frances M. Page, *The Estates of Crowland Abbey: A Study in Manorial Organization* (Cambridge, 1934), pp. 19–28.

167   The subsidy of 35 Eliz. indicates how wealthy the Huttons were compared to their neighbors: John Hutton was assessed on £30 land, while the next highest assessments were of John and Thomas Giffard and John Boyden on £5 goods: PRO, E179/82/296.

168   *VCH, Cambs.*, vol 1, p. 427, n. 1.

169   In 10 and 14 Eliz., half of the assessed were Giffards, as were nine of fifteen assessed in 35 Eliz.: PRO, E179/82/248, /257, /296. See wills of William, Thomas, Alexander (EPR, CW1597), Ralph (CW1602), and William (CW1604). Only William the elder (CW1563) described himself as "yeoman."

170   See Anne Reiber DeWindt, "Local government in a small town: A medieval leet jury and its constituents," *Albion* 23 (1991), 627–54, esp. 628–35.

171   DeWindt, "Local government (n. 170)," p. 629; *VCH, Cambs.*, vol. 9, p. 81, 84.

172   *VCH, Cambs.*, vol. 5, pp. 37–9; Royal Commission on Historical Monuments, *An Inventory of the Historical Monuments in the County of Cambridge*, 2 vols to date (London, 1968–), vol. 1, pp. 63–71.

173   PRO, E179/81/161.

174   PRO, E179/82/211, /219.

175   PRO, E179/82/234, /248; E179/83/308, /316.

176   EDR, D/2/2, ff. 5–6, 7v–8v, 14v, 33, 38–40A.

177   EDR, D/2/3, ff. 89v–95.

178   EDR, D/2/7, ff. 375–6v; D/2/11, ff. 1–2v, 11, 26.

179   EDR, B/2/5, p. 97.

180   EDR, B/2/9, f. 20.

181   *VCH, Cambs.*, vol. 1, p. 422; vol. 5, pp. 243–4; Lysons, *Magna Britannia* (n. 166), vol 2, p. 243. Because of land added in the 1300s, when Henry VIII received it, Orwell manor included more than half of the Domesday hideage.

182   *VCH, Cambs.*, vol. 5, p. 249.

183   Ibid., pp. 247–8. In 1535, the rectory was valued at £19 17s 7d, and the vicarage at £7 10s.

184   CCCC, MS 588, f. 15.

185   EPR, CW1566.

186   EPR, CW1580.

187   EDR, G/2/19, f. 56; B/2/11, ff. 177, 191, 201v; B/2/12, ff. 4, 20. Holland eventually settled at St Bride's London in 1594, remaining there until his death in 1603.

188   Spufford, *Contrasting Communities* (n. 116), pp. 97–8.

189   Ibid., pp. 99–111.

190   EDR, D/2/10, ff. 164v, 166, 169, 170; B/2/9, f. 9v.

191   EDR, D/2/14, f. 31; D/2/16, pp. 21, 107 (Rowning's fine is noted on a loose slip of paper in D/2/16); B/2/12, ff. 82v, 94; B/2/17, ff. 93, 114v, 173.

192   CRO, L1/130. His father left him a house and land burdened with bequests to three unmarried daughters: EPR, CW1563.

193   He appears in neither CRO, L1/130 or L63/49; see EPR, CW1605 (Rutt).

194   EPR, CW1591; CRO, L1/130; L63/49.

195   EDR, B/2/16, ff. 51v, 58v.

196   EDR, B/2/18, ff. 50v, 93v.

197   A scribal note reads "She is mad": EDR, B/2/18, f. 101.

198   EDR, B/2/18, f. 204.

199   EDR, D/2/5, f. 53 (*"docet fortunas populorum"*).

200   EDR, D/2/10, ff. 48, 60, 169v; B/2/9, ff. 4, 9v, 18.

201   EDR, B/2/11, f. 128v; B/2/16, f. 35; B/2/17, f. 28.

202   EDR, B/2/11, ff. 128v, 139.

203   EDR, B/2/18, f. 16v.

204   PRO, E179/82/248, /257. Dry Drayton had twenty assessments, but only ten different surnames.

205   CRO, L1/130, pp. 1–3, 5–7; L63/49.

206   Ibid.; EPR, CW1594.

207   EPR, CW1597 (Brock); CW1605 (Johnson); CRO, L1/130, pp. 1–3.

208   In a defamation case, three witnesses from West Wratting testified to conversation heard at the tailor's shop in Weston Colville: EDR, D/2/19, ff. 217v–19v; John Vale and John Cutchie went from Willingham to Thomas Heeth's alehouse in Weston Colville: EDR, D/2/4, ff. 36–7v.

209 When John Cutchie was thirty-eight years old, he said he had moved from Borough Green fifteen years earlier. Richard Webbe of Weston Colville, aged twenty-eight, had been born in Brinkley and lived in Carlton until he was twenty-one: ibid., f. 37. John Stelling, aged thirty, was born in Weston, raised in West Wratting, and moved back to Weston when he was twenty-four: ibid., f. 37v.

210 John Bye, yeoman of Brinkley, left lands in Willingham to his son John: EPR, CW1597; William Gynne of Brinkley had a copyhold in Carlton which he left to his mother: CW1588; Jeffrey Marsh, yeoman of Carlton, had ten and a half acres of freehold in Weston Colville purchased from Thomas Vale for his son Jeffrey: CW1592; John Tylburk of Carlton left his wife a copyhold in Balsham: CW1537.

211 *VCH, Cambs.*, vol. 6, pp. 183–5.

212 Ibid., pp. 149–51.

213 PRO, E179/81/134.

214 BL, Harl. MS 594, f. 194v.

215 ULC, MS Plan 550R.

216 PRO, E179/244/22.

217 PRO, E179/81/134.

218 BL, Harl. MS 594, f. 194v; PRO E179/244/23.

219 Spufford, *Contrasting Communities* (n. 116), chap. 3; idem, *A Cambridgeshire Community: Chippenham from Settlement to Enclosure*, Department of English Local History, University of Leicester, Occasional Papers vol. 20 (1968).

220 In addition, forty-five enclosed acres of demesne of the manor of Moynes, seventy-six of Leveretts and 113 of Colvilles were held by unnamed lessees.

221 Totals derived from ULC, MS Plan 550R, with the assistance of Margaret Spufford.

222 Assessments are taken from PRO, E179/81/134; E179/82/213, /236, /248, /257; E179/83/307.

223 EPR, CW1553.

224 EPR, CW1557.

225 See Carlson, "Churchwardens of rural Cambridgeshire (n. 96)."

226 EPR, CW1594.

227 EPR, CW1585 (Grigg), CW1587 (Bridge).

228 ULC, MS Plan 550R.

229 EPR, CW1597, CW1599.

230 Westley's home is not stated, but he was apparently not from Weston Colville. EDR, D/2/4, ff. 35v–7v; D/2/11, ff. 202–6v; B/2/18, f. 23v; D/2/22, f. 15.

231 EDR, D/2/19, ff. 213v, 217v–20v; B/2/17, ff. 10, 20v.

232 EDR, B/2/3, p. 78; B/2/12, f. 129v. Deekes was quarrelsome by nature, quarreling also with James Culpie in Carlton church, though he was not presented for it. The incident came to light when Culpie was presented for not receiving communion and claimed that he did not because he was not at peace with Deekes who had defamed him as a thief and a villain: B/2/11, f. 69. No records indicate whether Culpie took him to court over this defamation. (Since the accusation was of a common law offense, the defamation suit would have been heard in a royal court.)
233 EDR, B/2/17, ff. 25, 76v.
234 EDR, D/2/10, f. 147; B/2/17, ff. 129, 181v.
235 EDR, B/2/16, ff. 6v, 22, 43; B/2/7, f. 188.
236 EDR, B/2/12, ff. 26v, 39, 44.
237 Ibid., ff. 26v, 39.
238 EDR, B/2/17, f. 188v.
239 EDR, B/2/18, f. 41.
240 EDR, B/2/17, ff. 211v–12v.
241 EPR, CW1605.
242 EDR, D/2/14, f. 34; B/2/11, f. 205; B/2/13, f. 171v; B/2/18, ff. 214, 215.
243 EDR, B/2/11, f. 165. For other cases, see B/2/11, ff. 67v, 93v, 118v, 123v; B/2/12, ff. 26v, 115, 115v; B/2/17, f. 169v.
244 EDR, B/2/11, f. 107; B/2/12, ff. 47v, 60v, 77v; B/2/13, ff. 71, 84, 114v, 126, 140v, 154v; B/2/16, f. 61.
245 J.R. Ravensdale, *Liable to Floods: Village Landscape on the Edge of the Fens A.D. 450–1850* (Cambridge, 1974); Spufford, *Contrasting Communities* (n. 116), chap. 5.
246 J.R. Ravensdale, "Landbeach in 1549: Ket's rebellion in miniature," in *East Anglian Studies*, ed. Lionel Munby (Cambridge, 1968).
247 PRO, E179/81/126, /163; E179/82/215, /235, /248, /257, /296; E179/83/315; CCCC, Archives **XXXV**, 170.
248 John Teversham married into the Thurlow family and presumably came by his position in that way, but the others married outside of the parish, so it is not possible to trace the impact of their marriages on their status in Landbeach.
249 EDR, B/2/16, ff. 147v, 155v; B/2/17, ff. 2, 153, 165v.
250 W.K. Clay, *A History of the Parish of Landbeach in the County of Cambridge*, Cambridge Archaeological Society octavo publications, 6 (Cambridge, 1861), p. 31.
251 BL, Harl. MS 524, ff. 198–201. While the register shows a natural increase of thirty from 1549 to 1563, reports from 1558, the peak year of the influenza epidemic, are missing.
252 PRO, E179/84/437.
253 EDR, D/2/10, f. 143v; B/2/18, f. 244.

254 EDR, B/2/9, f. 30; B/2/11, f. 150; B/2/12, f. 106; B/2/17, ff. 150v, 163v; B/2/18, ff. 39v, 46, 93, 145v–6.

255 EDR, B/2/11, f. 79v; B/2/13, f. 94; B/2/16, f. 83.

256 EDR, D/2/7, ff. 221, 224; D/2/11, f. 200; D/2/12, *passim* (*Sankester* v. *Cooke*); D/2/20, *passim* (*Clark* v. *Clifton*); B/2/16, ff. 83v, 147.

257 Testamentary: EDR, D/2/7, ff. 38v, 222; D/2/12, *passim* (*Warwick* v. *Spackman*); D/2/13, *passim* (*Paternoster* v. *Hutch*, *Draper* v. *Hull*); D/2/15, *passim* (*Herne* v. *Gotobed*); D/2/20 *passim* (*Kippes* v. *Steven*). Matrimonial: D/2/2, f. 52; D/2/3 *passim* (*Jeye* v. *Lane*); D/2/7, f. 169; D/2/15, *passim* (*Foot* v. *Warwick*, *Baytham* v. *Lane*); Norwich Diocesan Record Office, ACT 21/24a, *passim* (ca. Cowling); B/2/11, f. 152v; B/2/13, f. 14v.

258 EDR, D/2/5, ff. 95v, 98, 100v; B/2/4, p. 169; B/2/6, pp. 83, 100; D/2/10, ff. 25, 43v, 52v, 216, 219v; B/2/9, ff. 13, 16v, 27; B/2/11, ff. 78v, 114, 133v; B/2/12, ff. 106v, 121; B/2/13, ff. 63, 105, 146v; B/2/16, ff. 37–8v, 46v, 76v, 91v; B/2/18, ff. 54v, 96.

259 It is possible that the parish had chosen to prosecute such cases in Quarter Sessions since Nicholas Ward, presented for incontinence, proved that he had been found innocent of that charge already by the Quarter Sessions: EDR, B/2/11, ff. 78v, 114, 133v.

260 E.E. Evans-Pritchard, *Nuer Religion* (Oxford, 1956), p. 128.

Select Bibliography

In the interests of reducing printing costs, this bibliography contains only a selection of printed secondary works in English which address issues central to this study. It is intended primarily for students and nonspecialists. Those seeking additional sources on these topics or on more peripheral topics covered in this book should consult my footnotes, which contain complete references to all primary and secondary works, printed and unprinted, which I cited or consulted.

Adams, Norma, "*Nullius filius*: A study of the exception of bastardy in the law courts of Medieval England," *University of Toronto Law Journal*, 6 (1946), pp. 361–84.

Amussen, Susan Dwyer, *An Ordered Society: Gender and Class in Early Modern England*, Oxford, 1988.

Anderson, Michael, *Approaches to the History of the Western Family*, London, 1980.

Ariès, Philippe, "The indissoluble marriage," *Western Sexuality: Practice and Precept in Past and Present Times*, ed. Philippe Ariès and André Béjin, Oxford, 1985, pp. 140–57.

Aveling, Hugh, "The marriage of Catholic recusants 1559–1642," *Journal of Ecclesiastical History* 14 (1963), pp. 68–83.

Barnes, Patricia M., "The Anstey case," *Medieval Miscellany for Doris Mary Stenton*, ed. P.M. Barnes and C.F. Slade, Pipe Roll Society, new ser., 36 (1960), pp. 1–24.

Barstow, Anne Llewellyn, "The first generation of Anglican clergy wives: Heroines or whores?," *Historical Magazine of the Protestant Episcopal Church*, 52 (1983), pp. 3–16.

—— *Married Priests and the Reforming Papacy: the Eleventh-Century Debates*, New York, 1982.

Bennett, Judith M., *Women in the Medieval English Countryside: Gender and Household in Brigstock Before the Plague*, Oxford, 1987.

Berlatsky, Joel, "Marriage and family in a Tudor elite: Familial patterns of Elizabethan bishops," *Journal of Family History*, 3 (1978), pp. 6–22.

Boulton, Jeremy, "Economy of time? Wedding days and the working week in the past," *Local Population Studies*, 43 (1989), pp. 28–46.

Bowker, Margaret, "The Commons Supplication Against the Ordinaries reconsidered in the light of some archidiaconal acta," *Transactions of the Royal Historical Society*, 5th ser., 21 (1971), pp. 61–77.

Brett, Martin, *The English Church under Henry I*, Oxford, 1975.

Brooke, Christopher, "Gregorian Reform in action: Clerical marriage in England, 1050–1200," *Cambridge Historical Journal*, 12 (1956), pp. 1–21.

—— *The Medieval Idea of Marriage*, Oxford, 1989.

Brundage, James A., *Law, Sex, and Christian Society in Medieval Europe*, Chicago, 1987.

—— "Rape and marriage in the Medieval canon law," *Revue de Droit Canonique*, 28 (1978), pp. 62–75.

Campbell, Bruce M.S., "The population of early Tudor England: A re-evaluation of the 1522 muster returns and 1524 and 1525 lay subsidies," *Journal of Historical Geography*, 7 (1981), pp. 145–54.

Carlson, Eric Josef, "The churchwardens of rural Cambridgeshire," *The World of Rural Dissent, 1520–1700*, ed. Margaret Spufford, Cambridge, 1994.

—— "Clerical marriage and the English Reformation," *Journal of British Studies* 31 (1992), pp. 1–31.

—— "Courtship in Tudor England," *History Today* (August, 1993), pp. 23–9.

—— "The historical value of the Ely Consistory probate records," in *Index of the Probate Records of the Consistory Court of Ely 1449–1858*, ed. Elisabeth Leedham-Green, 3 vols (London, forthcoming), vol. 1, pp. xvii ff.

—— "The marriage of William Turner," *Historical Research*, 65 (1992), pp. 336–9.

—— "Marriage reform and the Elizabethan High Commission," *Sixteenth Century Journal*, 21 (1990), pp. 437–51.

Casey, James, "Household disputes and the law in early modern Andalusia," *Disputes and Settlements: Law and Human Relations in the West*, ed. John Bossy, Cambridge, 1983, pp. 187–217.

Cheney, C.R., *From Becket to Langton: English Church Government 1170–1213*, Manchester, 1956.

—— "Legislation of the Medieval English Church," *English Historical Review*, 50 (1935), pp. 193–224, 385–417.

—— *Medieval Texts and Studies*, Oxford, 1973.

Cheney, Mary, "The Compromise of Avranches of 1172 and the spread of canon law in England," *English Historical Review*, 56 (1941), pp. 177–97.

Clark, Sandra, *The Elizabethan Pamphleteers: Popular Moralistic Pamphlets, 1580–1640*, London, 1983.

Clebsch, William, *England's Earliest Protestants, 1520–1535*, New Haven, Conn., 1964.

Corbett, Percy E., *The Roman Law of Marriage*, Oxford, 1930.

Cornwall, Julian, "English population in the early sixteenth century," *Economic History Review*, 2d ser., 33 (1970), pp. 32–44.

Cressy, David, "The seasonality of marriage in old and new England," *Journal of Interdisciplinary History*, 16 (1985), pp. 1–21.

Darby, H.C., *The Domesday Geography of Eastern England*, Cambridge, 1952.

Davies, Kathleen, "The sacred condition of equality: How original were puritan doctrines of marriage?," *Social History*, 5 (1979), pp. 563–78.

Dibdin, L.T., *English Church Law and Divorce*, London, 1912.

Donahue, Jr., Charles, "The canon law on the formation of marriage and social practice in the later Middle Ages," *Journal of Family History*, 8 (1983), pp. 144–58.

—— "The policy of Alexander the Third's consent theory of marriage," *Proceedings of the Fourth International Congress of Medieval Canon Law*, ed. Stephan Kuttner, Monumenta Iuris Canonici, C:5, 1976, pp. 251–81.

—— "Proof by witnesses in the church courts of Medieval England: An imperfect reception of the learned law," *On the Laws and Customs of England: Essays in Honor of Samuel E. Thorne*, ed. Morris S. Arnold, *et al.*, Chapel Hill, N.C., 1981, pp. 127–58.

—— "Roman canon law in the medieval English Church: Stubbs vs. Maitland re-examined after 75 years in the light of some records from the church courts," *Michigan Law Review*, 72 (1974), pp. 647–716.

Duby, Georges, *The Knight, the Lady and the Priest: The Making of Modern Marriage in Medieval France*, trans. Barbara Bray, New York, 1983.

—— *Medieval Marriage: Two Models from Twelfth-Century France*, trans. Elborg Forster, Baltimore, 1978.

Duggan, Charles, *Twelfth-Century Decretal Collections and Their Importance in English History*, London, 1963.

Duncan, G.I.O., *The High Court of Delegates*, Cambridge, 1971.

Emmison, F.G., *Elizabethan Life: Morals and the Church Courts*, Chelmsford, Essex, 1973.

Flandrin, Jean-Louis, *Families in Former Times: Kinship, Household and Sexuality*, Cambridge, 1979.

Frazee, Charles A., "The origins of clerical celibacy in the western church," *Church History*, 41 (1972), pp. 149–67.

Gillis, John, "Conjugal settlements: Resort to clandestine and common law marriage in England and Wales, 1650–1850," *Disputes and Settlements: Law and Human Relations in the West*, ed. John Bossy, Cambridge, 1983, pp. 261–86.

—— *For Better, For Worse: British Marriages 1600 to the Present*, New York, 1985.

Goldberg, P.J.P., "Marriage, migration, servanthood and life-cycle in Yorkshire towns of the later Middle Ages: Some York cause paper evidence," *Continuity and Change*, 1 (1986), pp. 141–69.

——, ed., *Woman is a Worthy Wight: Women in English Society c. 1200–1500*, Wolfeboro Falls, N.H., 1992.

Goody, Jack, *The Development of the Family and Marriage in Europe*, Cambridge, 1983.

Gray, J.W., "Canon law in England: Some reflections on the Stubbs-Maitland controversy," *Studies in Church History*, 3 (1966), pp. 48–68.

Haigh, Christopher, "Slander and the church courts in the sixteenth century," *Transactions of the Lancashire and Cheshire Antiquarian Society*, 78 (1975), pp. 1–13.

Hair, P.E.H., "Bridal pregnancy in earlier rural England further examined," *Population Studies*, 24 (1970), pp. 59–70.

—— "Bridal pregnancy in rural England in earlier centuries," *Population Studies*, 20 (1966), pp. 233–43.

Hajnal, John, "European marriage patterns in perspective," *Population in History*, ed. D.V. Glass and D.E.C. Eversley, Chicago, 1965, pp. 101–36.

Helmholz, R.H., *Canon Law and the Law of England*, London, 1987.

—— *Marriage Litigation in Medieval England*, Cambridge, 1974.

—— *Roman Canon Law in Reformation England*, Cambridge, 1990.

Herlihy, David, "Making sense of incest: Women and the marriage rules of the early Middle Ages," *Law, Custom and the Social Fabric in Medieval Europe: Essays in Honor of Bryce Lyon*, Studies in Medieval Culture, 28, Kalamazoo, Mich., 1990, pp. 1–16.

—— *Medieval Households*, Cambridge, Mass., 1985.

—— and Christiane Klapisch-Zuber, *Tuscans and their Families*, New Haven, Conn., 1985.

A History of the County of Cambridge and the Isle of Ely, ed. C.R. Elrington, *et al.*, 9 vols to date, London and Oxford, 1938– .

Houlbrooke, Ralph A., *Church Courts and the People during the English Reformation, 1520–1570*, Oxford, 1979.

—— *The English Family 1450–1700*, London, 1984.

—— "The making of marriage in mid-Tudor England: Evidence from the records of matrimonial contract litigation," *Journal of Family History*, 10 (1985), pp. 339–51.

Howell, Cicely, *Land, Family and Inheritance in Transition: Kibworth Harcourt 1280–1700*, Cambridge, 1983.

Hurstfield, Joel, *The Queen's Wards: Wardship and Marriage under Elizabeth I*, 2d edn., London, 1973.

Hyams, Paul, *Kings, Lords and Peasants in Medieval England: The Common Law of Villeinage in the Twelfth and Thirteenth Centuries*, Oxford, 1980.

Hyma, Albert, "Erasmus and the sacrament of matrimony," *Archiv für Reformationsgeschicte*, 48 (1957), pp. 145–64.

Ingram, Martin, *Church Courts, Sex and Marriage in England, 1570–1640*, Cambridge, 1987.

Johnson, James Turner, *A Society Ordained By God: English Puritan Marriage Doctrine in the First Half of the Seventeenth Century*, Nashville, 1970.

Kelly, Henry Ansgar, *Love and Marriage in the Age of Chaucer*, Ithaca, N.Y., 1975.

—— *The Matrimonial Trials of Henry VIII*, Stanford, 1976.

Kingdon, Robert, "The control of morals in Calvin's Geneva," *The Social History of the Reformation*, ed. Lawrence P. Buck and Jonathan W. Zophy, Columbus, Ohio, 1972, pp. 1–14.

Kussmaul, Ann, "Time and space, hoofs and grains: The seasonality of marriage in England," *Journal of Interdisciplinary History*, 15 (1985), pp. 755–79.

Laslett, Peter, *The World We Have Lost*, 3d edn, London, 1983.

Leclercq, Jean, *Monks on Marriage: A Twelfth Century View*, New York, 1982.

Leites, Edmund, "The duty to desire: Love, friendship, and sexuality in some puritan theories of marriage," *Journal of Social History*, 15 (1979), 383–408.

—— *The Puritan Conscience and Modern Sexuality*, New Haven, Conn., 1986.

Logan, Donald, "The Henrician canons," *Bulletin of the Institute of Historical Research*, 48 (1974), pp. 99–103.

Macfarlane, Alan J., *Marriage and Love in England 1300–1840*, Oxford, 1986.

Maitland, F.W., *Roman Canon Law in the Church of England*, London, 1898.

Marchant, Ronald A., *The Church Under the Law: Justice, Administration and Discipline in the Diocese of York 1560–1649*, Cambridge, 1969.

Marsh, Christopher, "In the name of God? Will-making and faith in early modern England," *The Records of the Nation*, ed. G.H. Martin and Peter Spufford, Woodbridge, Sussex, 1990, pp. 215–49.

McGinn, Donald, *The Admonition Controversy*, New Brunswick, N.J., 1949.

McGrath, Patrick, "Notes on the history of marriage licences," *Gloucestershire Marriage Allegations 1637–1680*, ed. B. Frith, Bristol and Gloucestershire Archaeological Society, Record Section, 2 (1954).

Mitterauer, Michael and Reinhard Sieder, *The European Family*, Oxford, 1982.

Monter, E. William, "The consistory of Geneva, 1559–1569," *Bibliotheque d'Humanisme et Renaissance*, 38 (1976), pp. 467–84.

Murray, Jacqueline, "On the origins and role of 'wise women' in causes for annulment on the grounds of male impotence," *Journal of Medieval History*, 16 (1990), pp. 235–49.

Noonan, John T. "Marital affection in the canonists," *Studia Gratiana: Collectanea Stephan Kuttner*, 12 (1967), pp. 489–509.

—— "Power to choose," *Viator*, 4 (1973), pp. 419–34.

North, Tim, "Legerwite in the thirteenth and fourteenth centuries," *Past and Present*, 111 (1986), pp. 3–16.

O'Hara, Diana, " 'Ruled by my friends': Aspects of marriage in the diocese of Canterbury, c.1540–1570," *Continuity and Change*, 6 (1991), pp. 9–41.

Outhwaite, R.B., "Age at marriage in England from the seventeenth to the nineteenth centuries," *Transactions of the Royal Historical Society*, 5th ser., 23 (1973), pp. 55–70.

—— ed., *Marriage and Society: Studies in the Social History of Marriage*, London, 1981.

Owen, Dorothy M., "Ecclesiastical jurisdiction in England 1300–1550: The records and their interpretation," *Studies in Church History*, 11 (1975), pp. 199–221.

—— "The enforcement of the Reformation in the diocese of Ely," *Miscellanea Historiae Ecclesiasticae*, 3 (1970), pp. 167–74.

Ozment, Steven E., *When Fathers Ruled: Family Life in Reformation Europe*, Cambridge, Mass., 1983.

Palmer, Robert C., "Contexts of marriage in Medieval England: Evidence from the King's Court circa 1300," *Speculum*, 59 (1984), pp. 42–67.

Pollock, Frederick and F.W. Maitland, *The History of English Law*, 2 vols, intro. S.F.C. Milsom, 2d edn, Cambridge, 1968.

Powell, Chilton Latham, *English Domestic Relations, 1487–1653*, New York, 1917.

Powell, Edward, "Arbitration and the law in England in the late Middle Ages," *Transactions of the Royal Historical Society*, 5th ser., 33 (1983), pp. 49–67.

—— "Settlement of dispute by arbitration in fifteenth-century England," *Law and History Review*, 2 (1984), pp. 21–43.

Prior, Mary, "Reviled and crucified marriages: The position of Tudor bishops' wives," *Women in English Society, 1500–1800*, ed. Mary Prior, London, 1985, pp. 118–48.

Ravensdale, J.R., *Liable to Floods: Village Landscape on the Edge of the Fens A.D. 450–1850*, Cambridge, 1974.

Razi, Zvi, *Life, Marriage and Death in a Medieval Parish: Economy, Society and Demography in Halesowen 1270–1400*, Cambridge, 1980.

Reay, Barry, ed., *Popular Culture in Seventeenth Century England*, London, 1985.

Reynolds, Susan, *Kingdoms and Communities in Western Europe 900–1300*, Oxford, 1984.

Rich, E.E., "The population of Elizabethan England," *Economic History Review*, 2d ser., 2 (1950), pp. 247–65.

Roper, Lyndal " 'Going to church and street': Weddings in Reformation Augsburg," *Past and Present*, 106 (1985), pp. 62–101.

—— *The Holy Household: Women and Morals in Reformation Augsburg*, Oxford, 1989.

Rushton, Peter, "The testament of gifts: Marriage tokens and disputed contracts in north-east England, 1560–1630," *Folk Life*, 24 (1985–86), pp. 25–31.

Safley, Thomas Max, *Let No Man Put Asunder. The Control of Marriage in the*

German Southwest: A Comparative Study, 1550–1600, Kirksville, Missouri, 1984.

Schofield, R.S., "English marriage patterns revisited," *Journal of Family History*, 10 (1985), pp. 2–21.

Searle, Eleanor, "Seigneurial control of women's marriage: The antecedents and functions of merchet in Medieval England," *Past and Present*, 82 (1979), pp. 3–43.

Seaver, Paul S., "Community control and puritan politics in Elizabethan Suffolk," *Albion*, 9 (1977), pp. 297–315.

Sharpe, J.A., *Defamation and Sexual Slander in Early Modern England: The Church Courts at York*, Borthwick Papers, 58, York, 1980.

—— "Plebeian marriage in Stuart England: Some evidence from popular literature," *Transactions of the Royal Historical Society*, 5th ser., 36 (1986), pp. 69–90.

Sheehan, M.M., "Choice of marriage partner in the Middle Ages: Development and mode of application of a theory of marriage," *Studies in Medieval and Renaissance History*, new ser., 1 (1978), pp. 3–33.

—— "The formation and stability of marriage in fourteenth-century England: Evidence of an Ely register," *Mediaeval Studies*, 33 (1971), pp. 228–63.

—— "The influence of canon law on the property rights of married women in England," ibid, 25 (1963), pp. 109–24.

—— "Marriage and family in English conciliar and synodal legislation," ibid, 36 (1974), pp. 205–14.

—— "Marriage theory and practice in the conciliar legislation and diocesan statutes of Medieval England," ibid, 40 (1978), pp. 408–60.

—— "Theory and practice: Marriage of the unfree and the poor in medieval society," ibid, 50 (1988), pp. 457–87.

Short, Brian, ed., *The English Rural Community: Images and Analysis*, Cambridge, 1992.

Smith, Richard M., ed., *Land, Kinship and Life-cycle*, Cambridge, 1984.

—— "Marriage processes in the English past: Some continuities," *The World We Have Gained*, ed. Lloyd Bonfield, Oxford, 1986, pp. 43–99.

—— " 'Modernization' and the corporate medieval village community in England: Some sceptical reflections," *Explorations in Historical Geography: Interpretive Essays*, ed. Alan R.H. Baker and Derek Gregory, Cambridge, 1984, pp. 140–79.

—— "Some reflections on the evidence for the origins of the European marriage pattern in England," *The Sociology of the Family*, ed. C. Harris, Sociological Review Monograph 28 (1979), pp. 74–112.

—— "Some thoughts on 'hereditary' and 'proprietary' rights in land under customary law in thirteenth and early fourteenth century England," *Law and History Review*, 1 (1983), pp. 95–128.

Spufford, Margaret, *Contrasting Communities: English Villagers in the Sixteenth and Seventeenth Centuries*, Cambridge, 1974.

—— "The limitations of the probate inventory," *English Rural Society 1500–1800: Essays in Honor of Joan Thirsk*, ed. John Chartres and David Hey, Cambridge, 1990.

—— "Peasant inheritance customs and land distribution in Cambridgeshire from the sixteenth to the eighteenth centuries," *Family and Inheritance: Rural Society in Western Europe 1200–1800*, ed. Jack Goody, Joan Thirsk, and E.P. Thompson, Cambridge, 1976, pp. 156–76.

—— "Puritanism and social control?" *Order and Disorder in Early Modern England*, ed. Anthony Fletcher and John Stevenson, Cambridge, 1985, pp. 41–57.

—— *Small Books and Pleasant Histories: Popular Fiction and Its Readership in Seventeenth Century England*, London, 1981.

Stone, Lawrence, *The Crisis of the Aristocracy 1558–1641*, Oxford, 1965.

—— *The Family, Sex and Marriage in England 1500–1800*, New York, 1977.

Thirsk, Joan, ed., *The Agrarian History of England and Wales, Vol. IV: 1500–1640*, Cambridge, 1967.

Todd, Margo, *Christian Humanism and the Puritan Social Order*, Cambridge, 1987.

Treggiari, Susan, *Roman Marriage: Iusti Coniuges from the Time of Cicero to the Time of Ulpian*, Oxford, 1991.

Walker, Sue Sheridan, "Common law juries and feudal marriage customs in medieval England: The pleas of ravishment," *University of Illinois Law Review* (1984), pp. 705–18.

—— "Feudal constraint and free consent in the making of marriages in medieval England: Widows in the king's gift," *Historical Papers* (1979), pp. 97–110.

—— "Free consent and marriage of feudal wards in medieval England," *Journal of Medieval History*, 8 (1982), pp. 123–34.

Watt, Jeffrey R., *The Making of Modern Marriage: Matrimonial Control and the Rise of Sentiment in Neuchâtel, 1550–1800*, Ithaca, N.Y., 1992.

Watt, Tessa, *Cheap Print and Popular Piety, 1550–1640*, Cambridge, 1991.

Weir, David R., "Rather never than late: Celibacy and age of marriage in English cohort fertility, 1541–1871," *Journal of Family History*, 9 (1984), pp. 340–55.

Wemple, Suzanne Fonay, *Women in Frankish Society: Marriage and the Cloister 500 to 900*, Philadelphia, 1981.

Wrightson, Keith, *English Society, 1580–1680*, London, 1982.

—— "Two concepts of order: Justices, constables and jurymen in seventeenth-century England," *An Ungovernable People: The English and Their Law in the Seventeenth and Eighteenth Centuries*, ed. John Brewer and John Styles, New Brunswick, N.J., 1980, pp. 21–46.

—— and David Levine, *Poverty and Piety in an English Village: Terling, 1525–1700*, London, 1979.

Wunderli, Richard M., *London Church Courts and Society on the Eve of the Reformation*, Cambridge, Mass., 1981.

Yost, John, "The Reformation defense of clerical marriage in the reigns of Henry VIII and Edward VI," *Church History*, 50 (1981), pp. 152–65.

Index

Abduction Act, 85
absence from church/communion, 145, 146,
   152, 153, 167, 173, 178
Admonition Controversy, 47, 80–1
adultery, 11, 22, 75, 85, 136, 145, 149–50,
   153, 162, 167
Agrippa, H. C., 113
Alder, Joan, 52, 60
alehouses, 110, 125, 143, 147
Alexander III, Pope, 14, 16–18, 20, 23, 24,
   29, 30
Amussen, Susan Dwyer, 153
Anselm, Archbishop, 10–11
anticlericalism, 69–70, 144–5, 154
Arches, Court of, 72
Arthur, Prince, 67–8
Articles of Religion (1552), 52
Articles of Religion (1563), 64
Assertio Septum Sacramentorum, 37–8
Assumpsit, 31
Augsburg, 5, 6, 7

Bacon, Francis, 113
Bacon, Nicholas, 79
ballads, 106
Bancroft, Richard, 61
baptism, 160
Barnes, Robert, 54–5, 56, 57, 65, 138
Barrow, Henry, 48
Basel, 6
bastardy, 17, 30–1, 73, 85, 161
Batty, Bartholomew, 113–14
Becket, Thomas, 16, 17
Becon, Thomas, 55–6, 107, 118, 138
Best, Henry, 111
Beza, Theodore, 7
Biel, Gabriel, 4
Bishops' Book, The, 42–3
Blony, Nicholas de, 4
Boleyn, Anne, 68
Boleyn, Mary, 68
Bonner, Edmund, 44, 92
books, 41–2, 106
Bourchier, Anne, 83–4
Bowman, Christopher, 48
Bracton, Henry de, 27, 28, 30
Brett, Martin, 12
Brigden, Susan, 41

Browne, Anthony, 44
Bucer, Martin, 7, 47, 51, 76–7
Bullinger, Heinrich, 6–7, 55, 58, 73, 74,
   78, 107, 109, 115, 117, 129
Bunny, Edmund, 118
Burgh, Lord, 83

Calvin, John, 7
Cambridge University, 72, 156
canon law (general), 13–15, 67–74, 78–81;
   see also marriage
Capito, Wolfgang, 4
Capp, Bernard, 114
Carleton, George, 86
Carlton cum Willingham (Cambs.), 169–71
Carolingians, 18
Cartwright, Thomas, 47–8, 158
Castle Camps (Cambs.), 132
Cecil, Robert, 92
Cecil, Thomas, 86, 92, 133
Cecil, William, 60, 62–3, 90, 93
Chancery, 31–2, 88–9, 98, 136
chapmen, 111
Chapuys, Eustace, 39
charivari, 173
Charles V, Emperor, 39, 44, 51, 69
Chaucer, Geoffrey, 142
Cheke, John, 44
Chobham, Thomas de, 19
church courts (general), 9, 16, 31–2, 105,
   106, 142–3, 152–3, 156, 160–2, 164,
   174, 178, 179; *see also* marriage
churchwardens, 143–6, 147, 151, 153–4,
   155, 161, 162, 164, 168, 171, 172,
   176–7
Cleaver, Robert, 117–18
clerical marriage, 4, 18, 49–66, 90–1
Cnut, King, 10
Cobham, Elizabeth, 83, 85
Collectanea satis copiosa, 70–1
Collivacinus, Peter, 14
"common fame", 144, 147, 155
common law, 17, 30, 31, 32, 71
Compilatio Quinta, 14
Compilatio Tertia, 14
Complaynt of Roderick Mors, 67
Compromise of Avranches, 16–17
compurgators, 147–9, 161, 162

Constitutions of Clarendon, 16
Convocation, 51, 64, 69–71, 78–9
Cooper, Thomas, 61, 117
Council of Trent, 8
"The Country-man's Delight", 110, 116
courtship, 106–13
Coverdale, Miles, 55
Cox, Richard, 44, 60, 62, 74, 80, 156, 158, 159
Cranmer, Thomas, 43, 44, 45, 49, 50, 71, 72, 74, 75, 76, 77, 81, 83–4
Cromwell, Thomas, 39–40, 42, 50, 52–3, 72, 81
Crowley, Robert, 58
Croxton (Cambs.), 157–8, 163–5
cui in vita, 32

debt, 16, 17
Decretals, 14, 18, 20
Decretum, 14
Dedham classis, 81
defamation, 153, 161, 173, 178
Delegates, Court of, 93
Deloney, Thomas, 114
Denmark, 4, 7
Denny, Anthony, 44
deserted spouses, 147
disinheritance, 122
Dispensations Act (1534), 86
dispensations, 67–9
disturbances in/around churches, 143, 145, 152, 167, 173
divorce
    a mensa et thoro (separation), 22, 76, 77, 91, 93, 94, 95
    a vinculo (dissolution), 22, 24, 73, 75–6, 77, 83–5, 93
Donahue, Charles, 15, 23, 24, 88
Donne, John, 97–8
Douglas, Margaret, 82
dower, 25, 26, 29
Dry Drayton (Cambs.), 65, 106, 110, 139, 157, 158–63, 177
Duby, Georges, 18
Dudley, John, 44, 74
Dudley, Robert, 60

Edward I, King, 26
Edward II, King, 26
Edward VI, King, 44, 49–50, 51, 73, 83, 87
Elizabeth I, Queen, 47, 50, 58, 59–62, 64, 78, 79, 80, 86, 87, 97
Ely diocese, 19
Erasmus, Desiderius, 38, 55
Evans-Pritchard, Edward, 179
Evaristus, Pope, 18–19
ex officio cases, 143, 161, 164–5
excommunication, 17, 19, 25, 41, 71, 72, 75, 151

fickleness, 112–13
"The Fickleness of Woman", 112

Field, John, 80
Firn, Anton, 4
Fish, Simon, 70
Fletcher, Richard, 60
formedon, 32
fornication, 22, 131–2, 143, 151, 153, 155, 161, 165, 167, 172–3, 178
Foxe, John, 58, 79

Gardiner, Stephen, 44, 56, 70–1, 85
Geneva, 7–8
Gifford, George, 160
gift-giving, 111–12, 127, 135–6
Gillis, John, 127, 128, 130
Glanvill, Ranulf de, 26, 28, 30, 31
Godwin, Thomas, 61
Goodrich, Thomas, 156
Goody, Jack, 23
Grantchester (Cambs.), 106, 132
Gratian, 14, 18–19, 23–4
Greenham, Richard, 47, 49, 65, 115, 128, 131, 138, 139, 158–63
Greenwood, John, 48
Gregory IX, Pope, 14
Gregory VII, Pope, 13
Grey, Catherine, 97
Grindal, Edmund, 61, 94
Grosseteste, Robert, 17, 30
Gwent, Richard, 72

Hacksuppe, Simon, 173–4
Hadrian IV, Pope, 26
Haigh, Christopher, 53, 63
Harrington, William, 40, 131
Haugaard, William, 62
Hedio, Caspar, 4
Helmholz, Richard, 9, 25, 31, 92
Henry I, King, 10, 11, 12, 13, 27–8
Henry II, King, 15–18, 30
Henry III, King, 17, 26
Henry of Blois, Bishop, 12–13
Henry VIII, King, 37–40, 43, 49–51, 67–72, 79, 87
Henson, Herbert Hensley, 65
Herbert, George, 65
Herbert, William, 44
High Commission, 63, 89–92, 97, 98, 121, 129, 133–4, 136, 138
"The Highway to the Spital House", 116
Hohenlohe, 5
Holgate, Robert, 59
Honorius III, Pope, 14
Hooper, John, 54, 77, 84
Howard, Thomas, 44, 57, 81
Humana concupiscentia, 19

impotence, 21, 75
Ingram, Martin, 105, 140, 148
Innocent III, Pope, 14
insanity, 120, 155
Investiture Controversy, 9, 10, 13
Iolanthe, 95
Ipswich, Statute of, 61–3

Jersey, 88
Jewel, John, 61, 64, 80, 93
John of Salisbury, 18
Jordan, W. K., 74
Joye, George, 56–7
Julius II, Pope, 67–8

Karlstadt, Andreas, 4
Katherine of Aragon, Queen, 40, 67–71
Kaysersberg, Geiler von, 4
King's Bench, 31, 32
King's Book, The, 43, 45, 93
Kirby, Richard, 175

"The Lament of a Girl in Service", 110, 111, 115
"The Lamentation of Master Page's Wife of Plimmouth", 108–9
Landbeach (Cambs.), 174–8
Lanfranc, Archbishop, 10, 11
Lasco, John a, 76
Lateran Council IV, 19
Latimer, Hugh, 46, 76–7, 114
Lea, Henry Charles, 49
Lee, Edward, 92
leet juries, 162–3
Leges Henrici Primi, 11
Lever, Thomas, 78
Little Wilbraham (Cambs.), 110, 132
Lollards, 40–1, 53
Lombard, Peter, 20
Longland, John, 41
Louis the Pious, 18
Luther, Martin, 3, 5, 6, 37–9, 57, 67, 70, 87, 136
Lyndwood, William, 19

MacCaffrey, Wallace T., 79–80
"A Mad Kinde of Wooing", 116
Magna Carta, 26, 28
Maitland, F. W., 14–15, 20, 29, 32
manorial courts, 25–7, 31–2
mantle children, *see* bastardy
"The Marchant's Daughter of Bristow", 118
maritagium, 31–2
marriage
  age of, 75, 81, 106, 122
  banns, 25, 72, 74, 82, 93, 94, 95, 128–9
  betrothal, 20, 49, 75, 95, 123–7
  in Bible, 20, 24, 38, 40, 42–3, 45–7, 54
  bigamy, *see* precontract
  canon law of, 5, 18–25, 40, 67–87
  ceremony, 18, 43–9, 96
  of children, 21, 96, 107–8
  clandestine, 5, 18–19, 21, 22, 24, 26, 29, 40, 48, 72, 91–2, 93, 94, 95
  conditional, 20–1, 73
  confarreatio, 24
  consanguinity/affinity, 10, 21, 67–8, 73, 75, 77, 81, 82, 93–5, 115–16, 137–8
  consent, 18–29
  Continental Reformation and, 3–8
  of deaf and dumb, 73, 75
  on deathbed, 29
  disorderly, 143, 146–7, 152
  ecclesiastical jurisdiction over, 5–8, 71–2, 76
  economic condition and, 106, 116–17
  employers and, 119
  forced, 10, 21, 23, 25, 72–3, 75, 108
  Friedelehe, 24
  handfasting, *see* betrothal
  impediments (general), 5, 22, 72, 75, 136–8
  indissolubility of, 130–1
  intermediaries, use of, 125
  licenses, 72, 82, 85, 86
  litigation, reasons for, 140–1
  location of, 72, 75, 82, 94, 95, 125–7, 133–4
  love in, 114–15
  parental consent, 5, 6, 73, 75, 77, 85–6, 92, 94, 95–102, 107, 108, 109, 117–23, 138–40
  Prayer Book, use of, 124, 128
  precontract, 21, 82, 85, 89, 95, 150
  proof of, 134–5
  puritan views of, 47–9
  of recusants, 91–2
  ring, 46, 47, 127
  as sacrament, 3, 37–43
  second, 93
  secular jurisdiction over, 18, 25–33, 71–2, 88–92
  separatists views of, 48
  versus single life, 113–14
  solemnization, 129, 132–4
  spousals, *see* betrothal
  time of day, 95, 133
  time of year, 75, 85, 95, 132–3
  of villeins, 26–8
  in Visitation articles, 54, 59, 92–6
  witnesses, 123–4, 127
Mary I, Queen, 46, 47, 50, 53, 85
Matilda, Queen, 13
Matthew, Tobias, 60, 96
Melanchthon, Philip, 5, 50, 56
merchet, 28
Merton, Statute of, 17, 28, 30
ministers, duties of, 153–4, 158–9, 160
mobility, 110, 169, 172, 177
Mont, Christopher, 51, 60
More, George, 97–8
More, Thomas, 38–40, 42, 55, 57, 69
mort d'ancestor, 32

Neville, George, Earl of Westmorland, 90, 93
"A New Courtly Sonet of the Lady Greensleeves", 111
"A New Mery Balad of a Maid that wold Mary a Servyng Man", 122
Noonan, John T., 23–4
Norton, Thomas, 79
Nuer, 179

Nuremberg, 6, 7

Oecolampadius, Johannes, 7
Orwell (Cambs.), 157, 158, 165–8
Osiander, Andreas, 7, 83
Ozment, Steven, 8

Paget, Eusebius, 138
Paget, William, 73
papacy, 11–18, 54–5
papal judges-delegate, 13, 14
parish registers, 106, 135, 160, 165
Parker, Matthew, 58, 61, 62, 79, 93, 115,
    175
Parkhurst, John, 63, 95
parliament, 51–2, 58, 64, 69–71, 74,
    78–87, 89
Parr, William, 83–5
The Passionate Morrice, 117
penances, 149–50, 151, 162
Penry, John, 79
Peristiany, J. G., 149
Perkins, William, 113, 129
Philip of Hesse, 50–1, 60
Piers Plowman, 153–4
Piers, John, 61
Pilkington, James, 64
Pollard, Richard, 72
Ponet, John, 58–9, 64
Prayer Book, 47; see also marriage
pregnancy, 113, 131–2, 155, 167, 178
Prerogative regis, statute of, 26
presbyterians, 78–9, 81
presentments, 143–5, 155–6, 160–2, 165,
    167, 172–4, 178
Privy Council, 42, 44, 58–9, 83, 88, 97
prohibition, writ of, 16–17, 23, 31
puritans, 47–9; see also marriage

Raymond of Peñafort, 14
Redman, John, 51–2
Reformatio Legum Ecclesiasticorum, 74–9, 83,
    84
Rochester diocese, 19, 137–8
Roman law, 18, 21, 24, 25
Royal Visitation (1559), 59, 91
Rushton, Peter, 127, 135–6
Russell, John, 44

sabbath breaking, 11, 146, 173, 178
"Salomon's housewife", 114–15
Sampson, Richard, 43
Sandys, Edwin, 58, 95–6
Sarum Use, 44, 46
Saxony, 7
Schmalkaldic League, 43
service, 110, 119, 122–3
Seymour, Edward, 44, 73
Sheehan, Michael, 23, 24
Shudy Camps (Cambs.), 132
Six Articles, 50–1, 52, 55, 56
Smith, Henry, 129, 138
Smith, Richard M., 106

Spufford, Margaret, 159
Starkey, Thomas, 117
Stationers' Company, 42
Stephen, King, 12–13
Still, John, 61
Stockwood, John, 107, 138
Stone, Lawrence, 99
Strasbourg, 4, 7
Stratford, John, 19
Strickland, William, 79
Strype, John, 60
Stubbes, Philip, 107, 117
Stubbs, William, 14–15
Submission of the Clergy, 71, 80
suicide, 120
Supplication against the Ordinaries, 70,
    144
suspension, 151

Table of Degrees, 93–5, 115, 137–8
Taverner, Richard, 55
"Tell-Trothes New-Yeares Gift", 107
Ten Articles, 42
testamentary jurisdiction, 16, 17
Theobald, Archbishop, 15
Thirlby, Thomas, 44, 156
Thornborough, John, 60–1
tithes, 161, 164, 178
Tunstall, Cuthbert, 40, 44, 46
Turner, William, 52, 60
Tyndale, William, 39–40, 41, 55, 56, 57, 70

Vaughan, Stephen, 39–40
Vermigli, Peter Martyr, 74, 76–7, 84
Veron, Jean, 64
Vives, Juan Luis, 40

Walker, Sue Sheridan, 27
Walsingham, Francis, 97
wardship, 28–9
Warham, William, 69, 70
Warren, W. L., 16
Westminster I, Statute of, 28
Whitford, Richard, 40
Whitgift, John, 47–8, 61, 86, 97
widows, 10, 25–7, 112, 122, 167
wife-lease, 131
William I, King, 10, 11
William II, King, 10
wills, 100–1, 106, 139, 159–60
Winchelsey, Robert, 17
Wittenberg, 4
Wolsey, Thomas, 37, 41, 68–9
Wriothesley, Thomas, 44
Weston Colville (Cambs.), 169, 170, 171,
    172–4

Young, Thomas, 90, 93
youth, 106–7

Zell, Matthias, 4, 5
Zurich, 6, 7
Zwingli, Ulrich, 4